MICHAEL BRANDER

# The Complete Guide
# to Horsemanship

CHARLES SCRIBNER'S SONS · NEW YORK

*Dedication*
To Evelyn

*(handwritten)*
798.2
B73c
80290
oct 1972

# CONTENTS

## Book One

## The Approach to Horsemanship

CONTENTS

CONTENTS

# Book Three

# Horsemastership

# CONTENTS

# ILLUSTRATIONS

# AUTHOR'S PREFACE

This is only intended as an aid to horsemastership. It can be nothing more, for horsemastership can only be truly learned by keeping horses and riding them over a long period. Pony Clubs are an excellent thing to encourage the young to learn to ride and care for their horses, or ponies. Riding Clubs are a great help to the older rider, but learning about horses should be a continuous process over a lifetime. Each day out with horses should increase one's knowledge, even if only by some insignificant item about one individual horse. Very often with horses, however, people may want to ask a question and either did not know how to frame it properly, or there is no-one present to answer it correctly and it is forgotten. While running my own stud it seemed to me there was a definite requirement for such a book as this, which is intended to cover the entire gamut of horsemastership in logical progression from the novices approach onwards.

My thanks for his help with the veterinary section and anatomy of the horse are due to Mr. J. Ralston, M.R.C.V.S., who over the past twenty years has also earned my thanks many times over while handling our stock, both horses and dogs. My thanks for reading the typescript and commenting on it are also due to Rozann Whitaker, Fay Cullen and Ella MacGregor, although any mistakes are entirely my responsibility. Finally for reading typescripts and proofs, for advice and general assistance, as well as for the illustrations, my very heartfelt thanks go to my wife, Evelyn.

# BOOK ONE
*The Approach to Horsemanship*

# PART I
## The Introduction to the Horse

*Section 1    The Points and Conformation of the Horse*
The horse may conveniently be divided into three: viz:

A    The Forehand:
This consists of the head and the neck, the withers, the shoulders and the forelegs.

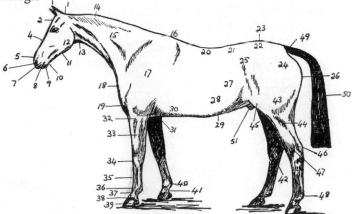

The Points of the Horse

1. The Poll. 2. The Forehead. 3. The Ears. 4. The Face. 5. The Nose. 6. The Nostrils. 7. The Muzzle. 8. The Lips. 9. The Chin. 10. The Chin Groove. 11. The Lower Jaw. 12. The Cheekbone. 13. The Throat. 14. The Crest. 15. The Neck. 16. The Withers. 17. The Shoulder. 18. The Point of the Shoulder. 19. The Chest. 20. The Back. 21. The Loins. 22. The Croup. 23. The Point of the Croup. 24. The Hip Joint. 25. The Point of the Hip. 26. The Buttock. 27. The Flank. 28. The Barrel. 29. The Belly. 30. The Floor of the Chest. 31. The Elbow. 32. The Arm. 33. The Forearm. 34. The Knee. 35. The Cannon. 36. The Fetlock Joint. 37. The Pastern. 38. The Coronet. 39. The Hoof. 40. The Fetlock. 41. The Heel. 42. The Chestnut. 43. The Upper Thigh. 44. The Lower Thigh, or Gaskin. 45. The Stifle. 46. The Point of the Hock. 47. The Hock. 48. The Ergot. 49. The Root of the Dock. 50. The Tail. 51. The Sheath.

21

B    The Body:
     This consists of the back and the chest, the loins, the flanks and the belly.
C    The Hindquarters:
     This consists of the hindquarters, the tail and the hindlegs.

But *N.B.*
1    Unless the various parts of the horse are balanced in relation to each other,
     the horse cannot be said to have good conformation.
2    It is generally preferable to have a horse which is so balanced, rather than
     one with some excellent points and some unsound.

Hence the above must be considered in greater detail, as follows:
Ai The Head and Neck
The points of the head and neck are as follows:

### The Tip of the Nose, or Muzzle
The convex area, which lies between the two nostrils:

i    It tends to be both prominent and highly sensitive.
ii   It is undesirable and unsightly for it to be flesh coloured, as this is generally
     indicative of coarse breeding.

### The Nostrils
The two nostrils lie one on either side of the tip of the nose or muzzle:

i    They should be large and wide:
     *a*    The hairs of the nostrils should be fine.
     *b*    If the hairs are thick and obvious it is a sign of coarse breeding.
ii   It is undesirable to have small or narrow nostrils, since this may impair the
     horse's breathing.

### The Lips
The upper and lower lips lie below the nostrils and above the chin:

i    They are very sensitive and in a well-bred horse should be thin and fine.
ii   It is a sign of coarse breeding if they are very thick and drooping.

### The Jaws and Teeth
Consist of the upper and lower jaw, each containing twelve molars, or grinders,
and six incisors, or biting teeth, also two tushes, or canine teeth, generally
absent in mares:

i    The lower jaw, as opposed to the upper jaw, is movable and articulates
     with the upper jaw behind in mastication:
     *a*    The lower jaw is operated by a powerful set of muscles visible on the
            cheeks.

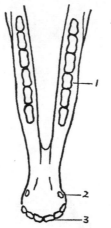

Key to the Jaw of a horse
1. Molars. 2. Tushes. 3. Incisors.

*b*    It is undesirable for the lower jaw not to fit accurately with the upper jaw, as this leads to digestive troubles.

ii    The space between tushes and molars is known as the bars. It is here that the bit rests. See pp. 66–67.

iii    Variations in the number of teeth:
The adult horse may have forty or forty-two teeth, the mare thirty-six or thirty-eight.

*a*    The variations are due to the presence, or absence, of small 'wolf' teeth in the molars and the normal absence of canine teeth, or tushes, in mares.

*b*    If they get in the way of the bit the wolf teeth may have to be removed.

iv    The Types of Teeth:
The Incisors are the nipping, or biting, teeth in front:

*a*    They are as follows: the middle two, the Centrals, the next, the Laterals, and the last on each side the Corners.

*b*    Behind the Corner Incisor is the Canine, or Tush.

The Molars are the grinders, or cheek teeth.

v    The Parts of the Teeth:
The various parts of the teeth are as follows:
*a*    The Fang: the hollow root within the jaw.
*b*    The Fanghole: the cavity in the fang.

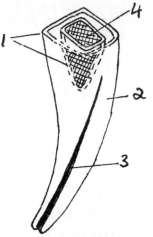

The Tooth
1. Enamel. 2. Ivory. 3. Fanghole. 4. Mark.

c   The Neck: the meeting place of the gum and the tooth.
d   The Crown: the visible portion above the gum.
e   The Table: the wearing or biting surface.
f   The Mark: a blackened depression in the table of the incisors, which grows out with the wear of the tooth indicating age. See Ageing, pp. 270–271.

*The Muzzle*
Includes:

i    The nostrils;
ii   The lips;
iii  The teeth.

*The Chin, Chin Groove*
The chin is the protuberance below the lower lip on the underside of the lower jaw:

i    The chin groove is the marked depression to be found behind the chin.
ii   The curb chain, when used, comes into action in the chin groove. See pp. 67–68.

*The Face, or Arch of the Nose*
That area between the tip of the nose and the forehead:

i    It is generally long, narrow and flat.
ii   It may be concave, i.e. dish-faced, or convex, i.e. roman nosed.

*The Cheeks*

On either side of the head below the eyes and above the jaw:

i   They should be moderately broad and flat.
ii  The muscles beneath operate the lower jaw and should be powerful.

*The Forehead*

That area between the eyes, the arch of the nose and the poll:

i   It should be broad and flat.
ii  Convexity of the frontals, or a bump between the eyes, caused by the intrusion of the orbits, or bony ridges, surrounding the eyes, is undesirable as generally indicating bad temper.

*The Eyes*

Should be a matching pair set well apart in the forehead:

i   They should be large, calm and intelligent looking, of the same size, colour and appearance.
ii  They generally give an indication of a horse's temperament:

    *a*   Small, sunken, 'pig' eyes generally indicate meanness of temper.
    *b*   One, or both, eyes with white round the pupil, i.e. a 'wall eye' indicates a wild disposition.
    *c*   Too large an eye, or too much white showing, generally indicates a wild and scarey temperament.

iii Deep sunken hollows above the eyes are undesirable as a sign of old age, or sickness.

*The Ears*

On either side of the poll above the forehead:

i   They are oval shaped, pointed at the tip and very sensitive.
ii  They are very mobile and indicative of temperament:

    *a*   They should generally be cocked and alert indicating an even temperament.
    *b*   They should not have a tendency to be frequently laid back, or constantly flickering, as this indicates an evil, sulky temperament, or a scarey disposition.

iii Long floppy ears are not desirable, but a horse with them may often prove quite a character.

*The Poll*

The area above the forehead and immediately behind the ears:

25

i   It is the anterior point of the neck.

ii  It is subject to injury passing through low doorways and similar places, resulting in poll evil. See p. 427.

*The Forelock*
A continuation of the mane:

i   It hangs forward between the ears over the forehead.

ii  It covers the poll.

*The Mane*
The mane extends from the poll to the withers:

i   It is composed of longer and tougher hairs than the rest of the body except the tail.

ii  In well-bred horses it is of fine hair, in coarser breeds it may be thick and coarse.

iii It may be flowing free in its natural state, or be plaited, or hogged, i.e. clipped. See pp. 182–4.

*The Throat*
The throat lies at the junction of the head and the neck:

i   It contains the gullet and windpipe.

ii  It should therefore in no way be restricted by the throat-lash of the bridle. See pp. 64–5.

*The Neck*
The junction between the head and the body:

Normal Neck          Bull Neck          Ewe Neck

i   It should be long and well shaped, tapering towards the head, with the head set on at the correct angle.

ii   The crest (see below) should be slightly convex, but not too pronounced.

iii   The crest should not be short and thick-set, i.e. 'bull-necked', resulting in the horse being too heavy in the forehand.

iv   It is undesirable for the neck to appear concave, rather than convex, from the withers, with the upper part straight:

    *a*   The result is rather like the neck of a sheep, hence is termed 'ewe-necked'.

    *b*   This may be caused by very poor condition in a young horse, in which case it can be corrected by correct feeding and schooling, otherwise it is due to poor conformation.

v   It is even more undesirable when the concave curve of the neck continues from the withers to the head:

    *a*   This is known as a 'swan neck' and is simply and solely due to poor conformation and cannot be corrected.

    *b*   A horse with a 'swan neck' inevitably has incorrect head carriage, with a tendency to 'star gazing'.

## The Crest
The crest is the upper side of the neck from which the mane grows:

i   It should be well muscled and more pronounced in the male.

ii   It should not be too pronounced (see above: *The Neck* iii) as in some coarser breeds, since this detracts from the horse's appearance and is liable to make it too heavy in the forehand.

## The Jugular Groove
The jugular groove is the marked furrow along the lower side of the neck:

i   This contains the jugular vein.

ii   It stands out prominently if a finger is pressed on it.

## The Conformation of the Head and the Neck

i   The head should be neat and well formed with a broad flat forehead and large open nostrils.

ii   The skin should be fine and thin, showing the muscles and veins, with the jaw muscles notably prominent.

iii    The eyes should be large and calm and the ears should be cocked and alert.

iv    The neck should be long and well shaped, forming the correct angle with the head and the body.

v    The two should form a well-balanced entity in relation to the conformation of the horse as a whole.

## Aii The Withers
The withers are the prominence where the upper part of the neck joins the body, caused by the first spinal vertebrae:

i    They should start at the base of the crest and should be highest at the top of the shoulder and gradually slope into the back.

ii    It is preferable to have prominent withers sloping well back, because:

    *a*    This generally indicates good action in front.
    *b*    It makes saddle fitting comparatively simple. See pp. 58–9.

iii    Very high withers may indicate good action in front, but:

    *a*    They are more liable to injury through ill-fitting saddlery.
    *b*    They are likely to be difficult to fit satisfactorily.

iv    In very rare cases of exaggerated conformation where there are very high withers in conjunction with a greyhound-shaped body, it may be necessary to fit a breastplate to prevent the saddle slipping backwards.

v    It is undesirable to have low withers for the reverse reason, i.e. the saddle may slip forwards:

    *a*    This is especially the case when so overlaid with fat as to be almost indistinguishable, as in many over-fat ponies.
    *b*    In this event a crupper must be fitted to keep the saddle from slipping forwards.

vi    The length from the withers to the elbow should be roughly the same as from the elbow to the fetlock.

## Aiii The Shoulders
The shoulders lie on either side of the body extending from below the withers to the humerus, or upper arm:

i    They should be long, sloping and well muscled.

ii    The slope of the shoulder should be about 45°:

· Good Shoulders                    · Short Straight Shoulder

*a*   The horse should not have too upright a shoulder since this restricts freedom of movement.

*b*   From the point of the shoulder, i.e. the foremost point of the shoulder, the upper arm, or humerus, should slope back to the point of the elbow at approximately right-angles.

iii   A line from the point of the shoulder should drop direct to the toe.

Aiv The Forelegs
The points of the forelegs are as follows:

*The Elbows*
The joint between the humerus, or upper arm, and the forearm, on either side of the body:

i   The elbow should be well developed muscularly and large.

ii   The angle of the humerus from the point of the elbow to the point of the shoulder, should form a right-angle with the slope of the shoulder.

iii   Viewed from the side the foreleg should be vertical below the elbow.

iv   A line dropped vertically from the point of the elbow should go through the centre of the knee and reach the ground touching the heel of the hoof.

v   The length from the elbow to the withers should be roughly the same as from the elbow to the fetlock.

*The Forearms*
The forearms extend from the knee to the elbow on each foreleg:

i   Their length should be greater than from the knee to the ground.

29

ii    They should not be too short, since this indicates lack of speed.

*The Chestnuts*
In the forelegs the chestnuts lie on the inside of the forearm above the knee (in the hindlegs inside hind cannon below the hock):

i    They are a horny outgrowth.

ii    The distance from the fore-chestnuts to the ground should roughly equal the length of the head.

*The Knees*
The knee is the joint in each foreleg between the forearm and the cannon:

· Weak, or Calf Knee

· Over at the knee

· Correct Position of Forelegs

· Knock Kneed and Splay Footed

· Bandy knees

i    They should be large, bony, well developed, flat in front and a matching pair.

ii    Seen from the side the leg should be straight at the knee:

    *a*    The knee should not bend back, this is known as 'calf-kneed' and a sign of weakness.

    *b*    The knee should not bend forward, known as 'over at the knee', also a possible sign of weakness.

iii    Viewed from the front the legs should appear absolutely straight from the point of the shoulder through the knees to the feet:

    *a*    The knees should not seem to approach each other, i.e. 'knock-kneed', as this leads to poor movement or action.

    *b*    The knees should not seem to bend outward, i.e. 'bandy-kneed', as this also leads to a poor action.

## The Cannons

The shin bones, or the bone from below the knee to the fetlock on either foreleg (the shank bones on the hindlegs).

i    They should be short and strong.

ii    The circumference of the cannon below the knee should be very considerable:

    *a*    If this is not the case the horse may be described as 'short of bone', or 'lacking bone'.

    *b*    Another description of the same condition is 'tied in below the knee'.

## The Fetlocks (and Ergots)

The joint between the cannon and pastern on each leg:

i    It should be well developed and strong.

ii    It should match the one on the other foreleg, or hindleg.

iii    In coarse breeds subject to the growth of coarse hair, or 'feathering'.

iv    At the rear of each fetlock joint is the horny growth known as the 'ergot', a vestigial remains of a footpad.

## The Pasterns

The part of each leg between the fetlock joint and the coronet:

i    It should be moderate in length and sloping, one of a matching pair:

    *a*   The slope should be about 45° in front, continued by the hoof about the same angle.

    *b*   The rear pastern should be slightly more upright, as is the rear hoof

ii   The pastern should not be too short and straight in front, because:

    *a*   This results in direct concussion and a jolty ride.

    *b*   It is a possible source of weakness.

· Foreleg too straight       · Pastern too sloping

iii  The pastern should not be too long and sloping, especially behind, because:

    *a*   It has to take a great deal of strain.

    *b*   It is a likely source of weakness.

### The Coronets

The lowest point of the pastern immediately adjoining the hoof on each leg:

i    It is the junction of the leg and the hoof.

ii   It is also known as the coronary band, or coronary cushion, although this is more correctly the bulge above the coronet.

### The feet

The hooves of the horse, covered with a horney outer covering growing downwards from the coronary band:

i    They should neither be too large, nor too small, but of medium size, dependent on the size of the horse:

    *a*   The two forefeet should be a matching pair, sloping at an angle of about 45° and each pointing straight forwards.

b   The two rear feet should also be a matching pair, but like the rear pasterns sloping slightly more steeply.

c   The horn should be tough and dark in colour, without rings or cracks, each of which are a sign of weakness, or disease.

ii   If either fore or hind feet are not a pair this is generally a sign of weakness or disease.

iii   The feet should not be small and upright, i.e. 'boxy', as this is generally a sign of weakness or disease.

iv   The feet should not be large, flat and dish-like:

a   This is a sign of coarse breeding and looks clumsy.

b   It is also a source of weakness.

v   The feet should not point inwards, i.e. 'pin-, pigeon- or hen-toed,' as this implies a poor action, or movement.

· Hen Toed

vi   The feet should not point outwards, i.e. 'lady-toed' or 'splay-footed', as this may lead to dishing and possible injury, i.e. swinging the feet outwards in movement. See p. 253.

*The Heels*
The lower rear part of the wall of the hoof:

i   The two bulbs of the heel, or cushions of the heel, should be prominent and well apart at the rear of each hoof.

ii   The heels should not be shrunken, i.e. contracted, as this is a sign of weakness, disease, or bad shoeing.

*The Sole, the Frog and the Bars of the Foot*
These consist of the following:

i    The Sole:

The sole is similar to the wall of the hoof and is bounded by the wall and the bars: being roughly crescent shaped:

    *a*    It should be arched, firm and thickest at the perimeter.
    *b*    It should not be flat, or spongy.
    *c*    It has a soft fleshy sensitive sole inside the outer cover.
    *d*    This shows as a white line where it joins the outer hoof.

ii    The Bars of the Foot:

The bars divide the sole from the frog and are a continuation inwards, towards the point of the frog, of the walls at the heels:

    *a*    The bars grow down from the sensitive sole and must not be cut away, or contracted heels and frog will result.
    *b*    Between the bars and the frog is a groove which allows the frog to expand when the body weight presses it to the ground.
    *c*    The bars support the wall at the heels and allow for expansion of the heels when the frog expands under body weight.

iii    The Frog:

The frog is the V-shaped fibrous formation between the bars:

    *a*    It should be large and well developed, expanding sideways when the horse's weight is placed on it, hence should not be pared.
    *b*    The frog should never be small and hard, or unduly spongy, as either of these conditions indicates bad management and possibly disease, or weakness.
    *c*    In the centre of the frog is the frog cleft, which should be shallow, rounded, clean and sweet smelling.
    *d*    At the base of the frog on either side are the bulbs of the heel.

Bi The Back and the Chest

The points of the back and the chest are as follows:

*The Back*

The region between the horse's withers and loins:

i    It should be short, flat and well muscled:

    *a*    If extremely short it indicates great strength, but also, probably, lack of speed.
    *b*    If very long it indicates possible weakness.

ii    A hollow 'sway' back is undesirable as a sign of weakness, injury, or old age.

iii  When a prominent convex spinal column is visible, this is known as a 'roach' back and is a sign of strength.

*The Chest: including the Girth, Brisket and Ribs*
The region below the horse's back and behind the forelegs containing the heart and lungs:

i  The chest should be deep and moderately wide, but:

   *a*  Excessive width, i.e. a 'barrel chest', is uncomfortable for the rider and difficult to fit with a saddle: on the other hand.
   *b*  A shallow chest is obviously not likely to have the lung or heart room required for staying power.

ii  The girth is the circumference of the chest immediately behind the forelegs:

   *a*  It should be large, see chest above.
   *b*  It should equal the length of the head.
   *c*  At lowest level should be below the point of the elbow.

iii  The brisket is the lowest part of the chest and should be well muscled.

iv  The ribs should spring out well to give plenty of heart and lung room:

   *a*  The horse should be 'well-ribbed-up', i.e. with the posterior ribs close to the point of the hip. See Hindquarters, pp. 36–8.
   *b*  Shortness of the back ribs is most undesirable, resulting in not being 'well-ribbed-up' as above.
   *c*  The ribs should be deep and convex, not flat.
   *d*  The curve of the ribs forms what is known as 'the barrel'.

Bii The Loins
That part of the back immediately behind the saddle:

· Sway Back

i    They should be broad and well arched.

ii   It is essential that they are strong and well muscled.

iii  Too long loins are generally a sign of weakness.

Biii The Flanks and the Belly
That area behind the ribs and below the loins, extending down to the lower line of the body:

i    The flanks and the belly contain the stomach and the large intestine.

     *a*    The belly should about equal the chest in breadth, but should taper gradually towards the flank.
     *b*    The straighter the lower line of the body the more likely the horse is to be a stayer.

ii   The horse should not have a concavity behind the girth:

     *a*    This is referred to as 'being tucked-up' and is either a sign of a bad doer, or of sickness, or poor management.

     *b*    In extreme cases this may be termed 'herring gutted' and is a sign of weakness, particularly lack of posterior ribs, although possibly due to lack of care.

iii  The horse should not have too much belly:

     *a*    This may be termed looking 'as fat as pig, barrel, etc.'
     *b*    This may be due to being 'just up from grass'. See pp. 210–12.
     *c*    It may be due to being in foal, or a sign of sickness. See pp. 340–1.

iv  Heaving flanks are a sign of exhaustion, or sickness.

Ci The Hindquarters
That part of the horse between the rear of the flank and the root of the tail, reaching down to the gaskin.
The points of the hindquarters, or quarters, are as follows:

*The Croup*
The upper part of the hindquarters from the loins to the root of the tail:

i    The croup should be convex and well muscled:

     *a*    A sloping croup may not appear as presentable, but it is not a sign of weakness.
     *b*    When a noticeable bump is present on the croup, it is termed the 'jumper's bump' and supposedly is a sign of jumping ability, for no good reason.

ii    The croup should be muscled in proportion with the rest of the hindquarter or the overall conformation may be marred.

· Well shaped croup

*The Point of the Hip*
The bony protuberance about a hand's width behind the posterior rib on either side of the horse:

i     This is not a true hip; it is the external point of the pelvis:

    *a*    It is easily injured passing through doorways and similar obstacles unless care is taken.

    *b*    A 'dropped hip' is therefore likely to be due to an injured pelvis and is an extremely serious matter.

ii    Breadth between the points of the hips is desirable, as is muscular development of the hindquarters, but, as above, only in proportion to the rest of the body.

iii   When the points of the hips are extremely prominent due to poor condition and lack of muscle this is sometimes referred to as 'ragged hips'.

iv    The distance from the point of the hip to the point of the hock should be about two and a half times the length from the point of the hock to the fetlock joint.

*The Buttocks*
That part of the hindquarters below the root of the tail and behind the thighs:

i     They should be long, rounded and well developed muscularly.

ii    The points of the buttocks project a little below the root of the tail on either side:

a    The point of the buttock, the point of the hock, and the rear of the fetlock joint should all form a straight line vertically.

b    The distance between the point of the buttock and the point of the shoulder should be about two and a half times the length of the head.

c    Lines taken from the point of the hip to the point of the stifle and thence to the point of the buttock and so back to the point of the hip should form an equilateral triangle.

*The Stifle*

The junction of the tibia and the patella; the true knee:

i    The prominence at the forward point of the stifle is known as the point of the stifle:

a    It should appear well developed and prominent.

b    Any weakness or injury here is likely to be a source of trouble and lameness.

ii    The distance from the croup to the stifle and from the point of the stifle to the point of the hock, should be equal and about the same length as the head.

*The Sheath*

Only found in a gelding or an entire, i.e. a stallion:

i    A fold of loose skin protecting the forward end of the horse's penis.

ii    It should be large and well formed.

Cii The Tail

The points of the tail are as follows:

*The Dock*

The root of the tail:

i    This includes the bare underside, as well as the side on which the hair grows.

ii    On a well-bred horse this should be carried well away from the body.

*The Tail*

All beyond the dock, or root of the tail:

i    This should be well set up, strong and muscular and covered with fine hair:

a    It is a sign of common breeding for the hair to be very coarse.

b    The appearance of the horse is not enhanced if the tail is set on too low.

ii   Good tail carriage, well away from the body, adds greatly to a horse's appearance.

Ciii The Hindlegs
The points of the hindlegs are as follows:

*The Gaskin, or Second Thigh*
The gaskin or second thigh, lies between the stifle and the hock joint:

i    It should be clear, well defined, broad and muscular.

ii   It is undesirable for it to be underdeveloped, weak, or undersized.

*The Hocks*
The joint on the hindleg between the gaskin and the hind cannon:

i    It is particularly important that these should be a matching pair, strong, powerful and well developed.

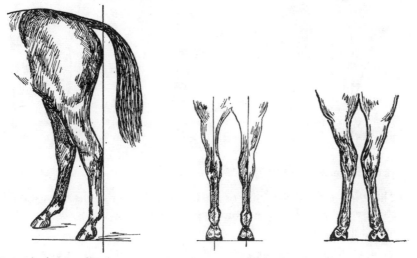

· Normal relation of hock to quarters   · Correct position of hindlegs   · Cow Hocks

ii   Seen from behind the leg should be perfectly straight:

a    As a guide the point of the buttock, the point of the hock and the fetlock joint should be in one vertical line.
b    If the hocks are bent outwards, i.e. 'bandy-hocked', or:
c    If the hocks are turned inwards, i.e. 'cow-hocked', or:
d    Any other deviation from the normal is a fault and possible source of weakness.

iii   Seen from the side the hock should be broad in all parts:

    *a*   As a guide a line from the top of the thigh should pass through the front of the hock joint and reach the ground midway between the toe and the heel.

    *b*   If the hocks are too bent, i.e. 'sickle-hocked' (or the foot too far back), the tendons are liable to be strained.

    *c*   If the hocks are too straight (or the foot too far forward), this causes concussion and is a source of weakness.

    *d*   Any deviation from the normal is a fault and possible source of weakness.

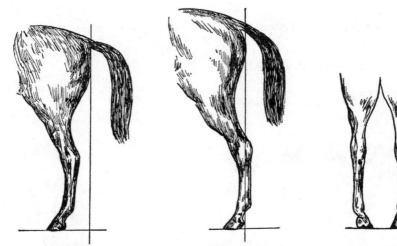

Hock too far under     · Leg too far behind     · Bandy Hocks

iv   The distance from the point of the hip to the point of the hock should be about two and a half times the length from the point of the hock to the fetlock joint.

v   With such measurements a horse might be termed 'well let down'.

The hind cannon, or shank, bones, chestnuts, fetlocks, pasterns, coronets and feet are as above, with the differences noted.

*Section 2   The Action*
After studying the points individually and the conformation as a whole the horse cannot finally be evaluated until it has been seen moving:

*1*   Its action or gait must be studied from the side, also from both front and rear.

2 It must be both walked and trotted in hand over a hard level surface for at least a dozen yards or so.

i From the side at the walk:

    *a* Its action should be long and free.
    *b* The hindfeet should step just in front of the prints of the forefeet.
    *c* The length of each diagonal should be the same.
    *d* The feet should be picked up freely, without stumbling, or dragging the hindfeet.

ii From the side at the trot:

    *a* The movement should be lively and the feet picked up cleanly.
    *b* Each beat should be clear and well marked.
    *c* Each diagonal should be equal to the other.
    *d* There should be no dragging of the hind toes.

iii From the front and rear:

    *a* The action should be straight.
    *b* There should be no throwing out of the feet, i.e. dishing.
    *c* The forefeet and hindfeet should take the same track.
    *d* There should be no turning in of the toes, or brushing against fetlocks or coronets.

*Section 3   The Colours and Body Markings of the Horse*
To try to standardize descriptions of colours and markings the Royal College of Veterinary Surgeons have issued their own recommendations, which are included in the following:

*The Whole Colours*
The whole colours are all one body colour except for the mane and tail and any white body markings, as follows:

i Bay:
Bay varies considerably in shade, from a dull red approaching brown, to a yellowish colour approaching chestnut: almost always with black points; i.e. black from the knee down: three main shades:

    *a* Bay: includes bright bay;
    *b* Dark Bay;
    *c* Light Bay, includes mealy bay.

ii Bay-Brown:
Predominating colour brown, muzzle bay.

iii Black:
Melanistic pigment general throughout the body, coat, limbs, mane and tail with no pattern factor present other than white markings.

iv Black-Brown:
The predominating colour black, with muzzle, and sometimes flanks, brown, or tan.

v Brown:
A mixture of melanistic and chocolate pigment, without yellow, in the body coat: distinguishable from bay, or chestnut, by the muzzle coloration.

N.B. If in any doubt as to colour, always check muzzle and eyes.

vi Chestnut:
There are three shades of chestnut:

a   Chestnut: including, bright, golden and red chestnut;
b   Dark Chestnut: including liver and mahogany chestnut;
c   Light Chestnut: including sorrel.

vii Cream:
A body coat of a cream colour, with unpigmented skin: the iris of the eye is deficient of pigment and may be devoid of it, giving the eye a pinkish appearance.

viii Dun:
A black coloration of the skin of the horse: of two kinds:

a   Blue Dun:
The colour of the coat a dilute black evenly distributed (giving a blue colour) with or without a dorsal band, or withers stripe or eel stripe always a black mane and tail.
b   Yellow Dun:
A diffuse yellow pigment in the hair, with, or without, a dorsal band, withers stripe, or bars on the legs. Striping is correlated with dark pigment on the head and limbs: when striping is absent the limbs will approximate to the colour of the body coat.

N.B. The primitive colour of the horse appears to have been a sandy dun, with a black 'eel stripe' down the back and black points.

ix Grey:
Body coat a varying mosaic of black and white hair, with skin black: with increasing age the coat grows lighter in colour:

*a* There are many variations of grey according to age and the season of the year: e.g. light, dark, dappled and flea-bitten.
*b* In horses of this colour any distinctive hoof markings may be useful for purposes of identification.

x Palomino:
(Not included by R.C.V.S.) A particular golden colour 'of a newly minted coin' with white mane and tail. May be:

*a* Light Palomino ⎫
*b* Medium Palomino ⎬ Mane and tail varying from silver to flaxen.
*c* Dark Palomino ⎭

*Broken Coloured*
Broken coloured, or more than one colour, may be:

i Odd Coloured:
The coat consists of a mixture of more than two colours, tending to merge into each other at the edge of the patches, with irregular body markings not classifiable as Piebald, or Skewbald.

ii Piebald:

A combination of black and white in irregular patches:
*a* It may be in large and striking patterns and combinations.
*b* In the U.S.A. this is known as a Pinto.

*The Body Markings*
Marks on the body in addition to the basic colouring by which the horse may be described for identification purposes:

i Black Marks:
Small areas of black hairs on white, or any other colour in any part of the body. (This covers the term 'Ermine Mark'.)

ii Flecked:
Small collections of white hairs distributed irregularly in any part of the body: may be described as heavily flecked or lightly flecked.

iii Grey-Ticked:
Isolated white hairs sparsely distributed through the coat in any part of the body.

iv Mane and Tail:
The presence of odd-coloured hairs in the mane and tail should be noted where they occur.

v  Patch:
This is used to describe any large, well-defined irregular area of hairs differing from the general body colour.

vi  Spots:
Small, more or less circular, collections of hairs differing from the general body colour, distributed in various parts of the body.

vii  Zebra Marks:
Striping on the limbs, neck, withers or quarters.

*Limb Markings*

i  White Coronet:
The hair immediately above the hoof, white.

ii  White Heel:

 a  The heel as from the back of the pastern to the ergot.
 b  Where white is confined to one or both bulbs of the heel it should be so specified.

iii  White Pastern:

 a  'Pastern' as from immediately below the fetlock joint down.
 b  Any variation of extent defined: viz, half pastern, three-quarter pastern.

iv  White Fetlock:

 a  'Fetlock' defined as the region of the fetlock joint down.
 b  Any variation of the white should be defined as above.

Sock

Stocking

v   Sock:

    *a*   Common usage for white marking to half-way up cannon.

    *b*   R.C.V.S. recommend precise definitions; e.g. white to middle of cannon, or shank: with variations noted.

vi   Stocking:

    *a*   Common usage for white marking to the region of knee or hock.

    *b*   R.C.V.S. recommend 'white to knee, or hock': variations noted.

*Head Markings*

i   Blaze:

Blaze

Star

Star, Race and Snip

Star and Stripe

45

    *a*    A white marking covering almost the whole of the forehead between the eyes.

    *b*    It should extend down the face the whole width of the nasal bones.

    *c*    It may have variations or addition which should be included in any description.

ii    Lip Markings:
These should be accurately described, whether including the whole or a portion of either lip.

iii    Snip:

    *a*    A single white mark in the region of the nostrils.

    *b*    It may vary in size or position, or may be joined to a stripe.

iv    Star:

    *a*    A white mark on the forehead.

    *b*    The size, shape and position may vary considerably and should be described accurately.

v    Stripe:

    *a*    A narrow white mark running down the face vertically.

    *b*    May be joined to a star or snip, but not wider than the nasal bones.

    *c*    Also known as a rase, race, rache, reach, streak, and strip.

vi    White Face:

    *a*    White covering the forehead and front of the face, extending laterally towards the mouth.

    *b*    The extension may be unilateral, or bilateral, i.e. on one side or both, and should be described accordingly.

vii    White muzzle:
White including both lips and nostrils.

*General Markings*

i    Mixed:
Used to describe a marking consisting of the general colour mixed with many white or lighter-coloured hairs.

ii    Bordered:
Used where any marking is circumscribed by a mixed border: viz: bordered star, bordered stripe.

ii   Flesh marks:
Patches where the pigment of the skin is absent should be described as flesh marks.

iv   Adventitious marks:
Permanent marks, but not congenital: i.e. due to galls, branding, etc. These should be described wherever they occur.

*Section 4   Terms describing a Horse's Sex, Age and Height:*
i   The following terms are used for both sex and age:

   *a*   Colt: a young entire, i.e. uncastrated horse (also used of racehorses up to three years of age).
   *b*   An entire: an uncastrated, or ungelded, horse: a colt, or stallion.
   *c*   Filly: a young female horse, up to three years of age.
   *d*   Foal: a young horse of either sex: this may be qualified, viz: a filly foal, a colt foal.
   *e*   Gelding: a castrated male horse.
   *f*   Horse: used generally to mean an animal of either sex, but strictly means a stallion, or entire.
   *g*   Mare: a female horse over three years.
   *h*   Yearling: a foal becomes a yearling at a year old.

ii   Terms used in ageing a horse, i.e. referring to its age, are as follows:

   *a*   Rising: this means approaching, i.e. nearly six would be termed rising six.
   *b*   Off. means passed, i.e. over six years old is termed six off.
   *c*   Aged: means over nine years old.

iii   A horse's height is measured from the highest point of the withers to the ground:

   *a*   These measurements are normally given in gradations of 4 inches known as hands.
   *b*   A hand may be subdivided in inches: 0·1, 0·2 or 0·3.
   *c*   Thus a measurement of 12·3 hands equals 51 inches.
   *d*   Hands may be abbreviated in print thus: h.h.
   *e*   Any horse of 14·2 h.h., or under, is termed a pony. See below.

*Section 5   British Horses and Ponies*
The British horses and ponies may be divided into heavy and light draught horses, saddle horses and ponies.

*The Heavy Draught Horse Breeds*
The various breeds of heavy draught horses are as follows:

i  The Shire:
   It is generally assumed that they are descended from 100 heavy war-horse
   stallions imported by King John from the Low Countries:

   a  They stand 17 hands high and weigh up to a ton.
   b  They may be of any colour and are notable for the profuse feathering
      on their massive legs.
   c  They are extremely powerful, docile and hard workers.

ii  The Clydesdale:
    The Clydesdale supposedly originates from a team of Flemish black horses
    imported in 1693 by the Duke of Hamilton in the Clyde valley:

    a  They stand from 16 to 17 hands and are lighter and more active than
       the Shire, though probably of similar war-horse origin.
    b  They may be of any colour, though commonly bay with a white face.
    c  The feathering on the legs is finer and not as heavy as the Shire.
    d  In quality and carriage the Clydesdale exceeds the Shire.

iii  The Suffolk Punch:
     Undoubtedly descended from a native breed of horse in East Anglia in
     existence for the past 500 years, of remarkably uniform type:

     a  They stand only 16 hands high, on short legs, free from feather, but are
        deep in the body with a powerful crest and good head.
     b  They may be of varying colours of chestnut with very little white,
        but the most favoured colour is reddish-chestnut.
     c  They are extremely tough and hardy and accustomed to the vagaries
        of the English climate.

iv  The Percheron:
    The Percheron was only imported from France after the 1914–18 War:

    a  They stand over 16 hands and are built somewhat like the Suffolk
       Punch.
    b  They are generally either black or grey.
    c  Docile and intelligent, they are accepted as particularly hard workers.

*The Light Draught Horse Breeds*
The breeds of light draught horse are as follows:

i  The Cleveland Bay:
   The Cleveland Bay is a large breed of carriage horse, bred in Yorkshire and

probably of war-horse origin with strong infusions of Arab and Thoroughbred blood, resulting in a very handsome horse:

a    The breed stands from 15·3 to 16·2 hands.
b    They are bay coloured with black mane and tail and black points.
c    They are noted for their reliability and all-round utility, as well as
     handsome appearance; also making a useful hunter or saddle horse.

ii   The Yorkshire Coach Horse:
     The Yorkshire Coach Horse has been bred in Yorkshire for 300 years and
     is lighter and faster than the Cleveland Bay:

a    They stand between 15 and 15·2 hands.
b    They are bay, or brown, with black mane and tail and black points.
c    They are frequently crossed to produce hunters and saddle horses or
     improve other breeds abroad.

iii  The Hackney Horse has been in existence as a breed for over 200 years, but
     the Hackney Stud Book was started less than 100 years ago:

a    They stand from 15 to 16 hands with the characteristic high-stepping
     hackney action and arched neck.
b    They may be all colours, though greys are rare and four white feet are
     valued.
c    A delight to drive and full of fire and life, now principally bred for the
     show ring, where their spectacular action may be seen.

iv   The Hackney Pony:
     Bred from the Hackney Horse and Welsh ponies, they have the same out-
     standing action:

a    They should only stand 14·2 hands.
b    They are commonly chestnut, bay and brown.

*The Saddle Horses*
The Saddle Horse breeds and types are as follows:

i    The Thoroughbred:
     The Thoroughbred has both parents registered in the General Stud Book,
     a register kept since 1791, although records go further back:

a    The Godolphin Arabian, the Darley Arabian, the Alcock Arabian and
     the Byerley Turk are amongst the seventeenth- and eighteenth-century
     imported horses which greatly influenced the breed.
b    The height may vary from 15·2 hands upwards, even exceeding 17
     hands.

*c*   The colours may vary from bay, brown, chestnut, to black and grey.
*d*   The head is lean and fine, the eyes intelligent and the body, conformation and action suggesting speed and quality.

ii   The Arab:
The Arab may be registered as Pure Bred, Part Bred, or Anglo-Arab, i.e. Thoroughbred/Arab cross, with the Arab Horse Society:

*a*   The Arab comes from the shores of the Mediterranean.
*b*   They are seldom over 15 hands and the colours may vary from bay, chestnut, brown, white, or grey: black is uncommon.
*c*   They are distinguished by their small head, concave profile, arched neck and gracefully carried tail.
*d*   They are full of courage and intelligence and of immense staying power.
*e*   They make an ideal cross with almost any native breed to cure faults and weaknesses.

iii   The Hunter:
The hunter is a type rather than a breed; hence it is difficult to set any standards for colour, or size, although it may be registered in the Hunter Stud Book:

*a*   A hunter type is one that can follow hounds across country, carry weight and stay.
*b*   It will require blood, quality, good conformation and action.
*c*   The hunter must be able to gallop and stay, hence must have depth of chest, powerful loins, a strong back and be well ribbed up, with plenty of bone.
*d*   The hunter may vary from 16 to 17 hands, but about 16·2 is the preferred height.
*e*   Subdivisions of hunters are lightweight hunters, carrying up to 13 stone 7 lb: middleweight hunters, carrying up to 14 stone 7 lb and heavyweight hunters carrying over 14 stone 7 lb.
*f*   The best type of Thoroughbred carrying these weights is the ideal hunter type; but failing that either a Thoroughbred cross, or Cleveland Bay cross, or similar.

iv   The Hack:
The hack is also a type of horse, not a breed, and there is no Hack Stud Book; it is the term loosely used to describe any horse simple ridden for pleasure:

*a*   A show hack should be a small thoroughbred type, under 15·3 hands.

*b*    The classes for hacks vary from under 15·1 to under 15·3 and even the smaller hack must move like a horse, not a pony.

*c*    The show hack should have a small fine head and good arched neck carriage and must be an outstanding mover.

*d*    He must also be extremely well schooled.

v    The Cob:
The cob is also a type not a breed, being a term used to describe a stocky, thick-set, small, powerful horse over 14 hands, but not over 15 hands, i.e. between horse and pony size:

*a*    The typical cob is the type of dual-purpose ride and drive horse favoured by farmers in the past.

*b*    The height of a show cob is limited to 15·2 hands; the body should be powerful, with small head and arched neck, short strong back and powerful quarters, and good tail carriage.

*c*    Used to be docked before the Act of 1955, now greatly improved with full tail.

*d*    Breeding generally accidental from half-bred or cart-horse mare and thoroughbred stallion, or similar, but may be deliberate.

vi    The Polo Pony:
The polo pony is also a type rather than a breed and is a pony in name only, not now being restricted in size, although at one time limited to 14·2 hands:

*a*    The polo pony requires a long neck with excellent flexion, good shoulders and a short back with well-sprung ribs and very powerful quarters and hocks: they must be courageous.

*b*    Bred from Thoroughbred hunter crosses and Welsh Cob blood, also Argentine stock crossed with Thoroughbreds.

*The Pony Breeds*
The term pony includes, by general definition, any horse under 14·2 hands: The native breeds of pony in Britain are as follows:

i    The Shetland:
The Shetland is probably the best-known breed of pony in Great Britain, as well as being both the smallest and one of the oldest:

*a*    The maximum height for the breed stud book is 42 inches: it is measured in inches, not hands: the smallest known is 26 inches.

*b*    The breed is known in all colours, although white is disliked.

*c*    The head is small and fine, the body neat and compact, the mane and tail profuse.

    *d*    They are sure-footed, intelligent and docile, as well as strong and courageous and full of character: must be well handled.

ii    The Highland:
There are three breeds of Highland pony, the Barra, the Mull and the Garron; all are sufficiently hardy to live out on the hill throughout the year:

    *a*    Depending on the breed the size may vary from 12·2 to 14·2 hands.
    *b*    Most colours are common, but dun to cream with a black eel stripe down the back and black points to the legs is preferred.
    *c*    The head is broad between the eyes with wide nostrils and dished face, plentiful mane and tail.
    *d*    The pony is gentle, sure-footed, intelligent and strong, used for carrying deer on the hills returning from stalking, also for pony trekking.

iii    The New Forest:
The New Forest pony, as the name suggests, comes from the area of the New Forest in Hampshire, where they were noted in the tenth century:

    *a*    It may not grow much more than 13 hands; certainly not more than 14 hands or thereabouts.
    *b*    It is generally found in bay, or brown, but may be any colour.
    *c*    Owing to the poor grazing available, accustomed to surviving on very little, but also sometimes lacking substance.
    *d*    They are inclined to be short in the neck, but with good shoulders, short back and strong loins and quarters.
    *e*    They are surefooted, easily made and schooled, and make a good mount for a child, or a useful harness pony.
    *f*    They are very quickly made traffic-proof, generally of good temperament and cross well with an Arab.

iv    The Exmoor:
The Exmoor breed found in Devon and Somerset is an extremely hardy pony and makes a fine child's mount:

    *a*    It generally measures under 12·2 hands, but is a good weight carrier.
    *b*    The colours vary from bays to brown, with characteristic mealy-coloured nose, which is a distinctive feature of the breed.
    *c*    The head is small, with a flattish profile, wide nostrils and forehead and small ears.
    *d*    It also makes a useful harness pony.

v   The Fell:
The Fell pony is similar to the original Dales pony, but hails from the west side of the Pennines, or Lake District, used as a pack-horse from the lead-mines to the sea:

a   The Fell is generally 13·2 hands and not exceeding 14 hands.
b   The colours vary from brown, bay, black, grey, to dun, but they are never chestnut.
c   Short-legged, but fast and active, they are a sturdy, strong animal, sure-footed and a useful weight carrier for their size.
d   They have a considerable mane and tail and silky hair at the fetlocks, useful as a saddle or harness pony.

vi   The Dales:
They were originally pack-horses similar to the Fell ponies, but found east of the Pennines: they now have much Clydesdale blood:

a   The best description of the Dales pony today is 'a miniature cart-horse:' although they do not exceed 14·2 hands.
b   The colours are chiefly black, brown, bay and grey.
c   They are sure-footed, have marked trotting abilities and great powers of endurance.
d   They have a short, well-arched neck, short strong back, fine hair at the heels and good legs and feet.
e   They are docile and easily made and schooled either for riding or driving.

vii   The Connemara:
The Connemara is a hardy compact pony from the West of Ireland, dating back several centuries and much influenced by Arab blood:

a   They generally stand between 13 and 14 hands.
b   The most popular colour is grey, but black, brown and bay are common.
c   Although sometimes inclined to be straight in the shoulder, they are a useful combination ride and drive pony, equally useful in either sphere.

viii   The Welsh Cob:
The only type of cob which has an actual name, the breed has evolved from the old Welsh Cart-horse through many crosses including Thoroughbred:

a   They vary from slightly under 14 hands to 15 hands.
b   The colours also vary, but bay, browns and greys are favoured.

  *c* They are a very strong ride and drive type, short-legged and fast trotters.

  *d* They have a silky mane and heel tufts.

ix The Welsh Mountain Pony:
The Welsh Mountain Pony is a hardy, spirited little native pony strongly resembling the Arab in appearance:

  *a* It seldom exceeds 12 hands.

  *b* Like the Welsh Cob above, it is generally bay, brown, or grey.

  *c* It can cope with extremely heavy weights very easily whether in harness or being ridden.

  *d* The breed crosses particularly well with the Arab.

x The Dartmoor Pony
The Dartmoor Pony is a well known little pony native to Dartmoor.

  *a* It does not exceed 12·2 h.h.

  *b* It is generally bay.

  *c* It is handy and a good child's pony.

# PART II
# The Saddle, Bridle and Ancillaries

*Section 1    The Saddle*

The saddle is basically a seat for the rider on the horse's back which has been developed since about the fourth century A.D.

i   Purpose:
    It is equipped with stirrups and held in place by a girth round the horse's belly. Its purpose is twofold:

*a*   It is intended to ease the rider.

*b*   It is also intended to ease the horse by distributing the rider's weight

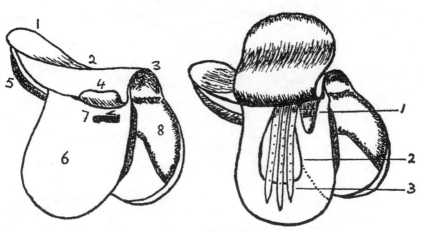

Parts of the saddle

1. Cantle. 2. Seat. 3. Pommel. 4. Skirt over       1. Part of the front arch of the tree.
spring. 5. Rear part of panel. 6. Flap.            2. Sweat flap. 3. Girth leathers.
7. Spring bar. 8. Front part of panel.

evenly over the strongest parts of the horse's back and preventing pressure on any vulnerable parts.

ii  Parts:

The parts of the saddle are as follows:

Interior:

a   The saddle tree: the framework of the saddle, consisting of two side-bars, or panels, joined by a metal, or alloy, arch at front and rear. Laminated wood, or fibreglass, may be used for modern trees. This provides resilience equivalent to a spring tree.

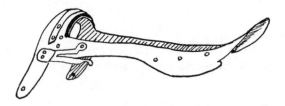

Conventional Saddle Tree

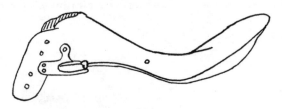

Spring Tree

b   Spring tree: this is a type of saddle tree so called due to the insertion of a light piece of steel on either side of the tree in the panels at their widest point, to provide spring or resilience in the seat of the saddle and thus intensify the rider's action.

c   The front arch, or gullet: the front part of the tree, shaped to curve round the withers.

d   The head, or pommel: the rounded top of the front arch, or gullet, which may be cut back to make room for the withers. In a spring tree is generally cut back at 45°.

e   The points, or burrs: the two wings which project on either side of the withers.

f   The bars: the metal clips, generally recessed on either side of the saddle tree to hold the stirrup leathers; usually equipped with a safety catch, which should be left open in use.

g   The back arch, or cantle: the junction of the two side-bars, or panels, at the rear of the saddle tree.

Exterior:

a   The seat: a shaped piece of leather, generally pigskin, fitted on to the tree over a webbing base.

b   The skirts: welted to the waist of the seat, they cover the bars on either side.

c   The flaps: the large shaped leather portion of the saddle, which receives the knee and thigh of the rider. Of differing cut with types of saddle. May include knee-rolls for jumping.

d   The surcingle slot, or loop: in the rear of the flap to take the surcingle when used, i.e. broad leather strap fitting over the saddle and girths for extra security.

e   The panels, on which the saddle rests on the horse's back: may be full, short or cut to particular shapes; may be covered with linen, serge or leather and stuffed with wool or felt. Leather last the longest, but requires attention to keep it soft and pliable.

f   The channel: the hollow between the two arches, or padded parts of the saddle tree. Should not touch the horse's spine at any point.

g   The pommel: the front arch of the saddle; D-rings on each side.

h   The cantle: the rear arch of the saddle, D-rings on each side.

iii   Types of saddle:

a   All-purpose, or general purpose: a modern saddle, with spring tree

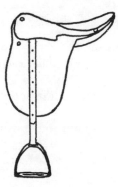 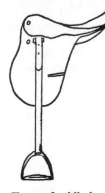 

Types of saddle *l. to r.*
Show, Hunting, Forward Seat.

    and dip, with moderate forward flaps, suitable for hunting, hacking, dressage, and cross-country work.

*b*    Army, or universal: a skeleton saddle resting on a folded blanket, or numnah-pad, thus fitting any type of horse.

*c*    Dressage: with dipped seat and straight flaps, designed to place the rider over the centre of gravity.

*d*    Hunting, or conventional English saddle: generally with a little dip in the seat.

*e*    Jumping: generally deep-seated with knee-rolls and panels set well forward.

*f*    Polo: generally deeper and with a higher cantle than the hunting saddle.

*g*    Racing: particularly lightweight with forward flaps, to avoid adding to the jockey's weight.

*h*    Show: generally with a straight-cut flap designed to show off the horse's front.

*i*    Side: fitted with two pommels, generally on the near side, for a lady to ride with both legs on one side under a habit.

*Section 2*   *Fitting the Saddle*

It is most important that the saddle fits the horse correctly and fulfils its proper functions:

i    To distribute the rider's weight evenly over the strongly muscled parts of the back, clear of the vulnerable spinal column; also:

    *a*    To avoid saddle galls; and

    *b*    To allow the maximum freedom of movement and comfort to the horse.

ii    The vertebral column must be kept free from any pressure throughout the entire length of the saddle:

    *a*    The channel must be clear of the spine throughout its length, or galls, or injury may result.

    *b*    The side-bars must distribute the weight evenly over the weight-bearing portions of the back, clear of the spine.

    *c*    To ensure this two fingers should pass easily under both arches, when the rider is in the saddle.

    *d*    Hence a wide-backed horse must have a wide tree and a narrow-backed horse a narrow tree.

    *e*    Due allowance must always be made for loss of condition after steady work.

*f* Similar allowance must be made when a horse is first brought in from grass.

*g* The fit of the saddle should be tested at fairly frequent intervals as a matter of course.

iii The withers must not be pressed or pinched in any way:

*a* The front arch should be at least an inch clear of the withers.
*b* Due allowance must be made for prominent withers.
*c* Broad withers will require a correspondingly broad arch.
*d* The front of the saddle must allow absolute freedom for the shoulder blades, i.e. both the front arch and the panel.

iv The rear end of the side-bars must not touch the loins:

*a* There is constant movement here and if it does a painful injury, or saddle gall, will quickly follow.
*b* The unprotected kidneys lie beneath the loins.
*c* A short-backed horse must therefore have a short saddle tree.

v Exceptional conformation of the withers may require special care:

*a* Very high withers and a 'greyhound conformation' may result in the saddle constantly slipping backwards on to the loins.
*b* A breastplate attached to the saddle is fitted so that the upper edge of the leather is three fingers' breadth above the breast-bone. See p. 80.
*c* The breastplate should allow the breadth of the hand between it and the flat of the shoulder.
*d* Very broad low withers overlaid with fat may result in the saddle constantly slipping forward.
*e* In such cases a crupper strap fitted to a crupper round the dock is attached to the rear of the saddle to keep it in position.

vi The saddle should be tested for correct fit by:

*a* Placing a saddle blanket on the horse's back.
*b* Placing the saddle in position on the blanket and tightening the girth.
*c* Mounting the horse.
*d* Testing the front arch, while the rider leans forward.
*e* Testing the rear arch, while the rider leans back.
*f* As stated above two fingers should pass easily under each.
*g* Check for blade-bone pressure by passing the fingers behind the shoulder blade while the foreleg on that side is held straight out in front by the toe of the hoof. It should be possible to do so without the fingers being pinched.

*h*   Each shoulder should be tested in turn.

*i*   Dismounting carefully, the saddle should then be removed and uneven impressions in the blanket should be looked for when the saddle is lifted off.

*j*   If there are any signs of uneven, or incorrect pressure, then the padding of the saddle should be altered accordingly.

N.B. When a saddle has been repadded it is always advisable to check the fit over the first fortnight as the padding settles.

## Section 3   Saddling-up
Saddling the horse:

i   The saddle should always be brought up over the croup from the near-side and placed gently well forward on the horse's back.

    *a*   It should then be slid gently back into its correct position thus smoothing down the hairs beneath it.

    *b*   The girth should be attached on the off-side and looped over the saddle.

    *c*   The stirrups should always be raised and not dangling on the ends of the leathers.

    *d*   The saddle should never be dumped on the horse without any warning being given of what to expect.

    *e*   Apart from a cautionary friendly word the free hand should be used to give the back a preparatory stroke or rub down.

    *f*   If the weather is extremely cold it may be as well to warm the saddle slightly before saddling-up.

    *g*   With horses known to suffer from 'cold back' it may be advisable not only to warm the saddle, but rub them down gently before saddling-up.

ii   When the saddle is in the correct position the girth may then be buckled into place:

    *a*   It should not be necessary to do the girth up tightly at once. This may be left until just prior to mounting.

    *b*   It is preferable merely to adjust the strap sufficiently at first to keep the saddle in position.

iii   If a numnah, blanket, or pad is being used, this should be placed in position before the saddle:

    *a*   A blanket is normally folded in four with the longer end across the horse, the free edges to the rear and near-side.

    *b*   The saddle should then be placed on top of it.

    *c*   It must be checked that the numnah, blanket, or pad is perfectly smooth, free of wrinkles and lifted slightly into the arches of the saddle, to prevent galls.

    *d*   The girth may then be done up as above.

### Section 4   *The Girths*

The broad straps encircling the belly to keep the saddle in place, with one, or generally two, buckles and straps at each end:

i    The girths are attached to the girth straps on the saddle, which are fitted to the saddle bars:

    *a*   The girths should pass under the horse's belly about 4 inches behind the point of the elbow, neither too close to restrict its movement, nor too far back to restrict the horse's breathing.

    *b*   The off-side straps should be buckled before the saddle is placed in position on the horse's back.

    *c*   The girths should generally be done up from the near-side, except in unusual circumstances, as in training a youngster.

    *d*   When the girths are fastened, as above, the saddle should be held firmly in place.

ii    Girths are generally made in sizes from 36 inches to 54 inches long and from $3\frac{1}{2}$ to 5 inches wide. They may be made from:

    *a*   Leather—of three principal types: the Balding, double straps crossing over at the middle to allow plenty of elbow room and prevent chafing; the Atherstone, tapering in the centre for similar reasons; the Three-Fold, folded in three, sometimes with a serge centre to retain grease. All last for years, but require attention to keep them clean and soft.

    *b*   Webbing: generally supplied with a single buckle each end and two girths used. Webbing must be kept well brushed.

    *c*   Cotton cord: these require washing and thorough cleaning and tend to rot with sweat.

    *d*   Nylon cord: these are easier to keep clean and wash, as well as being softer and less likely to gall the horse than cotton. Amongst the best types of girth produced.

    *e*   Elastic, rawhide, hemp, twisted wool and other materials may be used for girths also, but the above are the most common.

### Section 5   *Girthing-up*

The girths should not be tightened until the horse is also bridled and is ready to be mounted:

i    They should then be gently tightened to the required degree of tightness; always remembering:

  a    The better the rider the looser the girth he requires; it should only require to be sufficiently tight to keep the saddle in place.
  b    A girth should never be excessively tight and should allow a finger to be placed under it quite easily.
  c    The finger should be inserted from the rear, so that when it is withdrawn the hair is smoothed down correctly.
  d    It is entirely unnecessary and wrong to use force or violence to do up a girth.
  e    This only encourages the horse to blow itself out to prevent the girths being tightened.
  f    A horse which is regularly girthed correctly will not resort to this common trick; it points to poor horsemastership.
  g    Should it be necessary to do so, it is always possible to tighten the girth from the horse's back, by swinging the leg forward, then lifting the flap and tightening the girth.

ii    Girth galls are generally to be found only:

  a    Through carelessness in adjusting the girth, allowing friction, or leaving dirt on the girth, or similar bad horsemastership.
  b    When a horse is ridden for too long in very soft condition.
  c    The horse should not be worked until they are cured.
  d    A girth sleeve, of rubber, or sheepskin, round the girth may be used to prevent them appearing or recurring.

*Section 6    The Stirrups, or Stirrup-irons*
A pair of metal hoops, generally bell-shaped, in which the rider's feet rest, at the correct angle, taking weight from thighs and knees:

i    They must be large enough for the rider's boot:

  a    The rider's boot must be able to enter them and withdraw from them easily.
  b    It is extremely dangerous to ride with stirrups which are too small, which may catch the feet in the event of a fall, causing the rider to be dragged.

ii    They should be heavy and hang well; they may be made of:

  a    Stainless steel: these have the advantage that they do not require much cleaning.

<blockquote>

_b_    Nickel: in which case the stirrup leathers will require care and cleaning regularly to prevent rotting.

_c_    Steel: these will require burnishing to prevent them rusting.

_d_    Chromium: these need least cleaning of all.

</blockquote>

### Section 7   _The Stirrup Leathers, or Leathers_

The leather straps by which the stirrups are fastened to the saddle, generally 4 feet to 4 feet 6 inches long and $\frac{5}{8}$ to $1\frac{1}{8}$ inches wide, with a buckle at one end:

i    They may be made of cowhide, rawhide, or buffalo hide (red leathers), the last being easily the strongest and hardest wearing, if obtainable:

<blockquote>

_a_    The side-bars of the saddle to which the leathers are hooked should never be done up, so that the leathers will slide off easily should the rider fall and be dragged.

_b_    The free end of the leathers should be tucked under and backwards, making less thickness under the leg.

_c_    This also makes adjustment on horseback easier.

_d_    As a rough guide to the length of leathers required, the irons should fit under the armpit when the tip of the fingers reach the top of the leathers at the side-bar.

</blockquote>

ii    They should be marked Right and Left (R and L):

<blockquote>

_a_    They should have matching holes punched evenly in each pair.

_b_    It is an advantage if the holes are numbered.

_c_    They should be changed over weekly, as the nearside gets the greatest strain due to the rider mounting and dismounting.

_d_    When changed over they will tend to hang wrongly and should be twisted from the stirrup to the bar until the natural 'hang' is correct.

</blockquote>

iii    Before and after riding the stirrups should be slipped up the leathers to the stirrup-bars:

<blockquote>

_a_    The leathers should then be slipped down inside them.

_b_    This keeps the stirrups up out of the way, preventing them swinging free and hitting the horse, or the rider when removing the saddle.

</blockquote>

iv    The leathers should be inspected regularly for wear:

<blockquote>

_a_    They should be oiled and cleaned regularly; but:

_b_    Worn leathers should be discarded promptly.

_c_    If not discarded as soon as wear is discovered they may be the cause of a bad accident.

</blockquote>

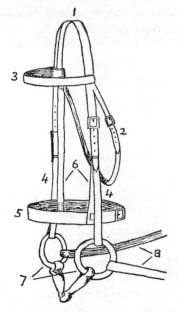

Parts of the Bridle

1. Headpiece, or Crown piece. 2. Throatlash. 3. Browband. 4. Cheek Strap or bit.
5. Noseband. 6. Cheekpiece of noseband. 7. Snaffle rings. 8. Reins.

*Section 8    The Bridle*
The parts of the bridle are as follows (double-bridle):

i    The head-stall, head-piece, or crown-piece:
    *a*    It passes from the bit on one side, over the poll and behind the ears, to the other side of the bit.
    *b*    Hence the double bridle requires two head-stalls, one for the bit, or curb-bit and one for the bridoon, or snaffle: the latter fits through the brow-band under the former.
    *c*    The head-stall should fit parallel to and behind the cheek-bone, or zygomatic ridge.
    *d*    This part behind the cheek-bone, between the bit and the head-stall, is known as the cheekpiece of the bridle and may be a separate piece or all part of the head-stall.
    *e*    The head-stall, or cheekpiece, may be fastened to the bit by stitching, buckles, or hook-studs.
    *f*    The head-stall should be fastened by a buckle on the near-side at the top of the cheekpiece.

ii The throat-lash, or throat-latch:

    *a*  It holds the head-stall in position, passing round the throat.

    *b*  It should admit at least three fingers between it and the throat.

    *c*  There should be no danger of it being too tight and choking the horse. Serious injury to the larynx might result.

    *d*  It should only be tight enough to prevent the head-stall falling off.

iii The nose-band:

    *a*  It passes round the top of the muzzle and is adjustable by means of a buckle below the jaw.

    *b*  It should be the breadth of two fingers below the cheek-bone or zygomatic ridge.

    *c*  It should be possible to insert two fingers between it and the nose.

    *d*  As a rule it is separate from the bridle and has its own head-stall, which fits through the brow-band loops inside the bit head-stall.

    *e*  It should be sufficiently rigid to keep it horizontal over the horse's nose. It should not droop.

    *f*  Its purpose is largely decorative, but a martingale may be fitted to the lower part of the nose-band. See standing martingale, p. 78.

    *g*  There are various other types of nose-band intended for various purposes. See pp. 76–7.

iv The brow-band:

    *a*  This should be roomy and allow full play for the ears.

    *b*  The brow band loops should allow room for the nose-band head-stall, as well as the two head-stalls of a double bridle.

    *c*  Coloured brow-bands are to be avoided, as they detract from the horse's appearance.

v The reins:
The reins are fastened to the bit on either side: in a double bridle there are two pairs: the upper reins are the bridoon, or snaffle, reins and the lower are the bit, or curb-bit, reins:

    *a*  In a double bridle they are invariably of leather, about 4 to 5 feet long, and generally thinner than a single snaffle-rein.

    *b*  Reins may vary from $\frac{5}{8}$ to 1 inch in width and may also be of nylon, webbing, or part rubber, but in general should be narrow and thin rather than broad and thick.

    *c*  They may be plaited, or laced, i.e. with a leather thong laced through them, or partially covered in rubber, to provide a good grip in wet conditions.

    *d*    They may be fastened to the bit, either by stitching, by buckles or by hook-studs.

vi   The bit and bridoon:

The bit, or curb-bit, is used in conjunction with the bridoon, or snaffle, to make up the double bridle. The parts of the bit, or curb-bit (generally a Weymouth, or Ward Union type), are as follows:

    *a*    The bar mouthpiece, with a port, or central curve, which normally lies flat on the tongue and raises the mouthpiece off the sensitive bars of the mouth; when the bit rotates in action the tongue fits into the port and the mouthpiece presses on the bars; hence the deeper the port the more severe the bit. See p. 73.

    *b*    The arms attached to the ends of the bar mouthpiece (fixed in a Weymouth bit, movable on a Ward Union bit) are known as the upper and lower cheekpieces, or cheeks or branches, of the bit.

    *c*    The upper cheekpieces each have a ring, known as the eye of the bit, at the upper end to which the cheekpiece of the bridle is attached, also a hook to take the curb-chain.

    *d*    The lower cheekpieces each have a small ring half-way down to which the lip strap is attached.

    *e*    At the lower end of each lower cheekpiece is a ring for the curb-rein.

    *f*    The longer the lower cheekpiece in relation to the upper cheekpiece the greater the leverage and the more severe the bit. See action, pp. 68–72.

    *g*    The upper cheekpiece must not be too long or the function of the curb-chain and of the bit itself will be valueless, or else actively harmful. See action, pp. 67–8.

The parts of the bridoon, or snaffle, are as follows:

    *a*    A simple mouthpiece jointed at the centre.

    *b*    A ring at each end of the mouthpiece to which the cheekpiece of the bridle is attached above and the reins below.

*N.B.*, as noted above:

    *a*    The bridoon, or snaffle, requires a separate head-stall fitting through the brow-band under the bit, or curb-bit, head-stall.

    *b*    The bridoon, or snaffle, also requires its own pair of reins, which are the upper pair of the two pairs and are held above and separate from the bit, or curb-bit, reins. See pp. 92–3.

vii  The curb-chain:

The curb-chain is a chain of steel, or stainless steel, of some nineteen links, which is hooked into place on the hook attached to the ring at the top of each upper cheekpiece:

a   It should be thick, as this is more humane and less likely to cause unnecessary pain if injudiciously used.

b   For the same reason and because its true function is then lost it must on no account be put on incorrectly, i.e. twisted, or badly fitting, too tight, too loose.

c   If the curb-chain is rough, or is causing pain beneath the jaw, the whole reason for fitting the curb-chain is nullified, i.e. its operation is intended to cause the jaw to flex and this may cause the horse to brace against the pain. See Action of bridle, pp. 68–9.

d   One end should be hooked on to the far-side hook and the curb-chain should then be twisted until the links lie flat.

e   One, two, or more links are then taken up to make the chain the right length and the last link is given an extra half-turn before being hooked on the near-side hook.

f   It should be possible to pass at least two fingers inside the curb-chain when the bit rein is relaxed.

g   When fitting correctly the curb-chain should lie flat against the chin groove when the curb-rein is tightened; on no account should it lie above the chin groove.

h   The correct length of the curb-chain should be such that when the cheekpieces of the curb-bit are at 45° from their normal position it is taut.

viii  The lip-strap:

The lip-strap is a short thin strap attached to the small rings about half-way down the lower cheekpieces of the curb-bit, also to the centre of the curb-chain, either through a small ring attached to the curb-chain for that purpose, or through one of the links:

a   Its purpose is to prevent the curb-bit from turning forwards in the horse's mouth and reversing itself, or becoming upside down, when the horse throws its head up suddenly, also to stop the horse taking hold of the cheekpieces in its lips.

b   It also helps to keep the curb-chain in place and may even sometimes take the place of the curb-chain if the chain bothers the horse, but it should then be adjusted accordingly.

## Section 9   The Fit and Action of the Bridle

The fit of the bit and the bridoon is a matter of individual care for each horse, since no two are alike:

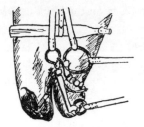

The Curb Chain and Lip Strap: Correct Fitting

i  The bit. The bit, or curb-bit, should be adjusted to come midway between the corners of the mouth and the incisors, or about an inch above the tushes of a horse and 2 inches above the incisors of a mare, across the bars of the mouth:

  a  There should be about ¼ inch play on each side, so that it neither pinches the lips, nor slides from side to side. If it is over-large it will slide to one side and cause a one-sided mouth.

  b  Pressure on the reins rotates the bit, pulling the lower cheekpiece back and the upper cheekpiece forward, inducing a lever action on the bars of the mouth: as stated above, when the cheekpieces are 45° from normal the curb-chain should be taut in the chin groove; this exerts pressure via the mouthpiece on the sensitive bars of the mouth—the greater the port in the mouthpiece the more severe the pressure; hence the port should never be too severe.

  c  The longer the lower cheekpiece compared with the upper cheekpiece the greater the leverage obtainable, hence the more severe the bit, but if the upper cheekpiece is too long the curb-chain may not fit correctly and another bit should be used: incorrect fit here, or elsewhere, falsifies the action.

  d  The action of the curb-bit and curb-chain is to induce the horse to open the lower jaw slightly to gain relief from the pressure on the sensitive bars of the mouth, i.e. to relax the jaw and flex the neck muscles.

  e  It is thus possible by judicious use of the bit, or curb-bit, to position the head correctly horizontally.

ii  The bridoon. The bridoon, or snaffle, fits above the curb-bit, just touching the corners of the mouth without wrinkling them:

  a  The snaffle acts on the corners of the lips and tongue, if the reins are pulled straight back, or upwards.

  b  This has the effect of raising the head, so that by judicious use of the snaffle the head can be positioned correctly vertically, i.e. raised and lowered.

iii  By correct use of the bit and bridoon combined with the other aids (see pp. 290–307) the horse can be trained to the highest degree of advanced equitation.

iv  The fitting of the bit and bridoon is a matter of individual care for each horse, since no two are alike. This cannot be repeated too often.

*Section 10  Bridling*
The act of putting the bridle on the horse (a double-bridle):

i  The bridle should always be put on from the near-side, while standing level with the horse's head:

   *a*  The nose-band of the bridle should first be undone to avoid it getting in the way.
   *b*  The reins should then be looped over the horse's neck with the right hand, to provide control if necessary.
   *c*  At the same time, the horse's muzzle should be gently but firmly held by the left hand also holding the top of the head-stall.

ii  The head-stall should now be transferred to the right hand and lifted up towards the horse's ears:

   *a*  At the same instant the left hand slips the bridoon and bit into the horse's mouth.
   *b*  As the bit is accepted the left hand holds the muzzle down and the right hand slips the head-stall gently over the ears and into position.

iii  There should be no fuss or struggle involved, or the horse may be reluctant to accept the bridle on the next occasion:

   *a*  If the horse is reluctant to open his mouth to receive the bit, the left thumb should be inserted gently behind the incisors and the bit slipped in as his mouth opens.
   *b*  Care must be taken of the horse's eyes and ears as the head-stall is being placed in position.

iv  The nose-band and throat-lash, or throat-latch, should next be fastened and correctly adjusted, while the fit of the bit and bridoon and the rest of the bridle should also be checked automatically.

v  The curb-chain should then be adjusted and hooked into position:

    *a*    The action of the curb-bit and the curb-chain should then be tested to make sure they are correct.

    *b*    Finally the lip-strap may be secured in position.

vi    If the horse is reluctant to lower his head, or is difficult to bridle, the following method may be used, from the near-side, facing the same direction as the horse, level with his head:

Putting on Snaffle Bridle: arm under jaw.

    *a*    The reins should first be looped over the horse's neck to provide control if necessary.

    *b*    The bridoon and the bit should be held in the left hand, thumb upwards.

    *c*    The nose-band may be unfastened to ease the bridling if desired.

    *d*    The muzzle should be held gently but firmly down by the right hand holding the cheekpieces of the bridle; the right arm under the jaw. See illustration.

    *e*    The bridoon and bit should be gently inserted into the mouth with the left hand, the left thumb inserted, as above, if required.

    *f*    As the bit is accepted the right hand raises the cheekpieces and hence the bridoon and bit into position and the left hand then takes over from the right.

    *g*    The right hand is then transferred to slip the head-stall gently over the ear and into position.

    *h*    The bridle is then adjusted as above.

vii    If the horse is to be left in the box for a short time after bridling, loop the reins behind the stirrup leathers, ensuring that they are even, but in that case do not do up the curb-chain. (*N.B.* The stirrups should be slipped up the leathers as noted above):

*a* The reins should on no account be left loose around the horse's neck, as if he tosses his head and they trail to the ground he might then put his foot on them and either break them or give himself a bad jab in the mouth.

*b* If the horse is left and by misadventure succeeds in getting the reins loose as described, he is less likely to injure himself if the curb chain is not in position.

viii Frozen bits. A really cold bit should never be put into the horse's mouth without warming it first:

*a* Frozen metal sticks to the skin and may cause severe burns.

*b* The harness-room where the bridles are kept should be warmed, but in really cold weather always ensure that the bit is warm enough before inserting it in the horse's mouth.

## Section 11  *Bits, Bitting and Bitless Bridles*

There are many varieties of bit, but all are variations on the two principal types:

i The Snaffle:
The basic snaffle, as above, is simply a jointed mouthpiece with a ring at each end. Other varieties are as follows:

*a* The cheek snaffle, with fixed upper and lower cheekpieces to prevent it pulling through the mouth.

*b* The egg-butt snaffle: large rings attached to the mouthpiece with a swelling thickness of metal to prevent chafing or pulling through the mouth.

*c* The D-ring snaffle: large D-rings with the same object as the egg-butt.

*d* The Australian loose-ring cheek snaffle: fixed cheekpieces and separately attached rings (similar variations known as the Spanish Riding School snaffle and the Fulmer).

*e* The straight-bar snaffle, and half-moon vulcanite bar snaffle, or mullen-mouth snaffle, are all bar snaffles.

*f* The twisted snaffle, i.e. a jointed but twisted mouthpiece, is more severe than a plain mouthpiece.

*g* The chain snaffle: with a chain mouthpiece; very severe.

*h* The rubber snaffle: a very mild bit for a horse with a soft mouth; merely a broad rubber bar with rings at each end.

  *i*  The roller snaffle, i.e. with a number of loose 'rollers' or keys round the mouthpiece, which encourages the horse to mouth and play with the bit; good for improving a hard mouth.

  *j*  The gag snaffle: the cheekpieces of the bridle and the reins are in one piece running through the rings of the snaffle; it has a double action on the poll and the corners of the mouth; very severe (note comment below).

  *k*  The Hitchcock gag snaffle: a variant where the cheekpiece goes from the bit to a ring on the head-stall, back to a ring on the bit and thence to the reins; it has a strong raising effect. Neither of these are suitable for the inexperienced and the experienced should have no need of them.

*N.B.* As noted above the materials used in the bit may vary from rubber to vulcanite, steel, nickel, or chromium-plated steel. (The first two are mild and the last more easily cleaned.)

ii  The Curb:

The basic curb consists, as above, of a mouthpiece of various patterns attached, either fixed, or movably, to uprights divided into upper and lower cheekpieces: the upper cheekpiece has a ring at the end, the eye of the bit, to which the cheekpiece of the bridle is attached and also the hook for the curb-chain; the lower cheekpiece has a small ring about half-way down to take the lip-strap and a ring at the end to take the rein. Weymouth and Ward Union patterns have been noted above (see p. 66). Other varieties of curb are as follows:

  *a*  The Banbury: a straight-bar mouthpiece tapered to give room for the tongue in the centre; the mouthpiece is set in slots in the cheekpieces so that it can move up and down in the mouth and revolve.

  *b*  The Ninth Lancer: a straight mouthpiece, flat short lower cheeks with two slots for the reins, so that the severity may be varied; used as a mild polo bit.

  *c*  The Chifney: a long lower cheek in relation to the upper; the upper cheek is fixed, but the lower pivots round the mouthpiece; this makes it a severe bit, but ensures the curb-chain fits in the chin groove.

  *d*  The Liverpool: a driving bit and one of the best made for the purpose; it has a straight-bar mouthpiece with large cheek-rings set in the cheekpieces level with the mouthpiece; the lower cheek is flat and has two slots for the reins, which may also be fitted to the cheek rings, thus allowing a choice of three positions with corresponding mildness or severity.

  *e*  In this country, except for polo and driving, the curb is almost invariably used with a bridoon as part of a double bridle.

*f*    As noted above, the severity of the curb-bit depends on the height of the port in the mouthpiece and the length of the lower cheekpiece in relation to the upper cheekpiece; neither should be excessive.

*g*    Due to the sensitivity of the bars of the mouth, the broader the mouth-piece of the bit the more the pressure is spread, hence the milder the bit.

*h*    As noted above, correct fitting is all-important, and each horse requires a different fitting; apart from falsifying and possibly even reversing the true action of the bit, incorrect fitting may damage the mouth, deadening it, or making it one sided, or severely damaging the jaw or sensitive bars of the mouth.

When checking the width of the bit required a wooden ruler may be placed across the bars of the mouth, or interdental space, for exact measurement; if a bit is only a shade too large circular leather cheek-pieces may be inserted inside each of the cheekpieces of the bit.

iii    The Pelham:
This is a third large class of bits; an attempt to combine the merits of both bit and bridoon:

*a*    The basic Pelham, in addition to the rings for the curb-reins at the lower end of the cheekpieces, also has rings level with the mouthpiece to which the bridoon rein is attached; it also has a curb-chain, thus acting both on the bars of the mouth and the corners, but lacking the clear distinction of a double bridle. There are a variety of Pelham bits, as follows:

*b*    The Port-mouth Universal, Reversible, or Angle Cheek Pelham, is the old military reversible bit and has a lot to recommend it. It has a mouthpiece with a smooth and a serrated side; by turning the cheek-pieces either side may be used; it has snaffle rings and the lower cheek, set at an angle, is flat with two slots for the reins, one above the other, allowing a choice of severity; it can also be used for driving.

*c*    The Three-in-One: the bridle is not attached to the cheekpiece but to the rings for the snaffle-reins. Thus there is no displacement of the mouth-piece or upper cheek before the curb-chain begins to act.

*d*    The Kimblewick: an adaptation of a Spanish jumping bit; it has a large bridoon ring incorporating the lower cheek of a Pelham, thus producing a mild combination of snaffle and curb action.

*e*    The Globe Cheek: all the parts are fixed and the lower rings are loops from the lower cheekpiece.

*f*    The Scamperdale: the mouthpiece is angled back so that the cheekpiece avoids chafing the corners of the mouth.

73

Three-in-One

g   Others include the Hanoverian, with a high-port mouthpiece and rollers on the arms; the Rugby, with a fixed cheekpiece and independent snaffle-ring; there are also half-moon vulcanite, half-moon rubber, straight-bar, port-bar and jointed mouthpiece Pelhams, etc.

h   The Pelham is a useful bit, especially for a pony with a mouth rather too small for a double bridle, but compared with the double bridle it has distinct limitations when it comes to advanced equitation.

i   A Pelham should always be used with two pairs of reins: using one rein with split ends, as is sometimes seen, is pointless.

j   It is as important to ensure the correct fit of a Pelham as any other bit, and like any other bit it must not touch the teeth; the exact fitting may vary with the type of bit.

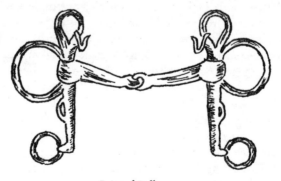

Jointed Pelham

iv   As will have been gathered, there is an embarrassing choice of bits and the tendency may well be to go on choosing more and more severe bits as each one fails; this should be avoided at all costs.

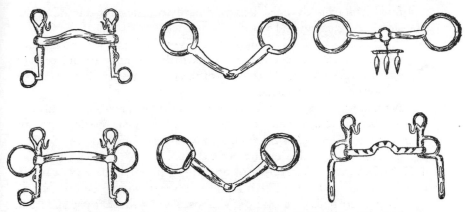

Bits: (*Top l. to r.*) i. Weymouth: or Curb. ii. Snaffle. iii. Mouthing Bit with keys.
(*Bottom l. to r.*) iv. Half-moon Pelham. v. Eggbutt Snaffle. vi. Reversible

v   For any advanced equitation the double bridle will fulfil all requirements:

   *a*   For general purposes a Pelham may be preferred by some.
   *b*   For general purposes others may prefer a simple snaffle, with possibly the addition of a dropped nose-band. See pp. 76–7.

vi   As noted above, the snaffle has the effect of raising the head when the reins are pulled upwards, acting on the corners of the lips and tongue:

   *a*   If the hands are held low, there is a downward nutcracker effect on the tongue, bars of the mouth and lower lips.
   *b*   There is also pressure on the poll through the cheekpieces of the bridle and the head-stall.
   *c*   With the addition of a dropped nose-band this is accentuated, but it must, of course, be used with care, knowledge and with sensitivity.

vii   No bit serves any useful purpose if the rider is straphanging, i.e. using it to preserve his balance and position in the saddle, or pulling his weight continuously on the horse's mouth:

   *a*   This leads to a hard mouth devoid of any feeling.
   *b*   It also leads to the horse leaning on the bit and taking control when he desires, as well as to poor action, lack of collection and indifferent schooling, etc.

viii   In order to prevent damage of this nature some riders prefer to use a bitless bridle:

   *a*   In its simplest form this consists of nothing more than a head-collar fitted with reins, the horse being primarily controlled by the aid of the rider's weight, legs and voice.

b   A more sophisticated version consists of a snaffle-bridle with nose-band, where the cheekpieces of the bit, which has no mouthpiece, are attached direct to the cheekpieces of the bridle and act directly on the nose-band and curb-chain.

c   A running rein may also be used with a dropped nose-band: this is a long second rein, attached to either side of the saddle, passing through the rings of the bitless bridle and back to the rider's hands, providing leverage to the action on the nose.

d   The Hackamore (of American origin) is a bitless bridle with a single rein; it operates through two solid cheekpieces and a nose-band, bringing pressure to bear on the nose and nostrils, as well as the jaw and back of the jaw:

The Snaffle Bridle: with dropped noseband

## Section 12   Drop Nose-bands and Others

There are several varieties of drop nose-bands, all of which have in common the object of bringing pressure to bear on the horse's nose as a means of control:

i   A dropped nose-band is a nose-band divided into two parts:

a   A front strap, which fits over the lower part of the nose.
b   A rear strap joined to it by a ring, which hangs at an angle to the front strap and over the snaffle-bit.
c   The nose-band is adjustable and may be tightened round the nose.
d   Originally used as a corrective for horses which got their tongues over the bit, or tossed their heads.
e   It may also be used as a means of halting a horse with the nose-band fitted low over the nostrils: when the reins are pulled the horse's

breathing is constricted and to gain breath the horse is forced to give his head, i.e. flex his head and jaw.

f    Its use with a standing martingale was rightly banned by the B.S.J.A., as this was no less than torture.

g    It has the advantage that when the horse pokes his nose or raises his head the pressure on his nose and poll, via the head-stall, is considerable, and immediate relief can be had by flexing his head and jaw; hence a useful training aid at all paces in experienced hands.

ii    A Grakle: two straps crossing over the nose, one passing over the bit and one under it and connected underneath:

a    The pressure on the nose is concentrated at the point of intersection.

b    A powerful counter to a confirmed puller, named after the 1931 Grand National winner, who wore it.

iii    A flash nose-band:
An ordinary nose-band with two straps sewn to the centre and crossing diagonally to fasten beneath the bit:

a    The intention is to obtain a similar effect to a drop nose-band; but:

b    Attach a standing martingale to the normal nose-band.

iv    A Kineton nose-band:
A severe type of nose-band originating in Kineton, Warwickshire:

a    It consists of a leather-covered metal front piece, with adjustable buckles at each end attached to two open metal loops which are in contact with the bit.

b    Pulling on the reins causes direct pressure on the nose, and the stronger the pull the greater the severity.

v    A cavesson nose-band:
This is simply a thickly padded nose-band, used on a training head-collar for lunging the horse, with a ring at front and sides:

a    It is inadvisable to have metal nose-bands even when thickly padded.

b    All leather nose-bands are preferable as less hard on the horse.

vi    A sheepskin nose-band:
One with a thick sheepskin covering over the front:

a    Supposed to prevent the horse from seeing shadows in front.

b    Hence sometimes also known as a 'Shadowroll'.

*Section 13   Martingales*
Generally attached to the bridle and intended as a purely temporary measure.

Their aim is usually corrective to improve poor head carriage due either to bad schooling or faulty conformation; the principal varieties are:

i   The Standing Martingale:
A broad leather strap attached to the girth at one end by a loop, passing between the horse's forelegs and attached to the nose-band by another loop at the other end:

The Standing Martingale

*a*   Both girth and nose-band are passed through the martingale loops; the martingale itself is adjustable by a strap and buckle for length.
*b*   The martingale is generally passed through the loop of a neckstrap to prevent it hanging down and becoming entangled with the legs.
*c*   The object of the martingale is to catch the nose of the horse when he raises it above the horizontal and prevent him tossing his head.
*d*   As a ready measurement of the correct length it should stretch from the girth, through the forelegs and up the shoulder to the top of the withers.
*e*   Sufficient room must be allowed for the horse to stretch his neck when jumping or galloping.
*f*   When used too short in conjunction with a dropped nose-band it meant that each time the horse extended himself at a jump he inevitably punished himself severely, hence was rightly banned.

ii  The Running Martingale:
A broad leather strap attached to the girth at one end by a loop, passing between the forelegs and bifurcated about a foot from the bridle, each division ending in a ring through which the snaffle-reins are passed:

*a*   This type of martingale also has a neck strap and is adjustable for length by a strap and buckle.

The Running Martingale

*b*    The object is to act on the bit and to a lesser extent on the nose-band and to check excessive head carriage.

*c*    Leather stops must be added to the reins to prevent the rings catching on the buckles of the reins.

*d*    The bib martingale is a variation used only by racehorse trainers for additional safety and so called due to a centre-piece of leather joining the two straps.

*e*    The Cheshire martingale is another variant attached direct to the bit-rings by snap-hooks. It is highly dangerous and not to be recommended.

*f*    The pulley martingale is another variation whereby, instead of bifurcating, the strap ends with a small pulley, through which runs a cord with rings at each end through which the reins run; supposedly allowing more flexibility in lateral movements of head and neck as required in show jumping.

*g*    The combined martingale: one in which both standing and running martingales are combined, i.e. nose-band and rein attachments, and combining the actions of both.

iii    The Irish Martingale:
A pair of rings joined by a short strap 6 to 8 inches long, through which the reins run (not strictly a martingale at all):

*a*    The object is to keep the reins together and prevent them being tossed about by an impatient or restless horse; or

*b*    To prevent the reins getting caught over the horse's head in the event of a fall.

*c*    Like the running martingale they require leather stops worn on the reins to prevent them catching on the rings of the bit.

*d*    Also known as a pair of spectacles, or a pair of rings.

The Irish Martingale

iv   The Market Harborough Martingale:
The main strap of the martingale is attached to two leather straps which pass through the ring of the snaffle and are attached to the rein:

a   Its action is to check the tossing of the head.
b   Its advantage is that it comes into action as a result of the horse's action not the rider's, and is instantly eased on returning to the correct head carriage.

*Section 14   Ancillaries*

i   Breastplate:
Its object is to keep the saddle from sliding backwards; there are two principal patterns:

a   A bifurcated leather strap with a loop for the girth and rings or buckles for attachment to the D-rings on the pommel of the saddle.
b   A broad breast-strap with a neck-strap to hold it in place and two straps to attach to the girths on either side under the flaps. See p. 59.

ii   Crupper:
Its object is to prevent the saddle from slipping forward:

a   It is effected by a loop of leather fitted round the root of the horse's tail and buckled to a D at the rear of the saddle.
b   It must be well padded and fit properly under the tail.
c   The crupper strap should allow two fingers to pass between it and the horse's croup or it is too tight.

iii   Neck-strap:
A thin strap round the neck in front of the withers and behind the mane with a loop for the main strap of the martingale:

a   May also be used for a breast-strap (see *ib* above).

b    Frequently used by beginners to hold on to in preference to the reins when jumping, thus avoiding jabbing the horse's mouth, and recommended for this purpose by some instructors.

iv    Rein Stops:
As mentioned above, small pieces of thick leather with a slit to pass over the rein, used to prevent the rings of the Irish martingale, or running martingale, from entangling with the rings of the bit.

v    Surcingle:
A leather, or webbing, strap passing over the entire saddle, through the surcingle slot in the flap of the saddle and behind the girths:

a    It should not be too tight.
b    If the girths are persistently slipping forward a strap between the surcingle and girths may help to hold them back.
c    Most commonly used and simple to keep a rug or numnah in position on the horse's back; if used with the former, also has pads to keep the weight off the spinal column. See pp. 186–9.

vi    Head-collar (and cavesson):
The head-collar should be of broad leather strapping and should fit easily without danger of galling:

a    There should be no danger that a horse may learn to slip his head-collar, this developing what may become a tiresome vice.
b    A neck-strap, or throat-lash, fitted to prevent slipping, or an attachment crossing below the jaw may be necessary.
c    At no time should the head-collar be so tight as to risk any danger of galling.
d    The cavesson used for lunging should be nothing more than a close-fitting powerful head-collar with a padded nose-band, but preferably without a metal reinforcement, which can jar a horse however well padded.
e    Such lunging cavessons sometimes have a rotating ring in the nose on a metal base, which is quite unnecessary.

vii    Halter:
The halter may be of rope; best made of nylon or terylene rope, which last longer and wears better.

a    It should be strong with canvas nose-piece.
b    It should be adjusted with a non-slip knot, to prevent it running too tight, if the horse pulls on it.

# PART III
# The Approaches

*Section 1   The Mental Approach*
The reasons for wishing to have anything to do with horses may be various and involved. Among the more obvious are the following:

i   A natural affinity with horses:

    *a*   It is only a few generations since horses were more common than motor cars and such a natural affinity may be inherited by people whose parents do not possess it.

    *b*   A love of horses without understanding of horses and horses' requirements is not enough in itself, but the latter can be acquired.

    *c*   A reasonable physique, co-ordination and sense of balance are also desirable, but these again may be acquired with practice.

ii   An upbringing with horses:

    *a*   By itself this does not necessarily imply real understanding of horses and many bad habits may have been learned.

    *b*   This can often have the opposite effect and inculcate an early fear of horses which may be difficult to overcome.

iii   A desire for exercise in the open air:

    *a*   Horse riding is amongst the finest exercise available, but this should not be the only reason for riding.

    *b*   Without an interest in and affinity with horses, this is not likely to bring real satisfaction.

iv   Social reasons, i.e. keeping up with the Joneses:

    *a*   This is a common, if undesirable, reason for wishing to have a horse or ride.

    *b*   Commonest among children, it is not unknown among adults, especially those with an unfulfilled childhood wish to have a horse.

c   This seldom leads to satisfactory results for horse or rider, if it is the only driving force involved.

## Section 2   The Mental Withdrawal

The reasons for wishing to have nothing to do with horses should also be considered:

i   They generally stem from one basic reason: fear.

a   This may even be an atavistic fear, but generally it is due to an early childhood fright, long-forgotten and deeply buried in the subconscious.

b   An early upbringing with horses may cause this, see ii*b* above.

c   Such subconscious fears are generally caused by injudicious and incorrect introduction to horses.

d   Such fear may be extremely hard, if not impossible, to eradicate.

ii   An unfulfilled childhood wish to have a horse may set up an inverted mental block, which may be reflected in a conscious dislike of horses. (A typical deprived childhood syndrome.)

a   This subconscious mental block may produce an aggressive hyper-critical attitude, scornful of horses and riders and all matters connected with them.

b   Such an attitude of mind was often found in infantry officers when criticising cavalry and is probably in part responsible for much anti-hunting criticism.

c   Since this psychological attitude is caused by ignorance rather than fear, it is sometimes more easily overcome than the latter, but the inhibitions are generally deep-seated.

iii   A physical or mental inability to ride, other than fear, may also result in an apparent dislike of horses:

a   Lack of co-ordination or balance, or initial vertigo, or similar reasons, are more common than might be imagined.

b   Careless introduction to horses in such circumstances may result in a permanent refusal to admit the inability, and a corresponding mental transference of blame to the horse, hence an apparent dislike of horses.

c   Pushing a novice beyond his capabilities can easily cause this type of psychological block.

d   This is commonest in children whose muscles are not sufficiently developed.

e   If the cause can be eradicated, this type of psychological objection may be overcome.

## Section 3  The Physical Approach

There are only a limited number of ways of having anything to do with horses and learning to ride:

i   For those fortunate enough to live in the country, with enough land and stabling available, the most desirable way is clearly to own and look after one's own horse or pony.

  a   In the case of a family owning several horses or ponies, the question of adequate tuition and supervision generally solves itself, since the parents or other adults are in a position to teach the novice adequately.

  b   In the case of the one pony-owner with non-horsey parents, or parents too busy to give instruction, the local Pony Club, or the nearest riding school are likely to be the principal sources of instruction.

ii   For those living in the country, without land or stabling available to keep a horse, there are still several alternatives open: costs must vary with locality and circumstances.

  a   It is generally feasible to rent a paddock in which to keep a horse or pony.

  b   Stabling, too, can generally be either rented or built comparatively cheaply.

  c   A nearby farmer or riding school will generally agree to keep a horse or pony for a moderate charge.

  d   It may be possible to come to some arrangement for hire of a horse or pony from a similar local source.

  e   In such circumstances, the cost of keep or hire may be debited against labour or services rendered, so that the total involved is not prohibitive.

iii   For most town-dwellers, unless they have access to the country at week-ends, a riding school, or riding club, is almost the only way to gain experience with horses.

  a   Riding schools and clubs vary considerably as to the facilities they provide and the quality of their horses.

  b   The best are generally residential and have every facility available, where the novice is given complete charge of a horse from the beginning and is trained to a high standard.

  c   The worst are mere hacking establishments, where dead-beat overworked old nags are hired out by the hour to all comers.

d    Fortunately, all riding schools now have to be registered and are liable to inspection, even so some are unlikely to be of much help to a novice.

e    For those who are content to remain a passenger on horseback, this will be enough.

f    Although most riding schools and clubs have to cater for a number of clients or members in the above category, they are generally only too pleased to have keen pupils, or good riders, and to encourage them with every facility at their command.

iv    Pony-trekking is becoming an increasingly popular aspect of riding throughout the country, and for many provides their first experience of horses.

a    In that some, at least, may be encouraged to learn more, this is a very desirable thing.

b    Where the trekking scheme is organised by an accredited riding school, there is likely to be some degree of tuition and the ponies are to some extent safeguarded.

c    Of necessity, however, the ponies are principally regarded merely as a means of transportation by people who are unaccustomed to riding, and many of those people will never be riders in any sense of the word.

d    Such ponies are generally ruined beyond redemption by the very nature of their task and become dead-beat slugs of the type already noted, iiic above.

e    In the cases where the pony-trekking is organised by accredited riding schools, they generally do their best to look after their mounts and match them to the expertise or otherwise of their riders. Too often, however, this form of riding would be better styled 'pony-wrecking'.

*Section 4    The Practical Approach to Horsemanship*
From the foregoing, it will be appreciated that the introduction to the horse is all important:

i    So that he knows what parts of the horse are being referred to, the novice should first be taught the points of the horse on a chart or dummy, or on a quiet, well-mannered old horse or pony.

a    To give him an idea of what to look for in a horse the conformation and appearance of the horse should also be outlined.

b    To help him distinguish one from another, the various colours and markings of the horse should also be explained.

ii   The parts of the saddle and bridle, their functions and fit, along with their ancillary harness, should also be described in detail.

  *a*   This is also ideally done on a dummy horse, or a well-mannered old faithful.
  *b*   By learning to put on the saddle and bridle correctly, the novice gains his first lessons in confidence even before mounting.

iii   The first lessons in the elementary basic principles of riding may also be taught either dismounted, or on a dummy or quiet old faithful, thus further increasing the novice's confidence:

  *a*   Among these are how to hold the reins, how to mount and dismount from the horse and how to shorten or lengthen the stirrups, or tighten the girth from horseback.
  *b*   The Seat, or rider's position in the saddle, the 'aids', the effect of the rider's weight, hands, legs and voice, and their effect on the control of the horse are also best taught in this way.
  *c*   At the same time, the novice should be practicing exercises for improving his riding muscles, balance and confidence.

iv   The interrelationship between horse and rider should be thoroughly examined.

  *a*   It is important that before he starts to ride the novice should begin to understand something of how the horse's mind works.
  *b*   It is equally important that he should be forewarned about the more common pitfalls to which he may otherwise succumb, and he should be ready to guard against them.
  *c*   If he has already spent some time looking after and grooming his own horse, so much the better.
  *d*   He will already have gained confidence in handling his horse, and they will have begun to know and understand each other.
  *e*   His initial confidence will have greatly increased and the likelihood of an early set-back will thus have been greatly reduced.

v   Only then should the novice start his first lessons on horseback, other than at the halt.

# PART IV
# The Approach to Riding : Dismounted or Mounted

The interrelationship of horse and rider is worth studying carefully: both psychologically as well as physically the rider must be on top.

*Section 1    The psychology of horse and rider*
The horse is far stronger than man, but the horse has only a limited reasoning power and cannot sort out problems like a human being, thus, the rider must control the horse by his superior brain power, and not by brute strength.

i    The human brain is far more complex than the horse's brain, but it requires considerable effort, at first, to understand how the horse's mind works.

   a    A horse associates things with the sensations he experiences when encountering them and he has a good memory. Also,
   b    The horse is very gregarious and a creature of instinct, both inheritances from his wild ancestors which must be remembered. But,
   c    The horse quickly accepts routine and will generally have a predictable reaction to most situations, so that it is up to the rider to be prepared in advance wherever possible.
   d    If the horse reacts, but is not checked by the rider, an undesirable behaviour pattern may be established, which may sometimes be hard to alter; this is the rider's fault, not the horse's, since it is by the converse, or the establishing of desirable behaviour patterns, that the horse is trained.

ii    An example of the above may be had, for instance, in the reaction of a horse to being clumsily bridled by a novice.

   a    A nervous, clumsy novice bungles his attempt to bridle the horse and slams the bit against the horse's lips and teeth, as well as rubbing the head-stall against the horse's eyes.

b    The horse is infected by the novice's nervousness and raises his head abruptly to escape the pain.

c    Next time the novice comes to bridle him, the horse associates the man and the bridle with pain and raises his head prior to being bridled.

d    The novice finds himself unable to bridle the horse and the horse has established mastery over man.

e    The horse may then be labelled 'hard to bridle', and thus are vices born. It may require some time and trouble to train him to accept the bridle willingly again.

iii    The rider, whether mounted or not, must always think ahead of the horse the whole time, like a driver anticipating the actions of pedestrians and other road-users.

a    He must be constantly alert for anything that may arise.

b    He must be ready to reassure the horse and impart confidence to him, even when he does not feel it himself.

iv    It must be remembered that the horse's hearing is very acute, but his vision, especially his side-vision, is not good.

a    Thus, the horse will react very readily to tones of voices to which he is accustomed, also to other sounds, such as music, or bugle notes.

b    He also reacts to sudden unexpected noises, or sounds coming from outside his range of vision, i.e. up from behind, and this, in particular, may make him react nervously.

c    Although his side-vision may not be good, the horse is liable to be very observant and will take note of the human expression and react to it as he might react to the tone of voice.

d    Because his hearing is acute and his side-vision, bad, it is always advisable to speak quietly to a horse when approaching him from the side or rear, so that he will not be startled.

e    When riding, it is especially important to ensure having control of the horse when being passed from behind, and it is advisable to reassure the horse by the tone of voice. Sudden unexpected movements, or objects seen out of the corner of the eye may cause a horse to halt or shy unexpectedly.

f    The rider should always be on the look out for anything which might cause such a reaction, and be prepared for it.

g    Should he fail to do so, he must reassure and calm the horse at once, if possible showing the horse the object which alarmed him and allowing him to examine whatever it was.

 *h* The horse should then be spoken to gently and confidently and urged to go forward.

 *i* It is important, however, to be ready for any recurrence, especially when passing the object again, and to be ready to overcome it.

 *j* A calm confident tone of voice is a source of great assurance to the horse.

v The rider must strive to learn from the horse's own reactions what to expect.

 *a* The horse's ears are a useful barometer of the horse's mind:

 *b* Cocked and alert generally indicates that all is well,

 *c* Flickering backwards and forwards indicates that something is worrying him, or that he is in an uncertain frame of mind,

 *d* Ears laid back and swishing of the tail indicate that he is feeling balky, or bad-tempered, and is possibly about to kick out.

 *e* The eyes rolling, or showing the white, may indicate nervousness or tension, as will sweating unduly without any physical reason.

 *f* Fidgeting, snorting, tossing the head, or sidling about, again, all indicate tension and nervousness over something.

 *g* Where necessary, the horse should be calmed in a reassuring confident tone of voice.

vi The rider must always ask himself the reason for any behaviour on the part of the horse which is not immediately explicable.

 *a* Such reactions as shying, baulking or obstinacy, may be due to a physical cause, such as a strained tendon or similar physical discomfort.

 *b* If the reason is a physical one, such as a strain, or gall, or similar cause, it should be remedied as soon as possible and the horse taken straight back to his stable.

vii The rider should always remember that when the horse reacts in an unexpected or tiresome way it is not the horse's fault.

 *a* The rider has failed to anticipate the horse's reactions and is to blame for not doing so.

 *b* He should not punish the horse for his failure.

 *c* He should seek to avoid any recurrence.

 *d* Each day out with the horse, they should both learn something fresh together.

viii The horse very quickly senses the attitude of mind of the rider.

 *a* Calm and confident behaviour will have a similar calming effect, even on a nervous horse.

    *b*    Nervous, uncertain behaviour will sometimes cause even a placid horse to react nervously.

ix   The rider who is nervous of a horse must learn to conquer his fear.

    *a*    He should always start with a calm and placid horse until he himself has gained confidence.

    *b*    More potentially good riders have been ruined by being over-horsed too soon than in any other way.

    *c*    Unless the rider has confidence in himself and his ability, he cannot communicate confidence to the horse.

    *d*    A horse will be quick to sense a rider's lack of confidence, and to take advantage of it.

    *e*    A rider who is constantly niggling at a horse, instead of being decisive, will cause it to turn balky, or sour, or bored.

x    The rider who cannot control his temper is never likely to be successful.

    *a*    A horse should be corrected, if correction is required, in a calm and even frame of mind.

    *b*    The man, or woman, who loses his temper loses control of himself and hence the bond between horse and rider is broken.

    *c*    A horse is likely to be nervous and afraid of a bad-tempered rider, unsure whether he is going to be hit, or jogged in the mouth, or why.

xi   The rider who is sure he knows it all is beyond hope.

    *a*    Each horse is as different from another as each human being not only in temperament and nature, but in the lessons it has learned.

    *b*    To achieve unity and understanding with any horse, it is necessary to have humility, and the rider who thinks he knows it all has a closed mind.

xii  The horse will react very favourably to the rider in whom he has confidence and whom he loves:

    *a*    The horse enjoys being caressed behind the ears where the mare caresses her foal.

    *b*    No real bond between horse and rider can be formed without this unity of confidence and feeling of mutual understanding.

    *c*    When being ridden, the horse and rider achieving perfection should attain a complete harmony of movement and instinctive understanding, making each for the moment an extension of the other.

The earliest lessons may be dismounted, or on a dummy, or quiet old faithful, and they should include:

*Section 2   How to hold the reins*
Certain basic principles are essential in riding, and the mechanics of holding the reins correctly are foremost amongst them.

i    While contact between the rider's hands and the horse's mouth, via the reins, should be continuous from the moment the reins are first held, it should never be heavy, or dead.

    *a*    Regardless of the horse's movements, the contact between the rider and horse, via the reins, should be light but firm when required: hence, the expression 'light hands': see pp. 101–2.

    *b*    There must be ready, fluid movement of the rider's fingers, hands, wrists, shoulders and body, to accommodate the movements of the horse's head at all times, as required.

    *c*    Hence, the rider must have acquired a good grip, good seat, balance and confidence before he can hope to acquire good hands, but constant practice from the start in the basic methods of holding, shortening and lengthening the reins is a considerable help in acquiring them.

    *d*    Since there is less likelihood of him jabbing the horse's mouth seriously, it is desirable that the novice should start his initial riding instruction with a snaffle bit and single rein. But,

    *e*    It is as well he should learn how to hold the reins of the double bridle, or Pelham, from the start.

ii    Both hands should be used on the reins by novices, or when riding and schooling young or difficult horses, or whenever instant and complete control may be required at any moment.

    *a*    When mounting the horse the reins must first be held in the left hand only, even if subsequently both hands are used.

    *b*    It is common practice when hacking to hold the reins in the left hand only, leaving the right hand free for carrying a hunting crop or whip, or for opening gates, etc.

    *c*    Since it may, at times, be important to have the left hand free, as when leading another horse on the inside, it is desirable to learn how to hold the reins in the right hand as well.

    *d*    Hence, it is important to learn from the first not only how to hold the reins in either hand, but how to transfer them from hand to hand quickly and easily without losing control of the horse.

    *e*    As a further aid to control of the horse, it is essential also to be able to lengthen and shorten the reins readily at will without any fumbling or confusion.

    *f*    N.B. Novices should always use both hands until they have attained a firm seat, or they are liable to develop a one shoulder forward position which is difficult to overcome.

iii Taking hold of the reins (snaffle reins only) correctly with the left hand, as for mounting, should be accomplished as follows:

 *a* Take the end of the reins in the right hand and raise them level with the withers.
 *b* The left, or near-side, rein should be outside the fourth, or little, finger.
 *c* The right, or off-side, rein should be grasped between the first and second fingers.
 *d* The slack, or ends, of the rein should be passed across the palm of the hand, and held between the first finger and thumb.
 *e* The ends of the reins should hang down the off-side shoulder.

iv Taking hold of the reins correctly with the left hand (double bridle) should be accomplished as follows:

 *a* Take the ends of the reins in the right hand and raise them level with the withers.
 *b* Place the little finger of the left hand between the two left hand reins with the curb rein outside.
 *c* The right hand reins should be divided by the first finger, with the curb rein again outside.
 *d* The spare ends of the reins should be crossed in the palm of the hand and hang down on the off-side.

v Another method of holding the reins in the left hand is as follows:

 *a* As iv*a* above.
 *b* As iv*b* above.
 *c* The right hand, or off-side, reins should be divided by the second finger, curb rein outside between second and first fingers.
 *d* The spare ends of the reins are then held between the first finger and thumb and hang down on the off-side.
 *e* The advantage of this method over the above is that it is easier to shorten them quickly by drawing them through the hands.
 *f* The disadvantage is that it gives less play to the right side of the mouth.
 *g* It is also maintained that the reins are more liable to slip.

vi How to hold the reins in both hands, snaffle only:

 *a* First, take hold of the reins in the left hand, as above.
 *b* Then, place the right hand on the right, or off-side, rein, with the little finger inside the rein.

c    Remove that rein from the left hand and allow the slack to pass between the first finger and thumb on eitherhand.

d    The slack, or spare ends of the reins, should hang down the off-side shoulder.

e    The hands should be about four inches apart.

f    The wrists should be slightly bent and the palms turned slightly upwards.

vii  How to hold the reins in both hands, double bridle:

a    First, take hold of the reins in the left hand, as above.

b    Then, place the right hand on the right, or off-side, reins with the little finger between the two reins and the curb rein outside.

c    Remove those reins from the left hand and allow the slack, or spare ends, to pass between the first finger and thumb of each hand.

d    The slack, as above, should hang down on the off-side shoulder.

e    The hands should be spaced, as above, in similar positions.

f    It should be noted that an alternative method preferred by some people is to ride with the reins reversed: i.e. with the curb rein inside.

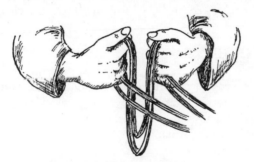

How to Hold the Double Bridle

viii When riding with the reins in the left hand, it may be desired to change over to the right hand.

a    The right hand should be placed over the left, the little finger of the right hand between curb and cheek rein of the off-side, or right hand, rein.

b    The second finger is then thrust between the other two reins and the slack of the rein passed over to the near-side, being grasped between finger and thumb as the left hand releases its grip.

c    This changeover should be practised frequently until it becomes automatic.

The Reins of the Double Bridle in One Hand

ix  When riding with the left hand only, it may happen that the rider requires to use both hands to control the horse, in which case viiia, above, is all that is required.

x   To shorten and lengthen the reins:

    *a*  It may be necessary, at times, when riding across country or starting to gallop, to shorten reins abruptly.

    *b*  If riding with all four reins in the left hand, simply grasp the slack of the reins in the right hand and draw them through the left hand to the length required.

    *c*  If riding with the reins in both hands, take them into the left hand and shorten them as above.

    *d*  To lengthen the reins, simply allow them to slip gently through the fingers to the length required.

xi  Making a bridge. This is the term used to describe the act of crossing the reins between the hands across the horse's neck.

    *a*  This is chiefly used in steeplechasing as a support for the rider if the horse pecks badly.

    *b*  It may be recommended for the novice in the early stages in lieu of a neck rein, or when the mane has been hogged, to give him extra confidence.

*Section 5 How to mount and dismount from the horse*
This is another of the basic principles of riding which should be mastered correctly from the start.

i  The horse is normally mounted from the left, or near-side, and the rider should be standing level with the horse's withers and facing towards the tail:

    *a*   The reins should be picked up correctly in the left hand, as described above, and drawn up by the right hand so that contact is maintained with the horse's mouth.

Mounting: 1st Phase

    *b*   The fingers of the left hand should then grip the crest of the horse's neck just in front of the withers and the horse should be under sufficient control to stop him moving forward or to one side, the ends of the reins being dropped on the off-side.

    *c*   The right hand next grasps the stirrup and turns it with the front towards the horse's side, while the left foot is raised and carefully put into it.

    *d*   The toe should be pointed downwards and the knee pressed against the saddle, and care must be taken not to let the toe tickle, or nudge, the horse's side.

e   The right hand then grasps the cantle of the saddle and with a spring from the right leg, and the support chiefly of the left hand, the body is raised upwards.

f   Should there be too much body weight on the right hand the saddle is liable to slip, or at least become crooked.

g   As soon as the left leg is straight, the right leg should be swung over the horse's croup, while the right hand releases its hold on the cantle and moves to the pommel taking some of the weight as the rider gently lets himself down in the seat of the saddle.

Mounting: 2nd Phase

h   The right foot is then slipped into the off-side stirrup, without nudging or tickling the horse's side and the left hand is removed from the horses' crest.

i   If both hands are being used on the reins, the right hand then takes over the rein, or reins, as described above, and the reins are held at the correct length required.

j   In any event, care must be taken to see that the horse is not allowed to move off until required to do so, due to being nudged with either foot or through contact with the mouth being lost, for, in this way, a bad habit can easily be set up.

ii   Mounting a difficult horse which constantly moves forward, or circles away from the rider, due to bad habits formed as above:

   *a*   The left hand should hold the near side rein extremely short, so that the horse's head is turned towards the rider as he mounts.

   *b*   The rider then mounts, as described above, but holding the horse's head round until he is in the saddle.

   *c*   The horse is thus unable to keep turning away from the rider, and, if trying to move forward will tend to circle towards the rider, thus facilitating mounting rather than the reverse.

iii   Dismounting:

   *a*   The horse should be brought to a halt and the reins shortened in the left hand, control of the horse being maintained.

   *b*   As the left hand grasps the crest, the right hand should grasp the pommel of the saddle and the right leg should be gently slipped from the stirrup, without nudging or tickling the horse's side.

   *c*   The body should be raised slightly on the left leg and hands and the right leg then swung over the croup, while the right hand is transferred to the cantle, most of the weight remaining on the left leg and hand.

   *d*   The left knee should then bend against the saddle flap and the right leg should be lowered to the ground. The left foot is then finally removed from the stirrup without nudging or tickling the horse's side, the whole action being one fluid movement.

   *e*   The reins should then be taken in the right hand near the bridle.

   *f*   Another method is simply to remove the left foot from the stirrups at the same time as the right and swing to the ground direct, with the weight supported on the pommel.

iv   Mounting and dismounting from the off-side:

   *a*   This should be practiced occasionally for the benefit of both horse and rider.

   *b*   Constant mounting and dismounting on one side lengthens the stirrup leathers on that side, even if changed regularly to even the wear.

   *c*   When mounting or dismounting from the off-side, the movements are exactly reversed.

v   Mounting and dismounting without stirrups:

   *a*   It is desirable to practice this also at intervals, but it is especially good training for the novice as it strengthens the muscles and increases the rider's confidence in himself.

b   The preparations are exactly as for mounting with stirrups, except that the rider stands square on to the side of the horse.

c   With left hand holding the crest and reins, and right on the cantle, the rider bends his knees and, springing up, straightens his arms, thus raising his body above the saddle.

d   The right leg is then swung over the croup and the right hand moves to grip the pommel, while the rider gently lowers himself to the seat of the saddle.

e   When dismounting, both hands are set on the pommel of the saddle, palms down, and the weight of the body is taken on them.

f   As the weight is taken on the hands the right leg is thrown back over and clear of the croup and the rider alights on his feet beside the horse.

g   The reins are then taken in the right hand near the bridle.

*Section 4   How to Shorten or Lengthen the Stirrups, or Tighten the Girths, from Horseback*

It is essential to be able to adjust the length of the stirrups correctly from the horse's back, and it is also good exercise for the novice, the foot remaining in the stirrup throughout.

i   With the reins in the left hand, it is easiest to adjust the off-side stirrup first:

a   Using the right hand, the turned-under free end of the stirrup leather should be loosened and the buckle disengaged.

b   Keeping the finger close to the buckle the disengaged tongue should then be guided into the required hole for the new length, either shorter or longer.

c   The buckle should then be pulled up to the supporting bar and the free end turned under the leather itself once more.

ii   To alter the near-side stirrup, it is only necessary to take the reins in the right hand and reverse the procedure as above.

iii   To tighten the girth, it is necessary to take the reins in the right hand, if it is intended to tighten them from the near-side.

a   The left leg should be swung forward and the flap of the saddle raised with the left hand.

b   The ends of the girth straps should then be grasped and gently tightened, as required.

c   In practice, it should seldom be necessary to tighten the girth in this manner unless a horse has a habit of blowing itself out when girthed, which is generally a sign of bad management.

*d*   To go through the motions, is good exercise for a novice.

*Section 5   The Seat*
The rider's seat is an amalgam of balance, grip and suppleness, differing for each rider with his physical proportions.

i   The rider must sit down on his buttocks and thighs, over the horse's centre of gravity:

  *a*   He must therefore sit well forward in the saddle, i.e. firmly in the seat.
  *b*   He must not sit back on the cantle with his weight towards the horse's loins, and he must sit squarely, not lop-sidedly.

ii   To attain the correct seat, it is essential to have the correct knee, thigh and calf grip:

  *a*   The knee should be at the height best suited to the physical proportions of the rider.
  *b*   Only the flat muscles of the thigh should touch the saddle, none of the large muscles at the rear of the thigh, otherwise the maximum power will not be obtained.
  *c*   The leg from the knee downwards should hang slightly behind the perpendicular and only the inside portion should come into contact with the flap of the saddle.
  *d*   If the back of the calf is used for gripping the saddle, this automatically forces the thigh and knee away and weakens the grip of the leg.
  *e*   The lower leg must, in any event, be available to apply pressure behind the girths and should be primarily used for that purpose (see pp. 114–19).

iii   Unless the stirrups are fitted correctly, it is impossible to attain the correct seat:

  *a*   The fit of the stirrups must again be dependent entirely on the physical proportions of the rider. But,
  *b*   If the rider sits loosely in the saddle allowing his legs to hang down freely, then squeezes the saddle with his knees and raises his toes, the position should be a guide for length.
  *c*   The stirrups should then be adjusted so that the bars are in line with the soles of the rider's boots.
  *d*   The stirrups are merely intended as a convenience to the rider.
  *e*   If they are too long, they are difficult to retain, if too short, the rider cannot use the lower part of his leg correctly.
  *f*   The toes, pointing naturally, should be raised in the stirrups and the

heels be down, thus gaining the maximum benefit for the riding muscles.

g  It is up to the rider whether he prefers to have the stirrup bars under the balls of the feet or the instep, i.e. have his feet right home in the stirrups; generally, the former is desirable, but sometimes the latter is more suitable.

h  In either position, the feet should be well pressed down against the bars and the heels down.

iv  A powerful grip of the muscles of thighs, knees and calves, good balance and pliant suppleness of the body, with practice, combine to produce a firm seat at all paces. In one rider, this may be gained in six months, in another, not in six years or milleniums.

*Section 6   The Aids to Riding*
The aids to riding should be explained, but cannot be practised effectively until the rider has a firm seat. They are as follows:

A  The Natural Aids. The position of the rider's weight, the legs, the hands and the voice.

B  The Artificial Aids. Whips, spurs, drop nosebands, martingales and similar appliances.

i  The position of the rider's weight.
   This is the most important of the natural aids, as it is independent of the sensitivity of the horse's mouth or sides.

a  The rider's centre of gravity is level with his hips and any alteration of the rider's body weight above that affects the horse's action.

b  The best parallel is that of carrying a man on one's shoulders, if he leans to one side it is necessary to put out a leg to maintain one's balance on that side.

c  Thus, by correct use of the rider's weight, the horse can be forced to lead with one or other leg, or to place one leg to one side or the other.

d  When turning on the forehand, the forelegs are held by the body weight inclined forward.

e  When turning on the haunches, the weight should, conversely, be to the rear.

f  When reining back, i.e. halting, the weight should incline forwards to remove the weight from the hindquarters.

g  When turning, the body weight is inclined inwards, and when at speed or over jumps it is inclined forwards.

ii    The legs:
The legs, i.e. from the calf downwards, below the knees, must be used quite independently of the arms or body, and unless the rider has a firm seat their use is liable to cause movements of the arms and body.

   *a*    The legs can act, resist or yield. Act, as when causing impulsion or forward movement; resist, or guide, as when preventing the horse from turning his quarters out to one side; yield, as when allowing the horse to back.

Leg position (*l. to r.*). i. Correct. ii. Wrong. Common Novice's Error. iii. Wrong

   *b*    Their primary use is to produce impulsion or forward movement, by application of both heels behind the girth.
   *c*    While applying the legs or heels, the position of the knees must in no way be altered, hence a firm seat is required before effective use can be made of the legs.
   *d*    The sides of the horse should be as sensitive as the mouth, and continual digging of the heels into the horse's sides must be avoided.
   *e*    Horses that are abused with spurs become deadened to the legs, as a mouth may be deadened by heavy hands.
   *f*    A sensitive horse will respond to delicate pressure of the calf, where another might need firm pressure and a sharp jab of the heels.
   *g*    In general, anything more than calf pressure should be regarded as punishment and the use of anything other than blunt spurs, even those with rowels clipped, ought to be quite unnecessary (see spurs, p. 103).

iii    The hands:
The hands, i.e. the fingers, wrists and arms, including shoulders, must be independent of all movements of the body, hence the rider must have a firm seat before he can have good hands.

   *a*    The hands act, resist and yield. Act, as when they turn a horse's forehand; resist, as when they prevent him moving forward; yield, as when he stretches his neck, i.e. jumping.

*b*   At times, as when jumping, it may be necessary to yield, or give, the whole arm from the shoulders, taking back contact with wrists only on landing, supple wrists and fingers then acting like a spring.

*c*   At times, it is necessary for the pressure on the mouth to be firm and unyielding, until the horse relaxes its jaws, then, instantly, the rider must relax also. Hence: 'give and take'.

*d*   Thus, good hands depend on a firm seat, supple fingers and wrists and an intelligent, or instinctive, anticipation of the horse's mind, i.e. as to when he is going to yield or require pressure.

*e*   At all slow paces, the hands give and take, but at faster paces the horse's forehand is supported by a gentle feeling, though not a dead pull.

*f*   By turning the backs of the hands, facing the horse's mouth, downwards, the sensitive edges of the little fingers transmit each movement of the horse's head through the reins to the rider's consciousness.

*g*   By rounding the wrists inwards, the degree of contact can be readily increased and the fingers of the hands lightly transmit the rider's wishes to the horse.

*h*   The hands should be held as if holding a pocket watch in them in order to tell the time, and they should act as a spring exerting light or strong pressure as the mouth of the horse demands.

*i*   On a puller, the reins should be firmly held and the horse's jaw drawn in towards his chest, and the hand is then fixed. As soon as the horse shows signs of relaxing, the pressure is released and the horse patted. Then, the pressure is taken up again, until the horse accepts that pulling is not worth it.

*j*   Good hands do not require severe bits and a puller will be cured with good hands and a snaffle-bit, where bad hands and a curb-bit failed to make any impression.

iv   The voice:

The tone of voice is all important and talking in a soothing tone will have a considerable calming effect on a horse.

*a*   Shouting will have the opposite effect, as will cursing, or the tone of voice employed when cursing.

*b*   Individual words of command can soon be taught and recognised, if the same tone of voice is used with them each time.

v   The Harmony of the Aids:

It is important that the aids should combine, in harmony at all times, to achieve the desired effect, e.g. to move forward, the legs provide pressure, the hands ease slightly, the body weight may incline slightly forward, the voice may urge the horse on.

a    The timing of the aids is thus all important, e.g. there should be a fractional pause between the legs providing pressure and the slight easing of the hands, above.

b    N.B. Whenever an aid is applied, there must be a result, or the horse will become deadened to it.

c    The aids must never be applied half-heartedly, indecisively, or in a niggling way, so that the horse becomes deadened to them.

vi  The lateral aids and diagonal aids:
The lateral aids are the use of the hand and leg on the same side and the the diagonal aids the use of opposing hands and legs, e.g. as in turning.

a    The explanation of the difference between the two types of aids should be made clear to the novice from the start.

b    It should be emphasized that the diagonal aids should be used from the very earliest stages.

c    If the novice is observed using the lateral aids, it should be pointed out to him, but in the early stages this is not important.

vii  The artificial aids:
Apart from the whip and spurs, these have already been examined at length. See pp. 76–80.
The Whip. The whip is a reserve force which the rider has at hand if the horse does not obey the pressure of the leg or requires punishment.

a    It should seldom require to be used in earnest.

b    It is a token of failure if resorted to often.

The Spurs. Spurs with rowels should never be used even when the rowels are clipped.

a    The only spurs which should be permitted are blunt spurs.

b    They should only be used when the rider has attained complete control and a perfect seat.

c    Neither spurs nor whip should be used by novices.

*Section 7   Exercises for Improving the Riding Muscles*
The following exercises are useful for improving the riding muscles and the novice's confidence if carried out on the dummy horse, or on a quiet old faithful standing still:

i   Rising in the saddle from the knee, at first, with stirrups and, later, without stirrups.

ii  Touching the foot with the hand on each side, at first, with stirrups and, later, without stirrups, the knees being kept firm in the saddle.

iii Leaning forward and touching the opposite toes, with and without stirrups, the knee again to remain firm.

iv  Leaning right backwards with the head on the croup and right forward with the head on the neck, with and without stirrups, the knees remaining firm in the saddle.

v   Turning round in the saddle from the hips to look behind to either side, without altering the position of the legs, with one hand on the horse's neck and the other on the cantle.

vi  Relaxing and then tightening the thigh and knee grip several times slowly in succession.

vii Swinging the lower part of the leg to the rear, the knee being kept firm in the saddle.

    *a*  This may be practised at first with only one leg, changing legs alternately.
    *b*  It may also be practised with both legs together.
    *c*  This teaches the use of the lower part of the leg and is, perhaps, the most important of them all.

*Section 8   The Aim at This Stage*
The aim at this stage is for the novice to have acquired:

i   A familiarity with the points of the horse and the parts and fitting of saddle and bridle, also the purposes of each and their accessories.

ii  An understanding of how the horse's mind works and how the horse is controlled by the rider.

iii Balance and practise in using thighs and knees to obtain a good grip.

iv  A correct seat, square in the saddle.

v   A working idea of how to hold the reins and what to do with his hands.

vi  A working idea of how to use his reins and legs to apply the aids to riding.

vii A corresponding sense of confidence in his ability to put these lessons into practise.

# PART V
## The Approach to Riding : Mounted

In the earliest stages of riding, the principal aim should be to give the novice confidence:

*Section 1   Methods of Inspiring Confidence in the Novice*
There are certain well-known and well-tried methods by which the novice's confidence is likely to be boosted. These are:

i   It is always preferable if the earliest lessons can be held in an indoor school.

    *a*   This provides privacy, and the novice is more likely to relax if he is not being watched by possibly critical eyes.

    *b*   It provides an enhanced feeling of safety compared with the open spaces, and the novice knows he cannot be run away with.

    *c*   It is also generally softer if he falls off, and, although falls should be avoided in the early stages, if possible, this is another point which increases the novice's confidence.

ii   In the early stages, it is desirable that both reins and stirrups should be used. (When confidence has been gained, they may be dispensed with from time to time.)

    *a*   Snaffle-bridles should be provided, preferably with a mild snaffle-bit, but if Pelhams are used the reins should both be attached to the cheek-rings of the bit.

    *b*   The stirrups may be attached to each other by a strap under the horse's belly, but this should not be continued for long as it tends to encourage an incorrect grip of the knees.

    *c*   In the earliest stages of all, a leading rein may be used, but it should be quickly dispensed with or it may tend to sap the movice's confidence in his own ability, rather than enhance it.

   *d*   It should, in any case, only be used outside, never inside the indoor school or manège.

iii   The novice should be allowed to make a bridge of his reins (see p. 94) or else he should be provided with a neck-strap to hold while he learns balance and grip at the various paces.

iv   As the novice's grip and balance improve, the various exercises already learned may be practised, first at the walk, then at the trot.

v   When the novice is gaining confidence, he may be lunged by the instructor in a circle with his arms folded, both at a walk and a trot.

   *a*   Brief spells of this with stirrups crossed and bareback, using a neck-rein if desired, will give the novice great confidence.

   *b*   When his grip and balance have improved sufficiently, a very small jump may also be included.

   *c*   Provided this training is carefully graduated according to the novice's progress, it can prove invaluable.

*Section 2   The Elementary Use of the Aids*
The elementary use of the aids must now be demonstrated to the novice, and as soon as he has begun to develop a firm seat he must start to practise them for himself.

i   To collect the horse:
To collect the horse is to bring his hindquarters under him and flex his head and neck slightly, i.e. to 'bring him up to his bit'. This is done by:

   *a*   Applying pressure with both legs, fractionally preceding,
   *b*   An equal slight tension applied on both reins.
   *c*   An uncollected horse is trailing his hindquarters and his head carriage is generally unbalanced.
   *d*   A collected horse is balanced and ready for the application of further indications, i.e. use of combined aids, from the rider.
   *e*   The walk, trot and canter are collected paces, but the gallop is an extended pace: see paces, below.

ii   To advance:
To cause impulsion, or forward movement, i.e. to make the horse go forward, the following indications should be given:

   *a*   The heels, or legs, should be used with a distinct tap behind the girth.
   *b*   The tension on the reins should be very slightly eased.
   *c*   The indication supplied by the reins should be fractionally, but almost imperceptibly, after the indication by the legs.

iii  To halt:

To stop, or reduce speed, i.e. to slow down from one pace to another, the following indications should be given:

- *a*  If the horse is collected, the reins are felt more strongly.
- *b*  The tension should be of the 'give and take' variety, not just a dead pull combined with the body weight slightly back.
- *c*  If the horse is not collected, he should first be collected by pressure of the legs, combined with tension on the reins, to prevent him merely going faster, i.e. driving him 'up to his bit' and collecting his hindquarters beneath him.
- *d*  As soon as the horse halts or alters pace, the tension should be relaxed.

iv  To turn to the left on the move:

To turn to the left on the move the following indications should be given:

- *a*  The left rein is slightly raised and the tension just felt.
- *b*  The right rein is kept low, pressed against the horse's neck.
- *c*  The right leg is used to provide impulsion and prevent the hindquarters flying out, also to cause them to follow in the tracks of the forelegs, i.e. diagonal aids.
- *d*  The left leg is used, if necessary, to provide impulsion and to keep the horse collected, or up to his bit, body weight slightly to the left.
- *e*  To turn to the right simply reverse the indications as above.

*Section 3  The Paces*

The paces that concern the rider of a schooled horse and to which the novice must accustom himself are:

i  The walk:

The diagonal legs move forward together and the pace is normally three and a half to four miles an hour.

- *a*  The hindlegs reach the ground just after the forelegs on the same side have left it.
- *b*  In a horse with a long stride, the hindleg imprint is ahead of the foreleg imprint; in a horse with a very short stride, it is behind (undesirable, as implying upright shoulder and hence jolty ride, see shoulder, pp. 28–29).
- *c*  Two feet are on the ground all the time, four feet part of the time.
- *d*  A horse should be made to walk out well, and it is the best pace to exercise a horse to keep it fit.
- *e*  The indications required to make the horse walk are as in 2ii above, i.e. equal pressure of the legs to cause impulsion.

ii   The trot:

The diagonal legs move forward together as in the walk and the pace is normally about eight miles an hour, although there may be a slow or a fast trot (also jog trot, which is undesirable).

    *a*   Two legs are on the ground most of the time, but there is a short period when there are no legs on the ground, very short at the slow trot, but considerable at the fast trot.

    *b*   The imprints of the fore- and hindfeet are together at the slow trot, but the hindfeet are a considerable distance in front of the forefeet at a fast trot—a much greater distance than at a walk.

    *c*   When trotting, the rider's body should be thrown up and slightly forward by the horse's action; it should not be lifted by a muscular action on the part of the rider.

    *d*   This slight rise is known as 'posting', i.e. 'to post'.

    *e*   To start with, it is better for the novice simply to sit still and learn to sit with the trot, rather than rise.

    *f*   The indications required to make the horse trot are as in 2ii, above, for impulsion: simply, pressure of the legs and a slight easing of the reins until the required pace is achieved, when the legs are eased and tension on the reins regained.

    *g*   To slow down from trot to walk, or to halt, as in 2iii, above.

iii  The commoner faults the novice should try to avoid, and their cures, are as follows:

    *a*   Sitting too far forward, thus rising on the fork and possibly 'pedalling' with the leg each time the body rises, i.e. the legs moving backwards and forwards like a pendulum.

    *b*   To cure the above, the body weight should be central, the stirrup lengths correctly adjusted, the knee firm in the saddle, the lower leg slightly back, the leathers taut and pressure on the irons, with the heel well down.

    *c*   Sitting too far back in the saddle, thus rising on the reins, generally with considerable exertion and the stomach leading, and probably with the legs pedalling forwards and backward.

    *d*   To cure the above, the body weight should be central, the body rising over the hands without any effort, the stomach in and the body supple from the hips: the leg movement cured as in iii*b* above.

    *e*   Rigidity and exertion in trying to post are best cured by encouraging body suppleness and letting the novice continue to sit with the trot until it comes naturally.

*f*   Rising too high, as much as an inch or more, posting, or showing daylight between seat and legs should be cured in the same way.

iv   The diagonals at the trot:
As the horse's off-fore comes to the ground, his near-hind also comes down: this is known as the right diagonal. The converse is the left diagonal.

*a*   As will be appreciated from the above, the horse alternates on his left and right diagonals.

*b*   The rider, when he rises at the trot, may rise on either diagonal.

*c*   If he comes down on the saddle as the near-fore and off-hind (left diagonal) comes to the ground, he is said to be riding on the left diagonal, i.e. his body rises up and down with the action of the near-foreleg.

*d*   Most horses are accustomed to being ridden on one or other diagonal, and will tend to throw the rider onto those legs by taking a half-step.

*e*   The effect of this is to put too great a strain on one set of legs and to make the horse more ready to turn on the free diagonal, hence more left-, or right-handed, i.e. freer on that rein.

*f*   Whereas it is difficult and uncomfortable to use the unaccustomed diagonal on an old horse, a young horse should be trained to accept each equally.

*g*   To change diagonal, the rider sits in the saddle for half a stride, rising as the other foreleg leaves the ground.

*h*   The importance of rising at the trot on the opposite diagonal to the leg on which he wishes the horse to lead at a canter should be mentioned. See pp. 300–5, leading with the chosen leg at the canter.

v   The canter:
This is a pace of three time and may vary from a slow canter of about five miles an hour to a fast canter of about nine miles an hour, or possibly more.

*a*   The legs come to the ground as follows: with near-fore leading; off-hind to the ground; then, right diagonal to the ground (off-fore and near-hind); then, leading leg; then all four legs off the ground and the horse lands on the off-hind and propels himself forward again.

*b*   The canter may be carried out with either pair of laterals leading, i.e. with the near-, or off-legs moving forward together: these are known as the laterals as opposed to the diagonals.

*c*   To be able to turn quickly and safely at a canter, the horse must be leading with the laterals on the side to which the turn is to be made, so, if not leading with those laterals, should be able to change to them quickly (see pp. 303–5 change of leg at the canter).

    *d*    When a horse is moving correctly with either pair of laterals leading, it is said to be moving 'united'. When moving in any other manner, it is said to be 'disunited'.

    *e*    When a trained horse turns at the canter, he will change to the correct leg, i.e. he will lead with the leg towards the side to which he is turning. When he does this, he is said to be cantering 'true'. If he leads with the other laterals, he is said to be cantering 'false'.

    *f*    A horse may therefore be cantering 'united' but 'false', though if cantering 'true' he must be 'united'.

    *g*    The indications required to make the horse canter are those for forward impulsion enhanced, i.e. the leg pressure is increased and the pause before easing the tension on the reins more noticeable. The weight is a little back, sitting down if at a trot, and the horse is literally squeezed into the canter from the base of the spine and the legs.

vi    The commoner faults the novice should try to avoid and their cures are as follows:

    *a*    Allowing the body weight to be too far forward and sitting rigidly, and generally, at the same time, shortening the reins, with the result that the rider bumps in the saddle, his legs are too far back and he loses control and starts to gallop.

    *b*    To cure the above, the body weight must be central, the body itself supple and moving in rhythm with the pace, the knee firm and legs pressing down in the irons, with the heels down and the lower leg just behind the perpendicular, not pressing against the horse's side, and the reins should be reasonably long, not too short.

    *c*    Allowing the body weight too far back, with the result that the lower leg is useless and the rider's weight bounces on the horse's loins; elbows generally flapping wildly.

    *d*    To cure the above, the body weight must be central and well down in the seat, the knees firm and the legs as in vi*b* above, shoulders not behind the perpendicular; the elbows should be still, but not stiff. As in vi*b*, rigidity must be avoided and the rider must move with the rhythm of the pace.

1–6 The Canter

*e*  The hands should not be allowed to rise upwards, but should be kept low, maintaining even contact with the horse's mouth throughout the motion of the pace.

*f*  Although the novice may be shown how to canter with the correct leg leading, it is unlikely he will succeed in doing so at this stage, especially if the horse is not well-schooled. For the moment, this should be ignored.

vii  The gallop:

This is an extended pace of four time, which may vary from about twelve miles an hour up to thirty, or more.

*a*  The legs come to the ground as follows: with near-fore leading, off-hind to the ground, near-hind, each of these coming, in turn, almost in a straight line under the horse. Slight pause; then, both hind-legs on the ground; then, on the right diagonal, i.e. near-hind/off-fore; then, on the off-fore only; then near-fore to the ground and off-fore leaves the ground; the body is then pivoted forward on the near-fore, the leading leg and the only one on the ground, taking all the strain; then, all four legs in the air and the horse lands on the off-hind again.

*b*  It is important to ride the horse equally on each fore-leg, due to the strain it undergoes.

*c*  As at the canter, the horse should turn at the gallop with the legs leading on the side to which he is turning.

*d*  If the horse needs urging, the rider should sit well down in the saddle with a firm grip, using his legs as necessary. He should have a continuous light feel on the horse's mouth to maintain control; the hands should be kept low.

*e*  If the horse gallops freely, the rider should lean the upper part of the body forward, taking his weight on the knees, thighs and stirrups and shortening the reins to maintain continuous feeling on the horse's mouth. The feet should be well home in the stirrups.

*f*  This is not a difficult pace to master, but practice should be had in galloping steadily, under control, and halting quickly and easily.

*Section 4  More Advanced Training for the Novice*
Once the novice has mastered the walk, trot and canter, and has developed a good sense of balance, it is time to start giving him further training to enhance his grip.

i   Short sessions with crossed stirrups should be given at the walk, then at the trot and canter.
ii  Short training periods should also be given with the arms folded at the walk and the trot, either on a leading rein, or free in the school, if the horse is to be trusted.
iii Walking and trotting with neither stirrups nor bridle is the next stage, and once the novice can accomplish this both safely and with confidence he is on his way to attaining a firm seat.
iv  It must be appreciated that each novice is likely to have a different rate of progress to the next, and what may seem easy to one may prove immensely difficult to another and vice versa, thus no time schedules can possibly be laid down for progress.

*Section 5  Elementary Jumping*
Elementary jumping should be brought into the novice's curriculum as soon as he is beginning to gain confidence without stirrups.

i   Riding over a bar on the ground:
    This is the best way to start, and it should be treated as if it was a full scale jump.

    a   The novice should hold the reins loosely by the end in one hand, or both.
    b   He may hold the neck-strap with the other.
    c   Approaching the pole, the body should be upright. As the horse reaches it, the novice should lean forward and tighten his grip.
    d   Once over the bar, the normal body position should be resumed.
    e   After a little practise at this the reins should be knotted on the horse's neck and the novice should be encouraged to fold his arms as he goes over the jump. If he still tends to be too tense, he may be encouraged to sing as he goes to loosen himself up.
    f   The next stage, as the seat improves, is crossing the stirrups and folding the arms before going over the bar.

ii  After a short while with the bar on the ground, it may be raised gradually from a foot to eighteen inches or two feet.

    a   The same graduated form of practice should continue.

   *b*    Although the jump is no effort to the horse, the novice should never be allowed to hold the reins to start with at this stage.

   *c*    A jumping lane is of great assistance in such training, but the jumps should still be restricted to about two feet high.

   *d*    As soon as the rider is fairly efficient with stirrups, he may have a session without stirrups.

   *e*    No reins should be allowed until he has perfect control over the position of his hands when jumping.

iii   Faults to watch for are pointing the toes down or clinging with the heels.

   *a*    The novice must also be watched for signs of nervousness.

   *b*    It must be remembered that this seems very frightening to the novice at first, and he must be encouraged as much as possible.

## Section 6   *More Advanced Methods of Turning*

i   To turn to the left on the haunches:

   *a*    The rider's weight should be kept back and slightly left.

   *b*    The forehand should be brought round with tension on the left, or direct, rein.

   *c*    The right, or indirect, rein should be applying less tension, but should be held against the horse's neck, i.e. neck-reining.

   *d*    The hindquarters should be prevented from flying out to the right by pressure from the right leg applying the diagonal aids.

   *e*    The horse may be kept up to his bit, i.e. collected, if required, by impulsion from the left leg.

   *f*    The forehand should move in an arc round the haunches, the near-hind leg acting as the pivot of the turn.

ii   The turn should be practised by the novice in four stages:

   *a*    At the halt, with the horse in a corner of the school, placed along one side with his tail in the corner, using the sides to prevent the horse moving back or letting his quarters fly out.

   *b*    At the halt, using the side of the school to prevent the horse backing, but using the legs to prevent the quarters flying out.

   *c*    At a halt, in the centre of the school, using the legs and reins to prevent backing or the quarters flying out.

   *d*    As the novice progresses, practise it on the move at the various paces, up to the canter, but only at a collected pace.

iii   The turn on the haunches is particularly good practise for the novice and for the horse:

    *a*   It teaches the novice co-ordination of legs and hands, and their correct use together.

    *b*   It also teaches him how to manoeuvre his horse handily and quickly.

    *c*   It teaches the horse obedience and lightness in the forehand as well as improving his balance.

    *d*   By this means, he can turn sharply at a fast pace and remain collected with his hocks under him ready to move on again.

iv  To turn to the left on the centre:

    *a*   The weight should be central and still.

    *b*   The left rein should be felt more strongly.

    *c*   The left leg should apply pressure well back, urging the quarters round, i.e. using the lateral aids.

    *d*   The right leg may apply pressure close to the girth to keep the horse up to his bit, if required.

    *e*   The right, or indirect, rein should be neck-reined.

    *f*   This turn cannot be used for a short turn at a fast pace, but may be used for changing direction after a full pass (see Section 8 below).

v  To turn to the left on the forehand:

    *a*   The weight should be a little forward.

    *b*   The forehand should be held in position with both reins, the left held a little more strongly.

    *c*   By sustained pressure from the left leg, circle the hindquarters round to the right, i.e. by use of the lateral aids.

    *d*   If necessary, the horse may be kept up to his bit with the right leg.

    *e*   As horses that are heavy in the forehand tend to try to turn on the forehand if possible, it is not generally desirable to turn in this way and always preferable to turn on the haunches.

    *f*   A turn on the forehand at speed will overweight and jar the forelegs, if it does not result in a fall.

vi  To turn to the right reverse the indications above. But *N.B.*:

    *a*   The rein providing the direct tension on the side to which the horse is being turned is known as the direct rein.

    *b*   The other rein is known as the indirect rein, or neck-rein.

    *c*   The rein or leg towards which the turn is being made is known as the inner rein or leg.

    *d*   The opposite rein or leg is known as the outer rein or leg.

    *e*   In an indoor school or manège, the inner rein or leg is that nearest the centre of the school or manège.

*Section 7   To Rein Back*
To rein back is to make the horse back a step at a time.

i   The horse should be collected with his hocks under him and is caused to step back by gently increasing tension on both reins:

   *a*   As soon as each step is made the extra tension on the reins should be immediately relaxed.

   *b*   After a brief pause the tension is felt again and another step is taken.

ii   The rider's weight should be kept a little forward to lighten the hindquarters and assist the horse in using them.

iii   The legs are used merely to keep the horse in a straight line:

   *a*   But should he run back, the legs must be closed to check him from doing so.

   *b*   Should he fight against the bit and fix his lower jaw, a strong pressure of the legs will have to be applied to force him to relax.

iv   The rein back is accomplished from the halt, walk, trot and canter, and the original pace should be resumed afterwards. The object is:

   *a*   It supples the horse, gets him onto his hocks, makes him light in the hand, improving his balance and collection, as well as teaching him to obey hands and legs.

   *b*   It teaches the novice rider to control and place his horse, as well as to use his hands and legs correctly and in harmony.

v   The commoner faults the novice should try to avoid, and their cures, are as follows:

   *a*   The horse running back out of control, due to heavy hands and weak legs, cured by greater pressure of legs and easing tension on reins, see iii*a* above.

   *b*   Too heavy and dead a tension on the reins may make the horse set his jaw and refuse to move. Correction is provided by strong pressure of the legs, as iii*b* above; as well as by easing tension. Cure is to avoid heavy pull on reins.

   *c*   The hindquarters flying out is prevented by leg pressure and the use of the direct rein.

   *d*   Lack of collection on halting. It is important to avoid halting with a low head carriage; it is corrected by feel on reins.

*Section 8   The Full Pass, or Passage*
In the full pass to the flank, the horse looks in the direction in which he is moving

and passes direct to the flank, i.e. moves sideways, by crossing the outer legs in front of and across the inner legs:

i   Bend the horse to the right by feeling the right rein, lean the weight very slightly to the right:

   *a*   The horse should always be bent in the direction in which he is moving and his jaw should be relaxed.

   *b*   When the horse is correctly bent, the rider, sitting square in the saddle, should be able to see the cheek and eye of the horse on the side towards which he is moving.

The Full Pass: Forelegs crossing

ii   In all lateral movements, the forehead must be slightly in front of the hindquarters, and the horse should never be allowed to step backwards.

iii  The forehand should be led with the open right rein:

   *a*   Cause the horse to cross the left legs in front and across the right legs with pressure from the left leg behind the girth, i.e. using diagonal aids—right rein, left leg.

   *b*   Support the horse and prevent him going forward with the right rein.

   *c*   Keep him up to his bit and prevent him running back with the right leg providing impulsion.

iv   Do not allow the horse to rush the exercise:

   *a*   Change the direction of the passage frequently.

*b*   When turning, turn on the centre.

*c*   Rest after a dozen steps or so.

v   When the horse's head is towards the wall of the school or manège, he is said to be moving with 'shoulder out', when towards the centre of the school with 'shoulder in'.

   *a*   Thus, the horse can right pass with the shoulder in or out.

   *b*   It can also left pass with the shoulder in or out. See pp. 298–302.

vi   For the pass to the left, the indications are reversed.

vii   It teaches the novice to use his hands and legs in harmony, also:

   *a*   To control the horse's forehand and quarters.

   *b*   To place the horse as required.

viii   For the horse, it is an excellent suppling and balancing exercise. Also:

   *a*   It makes him obedient and sensitive to leg and hand.

   *b*   It encourages him to carry his head correctly.

   *c*   It develops the muscles of the back, forehand and loins.

   *d*   It prepares the young horse for striking off with the correct leg at the canter and for the turn on the haunches.

The Full Pass: Hindlegs crossing

ix   The more common faults and weaknesses should be noted and corrected as follows:

a   The forehand and quarters should not move alternately or in fits and starts, i.e. the aids must be in harmony and the horse should move smoothly along the axis of the horse's body with the forehand and quarters moving on parallel lines.

b   The horse's head must be bent just behind the poll, not at the shoulder, towards the direction in which he is moving. If he bends the whole neck, the rider loses control of the forehand.

c   If the horse is moving laterally with his head turned in the wrong direction, i.e. away from the direction he is moving in, the balancing and suppling effect of the exercise is lost, so the head must be turned in the direction of movement, as above.

d   Exaggerated body movements on the part of the rider, with the inactive leg sticking out at an angle are common faults.

e   The rider, as well as the horse, should look in the direction of movements.

f   The horse's quarters must not precede the forehand and he must not be allowed to step backwards, i.e. he must always be collected and up to his bit.

### Section 9   The Half Pass to the Right

In this movement the horse gains as much ground to the front as he does to the flank, i.e. he moves at 45° in the direction in which he is facing.

i   The indications are the same as for the full pass, except:

a   The inner knee is closed more strongly to cause more forward impulsion or movement at each stride.

b   The feel, or tension, on the right rein is less than in the full pass.

ii   For the half pass to the left the indications are the reverse of those to the right.

iii   Most of the points above made for the full pass apply also to a large degree for the half pass.

### Section 10   Leading with the Chosen Leg and Changing Leg at the Canter

As soon as the novice has attained a firm seat, he should be shown the two methods of causing a horse to lead with the chosen leg at a canter.

i   Using the lateral aids:
An unschooled horse and unskilled rider may sometimes be taught the use of the lateral aids at first, but it is generally more sensible to start with the diagonal aids from the beginning.

*a*    To canter with the off-side laterals leading, the horse should be collected and impelled into the canter with the left leg and left rein slightly the stronger.

*b*    The rider's body weight should be slightly inclined back to the near side, along with the horse's own head pinning down the near-side laterals so that the horse is forced to strike off with the required leg, the off-fore, leading.

*c*    The head should at once be turned back in the direction of movement, i.e. left rein eased to match the right.

*d*    To canter with the near side laterals leading with lateral aids simply reverse the above indications.

ii    Using diagonal aids:
The more logical use of the diagonal aids, which in any event the rider should be taught afterwards, is given below, and see pp. 300–5.

*a*    To canter with the off-side laterals leading the horse should first be collected and impelled into the canter with the right rein and left leg slightly the stronger.

*b*    The rider's weight may, if required, be slightly to the off-side. The horse will be making a curve to the right. There is constant contact with the horse and no abrupt period of transition of reins immediately after leading off correctly.

*c*    To canter with the near-side laterals leading with diagonal aids simply reverse the above indications.

iii    When changing from a trot into a canter, the rider should be rising on the opposite diagonal to the leg on which he wants the horse to lead, i.e. rising on the off-fore and near-hind or right diagonal at the trot, then moving into a canter results in leading with the near-side laterals and vice versa.

iv    To change leg at the canter from off-fore and off-hind to near-fore and near-hind, the indications should be as follows:

*a*    Stronger left rein and right leg, thus ensuring that there is no deviation of the quarters from the straight.

*b*    The correct instant for making the change is when the off-fore comes to the ground, the aids are then applied and the horse should change in mid-air.

*c*    To change from near-fore and near-hind leading to off-fore and off-hind, simply reverse the indications.

v    In changing direction at the canter, the trained horse can be made to change the leading leg simply by the rider using his inner leg behind the girth (to change to the opposite leg) and shifting his weight towards the direction of the new turn, the change, as in iv*b* above, should be when the legs are in mid-air.

vi  As stated above, unless the horse is leading with the correct laterals on the side to which the rider wishes to turn he cannot turn quickly at the canter:

    *a*  Therefore, it is important to learn to change legs quickly at will. Also,

    *b*  It is an excellent suppling and balancing exercise for the horse, making him handy and obedient to the aids.

    *c*  It is the highest attainment of harmony and rhythm in the use of the aids for the rider.

vii  The following faults are the most common and should be avoided:

    *a*  Exaggerated movements of the rider's body, or jerking of the horse's head from one side to the other. The whole change should take place quite smoothly, without fuss or obvious movement of horse or rider.

    *b*  Failure to keep the horse collected and allowing him to get on his forehand when about to ask for the change, i.e. loss of contact with the bit.

    *c*  Incorrect use of the body weight when applying the aids. Leaning the body forward results in loss of leg power and swinging the weight to the side on which the change is being made is also a mistake; both may result in changing legs in front, but not behind, i.e. cantering disunited.

    *d*  Applying the aids at the wrong moment. They should only be applied when the leading leg comes to the ground.

*Section 11    More Advanced Jumping*

The novice has now gained a firm seat and is accustomed to using the aids and to jumping over small jumps. He may now be gradually trained to hold the reins when jumping:

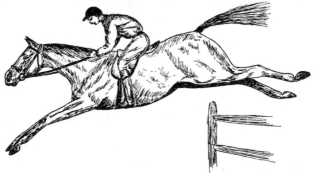

Extended Jump

i   The shoulders, wrists and hands must be given free play as the rider takes
    the jump, and as the horse extends its head and neck:

    *a*   The greatest care must be taken to avoid jabbing the horse's mouth,
    but contact should be maintained via the reins throughout.

    *b*   The reins should be held fairly long and the novice should be en-
    couraged to hold his hands low, as well as allowing them to go forward
    as he clears the jump, i.e. as the body is in the forward position clearing
    the jump, but contact is maintained.

ii  The commonest faults are:

    *a*   The body too far back, or failing to get forward as the horse raises its
    forehand, i.e. getting left behind at the jump. This is solely a question of
    timing and the rider may sometimes be taken by surprise when a horse
    takes off before he expects it to do so; when this happens, the reins
    must be allowed to slip through the hands to avoid jabbing the horse's
    mouth.

    *b*   The body may be too far forward on the approach. This means that
    the legs will be failing to provide correct impulsion; the horse will tend
    to be incorrectly collected; the jump may be taken too fast, and the
    take-off delayed too late, with the result that the fence is hit solidly,
    possibly causing both horse and rider to fall. The cure is to collect the
    horse correctly beforehand.

    *c*   On the take-off side: trying to lift the horse over the fence, i.e. raising
    the hands, keeping the body upright and failing to sit down and force
    the horse forward, lack of correct use of legs impelling the horse
    forward.

    *d*   On the take-off side: losing contact with the horse's mouth. Leaning
    forward too soon and letting the hands go forward too soon for fear of
    jabbing the horse's mouth, hence losing contact and control. A matter
    of timing.

    *e*   On the take-off side: the lower part of the legs stiff or badly placed, i.e.
    not sufficient impulsion and drive from the legs. Too much concentra-
    tion on timing or hands. Lack of harmony of the aids.

    *f*   On the landing side: drawing the hands back too soon. This can have
    the effect of jabbing the horse's mouth as badly as when crossing the
    jump itself. The horse must be given time to recover.

    *g*   Leaving the hands too long on the landing side is another common
    fault. The contact with the horse's mouth must be maintained through-
    out and slack reins after the jump mean loss of control on the far side,
    when the horse may require help from the rider, i.e. when it is pecking
    or stumbling, etc.

h   On the far side of the jump another common fault is bad leg position: the legs may be too far forward or too far back. The grip may have been shaken. Whatever the reason, the power of the legs to provide impulsion has been impaired, and this must be guarded against.

iii  From this stage onwards, the novice should ride horses which require to be ridden at their jumps, and he should be encouraged to ride them with determination.

a   He should increasingly, as a rider, begin to school the horses he is riding.
b   This does not mean to say that he should not still be learning something new from each one.
c   The process of learning, for both rider and horse, should continue as long as the rider is astride.

*Section 12   Presenting the Horse at the Jump*
In front of every jump, there is a suitable area from which the horse may take off with every chance of clearing the jump.

i   Correct presentation of the horse at a jump entails arriving at the take-off area correctly:

The Jump. (*Top l. to r.*) i. The Gallop. ii. Collecting. iii. Taking Off.
(*Bottom l. to r.*) iv. The Jump. v. Landing. vi. Preparing to Gallop on

a   As a rough guide the centre of the suitable take-off area lies about one and a half times the height of the jump in front of it.
b   The higher the jump, the narrower the area of the suitable take-off.
c   Presenting the horse at the jump successfully means bringing him collected and balanced into the take-off area and facing the jump with sufficient speed and momentum to clear it.

ii  The secret of arriving at the take-off area suitably collected and balanced, as well as with sufficient speed, is to choose a starting point some three paces before the take-off area.

    *a*  The horse should be ridden to the starting point and on arriving there fully collected is urged to regain his full jumping stride, without getting onto his forehand.

    *b*  Arriving at the take-off area with plenty of momentum, the aids are then applied and the horse should take off well, and should clear the jump successfully.

iii  If a misjudgment is made in selecting the starting point, it need not be disastrous:

    *a*  It may be possible to put in another quick stride and arrive in the take-off area successfully.

    *b*  Alternatively, it may be necessary to ride the horse to make him lengthen his last few strides, although the rider must be careful not to unbalance him in this event.

    *c*  It is important, however, to arrive in the take-off area in a balanced state, or the horse is hopelessly handicapped.

*Section 13  Exercises for Horse and Rider*
The following exercises may be practised in the indoor school or manège, or outside, benefiting both horse and rider.

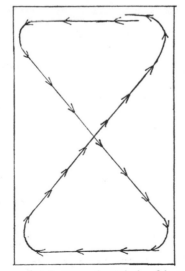

Figure of Eight Using the Whole of the School

123

i    The figure of eight:
     As its name indicates, the rider performs a figure of eight on horseback.

   *a*   The figure of eight may be taken at any pace up to the canter, either in the open, or in the indoor school or manège.

   *b*   At the canter, the leg should be changed when crossing over the centre of the figure of eight.

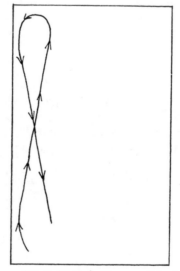

Figure of Eight Using a Quarter of the School

   *c*   The size of the figure may be large or small depending on the state of schooling of horse and rider.

   *d*   It is a useful suppling exercise for both horse and rider teaching balance and control.

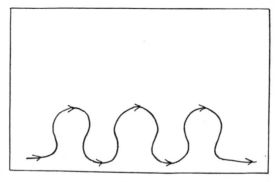

Serpentine

ii   The Serpentine:
As the name indicates, the rider performs a series of half-circles, generally three in the school or manège, and turns back to complete each circle on the reverse journey.

   a   The number of curves, or half-circles, depends on the space available and the degree of schooling of horse and rider.
   b   At the canter, the horse should change leg at the start of each fresh curve or change of direction.

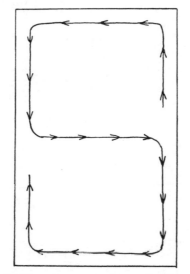

Right-angle turns to change direction

   c   This also is a useful suppling exercise, teaching both horse and rider balance and control.

iii   Circling in the corners of the indoor school or manège:
This may appear at first sight to be easy, but is, in fact, a difficult figure for the horse and rider to execute properly.

   a   The circles should first be made at the walk, then at the trot, and only when perfectly executed at these paces should the attempt be made to perform them at the canter.
   b   Nor should any effort be made to reduce the circles from a reasonably large size too soon. But,
   c   The horse should be made to go right into the corner, moreover, each turn must be made on the haunches and any attempt to make it on the forehand should be forestalled.

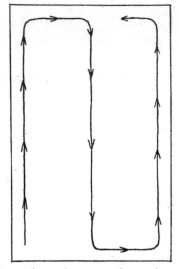

Using right-angle turns to change direction

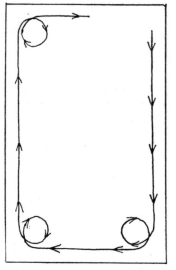

Circling, using the corner of the school

d    Finally, the horse should be going right into the corner and making such a tight circle that he is almost turning about on his haunches.

e    Again this exercise, properly executed, is of considerable value in suppling and teaching balance and control.

iv    Leading another horse or horses:
This should be practised both for the horse and rider's benefit.

    *a*    The led horse should generally be on the near-side, between the ridden horse and the traffic.

    *b*    The led horse's rein should be held flat against the reins of the ridden horse in the left hand.

    *c*    If the led horse is fresh, his rein should be held short about a foot from his head in the left hand, the ridden horse's reins being in the right hand.

    *d*    If the led horse tries to pull away, he should, at first, be given his head and only gradually brought under control, or he may pull the rider off his horse.

    *e*    If the led horse is saddled, the stirrups should be slid up the inside of the leathers and the lower end of the leathers passed downwards and in through the stirrups to stop them flapping and swinging about. See leathers, p. 63.

    *f*    When two horses are being led, it is usual to have one each side of the rider.

v    Vaulting:
This is an excellent physical training and suppling exercise, which not only gives the novice great confidence, but helps to make the horse steady and quiet.

    *a*    The horse should be led round by another horse and rider at a walk to start with and later at a trot—the stirrups and leathers may be removed, but this is not essential.

    *b*    The rider should be in the saddle in the correct position. When he is ready, he puts both hands on the front arch of the saddle, bends his arms and body well forward, throws his feet well up and out behind, and vaults clear of the horse and to the ground, still maintaining his hold on the saddle.

    *c*    The rider then runs forward a few paces, leaps forward in line with the fore feet of the horse, bends his head and body and throws his right leg up backwards, pulling with his arms at the same time. The momentum of the horse itself throws the rider into the saddle: the faster the movement of the horse the easier it is to get up.

    *d*    It is essential to vault clear of the saddle when dismounting, otherwise the rider may catch on the cantle of the saddle.

    *e*    It is essential to leap well forward before springing up again, otherwise the rider may get behind and land on the rear arch.

    *f*    It is also essential to hold the forward arch, both when vaulting off and when vaulting on again.

g If a vaulting pad is available, the exercise should be practised bareback and is easier for the rider, but not necessarily so for the horse.

h With a vaulting pad especially the horse may be lunged rather than led.

i A vaulting pad is easily constructed by any competent saddler with a pair of strong leather handles attached to the pads on a broad leather surcingle.

## Section 14 Hints for the Rider

The rider should know certain principles of horsemanship and certain accepted methods of dealing with common situations which arise.

i Certain principles of horsemanship cannot be too often repeated:

a Before mounting the saddle and bridle should be carefully examined to make sure that they fit and have been put on correctly. Check that the throat-lash and bits fit and that the curb-chain is flat.

b Check that the saddlery is clean, the buckles properly fastened and the saddle bar catches for the stirrup leathers are open.

c Make sure the leathers are the same length and that this is approximately correct; also that they are hanging correctly and that the loose ends are tucked under.

d Check the tightness of the girth, both before and after mounting and if loose tighten as required.

e Check that the shoes are all tight and the clenches are turned down, not projecting or loose (see pp. 169–171).

ii On horseback, there are also certain basic principles which should be borne in mind at all times:

a The first half mile should always be taken at a walk if possible, and the last mile returning should also be at a walk.

b If the above is done, there is no harm in allowing the horse a drink before starting, or as much as he wants to drink a mile or two from home, as long as the bit is removed to prevent him swallowing air and as long as he is walked the rest of the way. He will then be cool on reaching the stables and may be given some hay while being rubbed down or fed grain almost at once.

c Never sit in the saddle when there is no need for it, i.e. when gossiping with friends, or when stopping for any length of time: dismount and ease the horse whenever possible.

d When resting the horse for a few minutes take the opportunity of loosening the girths. If there is any grazing, let him have an opportunity to graze.

e   On long rides, get off and walk down the steep hills; it is as well to walk up steep hills also, since this eases both horse and rider.

f   Never ride in a slovenly manner, e.g. removing the legs from the stirrups when stiff, if feeling weary or stiff, get off and lead the horse for a change.

g   Never tie the horse up by the reins, either tie a piece of rope to the nose-band, or use a head-collar or halter if one is available.

h   Never let the horse get into the tiresome habit of jog-trotting—drive him up to his bit, i.e. collect him, and make him walk out by sustained leg pressure. Jog-trotting is often due to heavy hands and the horse being frightened of the bit, hence refusing to extend its neck, but it is a tiresome habit, upsetting to horse and rider, as well as other horses, and it is a sign of bad management. Do not allow it.

i   When on horseback the rider should be constantly on the alert anticipating any likely cause of trouble and preventing it occurring. The rider should especially be on the alert for any of the commoner vices which may occur and be prepared for them: there will usually be sufficient preliminary warning.

## Section 15   *The Clothes for Riding*

The principal point about clothes for riding is that they should be comfortable and practical:

i   It is useless if they do not fit and do not allow the rider to sit comfortably or move freely in the saddle:

a   If the rider is cramped by his clothes clearly he cannot ride properly.

b   Equally, if they are too voluminous this can be a bad fault. Badly cut breeches often have a wedge of cloth between the rider's leg and the saddle.

ii   They should be intended for riding:

a   Thin trousers or rubber boots are all very well in their way, but they do not help a rider to ride properly.

b   Jackets without a split do tend to catch in the saddle, and they can be tiresome when they are very long.

iii   If a lot of time has been spent grooming the horse and turning him out well, it seems a waste of labour if the rider does not then bother about his own appearance:

a   If the rider is proud of his horse he will want to look his best when out in public.

   *b*   In the indoor school or manège, it may be another matter.

iv   A hard hat, bowler or cap, is intended to save the rider from a knock on the head should he fall off:

   *a*   It should fit properly and be worn if there is any likelihood of the rider taking a fall.

   *b*   In the indoor school or manège, it may not be necessary.

v   Boots are another item that must fit well if worn:

   *a*   Rubber wellingtons, or similar sloppy footwear is useless for serious riding; hard leather footwear is essential.

   *b*   Calf boots unless they fit well may be more of a hindrance than an aid to riding, since the rider will be unable to 'feel' the horse properly.

   *c*   It pays in the long run to buy good boots.

vi   Jodphurs and jodphur boots are very comfortable wear for most purposes:

   *a*   Well cut riding trousers may also be very comfortable wear.

   *b*   Breeches, like boots, should be well made.

vii   A well-turned-out horse deserves a well-turned-out rider:

   *a*   Only after getting thoroughly wet once will a rider appreciate the value of good wet weather clothes.

   *b*   Only after they have been worn on a few such occasions will the riding clothes become really comfortable.

# BOOK TWO
## *The Care of the Horse*

# PART I
## Stabling

Ancillaries, such as the tack or harness room, dutch barn, food store and similar buildings, should be included in the term. Inevitably stabling must vary enormously and comparisons between large and small layouts, between those architect-designed and those converted by the owner from existing buildings, are pointless. But certain factors should remain constant between good stabling and bad, making the difference between comfort and discomfort for the horse. Amongst the factors are:

*Section 1   The Site*
Should be such as to receive the maximum of sun and air, but, at the same time protected, from the north winds. Also,

i   It should always be on throughly dry ground:

    *a*   High ground is thus generally preferable to low ground.
    *b*   Good drainage and good subsoil is essential.

ii   The subsoil is best of:

    *a*   Gravel.
    *b*   Sand or chalk.
    *c*   Rock or limestone.

iii   The foundations should be:

    *a*   Strongly built and solid.
    *b*   Protected from rising damp by damp courses.

iv   It is generally best to site the long sides with windows from east to west so that both sides get sunshine, but other factors include.

    *a*   The direction of the prevailing winds.
    *b*   Whether sunlight will be obstructed by trees or other buildings.

   *c*   A south to south-west aspect may be advantageous for getting sun and air, but only if protected from northerly winds.

   *d*   West or east aspects may be all right if protected from the wind.

v   Easy access should be available to surrounding paddocks; there should be good riding country round about.

## Section 2  Light

Whether daylight or artificial light, it is essential that the stabling should have plenty of each.

i   Stables should be well lit:

   *a*   With ample windows to allow for sunlight which is good for health.

   *b*   With good electric lighting, ensuring that all bulbs, switches and wiring are well protected and out of the horse's reach.

   *c*   The groom can thus see to do his work properly.

   *d*   It also ensures that any careless work can be seen at once.

ii   Dark stables are bad because:

   *a*   They are responsible for much weak eyesight and shying.

   *b*   They are less easily kept clean.

## Section 3   The Building Materials

These may be of brick, concrete, stone, timber or other materials, but it is desirable that they should have certain features:

i   They should provide effective protection against damp, or heavy rain, i.e. they must be completely weatherproof. They must also provide:

   *a*   Warmth in winter.

   *b*   Coolness in summer, i.e. adequate insulation.

ii   They should be fireproof:

   *a*   Since fire is one of the worst hazards in any stables.

   *b*   Because of the highly combustible nature of the horse's bedding.

iii   They should be strong and able to withstand heavy blows caused by horses kicking, fighting, rolling, etc.

iv   They should be of good quality: the use of poor materials, which may not last or cannot stand up to the wear and tear required, is a false economy. Regular checks are essential.

a   If wood is used, it will require annual attention in the way of tar or
    paint, but should then last effectively for years.

b   Whatever building materials are used, they will require regular inspec-
    tion and attention.

c   Unless small defects are repaired as soon as they are noticed, they may
    quickly develop into major damage requiring expensive repairs.


*Section 4   The Walls*

These may be built of brick, concrete, stone, timber, or other materials, as
above, but they should conform to the following:

i   They should be a minimum of twelve feet high at the eaves:

    a   Anything less than this is only really suitable for a foal or pony.
    b   Some of the so-called portable boxes are only eight feet high at the
        eaves.

ii  If built of timber, they must be on a brick or concrete foundation wall:

    a   If built of wood, they should have an asbestos, or similar, fireproof
        lining.
    b   If built of brick, they should be at least nine inches thick.

iii They are best built, whatever the materials used, with an airspace between
    an inner and outer wall:

    a   To prevent condensation.
    b   To provide coolness in summer and warmth in winter, i.e. adequate
        insulation throughout the year.

iv  They should have a damp course to prevent rising damp.

v   The inside walls are best lined with tiles or glazed bricks:

    a   Each of these are easily scrubbed down with disinfectant and kept
        clean.
    b   If ordinary bricks are used, they should be limewashed at regular
        intervals of about six months.
    c   If wood is used, it should be creosoted at intervals.
    d   If paint is used on an inside plaster wall, it should be oil-based, or
        similar type, with no lead or toxic content in case the horse should lick
        it.
    e   There should be no nails, splinters or projections which might injure
        the horse.

vi   There should be a ring for tethering the horse firmly imbedded in one of the walls of each box.

## Section 5   *The Roof*
The roof must be weatherproof; a sloping roof is generally preferable to flat in this respect.

i   The best type of roof is probably close boarded and tiled, or slated; this is weatherproof and provides good insulation.

    *a*   Roofing felt is an inferior substitute and does not last, also,
    *b*   Like wooden roofing shingles it is highly inflammable.

ii   It is undesirable to use materials which do not provide insulation against extremes of weather, such as:

    *a*   Corrugated sheeting.
    *b*   Asbestos sheeting.

iii   Without an inner ceiling a stable is liable to be lacking insulation.

iv   Rones, gutters and downpipes must be kept in repair and clean.

    *a*   They should be inspected frequently, especially in the autumn when they may easily become blocked by falling leaves.
    *b*   Unless they readily remove the water draining from the roofs, it may damage the walls or foundations.

v   The roof, or roofs, should be inspected at intervals for loose slates, tiles, etc.

    *a*   Any defects noted should be promptly repaired.
    *b*   Any metal work, rones, drainpipes, etc. should be painted at regular yearly intervals with bitumastic paint.

vi   A lightning conductor should be attached to the most prominent roof as an additional safeguard; in traditional style, it is often attached to a weather-cock.

## Section 6   *The Floors*
These are possibly the most important part of the stables and receive the greatest wear.

i   They may be constructed from:

    *a*   Concrete.
    *b*   Floor tiles or bricks.
    *c*   Granite setts or grooved slabs.

    *d*   Less desirably of wood or earth.

ii   The floor should be sloped to enhance drainage:

    *a*   The slope should not exceed 1 inch in 80;
    *b*   Otherwise, the horse will experience discomfort when standing.

iii  Suitable grooving for the floors is desirable and necessary:

    *a*   To provide drainage.
    *b*   To provide a grip for the horse's feet and prevent slipping.

iv  Deep drainage channels, or gutters, are undesirable:

    *a*   They may cause a horse to stumble, cast a shoe, or strain a sinew.
    *b*   They should be bevelled-off.
    *c*   Any steps should also be bevelled off and made smoothly sloping.

v   Any drainage covers in the floors should be regularly inspected for wear.

vi  Drainage in each box from a central trap is undesirable:

    *a*   It is old-fashioned, liable to block easily and insanitary.
    *b*   It is better to fill it in and cover it with a grooved concrete sloping floor.

vii  Wooden floors are very liable to be insanitary:

    *a*   They should be treated with disinfectant twice daily.
    *b*   Along with wooden walls, they should be checked daily for signs of splinters, rot, or unsoundness in any form.

### Section 7   *Doors and Windows*

The doors are an essential means of entrance and egress for the horse and, with the windows, also provide a source of light and air.

i   The doorways should be a minimum of eight feet high and four feet six inches wide:

    *a*   In most cases, half doors are preferable to full doors.
    *b*   They should be four feet six inches high and four feet six inches wide.
    *c*   Tops of half doors, which horses are liable to bite at, should be covered with a strip of metal.
    *d*   Any doors which are liable to be left open often should have a latch, or hook, to hold them in position despite strong winds.
    *e*   All doors should open outwards.
    *f*   Narrow doorways opening inwards are dangerous and a likely cause of injuries to the horse.

ii   Windows should also generally open outwards:

    *a*   Unless outside the reach of the horse, and
    *b*   Unless primarily a source of ventilation not light.
    *c*   They are best with metal frames, hence fireproof.
    *d*   If within reach of the horse, they should be covered by bars not more than three inches apart.

iii  In both doors and windows, the hinges, bolts, door handles, latches and locks must be heavy duty variety able to withstand considerable strain:

    *a*   They should also be simple to operate by hand, but difficult for a horse to manage successfully.
    *b*   In no case, should the bolts project so that the horse may injure himself on them.

iv   Some horses will succeed in opening any bolt within reach:

    *a*   In such cases, it is advisable to have a second bottom bolt on the lower half-door out of reach of the horse.
    *b*   This may be of the simple 'kick-over' variety.

*Section 8   Drainage*
This must include drainage of surface water, as well as drainage of waste from the stables; hence the importance of siting them on high ground to ensure the assistance of gravity:

i    Surface drainage, via open channels, is the simplest method:

    *a*   It is also the cheapest and easiest maintained.
    *b*   It is also amongst the most effective.

ii   Covered drainage systems must have a trap:

    *a*   This prevents noxious gases building up and returning to the stables with ill-effects on the horses.
    *b*   It should hold solid matter washed out of the stables.
    *c*   It should be easily and regularly cleaned.
    *d*   The cover for any such trap must be solid and non-slip.

iii  The worst form of drainage is that draining from the centre of each box and thence outside the stables:

    *a*   It very readily becomes blocked.
    *b*   It is old fashioned and inefficient.
    *c*   Where it is installed it is best to concrete it over and install surface drainage in its place.

*Section 9    The Boxes*
In any modern stables, boxes are preferable to stalls as, clearly, they provide the horse with greater freedom and comfort.

i    The size of boxes may vary from ten by twelve feet to around twelve by sixteen feet:

   *a*    Ten by twelve feet is suitable for a pony, but not really large enough for a full-sized horse.
   *b*    Twelve by sixteen feet is a good size of box suitable even for foaling purposes.
   *c*    The height should be twelve feet to the ceiling, as above.
   *d*    The doorways should be eight feet in height, as above.

ii    Each box should have its own fittings:

   *a*    These should include a manger, hay rack, if used, automatic water bowl, if used, and its own electric light and point.
   *b*    A tethering ring in the wall, as above, should also be fitted.

iii    Any stables, or stud, should include at least one isolation box.

   *a*    As the name implies, this should be isolated from the others.
   *b*    Any sick horses, especially those with possibly infectious diseases, should be quarantined there at once.
   *c*    There should be a strong overhead beam, or girder, available to support a horse in slings, if necessary.

iv    Foaling boxes should be sufficiently large, as above:

   *a*    They should be reasonably secluded and quiet.
   *b*    They should have a peephole available, so that the attendant can watch developments without disturbing the mare.
   *c*    In some cases, like stallion boxes, they are attached to a covered yard to allow the mare, or stallion, to exercise itself.

v    Boxes should be sited, if possible, so that their half-doors open on a central yard, or similar space:

   *a*    The horses looking out will find something of interest and are less likely to become bored.
   *b*    This, in turn, will help to prevent such vices as weaving, wind-sucking, or crib-biting, which are due to boredom.

*Section 10    The Manger*
This is the horse's feeding bowl, generally a fixture in the box.

i    The manger may be of porcelain, metal, or wood:

    *a*    Porcelain is probably preferable as more easily cleaned and, hence, more sanitary.

    *b*    Metal, generally cast-iron, is effective, but may need more thorough cleaning.

    *c*    Wood is least desirable, as it is liable to become insanitary and is readily gnawed by bored horses.

ii    It should be fitted at a height of about 3 feet:

    *a*    This allows the horse easy access to its feed.

    *b*    There is a theory that mangers should be at ground level since this is the natural position for the horse to feed, but

    *c*    This renders them more liable to be soiled and is insanitary; it may encourage eating the bedding, or dung, as well as being a possible danger to the horse.

iii    The manger should be large to prevent the horse bolting its food:

    *a*    It is preferably flat-bottomed, shallow and without a rim.

    *b*    It is thus easily cleaned of any leftover food or dung.

    *c*    It is preferably readily removable as required, but should not be easily knocked up by the horse.

iv    The manger should be inset and not projecting into the box:

    *a*    It may be necessary to build a brick or wooden partition beneath the manger.

    *b*    This could prevent the horse injuring its knees by accident.

v    Wooden mangers are liable to be gnawed and become insanitary (see i*c* above).

    *a*    The rims may therefore require lining with metal.

    *b*    This should be inspected daily since it could become dangerous.

*Section 11    Hay Racks and Hay Nets*
Rests, or containers, for hay to prevent it being wasted, or fouled, as it might be if merely placed on the ground.

i    Hay racks may be of metal, or wood:

    *a*    Metal, generally cast-iron, is preferable to wood.

    *b*    Wood is liable to be gnawed, and is less sanitary and lasting.

ii    If fitted, the hay rack should be flush with the manger:

a    The bars should be close fitting, no more than three inches apart.

b    There must be no danger of the horse catching a leg in them.

iii   Overhead hay racks are not desirable:

a    They cause dirt and dust to fall down into the horse's eyes and mane.

b    This can cause eye trouble and skin disease.

iv   Hay nets have considerable advantages over hay racks:

a    They can be prefilled, thus saving time and labour.

b    They can be adjusted for height to suit each horse.

c    The amount of hay a horse is eating can thus be accurately measured.

d    They result in less wastage.

e    They are inexpensive and can be readily replaced.

f    They take up no room in the stable.

g    They should be made from strong cord and should be well creosoted.

h    This last will discourage the horse from chewing at them when empty.

## Section 12   *Water*

A good water supply both for drinking and for washing down the stables is essential.

i    Water should be permanently available to every horse when stabled, except in some cases of illness:

a    Automatic drinking bowls in each box are excellent.

b    They are a great time and labour saver.

ii   If buckets are used to supply water:

a    One must be kept for each individual horse.

b    They should be named, or numbered, to distinguish them.

c    They should never be filled from a communal trough.

d    They should each be filled individually at a tap.

e    Any deviation from this is liable to spread disease, should any be present in the stables.

iii   If there are individual water bowls, or troughs, in each box:

a    These should be flush with the manger.

b    They should have a drain cock to ensure easy cleaning and sanitation.

c    They should have an easy means of filling, if not self-filling.

iv   Troughs should be of metal, generally cast-iron, with a cock for regular emptying and cleaning.

v   There should be at least one outside trough and one outside tap in every stable yard.

vi  In cold weather, it is advisable to fill buckets a little prior to watering to take the chill off the water.

## Section 13 *Fire Precautions*

Although, as already indicated, it is desirable to use fireproof materials in building the stables, it is also essential to take certain sound fire precautions.

i   It is not desirable to store hay in a loft over the stables:

   *a*  Even if the stables and ceiling are built of fireproof materials.
   *b*  In addition to the inflammable bedding, it is an unnecessary fire risk: spontaneous combustion in hay is common.

ii  Smoking should NEVER on any account be permitted in the stables or amongst forage or bedding.

iii Reliable fire extinguishers should be readily available near to each box:

   *a*  These should be checked regularly.
   *b*  Everyone around the stables should know how to use them.

iv  Everyone should also know what to do in case of fire:

   *a*  The position of fire hydrants should be clearly marked.
   *b*  It is as well to have an occasional fire drill.

## Section 14 *Ventilation*

The horse should have plenty of air available without any draughts.

i   If the doors and windows are adequate, there is no need for any other form of ventilation:

   *a*  It is, however, satisfactory to have a louvre board type of ventilator in the roof.
   *b*  This allows foul air to pass out.

ii  In the event of extremely bad weather, it should only be necessary to close or partially close, those doors, or windows, that are exposed.

iii Proper ventilation should ensure freedom from draughts liable to cause chills and colds:

   *a*  With correct ventilation, a more or less even temperature should be maintained, neither too warm, nor too cold.

*b*  Stables should always smell fresh if properly ventilated, never stuffy or too strongly of horses.

## Section 15  *The Feed Store*

The feed store should contain at least a week's supply of food.

i  It should be adjacent to the stables:

*a*  It should contain galvanised metal corn bins with at least a weeks supply of crushed oats, whole oats, linseed, chaff, bran, etc.

*b*  A boiler is essential to prepare boiled mashes and similar feeds.

ii  Water must be available on tap:

*a*  A sink for cleaning feeding utensils, etc., is also desirable.

*b*  Hot water should be obtainable from the boiler, when required.

iii  A pair of heavy-duty scales are an important item of equipment:

*a*  All incoming sacks should be weighed and checked.

*b*  Occasionally, the amounts fed should also be checked, especially if in any doubt.

## Section 16  *The Hay Barn or Hay Loft*

The hay should be stored in a separate storage shed, or loft.

i  The hay barn, or hay loft, should be adjacent to the stables:

*a*  As already noted, it should not be over the stables since this is an undesirable fire risk.

*b*  For convenience sake, however, it should be close at hand.

ii  It should preferably be built of fireproof materials:

*a*  It must be weatherproof.

*b*  It should be free from rats and other vermin.

iii  A dutch barn is quite effective, providing:

*a*  The whole of the weatherside is covered in.

*b*  The open front is covered for about a yard below the eaves.

*c*  The concrete floor is highest in the centre with a drainage slope all round.

*d*  Thus, any water blown inside will drain away at once.

## Section 17  *The Straw Barn*

The straw, or other bedding, may also be stored in a dutch barn.

i   This again should be adjacent to the stables for convenience and labour saving.

ii  It should also be kept free of vermin.

iii Depending on the size of the stables, the one barn may do for both hay and straw or other bedding.

*Section 18   The Corn Store*
When stored in bulk, oats require ventilation or they readily heat and deteriorate.

i   Ventilation of the stored oats can be achieved:

    *a*   By spreading them fairly thinly on a wooden barn, or corn loft, floor.
    *b*   By storing them in a ventilated hopper, which allows air to circulate through them.

ii  A corn-crusher, operated by an electric motor, should be kept close-by, for use as required.

iii The most satisfactory layout is as follows:

    *a*   The oats are stored, in bulk, in a ventilated hopper in a corn loft next door to the feed store.
    *b*   Beneath the corn loft is the crusher, connected by a chute to the hopper above, and ready for use as needed.
    *c*   A regular weekly quantity is passed through the crusher and moved next door to the feed store.

*Section 19   The Saddle, Harness or Tack Room*
The tack room is used for the storage of all saddles, bridles and other harness, or tack, i.e. tackle.

i   For convenience sake this should also be adjacent to the stables, but generally at the other end from the feed store:

    *a*   It should have ample room for racks for saddles, hooks for bridles, cupboard space for bandages, boots, etc., and storage of rugs, etc.
    *b*   It should have space for cleaning and drying saddlery, possibly separate in another room altogether.
    *c*   Whether in a separate room or not, there should be heating available to dry out wet clothing, bandages, etc.

ii  The room should be well ventilated and lit:

    *a*   There should be at least one good window and electric light, preferably overhead strip lighting.

*b* An even temperature should be maintained as far as possible, neither too not nor too cold.

iii Hot and cold water should be available:

 *a* There should be a good-sized sink.
 *b* This may be used to clean dirty, muddy bridles, saddles, bits, etc.

iv The tack room should always be kept in good order:

 *a* Saddles, bridles and harness should be clean and well kept.
 *b* It should smell of leather, saddle soap and oil, not of horse or sweat.
 *c* It is usually possible to gauge the efficiency of a stables from the state of the tack room and tack (see pp. 196–7).
 *d* A dirty, untidy tack room and dirty tack indicates bad management.

*Section 20 The Manure Pit*
The concrete pit in which the manure from the stables is stored prior to sale or use as fertiliser.

i It must be convenient to the stables to save labour:

 *a* It should not be too close to any buildings, as the ammonia is damaging to brickwork, as well as being bad for horses.
 *b* Also, it is insanitary and the fumes are unpleasant.

ii It should be built with a concrete floor and walls about four feet high:

 *a* The floor may have a slight fall to drain off the liquid manure to a drainage tank.
 *b* Access should be easy for depositing soiled bedding from the stables and for turning and removing the stacked manure itself.

iii It is generally sound practise to cover it with a corrugated sheeting roof to keep off the rain.

*Section 21 The Tool Shed*
It is desirable to have a convenient shed for storing the forks, shovels, brooms, etc., used for mucking-out:

i This should be close to the stables themselves.

ii A lean-to shed at the back of the stables, or to one side, should be quite sufficient.

*Section 22 The Stable Yard*
The space in front of the stables themselves is generally so-termed:

i    It should be kept clean, tidy and well ordered:

    *a*    It may be surfaced in expensive ribbed paving bricks, or

    *b*    Covered with a tarmac, or concrete surface.

    *c*    Alternatively, a cobbled surface may be preferred.

    *d*    Concrete and cobbles tend to be slippery, especially for young horses.

    *e*    Gravel, well rolled, is effective, but requires a lot of care.

ii   A grass covered centre-piece is usually effective.

*Section 23    The Indoor School or Manège, and Jumping Lane and Cavaletti*
A covered school, of course, is a considerable luxury, but an open manège is an effective substitute.

i    An indoor school or manège should measure 50 feet by 100 feet:

    *a*    For schooling over a full course of show jumps, it should be 100 feet by 200 feet.

    *b*    The walls should be 20 feet high.

    *c*    The roof should have sufficient slope to provide plenty of interior air space.

    *d*    Electric light for night work is essential.

ii   Half-way markers and quarter markers should be prominent on either side:

    *a*    This assists in school movements.

    *b*    It aids the rider to gauge distance.

iii  The floor surface may be of various kinds:

    *a*    Tan bark is quite often used, but is dirty and expensive; also,

    *b*    It is harmful to horse's feet.

    *c*    A mixture of two parts sand to one of sawdust has proved quite effective.

    *d*    Peat moss has proved amongst the best surfaces available.

    *e*    Loamy clay, well rolled is also a useful surface.

iv   The open, i.e. outdoor, manège should be surrounded with fencing:

    *a*    This should preferably be about six foot high and solid.

    *b*    This ensures privacy and no distractions for the horse or rider.

v    The floor surface may be as above.

vi   Jumping lanes consist basically of nothing more than a passageway in which one or more jumps are placed:

*a* Once the horse is in the passageway, it is urged down it and the easiest course left open to it is to clear the jumps.

*b* The horse may be ridden, or be jumping free, or be lunged down the jumping lane according to the type of lane and the requirements of the trainer.

vii A jumping lane may be circular, oval, or straight and may, of course, be of varying size, materials and costliness:

*a* It is quite common practice to build a jumping lane round an oval manège, which is thus totally enclosed, being entered by a gate in the side.

*b* It is also common practice to build a straight jumping lane down one side of a manège, open at each end.

*c* Temporary jumping lanes may also be erected comparatively simply against a suitable wall, or fence, or in an indoor school, or manège.

viii Side walls of a jumping lane may vary from four to five feet high to ten feet high, and from light paling to solid sleepers, depending greatly on the size and quality of the jumps likely to be placed in it.

ix Cavaletti, or nine foot long solid single bar jumps securely fixed to one angle of a matching pair of thick wooden cross endpieces, are invaluable for jumping training:

*a* By turning the wooden cross endpiece, the height of the bar may be raised from about a foot to eighteen inches or more.

*b* Used together with others cavaletti may produce endless combinations for jumping (see illustration, pp. 305–6).

*Section 24    Stabling for the One Horse- or Pony-Owner*
For the one horse- or pony-owner, stabling may be much less elaborate than the above, but that should supply a criterion for which to aim:

i Conversions of existing buildings can make perfectly good stables:

*a* In the case of a pony, it is permissible to scale down some of the measurements given above.

*b* In the case of a horse, it is highly undesirable.

ii A lean-to shed with a corrugated-iron roof is not sufficient for a horse or pony.

iii Some types of ready made prefabricated stables are excellent, others are not so good.

iv  In general the horse- or pony-owner should simply aim at achieving the best he can afford for his horse:

    *a*  Buildings that are old fashioned can readily be modernised.
    *b*  Buildings that were not originally intended as stabling may be readily adapted.

v  The ancillaries may be modified accordingly:

    *a*  Food store, corn store, hay and straw barns may be combined, as may the tool shed and tack room, and other combinations are possible.
    *b*  The outdoor manège may be reduced in size in a convenient paddock.

vi  The one horse-, or pony-owner must be prepared to adapt his ideas, but must also be determined to make the best of his circumstances.

# PART II
## Grooming

The skin of the horse is composed of two layers: the true skin, or dermis, and the outer skin, consisting of hair, hoof and horn, known as the 'epidermis'.

*Section 1   The Theory of Grooming*
The epidermis consists of layers of cells; fresh layers are constantly being produced by the dermis of which the outer layers form dandruff or scurf which is removed by grooming:

i   Sweat contains both salt and waste matter excreted from the system by the blood:

    *a*   These are partly absorbed by the dandruff or scurf in the horse's coat.
    *b*   Removing the scurf removes this waste matter, hence is good for the health of the horse.

ii   The true skin, or dermis, contains tiny glands beneath each hair:

    *a*   These secrete a fluid into the follicle of each hair.
    *b*   This keeps the hair smooth, soft and glossy.
    *c*   Massage is necessary to stimulate the action of these glands.

iii   The health of the whole body is benefited by stimulation of the blood supply:

    *a*   Increased blood supply means increased growth and health.
    *b*   Massage improves the health of the horse and the growth and condition of his muscles.

iv   Violent exercise results in an increased blood supply to the muscles and body surface, and enhances the danger of chills:

    *a*   If the body is then allowed to grow cold the horse may come out in a

cold sweat, resulting in a severe chill or congestion of the lungs, i.e.
pneumonia, or disease of the liver, or of the feet, i.e. founder.

*b*    This may happen if the horse is returned to the stables after severe
work without being allowed to cool down properly first, and is not
promptly given a thorough grooming.

*c*    Friction to the body is the best remedy.

*Section 2   The Reasons for Grooming*

Good grooming is as important a factor in keeping a horse in good condition as
good feeding.

i    Under domesticated conditions, good grooming is necessary to keep the
horse clean. Also:

     *a*    It keeps the horse free from chills and other diseases.
     *b*    It removes dandruff, sweat and body impurities.
     *c*    It stimulates the hair and sweat glands.
     *d*    It massages the muscles and increases the flow of blood, thus improving
the coat and the horse's condition.

ii    When wet, either from sweat or rain, the horse in stables requires drying
as he is unable to move around to keep himself dry as would a horse outside.

iii    The horse in stables requires massage of skin and muscles to increase his
bodily fitness.

*Section 3   The Grooming Tools*

Certain well-tried tools are required for grooming. These are:

i    The body brush:

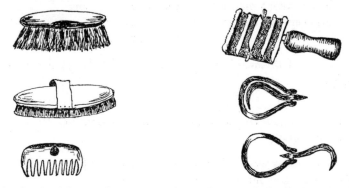

Grooming Tools: (*left, top to bottom*) i. Dandy Brush. ii. Body Brush. iii. Mane Comb.
(*Right, top to bottom*) iv. Curry Comb. v. Closed and Open Hoof Pick

The body brush is an oval-shaped brush with short bristles and a web loop across the wooden back.

a   The web loop is fitted over the back of the hand.
b   The brush is used for the removal of dirt and scurf.
c   It should stimulate the skin and provide massage.
d   It may be used in some cases on the mane and tail.

ii   The curry comb:
The curry comb is an implement of metal, or sometimes rubber, with four or five blunt serrated cross pieces set on a metal, or rubber, back, some five inches by four.

a   It may have a wooden handle, or hand loop to fit over the palm of the hand with the comb on the back of the hand.
b   It is used primarily for removing the excess scurf from the body brush.
c   The metal type should not be used on the horse, except possibly to remove dried lumps of mud that will not brush out.
d   The rubber type may be used anywhere, especially to remove hairs when the horse is losing his coat.

iii   The dandy brush:
A brush of stiff fibre, considerably longer and more bristly than the body brush.

a   It is usual to use the dandy brush all over the horse if unclipped, but when clipped out it is generally used only for grooming the legs and removing hard caked mud.
b   It is held and used in much the same way as a clothes brush on an over-coat.

iv   The water brush:
The water brush is approximately the same size as the dandy brush, but has much finer bristles.

a   When wet, the water brush may be used for damping the mane and tail and for washing the feet.
b   When dry, it may be used for grooming the face, or ticklish places not suitable for the body brush.

v   The sponges:
These may be of rubber, or natural growth.

a   They should be used for cleaning the eyes, nostrils, lips, also the dock and sheath, or the teats and udder of a mare.

*b*   It is preferable to have separate sponges for the various parts of the anatomy.

vi   The wisp:

The wisp is formed from a twisted rope of hay or straw, and is made as follows:

*a*   The twisted rope should be eight to ten feet long.
*b*   Two loops should be formed at one end.
*c*   The rope is twisted over and under each loop alternately.
*d*   The end is finally pushed through one loop and down the centre.

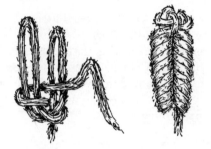

The Wisp; Half Made    Complete

The wisp is used as follows:

*a*   Used wet, or slightly damp, it removes grease from the horse's coat.
*b*   It is primarily used for massage.
*c*   It should be brought down with the full weight of the groom behind it in the direction the hair is lying.

Points concerning the whisp;

*a*   It is cheap and readily made as well as being an excellent means of providing massage.
*b*   A good substitute for it, also cheap and virtually everlasting, is a rectangle about the size of the hand, cut from the tread of an old car tyre.
*c*   The palm of the hand itself is an excellent, cheap and lasting source of massage.

vii   The stable rubber:

The stable rubber is simply a large clean flannel rag or duster.

*a*   It is used for the final wipe over and for putting the gloss on the horse after the general grooming.

*b*   It may be used as a substitute for the sponges, but then requires frequent boiling.

*c*   The full weight of the groom should be used behind the rubber, except, of course, on the head and ticklish areas.

viii The mane comb:
The mane comb is a flat metal comb with blunt ends.

*a*   It is used on both mane and tail.

*b*   It is particularly useful for untangling the tail, BUT,

*c*   The hairs of both mane and tail are easily damaged and it should only be used in experienced hands.

ix   The hoof pick:
The hoof pick is a blunt-ended hook:

*a*   It is used for cleaning out the feet round the frog, removing mud, stones, etc.

*b*   The hoof pick should always be used towards the toe, never towards the heel, and should not be forced down the frog cleft.

*c*   If used towards the heel, the frog or frog cleft might be damaged.

*d*   The hoof pick should never be sharp enough to damage the sole of the hoof, or puncture it.

x   The sweat scraper:
A half-moon-shaped strip of metal attached to a wooden handle, sometimes with a rubber edge to the metal piece.

*a*   Used primarily after racing, or games such as polo, where the horse is likely to return sweating to the stable.

*b*   It is primarily used simply to remove the surplus sweat at once.

*c*   It may also be useful on occasions when the horse returns very wet to the stables, but otherwise is not of great value.

*Section 4   The Method of Grooming*
It is necessary to know when, in what order, and how to use the grooming tools, as follows:

i   Times of grooming:
The horse should be groomed each morning and also on his return from exercise.

*a*   It should be possible to groom a horse in good condition inside half an hour.

153

b   After heavy exercise, when the horse is very dirty and sweaty, a good deal longer may be required.

c   The methods used and reasons for grooming may vary dependent on circumstances before and after exercise: also with each stables.

d   In the morning, the grooming is primarily to prepare the horse for exercise, i.e. it is a general conditioner and should not take long.

e   After exercise, the grooming may be primarily to aid recovery from that exercise, i.e. it is chiefly recuperative massage and is the important grooming of the day.

ii  Picking out the feet:
It is customary to pick out the feet and attend to them first whenever grooming the horse.

a   In the morning, the aim is to remove wet dung or any similar possible cause of thrush, i.e. disease of the frog (see p. 363).

b   After exercise, the aim is to remove any stones that may have been lodged between the frog and the shoe.

c   The hoof pick should only be used from the heel to the toe, checking the cleft of the frog, the sides of the frog and the inside of the shoe with especial care.

d   Start with the near-fore and near-hind, then move to off-hind and off-fore.

e   To raise forelegs run hand gently from shoulder to cannon, grasp pastern and raise the foot. Use hoof pick from heel to toe.

f   To raise hindleg, run hand gently from quarters to hock, grasp the fetlock and raise the foot. Use hoof pick from heel to toe.

g   In morning grooming, some people advise washing out the feet with cold water and the water brush to remove dung, etc. (N.B. the heels must not be wetted.)

h   The shoes should be checked to make sure they are not loose, that clenches are all tight and no nails missing etc.

iii Using the dandy brush:
As noted iii above, the dandy brush is used for removing dried mud or sweat, but its bristles are very stiff and it must be used with care.

a   Care must be taken especially in using it on ticklish or tender parts of the anatomy.

b   The area of the saddle patch and the legs are where it is principally likely to be used.

c   Care should be taken not to hit the legs with the wooden back of the brush.

*d*  Particular attention should be paid to the heels and fetlocks, but it should not take long to finish with this brush.

*e*  The heels should not be brushed when the legs are raised or the wrinkled skin may be damaged.

iv  Using the body brush and curry comb:
After the dandy brush, the body brush and curry comb should be used, as follows:

*a*  The body brush should be used methodically over the whole body, starting on the near-side at the top of the neck behind the ears.

*b*  From the ears, carry on down the neck, over the shoulders and barrel, over the ribs and belly, down the legs as far as the knee and hock, and then do the off-side.

*c*  On the near-side, the body brush should be held in the left hand and the curry comb in the right. These should be reversed on the off-side.

*d*  It is best to stand well away from the horse and use a stiff arm stroke in a semicircular movement mostly in the direction of the hair growth.

*e*  The brush should not be banged down heavily, but laid on gently with the full weight of the body behind each stroke.

*f*  Unless the horse is extremely dirty, it should be unnecessary to clean the brush on the curry comb more than three or four times on either side. Too frequent use wears out the bristles prematurely.

*g*  The dirt in the curry comb should be tapped out on the floor behind the horse, never in the manger where it might contaminate the horse's feed.

*h*  Some horses are extremely ticklish under the belly and thighs, and it may be advisable to use the water brush here as well as on the head.

v  Grooming the mane and tail:
The dressing of the mane and tail requires experience and patience. It should be done as follows:

*a*  They should be brushed out very carefully from the roots a lock at a time with one end of the body brush.

*b*  When the comb is used it should be dipped in olive oil to avoid breaking the hairs. Careless or inexperienced use of the comb or dandy brush, can easily ruin both mane and tail.

*c*  The mane should be brushed out beginning at the roots, from the poll, a lock at a time. Any burrs, or caked mud, should be removed by hand, if possible.

*d*  The tail is also begun at the top and the roots exposed by raising the hairs in small locks: working across the tail and downwards, dealing with burrs and caked mud as above.

   *e*  Plaiting the mane for showing, etc., is accomplished by taking three thin locks and plaiting them. The ends are turned under and the whole sewn with black thread. Generally seven to a dozen plaits are made (see pp. 182–3).

   *f*  The forelock is plaited separately and the number of plaits in the mane may vary considerably, but is never less than six.

   *g*  Tight plaiting should never be left in for more than twenty-four hours or the mane may fall out in chunks.

   *h*  Normally when the mane and tail have been brushed out they are left until after the use of the stable rubber on the horse, then they are smoothed down with a dampened water brush.

vi  Wisping:
The chief use of the wisp, as above, is to massage the horse, raising muscle, improving the coat and refreshing a tired horse.

   *a*  The wisp should be brought down with a bang and used very energetically on neck, body and quarters, but with care over the loins which have the unprotected kidneys beneath them.

   *b*  It should be used in the same order as the body brush, starting on the near-side and ending on the off-side.

   *c*  The wisp should be slightly dampened for better effect.

vii  Hand-strapping:
The use of the palm of the hand is an excellent means of massaging the horse.

   *a*  It is especially useful for drying the horse's back after removing the saddle.

   *b*  The hands should be slapped down on the body one after the other, with the weight of the body leaned on them.

   *c*  The forearms may be used as well as the hands and wrists, and firm pressure applied both with and against the hair.

   *d*  The hands should be kept slightly damp.

   *e*  This is also a useful method for removing loose hair when the horse is losing its coat.

   *f*  The legs, below knees and hocks, should be hand-rubbed each day in an upward direction.

   *g*  This stimulates the veins and lymphatic glands.

viii  The use of the stable rubber:
Following the wisping, or hand massage, the stable rubber should be used.

   *a*  As with the body brush and wisp, the full weight of the groom should be behind the rubber.

*b*    The rubber should be used in the same order as the body brush and wisp, starting on the near-side and having a care of the loins.

ix    The use of the sponges:
After the stable rubber has been used and the mane and tail brushed down with the damp water brush, last of all the sponges are used.

*a*    The eyes, mouth and nostrils should be carefully washed with cold water.
*b*    The dock as well as the sheath, or teats and udder, should then also be thoroughly washed and sponged.

## Section 5    *Washing the Horse*

The horse is not normally washed except as follows:

i    The sole of the foot, or the horn of the feet, if fouled by dung, are the only parts of the horse normally washed regularly.

*a*    This should be done outside the stable.
*b*    It is essential to ensure that the coronet and heels are kept dry.

ii    It may be necessary to wash white legs, or a grey horse marked by stable stains:

*a*    This should be done with soap and water and well rinsed out.
*b*    The horse should be promptly dried and massaged to restore circulation.

iii    The mane and tail should be washed out with warm water and soap at intervals, especially when scurfy:

*a*    When washing the mane the neck and head should not be wetted more than necessary.
*b*    The tail should be well rinsed by dipping direct into a bucket to avoid wetting the quarters unduly.

iv    The sheath should also be washed about once a fortnight with warm soapy water (particularly important with stallions).

*a*    The 'yard' or penis should be drawn out and good antiseptic soap used, e.g. Lifebuoy.
*b*    Horses which do not 'draw the yard', i.e. pass the penis properly, when staling require more frequent washing than others.

## Section 6    *Grooming after Exercise*

The grooming after exercise is the most important of the day, and much must depend on how the horse returns to the stable.

i  If the horse is tired after a hard day's exercise, but is not wet or sweating:

    *a*    It may be advisable to rug him at once, after loosening the girths of the saddle.

    *b*    Then, feed a hot gruel and hay.

    *c*    Examine his legs and feet and bandage his legs in wool bandages.

    *d*    Then, after about half an hour, remove the rug and start wisping and hand strapping to provide massage and improve the circulation.

    *e*    When the saddle is removed there is generally a wet patch underneath; this must be energetically hand-strapped to prevent lumps forming.

ii  A sweating horse should never be brought into the stables; it should always be walked back for the last mile.

    *a*    If a sweating horse is brought back he should be walked around outside with his girth and saddle loose until he is dry.

    *b*    If this is not possible he should be briskly wisped and rubbed down with handfuls of straw against the coat to dry him off, restore his circulation and prevent a chill, etc.

    *c*    The saddle should not be removed, but the girths loosened, as above, until the rest of the body is dry.

iii  If a horse is returned to the stables wet, it is advisable to try to warm him by trotting fast right up to the stable:

    *a*    The girth and saddle should be loosened and the entire back covered thickly with straw, or a sweat rug may be used instead.

    *b*    A night rug, inside-out, should then be put over the top to hold it in place.

    *c*    The horse's heels should then be thoroughly dried out first of all, followed by the belly and flanks.

    *d*    This should be followed by drying the throat, jowls and ears; the last should be pulled gently by hand until dry and warm (a gentle pull from the base to the tip).

    *e*    The night rug may then be removed and the body thoroughly dried-off, the saddle being removed last and the patch beneath thoroughly hand-strapped and sweat patches removed.

    *f*    Hand-strapping and wisping are more effective in these circumstances than anything else.

    *g*    The important point is to keep the circulation going and to prevent the horse catching a chill before he is thoroughly dry.

    *h*    If the horse is soaking wet and steaming when he comes in, a quick sponge down can do no harm, but the routine, as above, should then be followed.

iv  If the weather is extremely cold, and the horse is very muddy when he is
brought in, then grooming should start at once:

a  The girths should be loosened and the saddle left in place, but the
horse should be vigorously hand-strapped and wisped to maintain the
circulation and prevent him catching a chill, etc.

b  There is no harm in leaving the legs for half an hour until the mud has
dried and may be brushed off. (N.B. They should not be washed down
as this is liable to chill the horse in the stable.)

c  The grooming should then be completed in the normal manner.

v  If a horse breaks into a sweat after being dried and groomed, it is essential
to dry him off and groom him again:

a  He may be of a nervous disposition, or overtired, or chilled.

b  It may be advisable to feed a hot gruel or mash, drenched with a half
bottle of spirits or a quart of stout.

c  The horse should be kept under observation in case he has caught a
chill.

*Section 7  Checking the Grooming*
The grooming should be checked from time to time to ensure that a proper job
is being done.

i  Each leg should be picked up in turn:

a  The feet should be picked out and clean.

b  The heels should be dry and clean.

ii  The coat should be examined with the fingertips for scurf or grease by
running the hand against the hair:

a  Especially between the ears and between the forelegs.

b  Also on the top of the quarters and under the belly.

iii  Where the saddle and bridle or harness rest should be checked for any sweat
marks remaining:

a  Especially the forehead and round the ears.

b  Also the girth behind the elbows, and saddle patch.

iv  The eyes, ears and nostrils should be examined, also the sheath and dock.

v  The roots of the hair of mane and tail should also be closely examined for
scurf and dirt.

# PART III
# The Care of the Foot and Shoeing

The structure of the foot must be clearly understood if a real knowledge of the care of the foot and shoeing is to be attained. (As a horse is useless without sound feet some repetition must be accepted.)

*Section 1   The Parts of the Foot*
A clear distinction must be made between the inner parts of the foot and the outer parts.

i     The inner parts of the foot are as follows:

    *a*     The coffin bone, or os pedis, which lies behind the horn of the hoof and is the same shape as the hoof with a wing or projection on either side to which the lateral cartilages are attached (see *1*x below).

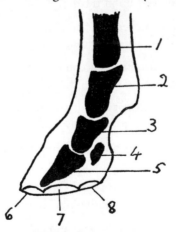

Cross Section of Foot and Pastern

1. Cannon Bone. 2. The First Phalanx, or Long Pastern Bone. 3. The Second Phalanx, or Os Coronae, or Short Pastern Bone. 4. The Navicular Bone. 5. The Third Phalanx, or Os Pedis, or Pedal, or Coffin Bone. 6. Toe. 7. Quarter. 8. Heel.

*b*    The navicular bone, or os navicular, which lies behind the coffin bone and is roughly boat-shaped.

*c*    Above the coffin bone, lies the lower part of the small pastern bone, or os coronae.

*d*    Also amongst the inner parts of the foot are: the lower ends of the flexor pedis perforans tendon and the extensis pedis tendon, the joint ligaments, the synovial membrane, the lateral cartilages, the sensitive laminae, the sensitive sole, the plantar cushion, the sensitive frog, the coronary band and the periopic ring.

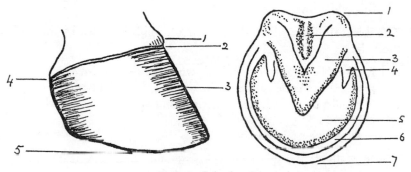

Points of the hoof

1. Coronary cushion. 2. Frog band. 3. Wall of hoof. 4. Bulb of heel. 5. Sole of hoof.

1. Bulbs of heel. 2. Cleft of frog. 3. Frog. 4. Bars. 5. Sole of hoof. 6. White line. 7. Wall of hoof.

ii    The outer part of the foot, or the horn container of the above, consists of the wall, the sole, the frog and the bars.

iii    The wall of the hoof is divided into the toe, the quarters and the heels.

iv    The wall of the hoof is covered on the outside with a cell-like skin known as the 'periople':

    *a*    This grows downward from the periopic ring.
    *b*    It prevents the hoof drying up or becoming brittle.

v    The wall of the hoof grows downwards from the coronary band and the rate of growth is about a quarter of an inch a month:

    *a*    It takes a year to grow to the toe and about six months to grow to the heel.
    *b*    If the coronet is damaged, the hoof below will not grow normally, but temporarily will be softer and should not have nails driven into it.

   *c*   The growth and quality of the horn can be improved by applying stimulants to the coronary band.

vi   The inner wall of the hoof is thicker and more upright than the outer wall, thus leaving a thick toe for wear:

   *a*   The inner wall is attached to the os pedis, or coffin bone, by numerous sensitive laminae or plates.
   *b*   These laminae may be seen as a white line between the sole and the wall of a freshly trimmed hoof.
   *c*   The blacksmith uses this as a guide line and always puts his nails outside this white line.

vii   The sole is similar to the wall of the hoof, and is bounded by the wall and the bars:

   *a*   It takes six months to grow down from the sensitive sole, which is attached to the underside of the os pedis, or coffin bone.
   *b*   It should be arched, not flat, firm, not spongey, and thickest at the perimeter.
   *c*   It should never be cut away.

viii   The bars divide the sole from the frog and are a continuation inwards, towards the point of the frog, of the walls at the heels:

   *a*   The bars grow down from the sensitive sole and must not be cut away, or contracted heels and frog will result.

Contracted Heel

   *b*   Between the bars and the frog is a groove which allows the frog to expand when the body weight pressed it to the ground.
   *c*   The bars support the wall at the heels and allow for expansion of the heels when the frog expands under pressure of the body weight.

ix   The frog is the V-shaped fibrous formation of elastic horn between the bars:

   a   It grows downwards from the sensitive frog and takes two months to grow.
   b   In the centre of the frog is the cleft of the frog, which should be shallow and rounded.
   c   At the base of the frog on either side are the bulbs of the heel.
   d   The frog is elastic and much softer than the wall, or sole, being intended to bulge outwards and expand the heel when bearing the weight of the body.
   e   Its function is to prevent concussion and provide a grip, or prevent slipping, when the body weight bears on it.
   f   Hence, the importance of NEVER paring the frog and always having frog pressure, i.e. of the frog bearing the weight of the horse at each pace.
   g   Above the sensitive frog is the plantar cushion, or frog pad, lying between the two wings of the os pedis, or coffin bone.
   h   The frog pad also lies between the two lateral cartilages and acts as an extra shock absorber and helps to expand the heel.

x   The Lateral Cartilages are placed just inside the top of the wall outside the plantar cushion on each side of the foot:

   a   They join the heel of the wall to the wing of the os pedis, or coffin bone, on each side.
   b   They are flexible, allowing movement of the heels of the wall and assisting in supporting the heels.
   c   The two are joined together by ligaments passing through the frog pad, or plantar cushion, and are attached to the sensitive laminae.
   d   If the lateral cartilages are injured, they easily become diseased, forming quittor and sidebone (see pp. 362, 369–70).

Section 2   *The Functions of the Parts of the Foot*
The parts of the foot function together as follows:

i   Normally the heel is the first part of the foot to touch the ground.
ii   The concussion is then absorbed by:

   a   The compression and lateral expansion of the frog and plantar cushion.
   b   By the flattening of the arch of the sole.
   c   By the descent of the os pedis, or coffin bone.
   d   By the elasticity of the fetlock joint and the leg.

iii The expansion of the frog and plantar cushion widens the heels.

  *a* This causes movement of the lateral cartilages causing them to act as valves for the venous circulation of the foot.

  *b* Hence, the reason why the foot circulation is impaired and the cartilages become diseased and ossified into sidebones if the frog pressure is removed (see pp. 369–70).

iv Too continuous concussion on a hard surface, i.e. road surface at a gallop, or lack of frog pressure may also lead to many other diseases of the foot, such as navicular, laminitis, etc. (see pp. 361–2).

*Section 3   The Shoeing Tools*

It is desirable to have a set of shoeing tools as follows:

i The shoeing hammer has a small head and curved claws:

  *a* It is used for driving in and 'clenching' the nails, hence it is not desirable that it should have a heavy head.

  *b* The claws are used for twisting off the ends of the nails projecting through the hoof.

  *c* In conjunction with the pincers, the hammer is then used to 'clench' or secure the twisted ends.

Shoeing Hammer

ii The pincers have handles a foot long and flat curved jaws:

  *a* They are used for removing the old nails and shoes.

  *b* Also in conjunction with the hammer, used to secure the clenches.

iii The buffer is a metal tool about six inches long with a chisel at one end and a punch at the other:

  *a* It is used to cut off the clenches preparatory to removing the shoes.

  *b* It is also used to punch out broken nails from the foot.

iv    The rasp is a file about sixteen inches long:

    *a*    It has one half of one side file-cut.

    *b*    The remainder is coarse-cut for taking down the ground surface of the wall of the hoof.

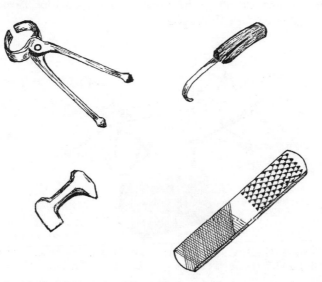

Shoeing Tools: i. Pincers (*top left*). ii. Knife (*top right*). iii. Buffer (*bottom left*).
iv. Rasp (*bottom right*)

v    The drawing knife is used to pare down the wall and remove ragged pieces of horn:

    *a*    It has a curved blade about six inches long.

    *b*    It must be kept sharp.

vi    The searching knife is used as a hoof trimmer and for examining the ground surface of the hoof.

*Section 4    The Smithy Tools*

It is desirable to know the names of the smithy tools, even if unable to use them. They are as follows:

i    The forge:
The forge may be portable or fixed.

    *a*    May have hand bellows, or power operated draught.

    *b*    It should be capable of producing a white heat in a short time.

ii   The Anvil:
     The anvil may be portable, or fixed.

    *a*   If portable likely to be a lighter version, i.e. 100 lbs. rather than 150 lbs.
    *b*   It is generally made of steel with a hardened steel top: the principal
       features are the hanging end, punching hole, tool hole, face, step, table,
       bic and throat (see illustration).

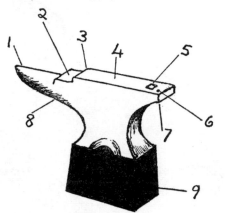

Anvil (155) parts: 1. The Bick. 2. The Table. 3. The Step. 4. The Face. 5. The Tool Hole.
6. The Punching Hole. 7. The Hanging End. 8. The Throat. 9. The Stand

iii  The fire tongs and shoe tongs:
     Each pair of tongs used for a separate purpose.

    *a*   The fire tongs, for holding the shoe in the fire, have long handles.
    *b*   The shoe tongs for working the shoe on the anvil have short handles.

iv   The turning hammer and sledgehammer:
     Each type of hammer has its separate purpose.

    *a*   The turning hammer used on the anvil has a flat face on one side and a
       convex face on the other and weighs 4 lbs.
    *b*   The sledgehammer is used by the assistant, or striker, to weld cut, or
       mould, when making shoes from bar steel; it weighs 9 lbs.

v    The shaping tools:
     The shaping tools are held by the blacksmith, while the striker uses the
     sledge on them:

    *a*   The swedge, or concave tool, to form a concave surface.
    *b*   The fuller, or blunt chisel, with a wooden handle, used to mould the
       fuller, or groove, in the ground surface of the shoe.

c    The pritchel, or counter sinker, used to punch the holes in the shoe for the nail heads to fit into.

d    The stamp, used to make the nail holes in the shoe: this and the previous tools must be the same size as the nails used.

*Section 5    The Mechanics of Shoeing*
There are certain principles involved in shoeing which must be fully understood, as follows:

i    Preparing the foot:
The hoof wall grows about a quarter of an inch a month, and it is general practise to reshoe once a month:

    a    It is thus necessary for the smith to use his knife and rasp to remove about this amount from the ground surface of the hoof wall preparatory to receiving the new shoe.

    b    It is desirable to make each foot of a pair as similar as possible to the other, but odd feet exist as in humans.

    c    The slope of the toe of the wall varies with the conformation of the foot; generally about 45°–50° in front and 50°–55° behind.

    d    The slope may be altered by the amount of toe, or heel, rasped or pared off the ground surface: feet of bad shape can sometimes be improved over a period of months.

    e    The pressure on the frog may also be greatly affected by the height of the heels: if too long the frog pressure is reduced and concussion increased, if too short the back tendons will be strained.

    f    When placed on a flat surface, every part of the ground surface of the wall should bear on it.

    g    Finally, the rasp is run round the outer edge to bevel it and prevent the horn from splitting.

ii    Fitting the shoe:
The shoe must be made to fit the hoof: the hoof must NOT be made to fit the shoe.

    a    When the foot has been prepared, the shoe should be heated in the forge and bent on the anvil so that the outer circumference matches the outside of the hoof exactly.

    b    The upper surface, or foot surface, of the shoe, must be a true plane, i.e. it must lie flat on the anvil and should be in contact with the hoof at all points: or the wall will be damaged.

    c    The shoe should then be heated to black heat only and placed on the foot for about three seconds, until smoke comes from the horn, thus sealing the ends of the horn fibres.

*d*   This also shows up any portion of the ground surface of the hoof which is not quite level and the rasp may then be used to remedy the defect. But *N.B.*:

*e*   Prolonged burning may do serious damage and a red hot shoe should never be held against the foot.

*f*   The length of the heel should be checked carefully, long heels on the fore-shoes may be torn off by the hind-shoes.

*g*   Too short a heel may cause corns due to the pressure on the end of the shoe.

*h*   If the shoes are being made by the smith, it is important to check whether any part of the hoof is not fit to receive a nail before punching the nail holes.

iii   The shoes:
The shoes should be made of the best mild steel, no heavier, or thicker, than is required to last until the next shoeing.

*a*   The weight of the ponies and hunters shoes may vary from four to twelve ounces and the width of the cover, or web, will be approximately three quarters of an inch (cover=width of metal, interchangeable with web, although this strictly also includes the thickness, i.e. the cubic area of metal).

*b*   The ground surface of the shoe may be either flat, or fullered, i.e. grooved, for about half its depth.

*c*   The fuller, or groove, should run closer to the outer edge of the shoe than to the inner; it provides a better grip.

*d*   The heads of the nails should fit into the fullering, and should not project.

*e*   Fullered shoes also generally have the inner edge of the shoe concave, or bevelled: this lessens the suction when crossing muddy ground, hence reducing the risk of losing a shoe.

*f*   The blacksmith, or farrier, may obtain the shoes ready-made, which is a great time-saver, but he should be able to make them from bar steel, either flat or fullered, as well as any special type of shoe required.

*g*   Even ready-made shoes will have to be made to fit correctly, either by use of the forge and hot-shoeing, or by cold-shoeing, i.e. simply using the anvil and machine-made shoes.

*h*   Parts of the shoes not mentioned above are the toe, heel and quarter, corresponding to the parts of the foot; also the branch, i.e. the complete side of the shoe from toe to heel, so there are two branches to each shoe.

iv   The nails:
The better the preparation of the foot and the fit of the shoe the fewer the nails required: only as many should be used as are needed to hold the shoe on securely:

a   Five nails in the fore-shoes, two inside and three outside, or six in the hind-shoes, are all that should be required for a hunter or pony: seven nails is the maximum.
b   Nails are not generally used at the toes, or heels, to allow for expansion at these points.
c   One side of each nail point is bevelled and the nail must be driven into the wall of the hoof with the bevelled side towards the centre of the foot: this drives the nail outwards.
d   If the nail were turned incorrectly, it would drive into and prick the sensitive sole, possibly causing serious injury.
e   The point of each nail should be examined before being driven in, and only nails of first-class quality should be used.
f   The nails should be the correct size to fit the hoof and not too large, e.g. carthorse size in a pony's hoof.
g   The nails must also fit the shoes: the hole must not be larger than the nail or vice versa.
h   Due to the fresh nail holes being too close to the old ones the feet will not generally stand being reshod more than once in three weeks.

v   Nailing on the shoe:
The first nail should be driven in towards the heel, i.e. at an angle to the surface of the shoe; this will tighten the clip, if there is one.

a   It is usual to drive the centre nails on each side first, and it is desirable that the points should come out about an inch up the wall of the hoof and that all the points should be approximately level.
b   It should be possible to tell by the sound if the nail is driving correctly.
c   If there is any doubt, or if the horse flinches at all, the nail should be withdrawn and the point examined for blood, i.e. a prick, but it may only have pressed the sensitive laminae, bruising it without pricking: this is known as a 'press' or 'bind'.
d   Faults are fine nailing, i.e. nails too near the edge of the shoe and insufficient grip, or coarse nailing, i.e. too far up and liable to be pressing on the sensitive laminae.
e   Each nail must be driven right home and the end is then at once screwed off with the claw of the hammer, but sufficient stub end must be left to form the 'clench'.

*f*     After all the nails are in, each must be hammered again to ensure it is home and while doing so the head of the pincers is held against the stub to flatten it down and form the clench.

*g*     The clench is then gently hammered down to rivet it over and if too big or jagged may be filed down a little. But *N.B.*, care must be taken not to damage the periople.

*h*     The clench must be large enough to hold the nail and shoe in place, but if too large will damage the hoof if the shoe is pulled off.

**vi   Clips:**

Clips are small triangular pieces on the outer edge of the shoe which fit into shallow nicks cut in the wall of the hoof.

Front Clip            Quarter Clip

*a*     There may be one on the toe, or sometimes, as in the case of harness horses, one on each quarter, or there may be none.

*b*     They do hold the shoe more securely on the foot, but should only be used when necessary.

*c*     The clip should be thin and almost flat; care must be taken that it is not bulging.

*d*     A bulge will press into the toe of the hoof and is a common cause of the disease known as 'seedy toe'. (See pp. 359–60.)

*e*     The clip must be bent to the slope of the foot while the shoe is being fitted, NEVER knocked into the wall after the shoe is in place: this may injure the hoof (see seedy toe).

**vii   Calkins:**

These are projections on the underside of the heels of the shoes made by turning the heel over:

*a*     They are generally used on hind-shoes only.

*l. to r.*) i. Shoe with Calkin. ii. Wedge Heel. iii. Badly Shod: Toe Dumped: Too short
at heel

> *b*   The object is to provide grip, but, by preventing frog pressure, they can be very bad for the horse.
> *c*   If used, they should never be high, but should be long and low.
> *d*   It may be on both, or the outer heel only, in which case the inside heel should be brought level by thickening: known as a 'wedge' heel.

viii Calks:
These may be screw, or drive, fitting into threaded, or specially shaped holes in the web and are removable, varying in length, shape and type.

> *a*   These are used sometimes in the winter in icy conditions, or for show jumping in greasy conditions.
> *b*   They have the advantage that they can be removed at night, or as required, but if too often removed tend to work loose easily.

ix  Removing the shoes:
It may be necessary for the owner to be able to remove the shoes, or a shoe, if nothing else, on occasions.

> *a*   The heads of each nail must be hammered home, so that the clench protrudes slightly. The ends of the clench may then be cut off with the buffer.
> *b*   The shoe should then be drawn out a little with the aid of the pincers.
> *c*   It should then be tapped into place again, and the nails left with their heads protruding are then easily drawn out by the pincers.
> *d*   The shoe must never be wrenched off with the nails in the foot as some of the horn may be torn off with it. Hence, if a shoe is half torn off, the importance of the owner being able to deal with the situation.
> *e*   All old clenches and nails must be carefully removed and damage to the periople kept to the minimum.
> *f*   If the shoes removed are to be used again, they are known as 'removes'.

x   Methods of restraint: the twitch and the trave:
In the case of extremely wild, young, or frightened horses, it may be necessary to resort to methods of restraint, although these are a condem-

nation of the handling and training the horse has received and are scarcely ever justified.

*a* The twitch is a short wooden pole, e.g. the end of a broom handle with a loop of soft rope threaded through a hole in the end.

*b* The loop is slipped over the upper lip of the horse and the wooden handle twisted until it is tight and the lip is bulging through it.

*c* The idea is to distract the horse's attention from shoeing, or similar treatment, by the pain in its lip.

*d* It is effective, but undesirable, as it inevitably breeds fear for the future and hence more violent reactions.

*e* There are various types of twitch, but they all work on the same basic principles.

*f* The trave is a wooden cage of stout timbers outside the smithy into which the horse is backed if intractable: generally used on young heavy draught horse breeds.

*g* One leg at a time, or all together, are fastened to the uprights of the trave to prevent kicking.

*h* It is neither effective nor desirable for the same reasons as the twitch, but in greater degree; is fortunately rare in this country. Both impractical and dangerous to use on a blood horse.

### Section 6 Special Types of Shoe
Various kinds of shoe may be required for different reasons, as follows:

i Tips:
These only cover the toe of the foot, extending from quarter to quarter.

*a* They are sometimes known as 'grass tips' as primarily intended to prevent the horn from splitting at the toe when out at grass.

*b* They are also used to provide extra frog pressure to counteract contracted, or diseased, frogs.

(*l. to r.*) i. Seated Out: Fullered Shoe. ii. Feather-edged Shoe. iii. Plain Shoe with Strip. iv. Three-quarter Shoe

*c* The rear ends may be tapered, or may be cut square and let into the hoof: the latter are stronger.

*d*　Two nails a side should be all that is required.

*e*　Care must be taken not to wear the frog and heels down too much on stony ground.

ii　Feathering:
A feather-edged shoe is one on which the web of one branch is less than half the normal width.

*a*　The inner side is feathered to prevent brushing or speedy cutting (see p. 354).

*b*　There may be no nails in the feathered branch.

*c*　Hind-shoes are more often treated in this way than fore-shoes.

*d*　The effect of the difference in weight is to swing the foot outwards.

*e*　These are merely an extreme example of side-weight shoes, i.e. shoes with the web weighted at the toe or one side to check faulty action or interfering.

iii　Bar shoes:
These have the heels connected under the frog and are used in relieving pressure on part of the walls.

*a*　Three-quarter and half bar shoes are often used for corns.

*b*　Bar shoes will tend to spread the heels if contracted.

*c*　Half bar shoes are used for sand crack (see pp. 362–3).

iv　Rocking shoes:
These have thick quarters and thin toes and heels and are used in cases of laminitis and dropped sole (see p. 361).

v　Rolled toe, or set-up shoes:
At the toe, half the width of the web is bent up at an angle of about 22°.

Shortened Toe to prevent tumbling　　　　Front View

*a*　The theory is that this is where the greatest wear comes in the shoe, and that by this means the shoe has longer life.

173

    *b*    The shoe may therefore be thinner and lighter, giving increased frog pressure, etc.

    *c*    Also liable to prevent stumbling.

    *d*    No clip is required, but the wall of the hoof must be rasped back to receive the rolled toe.

vi  A seated shoe:

A shoe with the upper surface, or bearing surface, bevelled at the inner edge, thus making little or no contact with the sole.

    *a*    Only necessary for flat feet or dropped sole.

    *b*    It is liable to be easily loosened in muddy going and collects dirt in the inner edge.

### Section 7  *Shoeing Faults*

Certain common shoeing faults are often seen and should be checked whenever possible.

i  Rasping the wall of the foot:

The outside of the wall, or periople, should never be rasped.

    *a*    The periople is necessary to prevent the horn becoming brittle.

    *b*    Rasping a notch to 'bed' the clenches, or rasping the clenches themselves are usually the reasons for this bad practice.

ii  Dumping the toe:

The toe of the foot should never be 'dumped', i.e. rasped down to fit the shoe: this is a very bad, but quite common, fault.

    *a*    It lessens the nail hold and reduces the width of the weight-bearing wall.

    *b*    It exposes the ends of the horn fibres and allows the horn to dry out.

iii  Paring the frog:

Neither the sole nor frog must ever be pared by the smith; but:

    *a*    From time to time a flake of horn, or 'false sole', may be lifted out with the hoof pick.

    *b*    Jagged pieces of frog may sometimes be trimmed.

iv  Other common faults:

Other very common faults which should be avoided are:

    *a*    The foot should not be rasped down to expose the white line all round.

    *b*    The heel should never be 'opened up' by paring away the wall at the heels and part of the sides of the frog.

*c*   Excessive burning with the hot shoe must not be permitted.

*d*   Clenching too tightly must also be prevented.

*e*   The horse must never be abused in the smithy or he will associate it with fear and be all the worse to handle on the next visit.

*f*   He should not require the use of the twitch, or trave: the former is a confession of bad training and the latter should not be allowed.

*Section 8*   *Checking the shoeing*

After shoeing, it is advisable to look for the following points:

i   With the foot on the ground:

    *a*   The shoe fits the foot.

    *b*   No dumping of the toe or rasping of the wall.

    *c*   Clenches even, flat and about one inch up, neither too high nor too low, nor driven through old nail holes.

    *d*   Clips, if any, flat and low.

ii   When the foot is lifted up:

    *a*   The shoe fits the foot: specially at the heels, neither too long nor too short.

    *b*   No paring of the sole or frog and no opening of the heels.

    *c*   No uneven bearing of the shoe, i.e. no daylight visible.

    *d*   Plenty of room for the frog to function.

    *e*   The nails all driven home.

iii   When trotted out that there are no signs of lameness.

iv   After exercise each day:

    *a*   That all the clenches are tight and no nails missing.

    *b*   That the shoe itself is tight and no signs of looseness or wear.

    *c*   There is no sign of warmth in the hoof indicating injury or disease.

    *d*   That there is no sign of lameness, e.g. pointing a toe or resting a foot.

# PART IV
# Clipping, Trimming, Plaiting, Hogging

*Section 1   The Reasons for Clipping*
The reasons for clipping are both practical and economic, as follows:

i   Clipping is essential for horses required to work hard during the winter months. A horse that has been clipped:

   *a*   Can stand more work without distress than a horse in its thick winter coat.
   *b*   Is much more easily groomed and cared for in the stables.
   *c*   Is much more readily kept in good condition.

ii   An unclipped horse will sweat much more readily and tire more easily when worked:

   *a*   It will take a long time to dry after sweating.
   *b*   It will be much more likely to catch a chill while drying.
   *c*   Proper grooming, i.e. removing the impurities and scurf caused by sweating, will be next to impossible.
   *d*   It is likely to lose condition quickly if worked hard.

*Section 2   The Time for Clipping*
The time for clipping must clearly vary with the individual horse.

i   The amount of coat a horse tends to grow must vary from horse to horse:

   *a*   A well-bred horse with a fine skin may only require clipping twice a season.
   *b*   A coarser horse may require clipping as much as four times a season.

ii   The time for clipping may also vary from year to year:

   *a*   Horses grow their winter coat during the autumn and it should not be clipped before it is fully developed.

 *b* If clipped too soon, the result will be patchy.

 *c* The later it is clipped, the less likely it is to require clipping again for some time.

iii When the horse begins to sweat unduly in normal work, it is generally a sign that it is time the coat was clipped.

*Section 3 The Types of Clipping*
The types of clipping may vary as follows:

i Fully clipped-out, i.e. clipped all over:

 *a* This is generally the case on the first time of clipping.

 *b* The second time of clipping may be as ii or iii below.

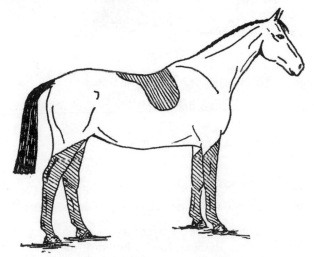

Hunting clip, leaving legs and saddle patch

ii Clipped-out, except for a saddle patch under the saddle:

 *a* The saddle patch may be left on fine skinned horses to give them some protection.

 *b* In a horse with long hair, this may be inadvisable as causing the horse to sweat too much under the saddle.

iii Clipped-out, except for the legs:

 *a* The legs may be left unclipped from a few inches below the elbow and from the hock, or point of the stifle, downwards.

 *b* This gives added protection from mud and thorns.

Trace clip

iv   Trace-high, i.e. from a line level with the trace:

    *a*   Primarily for a harness horse, this leaves a plentiful covering on the back.

    *b*   The legs may be left unclipped or clipped.

*Section 4   Types of Clipper*
The various types of clippers used are as follows:

i   The standard electric machine or hanging electric machine:

    *a*   The former is generally on a tripod base.

    *b*   The latter is generally hung from a hook, or overhead beam.

    *c*   Each may be plugged into the nearest electric point.

    *d*   Each only requires one man to operate it.

ii   The standard hand machine:

    *a*   This requires one person to operate the handle to provide the power for the machine and to hold the tripod steady.

    *b*   It requires a second operator to use the clippers.

iii   Hand clippers may be used for ticklish places or to finish off patches as necessary.

*Section 5   How to Clip*
Clipping should be done:

178

i   In a good light only, under experienced guidance at first, and the horse must be dry and cool, i.e. before exercise, not after:

    *a*  Always against the hair growth.

    *b*  Without any pressure on the blades whatever, merely lightly removing the hair at the speed of the machine.

    *c*  With frequent pauses to clean the blades of accumulated grease and dirt.

    *d*  No ridges should be left on the coat.

ii   Before starting, the horse should be thoroughly groomed to remove as much dirt as possible to avoid blocking the machine:

    *a*  The machinery should be carefully inspected before, during and after use.

    *b*  Only sharp, undamaged blades must be used, which will not grab hairs and thus hurt the horse and make it nervous of clipping.

    *c*  There should be no noise, or fuss, to avoid exciting the horse, thus needlessly making it apprehensive and troublesome to handle.

iii   While clipping the horse, he must be kept warm:

    *a*  While his head, legs, or belly are being clipped his body may be rugged.

    *b*  While clipping his forehand, his hindquarters may be rugged, or vice versa.

iv   A horse should not be clipped over the bedding or forage. Also:

    *a*  All hair should be carefully swept up and incinerated, or otherwise removed from harm's way at once.

    *b*  Should the horse eat any, it could make him seriously ill due to a hair ball forming in the stomach.

*Section 6   After Clipping*

Especially after the first clipping, the horse will be covered with grease and dirt.

i   A sharp trot with clothing on should raise a sweat fairly quickly:

    *a*  The horse should then be thoroughly groomed.

    *b*  A damp wisp is probably best to remove the grease, he should then be finished with the body brush and rubber as usual.

ii   It is important to remember to rug up sufficiently or the horse may very easily catch a chill after clipping.

iii   A few days after clipping, the coat may be singed, but this should only be attempted under experienced guidance:

*a* By that time a number of long cat-hairs will have formed, which require to be singed off.

*b* Singeing also seals off the ends of the clipped hairs and generally improves the look of the coat.

*c* A gas lamp, or paraffin burner, are probably the best types to use for this purpose.

*d* This should not be done near bedding or forage, and every care must be taken to avoid fire.

### Section 7   *Leaving the Saddle Patch*
A saddle patch left unclipped and correctly positioned looks quite smart and is a certain protection to the horse.

i The saddle should be put on in the normal position without girths or stirrups:

*a* The horse should then be clipped out round it.

*b* Care must be taken that the saddle is well forward and does not slip back.

*c* Nothing looks worse than a straggling saddle patch too far behind the correct saddle position.

ii The object is to give a fine skinned horse protection against saddle galls:

*a* If the horse is extremely long haired it may cause him to sweat unduly under the saddle:

*b* This may thus bring about the very thing it is intended to prevent, in which case the horse should be fully clipped-out:

### Section 8   *Leaving the Legs*
As already stated, the legs may be left unclipped from below the elbow and hock, or point of the stifle, downwards:

i The object is to provide protection against thorns and small cuts, and the danger of chills and cracked heels:

ii Too much hair on the legs may have the opposite effect, making it difficult:

*a* To notice small cuts, or thorns:

*b* To treat cuts and increasing the danger of infection.

*c* To dry the legs, thus enhancing the danger of cracked heels, rather than preventing it.

iii It may therefore be advisable:

*a* With thin-skinned horses to leave the hair on the legs.

*b*   With hairy-legged horses to clip them right out.

## Section 9   Trimming

The only tools required for trimming are a sharp pair of scissors; the hairs of the mane and tail may be pulled by hand.

i    Trimming should only apply to the mane, tail and heels:

   *a*   The horse's whiskers should be left untrimmed as they provide sensory perception when eating.
   *b*   The hair on the horse's ears may be trimmed, but not the inside hairs as they prevent rain entering the ears.

ii   The mane should be trimmed to an even length throughout:

   *a*   The hairs on the underside should be pulled to make it lie flat.
   *b*   The hairs underneath should also be pulled to thin it and prevent the mane growing bunchy.
   *c*   Pulling these hairs also helps to make the mane lie correctly on the off-side.

iii  The forelock should be thinned, as above:

   *a*   It should not be too thick, or too long and so hanging over the eyes.
   *b*   It should be trimmed so as to reach nearly to the eyes.
   *c*   Although it should fulfill its function of keeping off flies, it should not hinder the horse's vision.

iv   The tail should be trimmed by pulling the hairs from the underside:

   *a*   These hairs should only be pulled when the tail has grown particularly bushy.
   *b*   It is best done by passing the tail over the lower half of a stable door, unless it is certain that the horse will not kick.
   *c*   Only a few hairs at a time should be pulled and the tail should then be brushed and studied from a distance.
   *d*   It may be necessary to take some time, even a week or two, to improve a badly trimmed tail.
   *e*   Tail bandages should be used at night to produce the best results.

v    The tail may be trimmed square at the end, i.e. 'banged', or it may be tapered, i.e. 'swish-tail'.

   *a*   If banged, it is customarily cut level with the hocks and in movement raised slightly above them; a swish-tail is generally left longer.

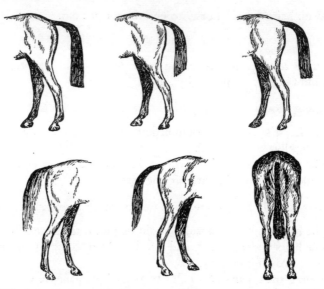

Tails: (*Top l. to r.*) i. Correct. ii. Cut without lifting to correct angle. iii. Too high (*Bottom l. to r.*) iv. Unpulled. v. Switch Tail. vi. Rear view well pulled tail

b    To trim so that it hangs square in movement, a banged tail must be cut at an angle with the inner hairs slightly shorter. Or

c    It may be held up under the dock, so that it is at the correct angle it should be in motion and cut square.

d    The tail only grows from six inches to a foot a year, therefore should not be cut too short.

e    A large pair of sharp scissors are required for the task.

vi  The heels should be trimmed at the fetlock joints with a pair of scissors, and preferably not too close:

a    The back of the fetlock should be trimmed short with the scissors, not clippers, and with increasing length above and below.

b    Unduly hairy heels are a sign of coarse breeding, and well trimmed heels give the horse a smart appearance.

vii Trimming much improves a horse's appearance and should be a regular fortnightly routine.

*Section 10    Plaiting the Mane*
Plaiting the mane consists of doing the mane up in a number of plaits, for show purposes, or to present a neat appearance.

i   An untidy mane will be much improved by being plaited:

   *a*  It is advisable to practise plaiting under experienced guidance at first.
   *b*  A chair is useful to stand on and a large needle and thread, or wool, is
      required to complete the task.

ii  The mane should be well brushed and slightly dampened with the water
    brush before starting to plait it:

   *a*  The number of plaits may vary from seven to a dozen and the width
      of mane required for each plait must be decided before starting.
   *b*  Standing on the chair to be level with the crest the portions of mane
      required for each plait should be divided off with the mane comb.
   *c*  Each portion of mane is then, in turn, divided into three equal locks
      with the fingers and plaited fairly tightly in the normal manner.
   *d*  About an inch or so from the end of the plait the thread, preferably
      black, is plaited into the centre and is then knotted round the ends of
      the plait to hold it securely.
   *e*  The plait is then doubled under from the middle and the thread, or
      wool, pushed through the mane at the crest with the aid of the needle
      and tied to hold the plait in place.

iii The forelock should be plaited in a single plait:

   *a*  It is generally doubled under in the same fashion as the mane plaits.
   *b*  Sometimes when it, or the mane, are very skimpy, it may be necessary
      simply to turn the end of the plait under and secure it.

iv  The mane should never be plaited too tightly:

   *a*  It should never be left plaited for more than twenty-four hours at a
      time.
   *b*  In either case, the hairs may tend to come out.

*Section 11   Hogging the Mane*
The mane may be hogged, or clipped right off, if required, and will take six to
nine months to grow long enough to be plaited again.

i   Hogging the mane should be done with the clippers in three stages:

   *a*  First, along one side of the crest.
   *b*  Then, along the other side.
   *c*  Lastly, along the top.

ii  It is important to avoid cutting the hair alongside the mane; only the
    bristles of the hog should be cut.

 *a* The hair between the ears on the poll must also be clipped.
 *b* The forelock should also be clipped off.

iii One of the principle reasons for hogging the mane is to save the trouble of grooming the mane:

 *a* But nothing looks worse than a bristly hogged mane, and this should not be permitted except when being grown again.
 *b* The mane should be hogged about once a fortnight.

# PART V
## Clothing

The term clothing covers the various rugs worn by the horse at various times, also their accessories, including amongst these bandages, knee caps, hock boots and other such ancillaries.

*Section 1    The Full Set, or Suit of Clothing*
The full set, or suit, of clothing is generally only used when the horse is travelling in a box, or for specialist purposes, as in racing. It consists of:

i  A quarter-sheet, hood, roller and breast-girth, fillet-string, or fillet-strap:

    *a*  It may be of wool, jute or linen.
    *b*  It is never used in the stables in normal circumstances.

ii  The hood covers the head and neck almost to the withers and down to the muzzle:

    *a*  It is attached under the neck and jowl by tapes.

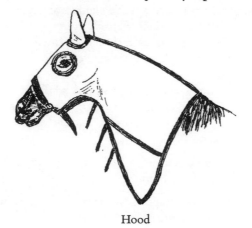

Hood

b There must be plenty of room at the eyeholes.
c The ear pockets must also be sufficiently large and roomy.
d It may be used to sweat a horse's throat when he has a cold, but it is not otherwise recommended for use in the stables.

iii The quarter-sheet is a rectangular sheet from three and a half to four feet long:

a It is kept in position by the roller and the breast-girth, the latter preventing it slipping back.
b The fillet-string, or fillet-strap fits beneath the tail and prevents the sheet being blown up; it joins the rear corners of the sheet.

*Section 2 The Day and Night Rugs*
These, with the accompanying horse blankets and bandages, come under the generic title of 'stable clothing'.

i The day rug is generally of light wool in a variety of colours, bound in a contrasting colour and with the owner's monogram:

a It fastens with a strap across the brisket and is held in place by a roller, generally sewn to the rug.
b The roller should be padded on each side of the spine to keep the weight off the spine and should fasten with a strap and buckle on the near-side.
c Sizes are measured from the centre of the brisket to the buttocks.
d They are generally available in three inch sizes, varying from four to six and a half feet.
e The summer weight version of the day rug may be either of linen or cotton in a checked or plain material.
f It may be necessary to add a horse blanket or ordinary blanket underneath the day rug for greater warmth in very cold conditions.
g With the addition of a hood in similar material, the day rug of either winter or summer weight may be converted into a full suit of clothing for travelling.
h If economy is necessary, the day rug can be dispensed with altogether and an ordinary jute or canvas rug, or a horse blanket, or ordinary blanket with a roller, used instead, but this should be shaped to fit across the brisket.

ii The night rug may be of canvas or jute, either partly or fully lined with a light weight wool or flannel lining:

a It also fastens with a strap across the brisket and is held in place by a padded roller, sometimes sewn to the rug.

*b*   Fillets, or thigh-straps, to keep the rug in place are seldom used nowadays, except in New Zealand rugs (see pp. 189–90).

*c*   The various sizes and measurements are as for day rugs (*id* above).

*d*   The night rugs are more likely to become soiled than the day rugs, hence must be of rougher and tougher material, less liable to be stained and readily washed.

*e*   The night rugs should be aired each day after use, hence the reason for the day rugs.

*f*   Additional rugs, or one or more horse blankets, or ordinary blankets, may be required to supplement the night rug in very cold weather.

*g*   A string sweat rug may be used under the night rug.

*h*   They are easily washed and dried.

iii   Gauging the number of extra blankets the horse requires in cold weather may require experienced guidance:

*a*   The amount of clothing required to replace the hair when a horse is clipped is approximately equal to one thick woollen horse blanket.

*b*   Horse blankets are gaily striped rough blankets in three weights very little different from army blankets, which may be bought cheaply from surplus stocks.

*c*   Two thin blankets generally provide greater warmth and insulation than one thick one, due to the air space between them.

*d*   The object of the rugs, or blankets, is not merely to replace the hair and prevent chills, but also, primarily,

*e*   To prevent the horse using up his food intake keeping warm, thus failing to benefit from it, i.e. losing condition.

*f*   Too many blankets, however, are worse than too few; they may make the horse soft and unable to withstand chills.

*g*   If in doubt as to whether the horse requires another blanket, it is generally best to leave him without it.

iv   It is essential that the rugs fit the horse properly, measured as above from the centre of the brisket to the buttocks:

*a*   They may shrink when washed, or lose their shape afterwards, hence should be carefully dried and stretched after washing.

*b*   When the breast fastening is tight, the buttocks should be properly covered, not bare, or the rug is too small.

*c*   When the breast fastening is tight, the rug should not be able to slip back over the withers; if it does so the rug is too large.

*d*   The roller must not be buckled up too tightly and the padding should be sufficient to ease any pressure on the spine.

  *e* It should be easy to slip the fingers behind the roller when it is buckled.

v The rug should be put on the horse with care, not flung on haphazard:

  *a* The rug should be folded so that when placed forward of the withers it can be unfolded over the quarters.

  *b* Then it should be gently slid backwards into position, thus ensuring that the hairs are all lying in the correct direction.

  *c* If a blanket is being put on underneath, it should be unfolded on the horse's back first in the same manner. The rug should then be unfolded on top of it, taking care not to disturb it.

  *d* Only when the rug is satisfactorily in place, should the straps and roller be fastened: it should be checked while doing so that the roller is not twisted and the rug not rucked up on the far side.

  *e* Night rugs should be checked last thing at night and if they have slipped should be replaced correctly, removing them before doing so.

  *f* When removing the rugs, they should be slid backwards over the tail, with the hairs not against them.

vi The rugs are an obvious means of passing infection round the stables. Hence:

  *a* Each horse should have his own rugs for his sole use: labelled, if necessary, with the horse's name.

  *b* When being aired during the day, the night rugs should not come in contact with each other.

  *c* When a strange horse comes into the stables, it should be provided with its own set of rugs.

  *d* Alternatively, it may be advisable to fit a thin cotton, or linen, sheet under the rug to prevent any danger of the rug being infected and requiring washing or disinfecting.

vii The rugs should never be worn outside the stables, except when travelling, as stated above:

  *a* A horse in good health should never be exercised in a rug unless it is intended to work up a sweat quickly just after clipping (see above, p. 179), or for some other special reason.

  *b* An invalid horse might be walked out in a rug if not fit for more than gentle exercise.

  *c* A rug might be taken on a visit to the smithy if the horse is likely to have a long and chilly wait, or:

  *d* When the horse is waiting to be boxed.

  *e* But in neither case should it be worn on the journey.

  *f* Any other course invites a chill.

*Section 3   New Zealand Rugs*
These are rugs designed to be used when a horse that has been clipped is being kept out in the open.

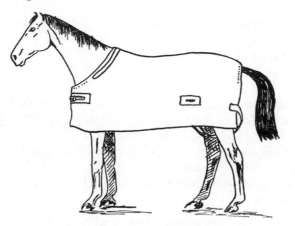

The New Zealand Rug

i   There are two designs principally used in this country:

    *a*   The Emston—the original introduced into this country.
    *b*   The All Weather.

ii   Both are of weatherproofed canvas lined with blanketing:

    *a*   Each buckles at the breast and is reinforced with leather above the withers.
    *b*   Strong leather straps with spring hooks are used instead of fillet strings.
    *c*   Both are made in pony, cob and hunter sizes.

iii   The Emston rug has no further fittings.

    *a*   The All Weather has a surcingle which passes through an opening at each side of the rug to avoid gathering it.
    *b*   It also has a crupper type attachment.

iv   Although there is no doubt that these rugs can be useful, care must be taken in their fitting and use:

    *a*   They are liable to need frequent adjustment and it is advisable to pad them over the withers and shoulders where, inevitably, they slide back to some extent.
    *b*   The leg straps of the Emston have to be sufficiently tight to keep it in place and must be kept extremely soft with neatsfoot oil.

    *c*    The surcingle on the All Weather is liable to need checking to make sure that it has not tightened or is chafing.

## Section 4   Bandages and Bandaging

As noted above, bandages come under the generic title of stable clothing, but strictly speaking, only a few uses of bandages are for that specific purpose; the title is scarcely applicable to other uses.

i    For warmth:

    *a*    Bandages used for this purposes are clearly part of the stable clothing.
    *b*    Thick woollen, or flannel, bandages about seven feet long are required as a protection against draughts and chills.
    *c*    These are put on comparatively loosely to avoid any danger of interfering with the circulation.
    *d*    They should extend from below the knee to cover the fetlock joint and the pastern.

ii    For cold water bandages to relieve heat and swelling:

    *a*    It is only by stretching a point that these can be regarded as stable clothing.
    *b*    Flannel bandages should be used and should be replaced frequently, or,
    *c*    A hosepipe should be connected to the top of the bandage and allowed to drip slowly.
    *d*    These also should extend from below the knee to cover the fetlock joint and the pastern.

iii    For support of strained muscles, joints and tendons:

    *a*    Again it is only by stretching a point that these can be regarded as stable clothing.
    *b*    Stockinette, or nylon/terylene cloth bandages should be used.
    *c*    They should be put on fairly tightly, but again not so as to interfere with the circulation.
    *d*    A pad of cottonwool should be wrapped round the leg before bandaging, otherwise the cannon bone, which does not require it, absorbs most of the support.
    *e*    These should also extend from below the knee to cover the fetlock joint and the pastern.

iv    For protection in polo, show-jumping, etc., or when travelling;

    *a*    These in no sense can be termed stable clothing, since they are specifically intended for use outside the stable.

b   They should be of stockinette, or nylon/terylene cloth as above, but generally are somewhat shorter.

c   A thick pad of cottonwool gam-gee, or foam rubber, should be wrapped round the leg before bandaging for even greater protection.

d   These bandages are restricted from below the knee to above the fetlock joint to prevent any possible restrictions of movement.

e   They are commonly fastened with a non-slip double bow on the outside about half way between the knee and the fetlock joint.

f   For cross-country work special gaiters are more commonly used.

v   For surgical purposes:

a   These also can in no sense be regarded as stable clothing.

b   They should be of linen and are shaped as the nature of the injury requires.

c   Their size and scope may be considerable and complex, and in general is best left to the vet.

vi   For keeping the tail neat—a tail bandage:

a   This may certainly qualify as part of the stable clothing.

b   The tail bandage which should be of cotton, stockinette, or nylon/terylene cloth can very easily be put on too tightly.

c   One of the best ways to keep them in place is to plait several locks of hair into the bandage.

vii   Care of bandages:

a   They should always be kept in sets of four for the legs.

b   Whenever dirty, they should be washed and thoroughly dried before being rolled up and stored.

c   They should be kept in a mothproof chest or cupboard, and should always be put away clean and ready for use.

d   They should be put away rolled up, with the strings outside them tied round them in sets of four to keep them tight.

e   Before putting them on, they should be unrolled and rerolled, so that the strings are inside: they are then ready to be put on.

viii   Bandaging the leg:

a   Hold the end of the bandage just below the knee, or hock, inside the leg with one hand.

b   Hold the bandage close to the leg with the other hand and let it unwind gently in a downward direction.

Putting on Leg Bandage

c   Maintain the angle of the spiral all the way down the leg covering the fetlock and pastern (*N.B.* except as in iv above).

d   At the coronet, turn and come up the leg again, until the point below the knee, or hock, is reached once more.

e   Then, tie the tapes in a non-slip double bow on the outside.

f   It is a help in keeping the bandage in place if the corner of the end first put on is turned down over the second round of bandage and then trapped by the final turn of all.

ix   Points to note on bandaging:

a   Do not exert any pressure or the circulation may be affected; this includes when tying the tapes.

b   Stockinette or nylon/terylene cloth bandages may have more pressure put on them, but even so must not be too tight and are best padded with cottonwool gam-gee or foam rubber, as above, to prevent this.

c   No bandages should be kept on longer than twelve hours without being removed.

d   After removing a bandage, massage the leg upwards to stimulate the circulation and the lymphatic glands.

e   If one leg of a pair is bandaged, it is essential to bandage the other to help take the additional strain: BUT

f   *N.B.* Do not become a bandage addict, bandage only when strictly necessary.

x   Tail bandages:
These may certainly be classified as stable clothing.

a   Their purpose is either to prevent the horse scrubbing, i.e. rubbing his tail in the stables or while travelling, or to keep the tail neat.

b   They should preferably be of cotton, although flannel or similar material will do.
c   They should be put on in much the same fashion as a leg bandage.
d   The bandage should be wound down from the root of the tail for about eighteen inches and then spiralled upwards again.
e   It should be fastened at the root of the tail on the outside with a non-slip double bow.
f   It should not be too tight in case it interferes with the circulation, but strands of the tail may be plaited into the bandage as it is applied.
g   It should only be tight enough to prevent it slipping, and the plaited strands should help to prevent this.
h   If the material is preshrunk, wetting it when in place is sometimes advocated.

*Section 5   Ancillaries*
Certain ancillary items of clothing should be included here as follows.

i   Knee caps:
    These should be worn when the horse is travelling, or if there is any danger of the horse slipping, in icy conditions, etc.

Knee Cap

a   There is a right and a left knee cap.
b   They should buckle above the knee with the buckle on the outside.
c   The lower strap should be left loose enough to provide play for the leg movement.
d   When stored, it is advisable to buckle them to each other to avoid loss.

ii  Tail guard:
    This is also worn when the horse is travelling, or when there may be a danger of the horse scrubbing its tail:

     *a*    The tail guard may be of leather or canvas.
     *b*    It may either tie or buckle into place.
     *c*    It fits close to the root of the tail and is about eighteen inches long.

iii  Hock boots:
These are also worn when the horse is travelling or when there is a danger of damaging the hocks:

Hock Boot

     *a*    They are protective padded leather boots which cover the hock.
     *b*    They strap on the outside.
     *c*    As with knee caps, there is a right and a left boot.
     *d*    As with knee caps, when stored, it is advisable to buckle them together.

Over-reach boots

iv   Overreach boots:
Not strictly part of the stable clothing, but sometimes worn when travelling.

   *a*   The object is to prevent injury from an overreach.
   *b*   A circular rubber boot which is fitted over the hoof and rests above the coronet. May be laced.
   *c*   Can often prevent serious injury to the coronet.

v   Brushing boots, or polo pony boots:
Boots fitted inside the fetlock to protect the leg from injury from the opposite leg.

   *a*   May be made from leather, or felt, with a padded protective portion inside the boot.
   *b*   Generally buckles on the outside, but there are many patterns.
   *c*   As with knee caps, pairs should be buckled together to avoid getting lost.

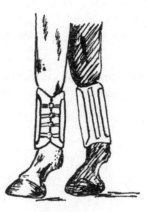

Brushing boots

vi   Eye-fringe:
Generally only fitted when flies are particularly troublesome in mid-summer.

   *a*   Where the mane is hogged and there is no forelock, they may give a horse considerable relief.
   *b*   They may be made of soft leather or string, generally attached to a separate brow-band which can be incorporated in the bridle or head-collar.
   *c*   Not often seen in Britain due principally to the climate.

*Section 6   Care of the Clothing and Harness: Tack Cleaning*
The standard of stable management can generally be gauged accurately by the state of the tack, i.e. tackle, including both clothing and harness, saddles, bridles, etc.

i   Clothing:
   The clothing should be clean and dry, well fitting and in good repair:

   a   Each morning stained clothing should be washed down, scrubbed, and put out to dry: while the day clothing is being worn.
   b   Any tears, or strained stitching should be promptly repaired before it is allowed to get any worse.
   c   Leaving torn clothing on a horse is asking for it to develop the tiresome vice of tearing and ripping its clothing.
   d   All buckles and leather parts should be cleaned with saddle soap or neatsfoot oil, care being taken not to stain the clothing itself.
   e   After washing, clothing should be dried, stretched and checked again for fit in case of shrinking.
   f   Spare clothing should be kept in a special cupboard or drawers in the tack room.

ii   The tack should be in good condition, clean and supple, but not polished, except in the case of patent leather work on the harness:

   a   It is essential that all grease, sweat and dirt are removed from tack after exercise.
   b   It is most important also that it is kept supple and pliable, and not allowed to become stiff, or hard.

iii   The sequence of cleaning is as follows:

   a   Undo all buckles, wash off the grease with warm water, dry thoroughly and rub vigorously with saddle soap.
   b   For the underside of saddle flaps, for sweat flaps, leather panels and girth tabs, neatsfoot oil well rubbed in will ensure that they remain supple and in good condition.
   c   On the seat of the saddle and outside of the flaps, the saddle soap must be worked well in to avoid staining the clothes.
   d   Buckles should be cleaned and wiped with an oily rag and, like all buckles or tabs, should be examined closely for wear.

iv   For black harness, a special harness polish is obtainable and should be used according to the instructions.

v  Linen or serge linings for saddles or collars should be thoroughly brushed:

    *a*  It may be necessary to sponge them to remove grease, using as little water as possible to avoid damping them too much.

    *b*  A blunt knife or scraper and a good brushing is probably quite enough to remove surplus grease or scurf.

    *c*  If they are soaking wet with sweat, they should be allowed to dry gradually in a suitable temperature in the tack room before being cleaned.

vi  Bits and stirrup-irons should be detached and washed separately in warm soapy water: if stainless steel or chromium plate, they then merely need drying with a dry cloth:

    *a*  A little polishing as required should then follow.

    *b*  They should, at the same time, be checked for any wear, especially in bits, which might damage the lips, or mouth: nickel is particularly bad in this respect.

# PART VI
# Bedding

The quality and quantity of the bedding provided for the horse has a very significant effect on his overall condition:

*Section 1    The Effects of Bad Bedding*
Bedding below standard in quality or quantity has an insidiously adverse effect on the horse's condition:

i    If the bedding is insufficiently thick and elastic, i.e. poor in quality, the horse will not be encouraged to lie down:

    *a*    He will remain standing throughout the night and consequently may not be as rested as he might have been.

    *b*    His work and condition may be adversely affected.

ii    If the bedding is poor in quantity as well as quality, the horse will suffer further:

    *a*    He will be standing in dung and urine.

    *b*    His feet will tend to suffer, even if thoroughly picked-out, and he may develop thrush.

    *c*    His eyes may be affected by the ammonia fumes.

*Section 2    The Desirable Qualities of Bedding*
The desirable qualities of bedding are as follows:

i    It should possess thickness and elasticity:

    *a*    To encourage the horse to lie down to rest.

    *b*    To ensure that the horse will not damage himself when doing so.

ii    It should possess either strong absorbent, or strong non-absorbent qualities:

    *a*    Either, so that the urine is absorbed promptly.

*b*   Or, so that the urine is allowed to drain away quickly.

iii   It should be light and easy to handle:

*a*   To facilitate laying the bed quickly and without effort.
*b*   To facilitate cleaning the stables or mucking-out.

iv   It should not be dusty, damp, or mouldy.

v   It should not be strong smelling, or contain harmful or irritating substances or bugs.

vi   It should not be edible, but if eaten should not have a harmful effect on the horse.

*Section 3   The Common Forms of Bedding*
The common forms of bedding in Britain are as follows:

i   Wheat straw.
ii   Barley straw.
iii   Oat straw.
iv   Peat moss, or moss litter.
v   Sawdust.
vi   Bracken.

*Section 4   Wheat Straw*
Wheat straw has the following advantages and disadvantages:

i   When obtainable in trusses, it is excellent:

*a*   It provides thickness and elasticity in the bed when suitably and correctly laid.
*b*   It is non-absorbent, and allows the urine to drain away quickly from the bed.
*c*   It is both light and easy to handle, either for bedding down or mucking-out.
*d*   It is neither dusty nor irritant and will not affect the horse adversely.
*e*   It is not readily eaten, but even if it were eaten would not have any ill effects.
*f*   It has a ready sale after use as compost, approximating closely to cost value in some districts.

ii   Its disadvantages are:

*a*   If obtainable at all, it is liable to be expensive.
*b*   It is more likely to be obtainable in bales which means that it has lost

half its value through having been crushed in a combine or bailer; it may then be absorbent and not as elastic.

## Section 5  Barley Straw

Barley straw has the following advantages and disadvantages:

i    It is more readily obtainable in most areas than wheat straw. But

ii    It is not as good bedding, even compared with baled wheat straw, because

   a    The barley awns tend to irritate the horse's sensitive skin and may affect the horse's eyes.
   b    It is not good for the horse if eaten, and is liable to cause colic.
   c    It is a short straw with few of the elastic or non-absorbent qualities of wheat straw.
   d    It will almost certainly have been crushed in a combine or bailer, hence may also be damp or dusty.

## Section 6  Oat Straw

Oat straw has the following advantages and disadvantages:

i    It is not as good as wheat straw, although preferable to barley straw, but is liable to be hard to obtain in some areas.

ii    As it is used as feed for cattle, it may prove expensive to buy:

   a    It is certainly likely to be eaten, but is not likely to be harmful to the horse.
   b    It will probably have been crushed in the combine or bailer with the disadvantages that follow from this.

## Section 7  Peat Moss

Peat moss, or moss litter, has the following advantages and disadvantages:

i    It is generally easily obtained and transport costs are not heavy:

   a    It is cheaper than straw in most instances.
   b    It is very absorbent and acts as a deodorant.
   c    It is warm, soft and elastic, hence encourages the horse to lie down.
   d    It occupies less space than straw and is easily stored under cover.
   e    It is not eaten by horses.

ii    Its disadvantages are:

   a    It requires about three hundredweight to make a bed for one horse.
   b    Hence, it requires considerable labour each day simply to move it.

*c*    Also, it is not as easy or as light to handle as straw.

*d*    It requires more frequent attention than straw to prevent it becoming fouled.

*e*    All droppings must be removed at once, if possible.

*f*    Wet patches of urine should also be removed promptly.

*g*    Because of its deodorant qualities, it is not always easy to make out which part of the bed has been soiled.

iii    Once accustomed to using it, there is no doubt that it has much in its favour, but equally there is no denying:

*a*    Although, economically, it may cost less to buy than straw.

*b*    It costs more in labour to use it efficiently.

*c*    If it is allowed to become fouled it very readily leads to foot trouble, in spite of picking out the feet frequently.

### Section 8    Sawdust

Sawdust has the following advantages and disadvantages as bedding:

i    If readily obtainable locally, from seasoned timber, it may be good cheap bedding:

*a*    It is warm, soft and elastic, encouraging the horse to lie down.

*b*    It is very absorbent.

*c*    It is not generally eaten by horses.

ii    Its disadvantages are:

*a*    If from green timber, it is no use as it heats on contact with urine.

*b*    If from an unreliable source, it often contains harmful objects, such as nails or splinters, which may injure the horse.

*c*    It is always liable to be messy and troublesome to handle in the stables.

*d*    It requires a considerable quantity to make a good bed and, hence, requires considerable labour.

*e*    It requires frequent attention to prevent it becoming fouled.

iii    Mixed with peat moss, it is generally much improved as bedding, but:

*a*    Even so, the entired bed will require turning each day.

*b*    As with peat moss, it is liable to lead to foot trouble.

### Section 9    Bracken

Bracken has the following advantages and disadvantages as bedding:

i    In a bracken area, it is plentifully available and free, but that is about all that can be said in its favour.

ii It has to be cut green and stacked like hay:

    *a* It is liable to be infested with bugs, which will irritate the horse and infest the stables.

    *b* It is neither sufficiently absorbent for drainless stables, nor sufficiently non-absorbent to allow urine to drain freely.

    *c* It is cold and harsh bedding, unlikely to encourage the horse to lie down, but it is better than nothing.

## Section 10 *Points on Bedding*

Various points on bedding should be noted, as follows:

i Rye straw:
Rye straw, if available, makes the best bedding of all; better than wheat straw:

    *a* It is extremely elastic and highly non-absorbent.

    *b* Unfortunately, it is virtually unobtainable.

ii Sand:
Sand is sometimes used as bedding in a warm climate:

    *a* Even then, it is an unsatisfactory form of bedding.

    *b* If there is salt in the sand, the horse is liable to eat it and suffer from sand colic as a result.

    *c* In this country, it is better not even considered.

iii For any form of bedding which the horse shows an inclination to eat, a spray with Jeyes Fluid, or similar disinfectant, is generally a sufficient deterrent.

## Section 11 *The Stable Tools*

The stable tools required for mucking-out and bedding-down are as follows:

i A light, four-tined hand fork.
ii A light hand shovel.
iii A stiff stable broom.
iv A hand skip, or canvas-covered frame, for scooping-up and removing droppings; this should always be on hand in the stable.
v A light hand barrow, preferably rubber tyred.

    N.B. All the above should be of the best quality available and kept in the best possible condition. Anything else is a false economy.

## Section 12 *Mucking-out*

Mucking-out should take place first thing every morning.

i   The procedure with a straw bed is as follows:

    *a*   All clean bedding should be sorted out and removed to one side:

    *b*   All soiled bedding should be removed with dung to the manure pit.

    *c*   Semisoiled bedding, which may be used again, should be removed to dry, or air thoroughly outside the stables. BUT *N.B.* it should not be mixed with the bedding from another horse in case of spreading infection.

    *d*   The stable should be thoroughly swept out with the stable broom.

    *e*   A light day bed may be left in position if the horse is to remain in the stable.

ii   The procedure with a peat moss or sawdust bed is as follows:

    *a*   All soiled bedding should be picked out and removed with the dung to the manure pit.

    *b*   The entire bed should then be turned and should be rolled or tamped neatly to prevent it being churned by the horse.

    *c*   A light garden roller or wooden dumper should be used on a bed at least eight inches thick; *N.B.* this should be added to the stable tools if peat moss, or sawdust, is to be used as bedding.

*Section 13   Bedding-Down*
Bedding-down should take place regularly at the same time each evening.

i   The procedure with a straw bed is as follows:

    *a*   The day bed should be thoroughly cleaned out, if soiled, and any droppings and soiled bedding removed to the manure pit.

    *b*   The semisoiled bedding, which has been thoroughly aired during the day, should next be used as the base of the fresh bed.

    *c*   The top of the bed and the edges should be of fresh clean straw.

    *d*   Sufficient bedding should be used to ensure that the horse will not suffer any injury if he lies down.

    *e*   The bed should be saucer-shaped, raised around the edges of the box, as the horse will usually scrape it into the centre.

    *f*   The bed should look and feel sufficiently inviting to encourage the horse to lie down.

    *g*   It should not only look clean and inviting, it should also smell clean and be clean.

ii   The procedure with a peat moss, or sawdust bed, is as follows:

    *a*   Any soiled bedding should be picked out and, using the shovel; removed with the dung to the manure pit.

    *b*   If necessary the bed may be given a quick roll: if much has been removed in the morning, fresh peat moss may now be added.

### Section 14   *The Invariable Rule*

The invariable rule of every stable should be that all droppings are removed with the hand skip, at once, on being observed, thus ensuring the maximum possible cleanliness of the bed and the clothing.

# PART VII
## Feeding and Fodder

In its natural state, the horse grazes constantly, passing small quantities of food almost continuously through its digestive system.

*Section 1    The Horse's Digestive System*
Before going on to feeding and fodder, it is essential that the horse's digestive system should be outlined.

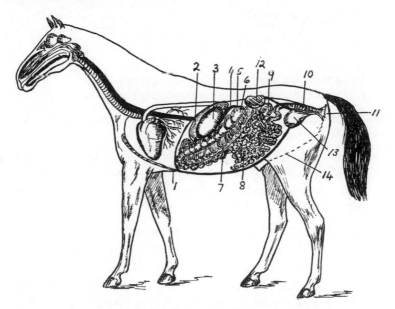

The Digestive System

1. The Diaphragm. 2. The Spleen. 3. The Stomach. 4. The Duodenum. 5. The Liver.
6. The Large Colon. 7. The Caecum. 8. The Small Intestine. 9. The Small Colon. 10. The Rectum. 11. The Anus. 12. The Kidneys. 13. The Bladder. 14. The Urethra.

i    The food is taken into the mouth by the lips and incisors:

    *a*    Mixed with the gastric juices from glands in the mouth and tongue, it is then ground to a paste by the molars.

    *b*    From the mouth, the food travels down the gullet to the stomach.

ii    The stomach is very small for the size of the horse, with a capacity of only 2–4 gallons.

    *a*    Near the stomach inlet, known as the 'cardiac orifice', the stomach lining is puckered, almost closing the opening.

    *b*    Hence, the horse cannot be sick.

iii    From the stomach, the food passes into the small intestine, or small bowel, which is 70 feet long:

    *a*    The horse has no gall bladder, and bile from the liver thus flows continuously into the small intestine.

    *b*    With fluid from the pancreas, this further helps to dissolve the food, much of which is absorbed into the body at this stage.

    *c*    To maintain the horse in health, however, the digestive process must be more or less continuous.

iv    The residue of the food next passes into the large intestine, which is 30 feet long.

    *a*    From there it passes via the colon to the rectum.

    *b*    It is then expelled from the body as droppings.

v    The stomach has a capacity of only 2–4 gallons, but the small and large intestines have a capacity of from 4–5 gallons.

    *a*    A horse may readily drink 4–5 gallons of water at a time which passes straight through the stomach to the large intestine.

    *b*    This may wash food through to the small intestine and cause colic: hence, always water before, not after, a meal.

vi    The stomach and intestines lie behind the diaphragm, the principal muscle used in breathing, on the forward side of which are the heart and lungs (see diagram).

    *a*    Hence, the horse should not be fed a heavy meal prior to severe exercise to avoid interference with the breathing or digestion.

    *b*    It is even possible that the diaphragm might be ruptured.

vii    The principles of feeding in accord with the horse's digestive system therefore are:

*a*   Feed little and often.
*b*   Water before, not after, feeding.
*c*   Do not work hard too soon after feeding: allow time for digestion.
*d*   Ensure that the horse has sufficient quantity, i.e. bulk, to keep the digestive system working.
*e*   Remember that the horse has a delicate digestive system and treat it with care; hence, always provide the largest meal of the day in the evening when there is the whole night to digest it.

## Section 2   *Feeding*

The object of feeding the horse is to maintain him in the best possible condition for the work required of him, and the secret of doing so is to balance the feeding accordingly.

i   All feeding must vary with the individual horse and be dependant on the individual horse's circumstances, i.e. it must depend on:

    *a*   The type and breed of horse, i.e. pony, thoroughbred or carthorse.
    *b*   The horse's size and condition, i.e. how much flesh and muscles.
    *c*   The amount of work the horse is expected to do and the nature of the work, i.e. fast work or slow, heavy work or no work.

ii   The principles of feeding above cannot be too often repeated, and others may be added to them, as follows:

    *a*   The horse should be fed little and often, i.e. a series of small meals throughout the day.
    *b*   The horse should be allowed time for digestion after a meal before any severe work: at least an hour should be allowed.
    *c*   The horse must have sufficient quantities of food each day, i.e. bulk, to keep the digestive system working, but the actual fodder making up this bulk must vary with the amount of work required, i.e. so much chiefly bulk-providing foods, such as hay, chaff or grass, and so much stimulating or heating foods, such as oats.
    *d*   No abrupt and radical changes of diet should be introduced or the horse's delicate digestive system may be upset.

iii   The horse should be allowed plenty of time for a meal, if possible, at least an hour and a half:

    *a*   While feeding hay he may be rubbed down.
    *b*   While feeding oats he should be left alone.

iv   The appetite is generally a good gauge of a horse's fitness, hence, condition:

    *a*    After severe work the appetite may be affected.
    *b*    In such conditions, never offer the horse grain or green food.
    *c*    Water, a gruel or bran mash, or similar easily digested foods, as under, should be offered first when a horse is very tired or off-colour.

v   The total bulk fed should be about 25–30 lbs. for a 15·2 hands horse:

    *a*    The amount of heating or stimulating foods, i.e. oats or other grains, beans, peas etc., must vary with the amount of work.
    *b*    The amount of hay must vary according to the amount of other food fed.
    *c*    Bran or chaff may be fed with the grain either to make up bulk or to slow up the horse's rate of eating.

vi  It is always important to try to make the horse eat as slowly as possible:

    *a*    This aids the digestion and allows the gastric juices time to work fully.
    *b*    Apart from feeding bran, or chaff, with the grain, as above, it may be advisable to place some large stones in the manger to prevent a greedy horse bolting his food.

vii Mangers must be kept scrupulously clean and sweet-smelling:

    *a*    Any old, sour, uneaten food must be cleaned out before a fresh feed is put in.
    *b*    Dust or dirt in a manger must be removed before food is put before the horse.

viii When the horse refuses food, it may be because:

    *a*    The horse is unduly tired and his appetite is affected.
    *b*    The food is tainted, unclean, or otherwise displeasing.
    *c*    The horse is ill, suffering from some form of sickness, chill, colic, or similar attack.
    *d*    Check at once for the reason and alleviate it as soon as possible.

ix  Horses are not naturally thin and when a horse is thin it may be because:

    *a*    He is bolting his food and is not gaining the maximum benefit from it.
    *b*    His teeth are uneven and he is unable to masticate his food properly.
    *c*    His feeding is in some way at fault, i.e. for some reason he is not getting as much as he should, or else it is the wrong sort of food.
    *d*    He is not getting enough water; a regular supply is essential to keeping a horse in good condition.
    *e*    For some reason he is nervous and not getting the benefit from his food.
    *f*    He is sickening for something, or is suffering from worms.

*g*   Check the various reasons and adjust the diet.

x   The horse's dung should be inspected regularly as a pointer to the horse's condition and his feeding:

*a*   Normally the dung should be moderately soft, well formed and brittle, neither fluid nor hard.

*b*   If the dung is too loose, the horse may require less laxative food; if too hard, the converse.

*c*   If the horse is passing whole, or undigested grain, he may need his teeth seen to, or he may be bolting his food.

xi   Feeding must never become a mechanical business:

*a*   It is important to avoid feeding too much of any type of food without variation.

*b*   In some cases, as with too much boiled foods, which cause a distended stomach, the results may be physically bad.

*c*   In all cases, the important thing to avoid is monotony.

xii   Accuracy in feeding is, however, imperative:

*a*   A good spring measure is sufficient for weighing hay in hay nets.

*b*   Accurate feed measures should be available in each bin of food.

*c*   A check of the amounts fed should always be kept.

*d*   Diet sheets for each horse should be worked out in advance and notes kept on the condition of each.

xiii   Examples of feeds for a 15·2 hands horse might be as follows:

*a*   In very light work:
   7.30 a.m.   2 lbs. hay, 1 lb. green food;
   12.00 p.m.   1 lb. oats, 1 lb. chaff;
   2.00 p.m.   2 lbs. hay, 2 lbs. green food;
   5.00 p.m.   1 lb. oats, 1 lb. chaff;
   7.00 p.m.   2 lbs. hay, 2 lbs. green food;
   9.00 p.m.   2 lbs. carrots, 8 lbs. hay.

*b*   In more severe work, e.g. hunting once a week:
   5.30 a.m.   2 lbs. oats, 1 lb. chaff;
   7.30 a.m.   2 lbs. hay, 1 lb. green food;
   12.00 p.m.   2 lbs. oats;
   2.00 p.m.   2 lbs. hay;
   5.00 p.m.   gruel, after hunting, or bran mash;
   7.00 p.m.   4 lbs. oats, 1 lb. chaff;

9.00 p.m.    8 lbs. hay, 2 lbs. green food.
With variations.

xiv  Watering is a most important aspect of feeding:

a   The horse should always be watered before a meal as the water is required in his system to aid his digestion (see vii above).

b   Horses that do not have water before them all the time should not be watered, more than a few mouthfuls, for an hour and a half after feeding grain.

c   Water does not remain in the stomach, but passes on through to the large intestines: it may cause the grain to swell in the small intestines and cause colic (see 2v above).

d   Horses should not be watered when hot, to prevent the internal organs being cooled down too suddenly and a chill resulting.

e   The most desirable arrangement is for the horse always to have water available.

f   The horse is a slow drinker and should never be hurried when being watered; he may raise his head slowly several times, but this does not mean he has finished.

g   The horse should drink 8–10 gallons a day, and 4–6 gallons is normal on return from exercise.

xv  All feeding is a question of trial and error to achieve the best results for each individual horse with the minimum of waste:

a   Each horse must be studied carefully.

b   The amount of work it is doing must be taken into account.

c   The condition it is in must also be considered.

d   The way the horse's condition varies with both food and work must be noted carefully.

e   The feed must be adjusted according to the work and the effect of both on the horse's condition.

f   It is essential to use imagination and to check the greedy feeder and tempt the dainty feeder.

g   The horse must never be fed the same unvarying, unimaginative feeds until it refuses them out of sheer boredom.

*Section 3    The Horse at Grass*
The horse at grass requires at least seven hours grazing to eat his fill, if no other food is fed.

i   The period during which the horse is kept at grass, and in which months of the year, must depend entirely on the particular circumstances of horse and owner:

a   If the horse is to be kept out all the year round, it must have supplementary feeding during the winter months when there is no grass available.

b   If in doubt about whether this supplementary feeding is required, the acid test is whether the horse leaves good hay put out for him untouched and continues grazing.

c   If the horse is to be kept out all the year round, its natural coat should be left untouched and it cannot therefore be expected to do any severe work. Before being saddled, it should only be lightly groomed to avoid disturbing the natural grease in its coat.

d   Sometimes, polo ponies and show-jumpers normally worked in the summer are wintered out to save the trouble and expense of keeping them in stables.

e   Hunters may be put out to grass during the summer months as a rest from work and a saving in trouble and expense.

f   A preferable arrangement may be to turn out the horse at night during the summer months, saving the horse from flies and the heat of the day and economising in bedding and feed.

g   In this way, the horse will only require a light day bed and small feeds of hay during the day, before being turned out in the late afternoon.

ii   Normally, grass should supply sufficient keep from May until October if required to do so, but much must depend on the nature of the grazing available and its extent, apart from the number of horses and similar variable factors.

a   The best time to turn horses into fresh pasture is when the grass is about four to six inches long and beginning to wave in the wind.

b   When the field has been levelled down, but not grazed bare, the horses should be removed. When the grasses have grown again, they may return.

c   This is known as 'rotational grazing'.

iii   It is thus essential to have a choice of grazing, and two small paddocks are generally preferable to one large one.

a   Horses are untidy grazers and will not feed near their own droppings, so that coarse, thick growth results in patches.

b   Pastures can therefore quickly become 'horse sick' unless carefully looked after and tended.

    *c*    As soon as horses have left a pasture, it should be chain-harrowed to spread the droppings.

iv   Timothy, rye grass, cocksfoot, meadow fescue and meadow grass are among the best grasses for the horse, but a good pasture will have a wide variety of suitable grasses and herbage (see hay, pp. 216–19).

    *a*    These will tend to mature at different times so that the rotational grazing will have to be varied from year to year to avoid spoiling the pasture.

    *b*    Chain-harrowing and rolling the pasture in the spring and winter, as well as applications of nitro-chalk and sulphate of ammonia in the spring, will help to produce good grazing.

v    Horses and cattle pasture well together because cattle tear off the longer grasses with their tongues, whereas horses bite the sward with their teeth, preferring the shorter grasses:

    *a*    Sheep on the other hand eat the centre of the plants, and do not graze well with horses.

    *b*    Grazing cattle and horses concurrently is not always advisable as some horses tend to chase cattle and might cause the loss of a calf, also in the case of horned cattle there is a risk of injury to the horse, especially in the case of young stock.

    *c*    Cattle should be grazed after horses to prevent the grass growing long and seeding, and horses will always find feeding in a field after cattle.

    *d*    Neither minds the other's dung, but each objects to its own.

    *e*    Intergrazing in this way helps to keep the pastures free from infection and disease as horses and cattle eat each other's parasites and thus kill their life cycles, e.g. the red worm in horses.

    *f*    Especially when grazing with cattle, the condition of the pasture should be constantly inspected to ensure there is sufficient for the horse.

vi   A plentiful supply of water must be available in each paddock, preferably piped to a trough with an automatic ballcock feed:

    *a*    Ponds and streams are liable to be a source of disease and infection and are not suitable; they are best fenced-off.

    *b*    If either is stagnant or fouled with mud or scum, the horse may refuse to drink from them.

    *c*    Troughs should be cleaned out whenever the horses leave the pasture, and checked for fresh supplies when they are first put out to grass.

    *d*    The pipes leading to them should be lagged, and in frosty weather they

Rye Grass

Sweet Scented Vernal Grass

Crested Dogstail Grass

Meadow Grass

Cocksfoot Grass

Meadow Foxtail Grass

should be checked twice daily, at least, and the ice on the water should be broken.

vii A shed should be provided in each paddock or pasture as a protection for the horse against bad weather, or excessive heat and flies:

 *a* It should be enclosed on three sides and open on the fourth, preferably the side facing south.

 *b* It should be about twelve feet high at the eaves and slated, tiled or thatched; preferably not roofed with corrugated-iron which lacks insulation.

viii The hedges or fences, and ground itself, should be inspected frequently, preferably daily, to ensure there are no possibly harmful stakes, jagged nails, broken bottles, holes or similar likely sources of injury to the horse:

 *a* There should be no barbed wire anywhere around a field with horses in it.

 *b* Agricultural implements must never be left standing in a field where horses are, or even where horses are going to be, since they are easily forgotten, e.g. a harrow in long grass could be lethal.

 *c* Gates and doorways should be wide and should be inspected each time they are used to make sure they are not worn.

 *d* Locks may be required on gates which adjoin public roads to avoid the risk of trespassers leaving them open and allowing the horses to stray.

ix The hedgerows and pasture should also be inspected for any poisonous plants or for potential access to them, i.e. over the fence, growing within reach:

 *a* The more likely poisonous plants which may be found are hemlock and cowbane, both like cow-parsley, also poison ivy, privet, laurel, yew and deadly nightshade.

 *b* Less common, but still dangerous, are laburnum, aconite, rhododendrons, boxwood, lupins, foxgloves and meadow saffron.

x If a horse is to be kept in condition while out at grass, some oats will need to be fed to him. (*N.B.* This does not apply to ponies.)

 *a* The horse at grass should be checked daily for condition and fitness.

 *b* Any sign of loss of condition should be noticed at once and the reason sought, e.g. failure of the water supply, or insufficient grazing left in the pasture.

xi The horse is a gregarious animal and should have the company of another horse at grass, if possible:

*a*  At the least, he should have the company of a donkey, or similar substitute, as a companion, e.g. cattle.

*b*  Otherwise, it may be found that he is constantly breaking out in search of company, or simply pining and not putting on any flesh.

xii  The horse should be introduced to grass slowly, and, as gradually, returned to the stable routine:

*a*  A short session at grass daily, steadily increasing the time allowed, is the way to avoid stomach upsets.

*b*  Abrupt transitions of diet are likely to upset the horse's sensitive digestion and are generally unnecessary.

xiii  When turning the horse out to grass, it is advisable to open the gate wide, take the horse into the field and then remove the head-collar and stand back; he will probably toss up his heels and set off at a gallop.

xiv  The ideal paddock for a horse at grass is situated in a wooden ring fence, lying on a gentle southerly facing slope, which is sheltered against the coldest winds, but is open to the sun all day. It is seldom found outside the Elysian fields, but most other paddocks can be improved with care and effort.

Deadly Nightshade

*Section 4    Green Food*

Green food is stable terminology for freshly cut grass.

i    It must be fed within twenty-four hours of cutting, and preferably as soon as possible:

    *a*    Otherwise it will start fermenting, i.e. heating, and will cause colic.

    *b*    Lawn cuttings start fermenting almost at once and are NOT suitable as feed for the horse.

ii    In spring or summer, green food is an invaluable addition to the feed:

    *a*    A few pounds mixed with hay, or chopped with grain, may be fed daily. BUT

    *b*    Too much should not be fed too suddenly, or it may cause an attack of colic.

    *c*    It has a high water content, therefore a little weighs quite a lot.

iii    Up to about 10 lbs. may be fed daily: BUT

    *a*    It has a laxative effect.

    *b*    If it causes scouring, i.e. loose bowel movements, the amount should be reduced.

iv    Good grasses in good condition should be chosen:

    *a*    Do not feed useless weeds or grasses short in feeding value.

    *b*    Do not feed grass that has been fouled in any way.

*Section 5    Hay*

Hay provides the main bulk food necessary for the horse in stables to remain in good health:

i    A horse of about 15·2 hands requires about 25–30 lbs. of bulk feed a day: and its annual consumption of hay is probably around 1½–2 tons:

    *a*    The normal practise is to feed a small amount in the morning, more at noon, more in the evening and the main bulk later on to allow the horse the night to digest it.

    *b*    The amount of hay to other foods must vary with the amount of work a horse is doing: the more work, the less hay.

ii    Hay is composed of grasses and herbage:

    *a*    Useful grasses for hay are: cocksfoot, crested dogstail, meadow fescue, rye grass, rough- and smooth-stalk meadow grass, sweet vernal, tail fescue, foxtail, timothy and yellow oat grass.

Common False Oat

Sheeps Fescue

Fiorin, or Marsh Bent Grass

Slender False Brome

    *b*   Useless grasses are: couch grass, barren fescue, bents, barren brome, darnell, slender foxtail, sheep's fescue, and wall barley. Ribbon grass, quaking grass and false oat.

    *c*   Common weeds are: coltsfoot, dandelions, buttercups, blackhead, marguerites, silver weeds, sedges, rushes, nettles and thistles.

    *d*   Herbage consists of: clover, trefoil, vetch, sainfoin and lucerne.

iii  Hay may be:

    *a*   Ley hay or seed hay, i.e. grown from seed as a rotation, or ley, crop, generally consisting primarily of a few varieties, thus being termed a timothy hay, a clover hay, etc.

    *b*   Meadow hay, i.e. grown on suitable land in permanent pasture, taken annually and notable for the variety of grasses and for its fineness, as well as for its pleasant smell.

    *c*   Water-meadow hay, i.e. grown on damp waterside fields, generally notable for coarse sedges and rushes.

iv  Hay should be cut when flowering and allowed to dry, or make, properly:

    *a*   If cut too soon, the nutriment is in the stalk.

    *b*   If cut too late, the nutriment is in the seed.

    *c*   If cut too late, the stems will be woody and there will be no flower heads or seed.

    *d*   If not allowed to dry, or make, properly it will heat in the stack, or bale, and become mow-burnt, or even fired.

v  Good hay should not be fed before it is at least six months old:

    *a*   It should be greenish in colour: not colourless or yellow.

    *b*   It should smell sweet and contain plenty of flowering heads.

    *c*   It should taste slightly sweet, never bitter.

    *d*   It should contain a plentiful variety of useful grasses and a minimum of useless ones or weeds.

    *e*   It may be as much as three times as nutritious as poor hay.

    *f*   Good hay is amongst the best and most nutritious food available, hence, it is most important to be able to recognise it.

vi  Hay is not good when:

    *a*   The colour has been completely washed out.

    *b*   It is very woody, or excessively dusty.

    *c*   The bales are badly mow-burnt, and it is obvious they have been overheating due to the hay not having been properly dry before it was baled.

vii If it has to be used, dusty hay should be thoroughly wetted before feeding to the horses.

viii It is always better to buy hay from a large stack than from a small one: estimate ten cubic yards to the ton.

    *a* The small stack always has more exposed in proportion to the large one.

    *b* The small stack therefore always has more weathered hay in proportion to the large one.

ix It is a common trick amongst unscrupulous dealers to water one or two bales in a load:

    *a* This increases the weight of the load.

    *b* Hence, it also increases their profit.

    *c* If this is discovered make a point of telling the dealer and avoid buying hay from him again.

x When examining hay before buying it, it is advisable to check several bales at random and examine their contents before agreeing to buy.

xi The hay may be fed chopped as chaff, or long, either in hay racks, which have considerable disadvantages (as noted above, pp. 140–141), or in hay nets as follows:

    *a* The hay nets should be filled over a small tarpaulin.

    *b* The seeds that fall down on the tarpaulin should be collected and form a useful addition to the chaff or feed.

    *c* Ten to twelve pounds can very readily be stuffed down into a hay net without any effort.

    *d* Several hay nets can be prepared beforehand at any spare convenient moment.

    *e* Shaking out the hay before stuffing the hay nets will also remove any impurities, foreign bodies, such as barbed wire, sticks or stones, or simply dust.

    *f* If very dusty, the hay nets should be doused with water as suggested above.

    *g* When given to the horse they should be tied with a non-slip knot at a convenient height for the horse, so that he does not have to stretch for it and yet is in no danger of catching his foot in the net, i.e. neither too high, nor too low.

*Section 6  Chaff*

Hay or oat straw, after it has been passed through a chaff-cutter, becomes chaff, i.e. chopped into short lengths.

i   It is mostly used as an auxiliary feed:

    *a*   Most commonly in nose-bags, mixed with oats for work horses.
    *b*   Mixed with oats in stables to prevent a horse bolting his feed.

ii  It is sometimes suggested that hay is better fed as chaff than long, as it is less susceptible to waste.

*Section 7   Oats*
Oats are the most suitable grain to feed to horses.

i   Oats a year old are best, as new oats are soft and unfit to feed to horses; they need time to dry out and mature:

    *a*   The oats should be plump, short and round.
    *b*   They should be hard, dry and floury if bitten.
    *c*   They should be pale yellow, white, or black.
    *d*   They should be beardless and uniform in size.
    *e*   The kernels should bulge through the husks.
    *f*   They should smell slightly sweet.
    *g*   They should be firm to the hand when a handful is taken up and squeezed.

ii  Inferior oats may be:

    *a*   Bitter tasting or dusty.
    *b*   Dark in colour.
    *c*   Long, thin and irregular in shape.
    *d*   Strong smelling.
    *e*   Soft to the feel when squeezed.
    *f*   Long of beard and thick of husk.

iii Damp oats become heated, but may be saved by kiln drying:

    *a*   If damaged badly by damp, they may become dark coloured and acrid smelling: this is known as 'foxy'.
    *b*   When dried foxy oats will turn dark brown, and may then be bleached to restore the colour, but they will then taste wrong.
    *c*   Mustiness and mouldiness may be smelt at once.
    *d*   Oats tainted by rats also smell strongly and will be refused by any horse.
    *e*   For this reason, it is advisable to avoid oats swept off a barn floor.

iv  Oats are a heating food, stimulating the horse and providing energy and, hence, must be strictly rationed according to the amount of work the horse is doing:

a   For a 15·2 hands horse in moderate work about 8 lbs. of oats a day is probably quite sufficient.

b   Never more than 4 lbs. should be given at any one feed.

c   A pony, especially if being ridden by a child, should seldom be given oats at all except under strict supervision.

d   Oats can be stimulating almost to the point of intoxication to judge by some horse's reactions and care must be taken to find how the individual horse reacts.

v   As with hay the normal procedure is to space out the feeding of the oats throughout the day, with the main bulk in the evening.

vi  Oats should be fed whole, except in the case of sick horses or old horses with inferior teeth when they should be fed crushed:

a   The crushing machine should only just break the kernel.

b   If the oats are crushed to flour, much of their goodness is lost.

vii Oats are generally best fed mixed with bran or chaff to prevent the horse bolting them without masticating them properly:

a   If the horse passes whole oats in his dung, first check the teeth which may need attention.

b   If the teeth are all right he is bolting his food and must be checked, as above, p. 208.

c   The proportions may vary from half oats to quarter bran and quarter chaff, or as preferred.

viii Whereas a horse at rest in the stables may require only say 1 lb. of oats a day, a horse working hard may require as much as 12–16 lbs. of oats a day:

a   It depends entirely on circumstances, how much is fed.

b   It also depends very much on the individual horse concerned.

c   All feeding is a matter for individual attention. BUT

d   The basic principle of all feeding should be 'little and often'.

ix  During illness, or after injury, oats should be expressly excluded from the diet altogether:

a   An exception may be oats steamed, or soaked, in hot water for about an hour, which are then a very good feed for an invalid horse.

b   Damped bran and extra hay should take the place of the ration of oats.

c   When again permitted, the ration of oats should be started gradually and slowly increased.

d   Abrupt changes of diet should be avoided whenever possible.

x    Oats are the best balanced of all horse foods, especially for fast work, but should be fed only according to the horse's requirements and reactions to them.

### Section 8   Beans

Beans are a very nutritious and heating food: either soya or field varieties.

i    They should be hard, dry, and light brown in colour:

    *a*    They should taste sweet and be free of weevils.
    *b*    Beans less than a year old are indigestible.
    *c*    If old, they become dark and deteriorate.
    *d*    They should be fed split, due to their thick husks.

ii    They are a useful feed for horses in pasture, during damp weather especially, or to help a horse recover lost condition:

    *a*    They are also a useful addition to the feed when the horse is working hard.
    *b*    Up to 3 lbs. a day is generally sufficient when the horse is working hard.

iii    In normal circumstances, 1 lb. a day mixed with the feed provides variety and is probably sufficient.

### Section 9   Peas

Peas are also a useful, nutritious and heating food:

i    They should be light in colour:

    *a*    The varieties are white, grey and blue peas.
    *b*    They should be hard, sound and dry.
    *c*    They should be fed with the tough skins split to make them digestible.

ii    Feed as with beans above.

### Section 10   Other Grains

Other grains are as follows:

i    Barley:
    Barley is not greatly used for feeding horses in this country, although it is commonly used in other countries.

    *a*    It should be plump, hard, wrinkled, yellow and non-smelling. But
    *b*    There are many new varieties which are perfectly good, but do not match this description: they all have a hard husk.
    *c*    It can be quite a useful feed, producing bone in youngsters. But

*d*  It should be fed boiled, or crushed, due to the indigestible husk.

*e*  It should be fed in rather smaller quantities than oats.

ii  Wheat:

Wheat is rarely fed to horses as price and the human demand for it militate against its use.

*a*  It should be round, plump and hard, non-smelling.

*b*  It can also be a useful feed, in small quantities.

*c*  It should be fed crushed and mixed with other grain or chaff.

iii  Maize:

Maize should be fed with other grains and is most popular in flake form.

*a*  It should be bright in colour, hard, dry and sweet to the taste.

*b*  It should be fed crushed and split and mixed with other grains or chaff: as it takes a long time to digest.

*c*  It is highly nutritious and best limited to about 2 lbs. a day. Generally used for heavy harness horses.

*d*  In flake form, still indigestible, but useful addition to oats, especially for ponies.

iv  Rice:

Rice is unlikely to be used as a feed in this country:

*a*  Without the husk, it is unsuitable feed, due to its lack of fibre.

*b*  The husks are very indigestible to horses unaccustomed to them.

*c*  In the East it is fed in small quantities crushed or boiled.

v  Rye:

Rye is also unlikely to be used as a feed in this country.

*a*  It is quite common on the continent.

*b*  It is very similar in analysis to wheat and is fed the same way.

*Section 11*  *Concentrates*

Concentrated foods, in the shape of nuts or cubes, are available:

i  They have an equivalent food value to oats and save time and labour in preparation:

*a*  There are several varieties produced, mostly fairly expensive.

*b*  They are generally reliable and should be fed as recommended, but one should never believe all manufacturer's claims.

ii  They should not be fed without variety, *ad nauseam*, the horse both deserves and appreciates imagination in his feeding.

*Section 12   Alternative Foods*
The following foods may be considered as alternatives, when desired, but should not be a first choice.

i   Draff or brewer's grains:
    The refuse of malt after brewing and extremely rich in nitrogen.

    *a*   They may be obtained wet or dried.
    *b*   If obtained wet, should be fed fresh as they soon turn sour.
    *c*   They should be mixed with other grains and treated with caution.
    *d*   Their food equivalent is about 5 lbs. of brewer's grains to 4 lbs. of oats.

ii   Malt culms:
    Another by-product of the brewing processes is the dried rootlets from sprouting barley in the malting chamber.

    *a*   Said to vary considerably in quality from good to very poor.
    *b*   Recommended to be fed scalded, or thoroughly moistened, mixed with other grains.
    *c*   It is suggested that it should be introduced carefully and a handful or two be added to the feed at the most.
    *d*   It is also recommended that bonemeal be added to make up its mineral deficiency.

iii   Silage:
    Cut grass or green crops packed with molasses and used principally for feeding cattle in winter in place of hay.

    *a*   Horses can become accustomed to silage fed in roughly the same quantities as hay, but
    *b*   It is smelly stuff to handle and, understandably, not highly popular, however nutritious it may be.

iv   Sugarbeet pulp:
    A byproduct of the sugarbeet industry.

    *a*   It has considerable food value, but must be balanced with hay and oats, not fed by itself.
    *b*   The pulp should be soaked for at least twenty-four hours before feeding.

*Section 13   Roots*
Some roots are very valuable feed for horses and may be extremely beneficial, others are not so good.

i    Carrots, mangels and parsnips are very good for horses, in that order:

    *a*    Carrots and parsnips should be fed whole, or sliced endways or pulped.

    *b*    They should never be chopped across, or the horse may choke himself on the pieces.

    *c*    Mangels should be chopped, diced, pulped, or fed whole.

    *d*    Some horses do not like parsnips, but all horses like carrots and mangels.

    *e*    Up to 4 lbs. a day is not too much for a 15·2 hands horse, even when working hard.

ii    Swedes and turnips are not such good roots for horses:

    *a*    Turnips are sometimes used for work horses.

    *b*    Swedes are inclined to have a laxative effect and most horses do not like them much.

    *c*    If fed, they should be chopped and added to the feed.

iii    Potatoes should not be fed raw, if at all:

    *a*    They should, if fed, be boiled and added to the feed.

    *b*    This is how they are said to be fed to horses in Ireland.

iv    All roots may be fed as follows:

    *a*    Boiled and still warm, but not too hot.

    *b*    Mixed with grain or chaff, either cooked, or raw and chopped.

    *c*    Never when frosted: this is liable to cause scouring, i.e. diarrhoea.

*Section 14   Bran*

Bran is the husk of wheat after the kernel has been ground into flour.

i    It should be quite dry, flaky and free from lumps:

    *a*    Its colour varies from yellow to yellow-red, dependent on the variety of the wheat.

    *b*    It should smell sweet.

    *c*    If chewed, it should be neither gritty nor sour tasting.

    *d*    If the hand is plunged into it, the fingers should come out floury.

ii    If sour or lumpy, it has been damp and this may cause poisoning should it be fed to the horse.

iii    Sand may sometimes be added to increase the weight:

    *a*    If a handful is thrown into water the bran will float. But

    *b*    If there is any sand present, it will sink.

iv It does not contain much nourishment, but it is a very valuable horse feed because:

    *a*    It aids digestion.

    *b*    It increases bulk.

    *c*    When fed in a mash it is mildly laxative.

    *d*    When fed dry it tends to be slightly constipating.

    *e*    It contains valuable salts, i.e. lime and phosphate.

    *f*    When mixed with oats, it helps to prevent horses bolting their feed.

    *g*    It is especially good for growing youngsters.

v Bran mash:
A bran mash is a very useful laxative feed. It is made:

    *a*    By placing 2–3 lbs. of bran in a bucket.

    *b*    Boiling water should then be added, but it must not be made too sloppy.

    *c*    An ounce of salt should be added to the mixture.

    *d*    It should then be stirred well with a wooden stick or spoon.

    *e*    The bucket should then be covered and it should be left to cook in its own heat.

    *f*    When it is cool enough to put a hand into the mixture, it may be fed to the horse.

    *g*    This should be sufficient for one horse.

*Section 15   Linseed*
Linseed is the seed of the flax plant.

i It is a most valuable conditioning food:

    *a*    The grain should be plump and well filled.

    *b*    It should be bright and shining and free from dirt.

    *c*    Because of the very tough husk, it should not be fed whole.

    *d*    It must be fed ground, soaked or cooked.

ii Boiled linseed is an excellent food for fattening a horse:

    *a*    It is made by boiling the whole grain slowly from 6–12 hours, stirring to prevent it burning.

    *b*    It may also be made by soaking the grain in cold water for 24 hours, stirring frequently.

    *c*    It will form a jelly which horses like very much indeed.

    *d*    Half a pound per day fed with other food is a suitable ration for a 15·2 hand horse.

iii   Linseed cake:

    *a*   Is the residue from which the oil has been extracted.
    *b*   May be fed broken up, or soaked in cold water for 12 hours.
    *c*   If soaked for too long, it may turn sour.
    *d*   Up to one pound a day is a suitable ration for a 15·2 hand horse.

iv   Linseed mash:

    *a*   Is made by boiling 1–1½ lbs. of linseed in water for 8 hours; fairly sloppy consistency, not too thick.
    *b*   Add two pounds of bran and an ounce of salt and stir.
    *c*   Cover and allow bran to cook until cool, as for bran mash.
    *d*   This is enough for one horse of 15·2 hands.

v   Linseed tea:

    *a*   Boil 1 lb. of linseed in 1 gallon of water and allow to simmer for 12 hours.
    *b*   A teacupful may be added to the evening feed.
    *c*   It is excellent for soothing the urinary organs and mucous membranes.

vi   Linseed oil:

    *a*   Raw linseed oil may be used as a substitute for linseed tea.
    *b*   Feed 2 oz. with the evening feed.

*Section 16   Oatmeal Gruel*
Oatmeal is excellent for making a gruel, but other meals may also be used, e.g. maize or bean meal.

i   Gruels should be very thin and sloppy, much more so than a mash, which should merely be wet:

    *a*   Put two handfuls of meal into a bucket of hot water.
    *b*   Stir and feed warm.
    *c*   This is excellent for a horse after a hard day's work in winter.

ii   A cold gruel is excellent in hot weather:

    *a*   This is made with cold water as for a hot gruel.
    *b*   It is very refreshing to a horse in very hot weather.

*Section 17   Sugar*
Sugar is best fed in liquid form as syrup and is an excellent fattener.

i   About 1 lb. added to the feed in the form of molasses, treacle, or syrup, is a suitable ration of a 15·2 hand horse:

    *a*   It may be fed by diluting 1 pint in boiling water, then adding up to 2 gallons of cold water per pint.

    *b*   Or it may be used in making up mashes, or boiled feeds.

ii  Lump sugar should not be given too frequently as a tit-bit:

    *a*   It may lead to vices.

    *b*   It can lead to licking mangers, walls and, eventually, to crib-biting.

*Section 18   Salt*

Salt is an invaluable addition to the horse's feed.

i   It is extremely beneficial to the horse's system:

    *a*   It purifies the blood.

    *b*   It helps to rid the horse of intestinal worms.

    *c*   It increases the thirst, which is extremely important.

    *d*   It also increases the disease-resistant qualities of the blood.

ii  It is not advisable to leave a lump of rock salt in the manger or a salt lick attached to the wall of the box:

    *a*   It is suggested that this may be a contributary cause of the stable vice of crib-biting.

    *b*   But if a horse is already a 'weaver' it may help to check this vice.

iii Rock salt should be stored in a dry place where it will not crumble.

# PART VIII
## Care of the Horse in Sickness

*Section 1    The Daily Checkover*
The first signs of any illness should be automatically noted in the course of the
day's routine by any experienced horseman.

i    The Appearance of the Healthy Horse:
     The horseman must know how the healthy horse should look.

   a    The horse is generally standing well, possibly resting a hind leg, but
        showing an interest in what is going on around him.
   b    The eyes are alert and the ears cocked and mobile.
   c    The skin should be loose and elastic, and the coat glossy.
   d    The membranes of the eyes, nose and mouth should be a bright
        salmon pink.
   e    The bowels should be moving freely and the droppings normal.

ii    Abnormal symptoms:
      Any alteration in the horse's normal behaviour should be noted as a matter
      of course, and the reasons for it analysed.

   a    Any sign of listlessness, moping, or loss of appetite, when being fed and
        mucked-out first thing in the morning should be noticed at once.
   b    Any unusual stance or posture, or a staring coat, should also be noticed
        and the reason looked for promptly.
   c    Any unusual sluggishness or nervousness, or signs of strain at exercise,
        or throughout the day, should also be seen at once.
   d    Any uneasiness, unusual breathing, excessive sweating, or abnormal
        droppings, should also be regarded as a sign of trouble and promptly
        looked into carefully.

iii    The droppings:
       When mucking-out the horse, or in the course of the day, the droppings
       should be examined as a matter of routine.

a   When stable-fed, the droppings should be golden brown passed in small balls, which break on the ground.
b   For grass fed horses, they should be more greenish in colour.
c   If too hard, or too soft, a digestive disturbance may be assumed.
d   They should not be slimy, or evil-smelling: this may be serious and points to ill health.
e   Worms, or eggs, may be found in the dung, but microscopic tests will be required to test the degree of infestation.

iv   The urine:
The manner in which the horse passes urine should be checked automatically.

a   A horse should pass urine at least five times a day, and never less than a quart at a time.
b   The urine should be thick and yellow in health, but may turn cloudy, or have a bright colour, when the horse is sick.
c   It is normal for the horse to grunt and straddle rather noisily when passing urine.

v   The membranes of the eyes, nose and mouth and skin:
When grooming these should be automatically noted.

a   The membranes of eyes, nose and mouth should be pink and moist.
b   Paleness indicates anaemia; redness indicates fever; yellowness indicates illness; purple spotting indicates impurities in the blood.
c   The coat should be lying flat and smooth, not harsh or staring, and the skin should feel elastic and supple, not dead.

vi   The stance:
When checking the feet in the morning and cleaning them out, any unusual stance or warmth in the feet or joints should be noted:

a   Pointing a forefoot invariably indicates foot trouble there: ordinarily a hindfoot may be rested, but that is all.
b   If both forefeet are painful, they will be spread well forward.
c   If the forefeet are apart this may indicate chest trouble.
d   If the hindfeet are well forward, and the horse backs only reluctantly, this points to trouble with the hindfeet.

vii   Other symptoms:
Other symptoms of sickness or pain may be:

a   Excessive sweating may be due to general weakness or pain, but healthy sweat should never form separate globules.

*b*  An increased rate of breathing: normally, the flanks should rise and fall about fifteen times a minute. Coughing and sneezing.

viii Checking temperature and pulse:
If in doubt about the horse's state of health, the temperature and pulse should be checked:

*a*  The temperature is taken by inserting an ordinary clinical thermometer, the bulb smeared with vaseline, gently into the rectum for three minutes: the reading should be between 100–101°F.

*b*  The temperature will normally be higher at midday and in the evening, but should not vary unduly apart from that. Anything over 102° is abnormal and 104°, or over may be serious.

*c*  The pulse rate is between 35–40 beats a minute and may be felt with the first two fingers at the inside of the elbow, or immediately above the fetlock, or under the lower jaw, where the sub-maxillary artery crosses the jaw.

*d*  While taking the pulse, also check the breathing: it should be noiseless, even and steady, at about ten to fifteen respirations a minute.

*Section 2  The Periodical Checkovers*
Certain checks on parts of the horse's anatomy and health should be routine.
i  The teeth:
The teeth should be checked over periodically, at least once a month, to ensure there are no ragged edges interfering with digestion:

*a*  The tongue should be grasped in one hand and held outside the jaws, while the other hand feels the surface of the teeth for ragged edges.

*b*  If any sharpness is felt, then a tooth rasp should be used to file down the edges.

*c*  Any more serious conditions found should be referred to the vet, e.g. lampas which is a swollen condition of the roof of the mouth generally caused by cutting the permanent teeth and is probably curable by Epsom Salts added to the drinking water.

ii  The sheath:
The sheath and penis should be periodically inspected and cleaned (see grooming, p. 157).

iii  The dung:
Apart from the daily check on the dung, a microscopic check should be made every six months or so, or whenever worms are suspected: a sample is sent to the vet to be checked.

*Section 3    The Checks for Lameness*
When lameness is apparent, but the reason for it is questionable, the following checks may be made:

i    Stance:
     By entering the stable quietly so as not to disturb the horse quite a lot may be told from the stance.

    *a*   As noted above, weight is generally equally distributed on the forelegs and only a hindleg being rested: although sometimes, as when very tired, the alternate foreleg may also be rested.

    *b*   If a foreleg is being pointed, note should be taken whether the heel or toe is taking the weight (the toe is generally rested in cases of laminitis and ringbone, the heel in navicular).

    *c*   In a case of slight lameness, the pastern of the lame leg may be slightly straighter than the pastern of the sound leg.

    *d*   If lame in the shoulder, the lame leg may seem to hang down, and may also be slightly behind the other foreleg.

ii   Checks at a stand:
     While standing still the legs should be compared for size and swellings.

    *a*   The hand should be run down each leg with the fingers down the tendons.

    *b*   Any tenderness, swelling, or heat should be felt.

    *c*   This should be regular practise when grooming.

    *d*   The feet should also be tested in the same way for heat, or for anything in the foot, or damage to the sole.

iii  Checks on the move:
     The horse should be walked out and trotted out in hand on a level surface

Lame in off-fore

directly away before being turned and brought back, then past and back once more.

a   The horse will take a shorter stride with the lame leg.

b   When lame in front, the horse drops his head as the sound foot touches the ground and raises it to take the weight off the lame leg.

c   If lame behind, the horse drops his head as the lame leg reaches the ground: the reverse of the above.

Lame in near hind

d   It may be noticeable when lame behind that the horse is leaning over to the other side to take weight off the unsound leg.

e   Lameness in the hindquarters is more apparent when the horse turns on the forehand.

f   If trotted up and down hill, a horse lame in the foot will go lamer downhill and a horse lame in the shoulder will go lamer uphill.

iv   Checks for shoulder lameness:
To check if the lameness is in the shoulder:

a   First, pull the horse's leg forward as far as it will go.

b   Then, flex the leg backwards as far as it will go.

c   Repeat this two or three times each way and if the horse flinches, or half rears, this indicates he is probably in pain.

d   As some horses object to this test, it is advisable to check both shoulders.

e   He may swing the leg slightly or catch the toe in the ground.

233

Test of Shoulder Lameness

Test for Shoulder Lameness

v   Checks for stifle lameness:
    To check if the lameness is in the stifle:

    *a*   If the horse is reined back he will tend to drag the toe of the leg on
          which he is lame.
    *b*   He will bend the hock and fetlock as little as possible on the side
          affected.

234

*Section 4    Treatment of Wounds*
Wounds in horses can often seem very shocking at first sight, but with care and sensible nursing are generally easily healed.

i    Shallow wounds:
Cuts, tears and galls all come into the category of shallow wounds and, at first, sometimes appear very unpleasant.

    *a*   If clean and without inflammation, it is best bathed with a mild solution of Dettol and water.

    *b*   Then, powder with sulphanilamide and leave to heal.

    *c*   If inflamed and dirty, it will require more careful bathing and removal of the dirt before it will heal.

    *d*   Hot fomentations may be required to reduce the swelling.

ii    Punctures and deep wounds:
Although these may not, at first sight, seem so unpleasant as shallow wounds they are, of course, far more dangerous.

    *a*   Punctures, being generally small, are easily overlooked and, as they very often heal from the surface first, they readily result in abscesses, which require reopening.

    *b*   If very small, an injection of penicillin may suffice to let them heal from the bottom upwards.

    *c*   If this is not enough, they may require more regular treatment with penicillin, or antibiotics, according to the vet's advice.

    *d*   In the case of deep wounds, it may be difficult to stop the bleeding: if veinous, the blood is a dull red, if arterial, the blood is a bright scarlet and spurting.

    *e*   Cold water compacts should stop veinous bleeding, but a tourniquet, or veterinary assistance, may be required to check arterial bleeding.

    *f*   The wound should then be bathed and syringed out with a mild solution of Dettol and water.

    *g*   Inflammation should be reduced with hot fomentations of Dettol and water, but only once the bleeding has been thoroughly checked.

    *h*   An antiseptic gauze dressing should be bandaged in place and changed daily, and the wound should be syringed out each time until it heals. Sulphanilamide or similar treatment may be applied as the vet directs.

iii    Wounds near joints:
These may be especially dangerous and should be watched carefully, if in doubt about them call the vet at once.

  *a* If there is any yellow discharge, this may be synovial fluid, or joint oil, escaping and is extremely serious.

  *b* Call the vet at once.

**Section 5** *Normal Nursing Practise*
Certain treatments for the horse are normal: viz.:

i Purgatives and laxatives:
Clearing out the bowels is often an essential prelude to treatment of the horse; it may be done in several ways:

  *a* By administering an aloes ball: about 3 drachms for a small pony and 5 drachms for a hunter.

  *b* By dosing with about 1 pint to 1½ pints of linseed oil.

  *c* By dosing with ½ lb. of dilute Epsom Salts, or by adding this to a bran mash.

  *d* In each of the above cases, the purgative should be preceded by a diet of bran mashes for a full 48 hours.

  *e* If suitable preparation is not made as above, the horse may suffer super purgation, or acute diarrhoea.

  *f* Smaller doses of Epsom Salts are handy as a mild laxative, as also are bran mashes and linseed mashes.

ii Balling:
This is a method of administering a medicinal ball.

  *a* The horse's tongue should be held in one hand, the ball held in the tips of the fingers of the other hand.

  *b* The hand should then be inserted into the mouth and the ball pushed beyond the back of the tongue before being released.

  *c* Another method is to insert a tube and blow down it, thus pushing the ball into the correct position.

  *d* Care must be taken that the horse does not blow first!

iii Drenching:
This is a method of administering a liquid to the horse.

  *a* A proper drenching bottle with reinforced mouthpiece may be used, or a pint-sized bottle with the neck bound with cord.

  *b* An assistant is necessary to hold the horse in position and ensure that the head is raised: this may either be done by hand or with a cord over a beam round the jaws.

  *c* The person administering the drench should either be tall, or else standing on a stool beside the horse's head.

*d*   The bottle containing the medicine to be administered is inserted behind the incisors and in front of the molars.

*e*   The horse's head is held up and the bottle tilted until the contents are swallowed.

*f*   Should the horse start to cough the head must be lowered at once and the drenching bottle also lowered, or the contents may go down the wrong way: this could be very serious.

*g*   Do not try to administer more than about half a pint at a time.

iv   Blistering:
Blistering is the application of an irritant to cause a severe inflammation as a counter to a more deep-seated condition, e.g. a sprained tendon or ligament in the leg.

*a*   Severe blistering can be extremely painful, and should not be attempted by the inexperienced except under veterinary supervision: it is seldom recommended nowadays.

*b*   It acts by attracting an increased blood supply to the affected parts.

*c*   It tightens the skin, acting as a natural bandage, and the pain restricts movement.

*d*   The horse may need to be tied up in the early stages to ensure that he does not bite his legs.

*e*   As with bandaging, it is necessary to blister both legs of a pair, even though only one is affected.

*f*   In milder form, it may be used to reduce swellings, sprains or bring abscesses to a head.

*g*   Strong horse liniments are, in effect, a mild blister, and rubbed in well can have remarkably good results.

*h*   These are all that should normally be required in the way of blistering, except on veterinary advice.

v   Routine:
The standard nursing routine should be followed in sickness.

*a*   The isolation stable should be kept dark and sudden noises should be avoided: it is highly desirable to give the patient peace and quiet.

*b*   One trusted attendant only should nurse the sick horse, and this may be nearly a full-time job in serious cases. The temperature and pulse should be noted regularly and recorded on a chart.

*c*   The horse should be kept warm, well rugged and bandaged, and the stables should be well ventilated.

*d*   Water must be constantly available and, if a bucket is used, should be frequently changed.

*e*   To maintain the horse's strength, it is desirable to tempt him with variety, ringing the changes in diet, but only a little at a time.

*f*   When the temperature is high, the food will probably remain untouched and should be removed.

*g*   An invalid diet should be adhered to: generally of a laxative nature: bran mashes, linseed mashes, green foods, carrots, roots, linseed and hay tea, and boiled barley.

*h*   Gruels, bread soaked in skim milk with a raw egg beaten into it and similar foods may be given to tempt the horse's appetite.

vi   Exercise and grooming:
In the case of the sick horse, these may naturally have to be suspended entirely, but as the invalid begins to convalesce they may be an important part of the nursing:

*a*   The convalescent horse should be walked in hand gently as often as possible.

*b*   Twice daily for short intervals is better than one long exercise period: the progress should be gradual.

*c*   It is important after serious illness not to exercise the horse too soon, or a severe relapse may be the result.

*d*   Grooming may be given to the convalescent horse as an important part of his recovery, enhancing the circulation and massaging his muscles but as with the exercise it must not be too severe and the build up should, be gradual.

*e*   Like the sick human it takes the sick horse time simply to recover the use of his muscles, and these must be built up again gradually.

*f*   As the exercise, so the diet should also be gradually altered accordingly.

*Section 6   Standard Precautions*
Certain precautions in stables are standard and always worth adhering to in order to avoid sickness spreading.

i   New arrivals:
It is always worth isolating new arrivals for the first twenty-four hours at least.

*a*   They should be examined by the vet to give them a clean bill of health before joining the others.

*b*   Any sign of sickness, or infectious or contagious disease they may have, will thus not be introduced to the stables.

ii   First signs of sickness:
As soon as the daily checkover shows signs of sickness in a horse, e.g. a high

temperature and running nose:

a    Isolate at once, rug well, keep warm in well-ventilated box, and CALL THE VET.

b    Ensure that all bedding is removed and the stable sprayed with disinfectant immediately.

c    Ensure that clothing, also saddles, bridles, buts and grooming kit belonging to the sick horse are isolated or disinfected: this is one of the commoner ways infectious or contagious diseases are passed through a stables.

d    Put the horse itself on a laxative diet, and cut down at once on the heating foods.

iii    Coughing, sneezing, running nose:
Any of these three, combined with a temperature, should be treated as potentially serious, as above.

## Section 7    Calling the Vet

The inexperienced horse-owner who suspects something is wrong should never try to diagnose it himself, but should at once call the vet.

i    Symptoms:
If the horse has developed symptoms as indicated above, there is clearly something wrong.

a    Incorrect treatment may well aggravate the illness.

b    The sooner correct treatment can be begun the better the chances of recovery.

ii    Hypochondria:
Some inexperienced horse-owners are always imagining that something is wrong with their horse.

a    The vet is inevitably a busy man and will not appreciate false alarms.

b    The horse-owner with hypochondria on behalf of his horse is like 'the boy who cried wolf'.

## Section 8    First Aid and the First Aid Chest

There should be a regular check on return from exercise or on coming in from grass for any cuts, bruises, or similar injuries, e.g. thorns.

i    Any such cuts, tears, or bruises should be treated according to their merit:

a    A minor bruise or swelling may be rubbed with liniment and watched for the next day or so.

 *b* A minor cut may be bathed, cleaned and dusted with sulphanilamide powder.

ii The first aid chest for one horse should contain the following:

One large roll of cottonwool.
Two, or more, 3 in. surgical bandages.
One, or more, elastic bandages.
One packet of Boracic Lint.
One packet of gauze.
One plastic puffer of sulphanilamide powder.
One, or two, tubes of penicillin provided by your Vet.
A 1 oz. bottle of Iodine.
One large bottle of Dettol.
One 2 oz. jar of Vaseline.
One bar carbolic soap.
One pair of scissors, preferably with curved ends, i.e. surgical.
One pair of forceps.
A syringe.
An enema.
A clinical thermometer.
One quart of linseed oil.
A 2 lb. packet of Epsom Salts.
One ½ bottle whisky or brandy.
One 1 lb. tin of cough electuary.
A tin of Stockholm Tar.
A ball of tow.
Proprietory liniments, etc. for mild blisters, etc.
Radiol Liniment and Bone Radiol, for splints, etc., are good.
Hoplemuroma, to encourage growth of horn, is also good.

# BOOK THREE
*Horsemastership*

# PART I
## Buying or Selling a Horse or Pony

Few subjects are more instinctively associated in most people's minds with double dealing and sharp practise, although most of the rogues have long ago been mechanized and have moved to the more profitable field of motor cars.

i   When it comes to buying a horse, the golden rule that seems to have been current since the days of the Romans has always been 'Caveat emptor', or 'Let the buyer beware'.

    *a*   Unfortunately, when it comes to selling a horse the reverse often holds good: 'Caveat venditor', or 'Let the seller beware'.

    *b*   There are pitfalls on both sides.

ii   Two more suitable saws today might be:

    *a*   Do as you would be done by.

    *b*   Everyone ends up with the horse they deserve.

*Section 1   Buying a Horse or Pony*
When buying a horse or pony, there are a number of factors which must be considered beforehand.

i   If the buyer himself has no particular preferences or bias, which is unusual, he should consider:

    *a*   The rider: the size, weight, age, experience and sex of the rider, all have a bearing on the most suitable type of horse or pony.

    *b*   The principal uses to which the horse, or pony, is likely to be put, i.e. hunting, hacking, harness work, etc.

    *c*   The sort of country where the horse or pony will for the most part be ridden, i.e. downland, moorland, banking country, etc.

    *d*   The sort of stabling and home background the horse or pony, is likely to have, i.e. clipped out in stables, or living rough at grass, etc.

  *e* The most suitable breed or type of horse or pony, which most closely matches all these varied requirements, i.e. arab, welsh cob, etc.

  *f* He must then decide the likely current market price for such a horse, or pony, and the maximum he is prepared to pay over that.

  *g* If he has not already done so, he must rid his mind of the idea that everyone wishing to sell a horse is necessarily out to try to cheat.

ii Once the buyer has decided what is required, he should next consider how he intends to find such a horse or pony:

  *a* If he has any knowledgeable friends and acquaintances, he may ask if they know of anything suitable, such as he has in mind.

  *b* This is very often the best way of learning of a suitable animal, which someone may have only just begun to consider selling.

  *c* There is also more than a grain of truth in the suggestion that buying a horse in this way is the best way to lose friends.

iii The buyer may visit various local riding schools and dealers to see what they have to offer that approximates to what he wants:

  *a* A reputable riding school or dealer cannot afford to risk that reputation simply to sell one horse or pony.

  *b* There are, of course, disreputable dealers and indifferent riding schools, but they should be avoided.

iv The buyer may advertise, in fairly general terms, for the sort of horse or pony he wants: in local, national and specialist press and journals:

  *a* It is generally advisable to start with the local paper and see what sort of response this brings, then go on to specialist or national level.

  *b* Many of the replies will be useless, but some may be worth following-up.

v Alternatively, the buyer may himself answer advertisements in similar papers, or journals, purporting to offer something like the horse, or pony, he desires:

  *a* In general, editors try to screen their advertisers to some extent, but inevitably some of these are extremely dubious.

  *b* The buyer can only use his common sense in sifting those that appear reasonable from those that are probably useless; then, he can go and look for himself.

vi Finally, the buyer can go to various horse sales and see whether there is anything up for sale that looks like the horse or pony he has in mind.

a   There is likely to be a good selection here, but the disadvantage is that it is not always possible to try the animal, and there may be no warranty with it.

b   The buyer must be very sure of his own judgment.

vii   Should the buyer find a horse or pony in any of the above ways that looks like what he is after he should:

a   Check it carefully for conformation and appearance: check the eyes and teeth, for vision and age (see ageing, pp. 270–272).

b   He should then run a hand down the legs to check for splints, spavins, curbs and similar defects, as well as lifting the feet to check the frogs and hooves (see pp. 160–163).

c   He should then have it led up and down in front of him, first at a walk and then at a trot, to check its action and movements, e.g. for dishing, brushing, etc. (see pp. 393–399).

d   If possible, he should then mount it and put it through its paces briefly, testing its mouth, schooling and reactions to the aids.

e   If possible, he should have his vet look the horse over with him to give him his opinion on its soundness.

f   If the horse or pony appears to be what he wants and to have no obvious defects, the buyer would then do well to ask for a warranty of soundness and any other details of which he is uncertain.

g   If, for some reason, he has not been able to test it as above, he should be all the more determined to ask both for a chance to do so and for a warranty.

viii   A warranty may mean a great deal, or may not be worth the paper it is written on:

a   A warranty should read something as follows:
'Received from Mr Blank the sum of £100 for a grey mare 15·2 hands, warranted 7 years old, sound, quiet to ride and drive, and free from vice. Signed . . .'.

b   Should it read: '7 years old, sound, warranted quiet to ride and drive, free from vice', it might be eleven years old and suffering from permanent lameness, as in this instance these points are not within the warranty, i.e. do not come after the word 'warranted'.

ix   Many people offer a horse or pony on a week's trial:

a   If the buyer is uncertain of his own ability to check the horse or pony as suggested in vii above, and if he thinks he wants it, he should certainly take such an opportunity.

b He can then have his veterinary surgeon check the horse or pony at his leisure.

c He can himself ride or test the animal as he wishes at his leisure, or the rider he is buying it for may test it.

d He must remember that the horse or pony is very probably upset and confused by an abrupt change of quarters and of handlers and may not give of his best: allowances must be made.

e In practise, any experienced horseman ought to be able to tell all he wants by riding a horse or pony and having it run up and down in front of him.

f The normal arrangement is that the prospective purchaser pays the costs of the journey, even if he decides to buy the horse, and the care of the horse is his responsibility from the moment of its arrival.

g Unless the prospective purchaser knows something of the people with whom he is dealing, this can sometimes prove an expensive business, with claims for damage to the horse or pony arriving unexpectedly after it has been sent back.

h It is always advisable to have any new arrival to the stables checked at once by the vet and equally advisable to have any animal checked by the vet before its departure: a veterinary certificate in these circumstances may often prove invaluable.

*Section 2    Selling a horse or pony*

This is the reverse of the coin and here, too, there are a number of snags and pitfalls to be considered:

i The first decision to make is on the price required and various factors must be taken into account:

a The age and degree of training and schooling are amongst the first factors to be considered.

b The conformation and action, the physical condition and presence, or absence, of any vices are the next equally important factors.

c The next factor influencing the price is the market demand for the type, or breed, of horse or pony.

d To some extent, the time of year may also influence the price, since demands for certain types of horse or pony are seasonal.

e It is probably advisable to decide on an asking price and a minimum price, but this must be up to the individual.

ii The second decision necessary to make, and to some extent bound up with the first, is whether it is desired to sell the horse or pony within any given time limit:

*a* It may be desired to move the horse, or pony, on to make room for another, or there may not be enough keep for him.

*b* The owner may wish to avoid the expense of keeping him on at livery, or be going away, or be unable to look after him.

*c* Alternatively, the owner may be happy to keep the horse or pony, until a really good home, or good price, is obtained.

*d* There may be no urgency about selling him and he may be kept quite easily at grass as long as required, but economically he is costing money all the time, hence his sale price is diminishing.

*e* Obviously, the time factor is important when it comes to obtaining a good price. hurried sales mean low prices.

iii The next decision to be made is by what means the horse or pony should be sold: the order, if no urgency is involved, will probably be as follows:

*a* Privately, through friends or acquaintances, passing the word around that he is for sale.

*b* This is only advisable if the horse or pony is virtually faultless and, even then, the remarks made above about losing friends still applies.

*c* You, or your friends, will be blamed for all real and imagined faults should anything go wrong and will get little thanks even if the horse, or pony, proves perfect.

iv The seller may try advertising in local, national or specialist press or journals:

*a* As with buying, it is generally advisable to start with the local papers and see what response there is from them.

*b* The advertisement should stick to the facts and avoid hyperbole, but this again is a matter for the individual.

v The seller must next decide whether he is going to allow the horse or pony to leave his stables on trial and for how long:

*a* If he does allow a trial, it should be for no longer than a week and he should make sure his vet provides him with a certificate of soundness beforehand: he should also insure the horse, if possible, though this is expensive.

*b* Should the horse or pony be injured on trial, the prospective buyer might well claim that it was due to the animal's vice and no fault of his: litigation might well follow with attendant costs rising all the time.

*c* In general, trials away from home are not a sound plan: the prospective purchaser should be offered any trial on the premises and the seller can then superintend matters and ensure the horse's safety.

    *d*    Allowing a horse off the premises is inviting trouble unless you know the person handling the horse well: the schooling of months can be ruined in a few hours by a heavy-handed rider.

vi  If the seller does not insist on providing a certificate of soundness with the sale of each horse, he has no redress when a purchaser returns the horse with faults caused by his bad handling or lack of care, e.g. lameness (see pp. 357–372).

    *a*    A certificate of soundness from a veterinary surgeon is a safeguard for both buyer and seller.

    *b*    No stock should be allowed to leave the premises without a certificate showing the horse to be sound at that time.

vii  The seller may prefer to sell his horse or pony through a dealer:

    *a*    In that event, he will simply have to pass the animal to the dealer and agree on a price.

    *b*    He will, of course, have to pay the dealer a percentage, but it may be that he will still obtain a better price without the attendant responsibilities.

viii  The seller may decide that his best course is to put the horse or pony into a sale:

    *a*    He will have to approach the auctioneers and make his entry for the sale according to their rules in good time.

    *b*    It is advisable to have the animal well turned out and led round the auction ring by its normal groom or attendant.

    *c*    Allowing the horse or pony to appear straight from grass and un-groomed, to be led round the ring by a stranger unaccustomed to the animal, or it to him and, hence, probably jibbing at every step, is automatically to lower the price considerably.

ix  A seller who is determined to hold out until he gets the price he asks may obtain it in the end, but by then his costs for keep may have more than cancelled his profits:

    *a*    It is often advisable to accept the first offer near the asking price, rather than hold out and end up the loser. But

    *b*    A horse that is valuable to one man may be valueless to another, i.e. a steeplechaser to a novice rider or a pony to a seventeen stone huntsman.

    *c*    It should also be remembered that there are degrees of unsoundness, so that while a horse might be unsound for one purpose, e.g. steeplechasing, he might be quite sound enough for another, e.g. hacking.

*d*   Both in buying and selling a horse or pony, the man or woman who knows horses has an obvious advantage over anyone who does not, but it is also important to be able to gauge your fellow-man.

*e*   Often, there is very little logic, and a great deal of emotion or instinct, involved in both buying and selling horses or ponies.

*f*   One logical certainty is that any horse which is completely unsound is an expensive horse, even as a gift.

*g*   Yet there is generally a buyer for any horse, if the price is reasonable, even if only, in the last resort, for meat.

# PART II
# Breeding

The aim and, incidentally, the fascination of breeding is to try to produce better stock, as the perfect animal has never been bred and there is always scope for improvement: horsemastership should include at least a working knowledge of the subject.

*Section 1    The Breeder's Requirements*
To run a stud farm successfully, there are certain basic requirements.

i   Sufficient knowledge:
    It is absolutely essential that the prospective breeder has a sufficient background knowledge to ensure success:

    a   Knowledge of the bloodlines of the stock with which he is dealing, whether Thoroughbred, Arab, pony or other stock, is an essential prerequisite.
    b   An eye for a horse, an understanding of conformation and action, of the correct alignment of bone and muscle, of temperament and horse psychology are also highly necessary.
    c   Knowledge of the care and management of horses, whether stallions, mares, or foals and young stock, is also essential: he must be a complete horsemaster.
    d   Finally, a knowledge of genetics, or the science of breeding, is also required.

ii  Sufficient business and organising ability:
    Unless the stud is run on a businesslike footing, and unless each detail of the organisation is correctly supervised, it will not be a success:

    a   Any farm today, and stud farms are no exception, requires considerable paper and office work: tax returns, government forms and more government forms, quite aside from ordinary business correspondence, constantly require attention.

*b*   The day to day organisation needs to be effectively planned and supervised.

iii   Sufficient capital:
It is essential to have enough capital not only to finance the initial expenditure on buildings and stock, but also to cover the first year or two:

*a*   There is unlikely to be any return on the capital investment for the first year or two until the young stock are sold.

*b*   It is bound to take several years to establish a reputation, and during this time there will be a constant drain on capital resources.

*c*   Even if the capital is readily available and money is no object, it is advisable to start cautiously.

*Section 2   The Choice of the Mare*
Before deciding to breed from any mare a number of points should be considered: as follows:

i   General appearance:
It is important first to assess the general appearance of the mare, rather than any individual faults, since no animal is fault free.

*a*   Next, the mare's conformation, constitution and temperament and general soundness should be critically examined.

*b*   Only then, should it be decided whether she is fit for breeding.

ii   Balanced judgment:
It is important to avoid any biased judgments.

*a*   Many breeders or owners of animals are genuinely quite unable to see any faults in their own stock, although quick to fault other people's: this is a fatal defect in a breeder.

*b*   It must be accepted that no animal, or human, is perfect and a determined effort must be made to look critically at the mare.

iii   The type of stallion:
If it is decided to breed from the mare, it is then necessary to decide what type of stallion would be best to mate with her:

*a*   It is no use mating a shire stallion and an Arab mare or vice versa: as with Bernard Shaw and the actress, the results might be all wrong, i.e. his legs and her brain.

*b*   Some people seem to have an objection to breeding pure stock and always want to experiment, but there is no future in breeding mongrels.

*c*    If a half bred mare is in question a Thoroughbred, or Arab stallion should be matched with her: there is no future in breeding backwards, i.e. away from perfection.

iv    Complementary points:
It is then necessary to decide which particular stallion to match with the mare (see further under 'Choice of Stallion', Section 3).

*a*    It is best if both mare and stallion are perfect, but since no animal is perfect they should at least be complementary to each other, i.e. one or other should make up the deficiencies of the other.

*b*    Where a mare has a fault, such as a badly set on tail, the stallion should be particularly fault-free.

*c*    Where mare and stallion both suffer from the same fault, the chances are that the foal will have it also.

v    Assessing faults:
It is necessary to distinguish between important faults and unimportant faults as follows:

*a*    If the quarters are sloping, rather than level and broad, as long as they are muscled this is not a serious fault; only if they are short and narrow, therefore weak, is this a serious fault (see pp. 36–37).

*b*    Although sickle hocks are not attractive, they do not detract from speed, or performance, and are only really bad if the hocks are also narrow and weak (see pp. 39–40).

Legs and feet too close together

*c*    If the horse has been over at the knee since birth, this is a sign of strength and is only a serious fault if caused by breaking-down due to hard work (see pp. 30–31).

*d*   Standing back at the knee, which is less easily noticed, is a more serious fault as a sign of weakness.

*e*   A horse with pin toes turning in is unlikely to strike itself, hence, this may be considered a less serious fault than splay feet (see pp. 30–31).

Dishing

Too wide in front

vi   Conformation:

In general conformation, brood mares should be wide and roomy, well-ribbed-up, broad and muscular over the loins and quarters:

*a*   Flat-ribbed, flat-sided, narrow-breasted mares, or those that are herring-gutted, are no use as brood mares.

*b*   Apart from the fact that they have little room for the heart and lungs, which affects their constitution, they have no room to carry the foal.

*c*   A foal from such a mare is bound to be a weak and sickly animal if it survives.

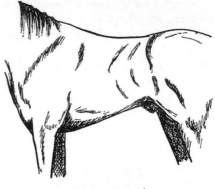

Herring Gutted

vii Constitution and temperament:
The mare's constitution and temperament are also all important, since a nervous, highly strung, poor doer is simply not worth breeding from either:

a  Defective conformation, as above, or general debility in a mare may be a congenital weakness due to bad health or a poor upbringing.
b  There is no point in breeding from such a mare as, even should the foal survive, it will be a poor sickly type itself.
c  The ideal brood mare is a good doer, always healthy and in good condition, with plenty of flesh on her and a calm, easy, confident temperament.

viii Colour:
The colour of the mare is often associated with her constitution:

a  A wishy washy colour tends to go with a weak constitution and a poor doer.
b  A good solid colour, clear and distinct, tends to go with a good healthy constitution.

ix  Soundness and unsoundness:
If the mare is sound, all is well, but, if unsound, this may not matter if the unsoundness has been contracted after birth and is not hereditary:

a  If a mare is lame, for instance, through having injured a muscle in an accident, she is perfectly safe to breed from.
b  Roaring, navicular, sidebones, curbs, ringbone and spavins, though theoretically not transmittable to a foal by heredity, should be looked on with suspicion.

*c*    All cases of defective wind, eyesight, curb, or bone or foot disease are better referred to the vet for his opinion on this point.

x    Difficult breeders:
Some mares are shy breeders, difficult to catch just right. Others have underdeveloped ovaries, or for other reasons are difficult breeders, or may not be able to breed at all:

*a*    Mares that are too fat, or alternatively in too hard condition, may be difficult to get in foal: they should be merely in good natural condition.
*b*    It is important to have the mare examined by a vet to decide her chances of breeding before wasting money on stallions and services.

xi    The aims of breeding:
The breeder should have a picture in his mind's eye of the sort of horse he hopes will result from any particular mating:

*a*    Thus, by knowing the background pedigrees, he should be able to judge if he is breeding for speed, stamina, etc.
*b*    If he is breeding from a hunter, or half-bred mare, he must consider how he wants the foal to develop when he comes to chosing the stallion, i.e. whether larger or smaller, etc.

xii    The Mendelian theory:
If the performance of the dam is good and the performance of the stallion is good, then the foal should also be good:

*a*    According to the Mendelian theory, propounded in 1854, the parents each pass their genes to their offspring and some genes are dominant and some recessive: the dominant genes will prevail in the offspring.
*b*    This is seen most clearly in the matter of colour, where grey is dominant to all other colours, which follow in the order bay, brown, black, chestnut.
*c*    Bay is thus dominant to all colours after it and chestnut is recessive to all the others: thus two chestnuts will produce a chestnut, but crossed with anything else this is unlikely. (Hence, how the Suffolk Punch has remained fixed.)

*Section 3*   *The Choice of the Stallion*
The choice of the stallion also involves a number of points which must be considered carefully, as follows:

i    Assessment of the stallion:
The first step is to look through the stud books of the various societies and study the lists of stallions and their fees:

a    If approached, the owners will be pleased to send particulars of the stallion's pedigree and records.

b    It is desirable to see each stallion and look him over carefully if thinking of using him: he should be particularly strong in any points where the mare is weak (see above).

c    Some stallions will be too expensive, but it does not pay to send a good mare to a cheap stallion, for the better the stallion the better the foal, at least, in theory.

d    It is certainly absurd to go to the nearest stallion simply because of the trouble saved, or the small saving in costs: this is being penny wise and pound foolish.

e    For the 45 guineas saved between a 5 guinea and 50 guinea service, the difference in the values of the respective foals might be several times multiplied: this is even more foolish.

f    It is always best to try to breed up, improve stock, wherever possible, i.e. if breeding from a half bred mare to use a thoroughbred or Arab stallion, rather than simply to cross for the sake of crossing, e.g. with Hackney or Cleveland Bay, or similar stallion.

g    Do not use any stallion that seems short of bone, or of nervous or uncertain temperament.

ii    Affinity with the mare:
There should be an affinity between the stallion and the mares he is covering:

a    Not only should they be complementary to each other, so that the faults of one are countered by strong points in the other (see above) but

b    They should also match reasonably for size, i.e. a 16·2 Thoroughbred stallion should not be covering a 14·2 pony mare, or a Shire stallion an Arab mare:

c    In general, the cold-blooded heavy draught type of horse and the hot blooded Thoroughbred or Arab types do not mix well:

iii    The Number of mares covered:
It is desirable to know how many mares a stallion is covering each year, and it is preferable these should be strictly limited to 40.

a    The premium stallion travelling the county may be serving sometimes up to six mares a day, which is too many.

b    The stallion should be limited both for his sake and the mares, since there is more likelihood of him being fertile.

c    In any event, the stallion chosen should have a good record for fertility.

iv    Fatness and fertility:
It is important that the stallion is fit for his job and in good hard condition:

*a*   A stallion cannot be fat and fertile.

*b*   To serve a reasonable number of mares effectively, he must be as fit and hard as he can be made.

*c*   Stallions may be exercised in hand, or put out in an exercising paddock. Alternatively, there is no reason why they should not be regularly ridden for exercise.

*d*   Liberties should not be taken with stallions, but they should not be treated as if they were liable to explode.

*e*   As far as possible, they should be treated like other horses.

*Section 4   The Service*

The service, or actual mating of stallion and mare, requires careful preparation and forethought.

i   The time for the service:
This is regulated by the fact that the mare has her oestrus periods, i.e. comes into season, for five days every three weeks from January to August.

*a*   The mare's pregnancy last an average of 340 days, or eleven months; the shortest known is 322 days and the longest 419.

*b*   It is desirable to have the foal in the spring, rather than in the bitterly cold weather early on in the year.

*c*   The normal aim will be to foal in April or May, hence, the mare is best covered in May or June.

*d*   An exception is Thoroughbred racing stock, which take their age from January 1st of the year born and are raced as two year olds, when a month or two's extra growth makes vast differences.

*e*   By watching the cycle of the oestrus carefully, it should be possible to take, or send, the mare to the stallion at the right date, but it is not desirable to send the mare away too close to the time, or the cycle may be upset.

*f*   When the mare has foaled, she will start her season again on, or between, the fifth and tenth day and should be sent with the foal at foot if necessary.

*g*   Theoretically, a mare may be covered at any age between 2 and 20, but extremes should be avoided and the mare should not be covered first until fully grown, when she is between 4 and 5.

ii   Reactions of the mare in season:
The reactions of the mare in season are usually obvious enough even to the casual observer:

*a*   The mare is liable to be sluggish and irritable.

 *b* She will object to having her quarters touched, lifting her tail and squealing and discharging small quantities of urine or mucous.

 *c* She will show a marked preference for the company of horses, even geldings: some mares are appalling flirts when in season.

iii The preparation of the mare:
The mare should be presentably groomed and her shoes removed before she is sent to the stud:

 *a* At the very least, her hind-shoes should be removed to prevent any danger to the stallion should she kick out at him.

 *b* It is as well that her head-collar should have her name on it to identify her, if she is unaccompanied.

 *c* She should have been thoroughly wormed to prevent any need for this once she is in foal.

iv The Introduction of mare and stallion:
It is generally advisable to introduce the mare and stallion with a stout barrier between them to prevent the mare lashing out should she be so minded:

 *a* It is generally quite convenient to lead the mare up to the stallion's box with the half door between them.

 *b* This will allow them to become acquainted and will provide a sufficient barrier to prevent a kicking match developing.

v The service:
For this, the mare should be held by one attendant and the stallion brought up within a couple of horse lengths and to one side behind her, so that they can see and smell each other.

 *a* The mare's head should be held high to check her should she show any sign of kicking out.

 *b* The stallion should be wearing a stallion bridle, i.e. bridoon with a divided chain attached to the bridoon rings and to a nine foot webbing or plaited leather leading rein.

 *c* The stallion should be held in position until he is ready and the yard fully showing.

 *d* A young stallion, especially, must be restrained from being too impetuous, to train him that here, also, he must await the command. A young stallion should never be used with a maiden mare.

 *e* The stallion should not normally be kept waiting, but allowed to mount when ready.

 *f* This will almost certainly be done with sufficient force to move the mare forward a few paces and at this stage the stallion handler should move the mare's tail aside and insert the penis correctly.

g  As the stallion gets his forelegs firmly in position, he will grasp the mare's flanks and the actual service will then only take a few seconds.

vi  After completion:
After the successful completion of the service, the stallion should be walked back to his box and the mare walked round for ten minutes or so.

a  This will prevent her getting rid of too much semen, although some will undoubtedly be wasted.
b  This scarcely matters since only one sperm out of millions is required to do the job.
c  Meanwhile, the stallion himself should have his sheath washed out with a mild disinfectant.
d  He may then be exercised in the normal manner: it is a distinct mistake to imagine that the service constitutes sufficient exercise for him.

vii  Checking the success of the service:
When the mare has been successfully served, it is then necessary to wait and see whether she repeats, i.e. comes into season again:

a  If she does, then the whole process must be repeated again.
b  If she does not come into season again, all should be well: she should be in foal: if she has not repeated after nine weeks.
c  It is advisable to take a blood test as confirmation after six weeks, or a urine test after ten weeks: the blood test is the more reliable.
d  When successful, the mare will tend to show signs of increased quietness and docility; as the months pass her stomach should show signs of expansion when viewed from behind.

*Section 5  The Care of the mare in foal*
A great deal must depend on the breed of the mare, but, in general, it is a mistake to pamper the in-foal mare.

i  Working the mare in foal:
Normally, the mare in foal may be worked as usual, though not too hard, for the first six to eight months:

a  Some pony mares and coarse breeds are perfectly capable of working more or less normally up to the last moment and then foaling quite happily by themselves, but this is not recommended.
b  Generally, after six to eight months, the work should be eased off and

259

the mare gradually turned out to grass with only very gentle exercise, preferably walked out, not ridden.

ii   Additional feeding and minerals:
Again, a great deal must depend on the nature and breed of the mare and the strength of her constitution.

a   A sturdy pony mare will probably not require anything in the way of additions to her normal diet, and will still produce a fine healthy foal and show no signs of ill-effects herself.

b   A delicate Thoroughbred mare may require extra feeding from the sixth to ninth month onwards and special care throughout.

c   Every mare in foal should be fed a tablespoonful of cod liver oil every fortnight at the very least.

d   The addition of mineral salts to the feed should in any event be standard procedure, and should be stepped-up during the last months to replace those used in forming the foal's bone.

e   Laxatives should be avoided until the last week or so of the pregnancy when bran mashes may be fed daily.

f   All hay fed to the mare throughout her pregnancy should be of the best quality only.

*Section 6   The Foaling*
Opinions differ as to whether it is best to allow the mare to foal inside or outside.

i   Inside or outside:
A very great deal, once again, must depend on the breed of the animal concerned.

a   With a pony mare or coarser breeds, it is probably as well to have the foal as naturally as possible in the open.

b   With valuable and highly bred animals, such as Thoroughbreds, or Arabs, it is probably advisable to have the foal indoors.

c   If the foaling is indoors, the whole process is more easily supervised and any abnormalities checked immediately.

d   Mares generally foal down in the middle of the night, and will not readily do so in the presence even of their regular attendant: hence it is advisable to stay out of sight until the foal has actually started to arrive.

e   It is desirable not to be continually disturbing the mare in her box, but to watch her progress through a convenient peephole.

ii   The preliminaries:
During the last month, the mare should be sleeping in the foaling box, which should be of ample size (see p. 139).

a    The box should have been very thoroughly disinfected and bedded down with plenty of fresh clean straw.

b    When it appears that the foaling is due shortly, it is advisable to have the mare examined by the vet.

c    He should be able to give an approximate date and advise whether he considers any complications, such as twins, or difficult presentation, to be likely.

d    If he thinks this possible he will be able to note the date and stand by if required.

iii   The preparations:
When it appears that the foaling is imminent, certain preparations should be made:

a    A bucket of warm water and disinfectant, clean towels, sterilised scissors, cottonwool, tape for a navel ligature, and a bottle of iodine will be required for the foaling.

b    An enema syringe, a bottle of liquid paraffin, a bottle of castor oil, a feeding bottle with a large teat, vaseline and disinfectant may all be required shortly afterwards.

c    A bran mash with Epsom Salts in it should be ready for the mare after the foaling.

iv    The signs of approaching foaling:
The signs that foaling is due fairly soon are as follows:

a    The first sign is generally that the udder begins to swell and grow obviously larger.

b    Sometimes, small yellow wax formations appear on the ends of the teats.

c    The vulva may swell very obviously.

d    The muscles on either side of the root of the tail may be seen to have dropped quite noticeably.

e    If at grass, the mare may start wandering off by herself into distant corners of the field.

v    The signs of imminent foaling:
The signs that the foal is due very shortly are:

a    Milk is visible and actually flowing from the teats down the hind-quarters in some cases.

b    The mare will become restless, lying down and then getting up again repeatedly: she will stop eating.

c    She may start kicking at her belly and switching her tail.

    *d*   The vulva is very enlarged and slack.

    *e*   The first labour pains may begin, there may be a discharge of fluids and the bag may appear.

vi  Foaling—first stages:
The actual order of events in normal circumstances is as follows:

    *a*   As long as the attendant can hear the mare munching her hay, there is no need for him to look at her through his peephole.

    *b*   The increasing restlessness of the mare will probably become more and more pronounced.

    *c*   Finally, as already noted, there should be the gush of fluid preceding the appearance of the bag.

    *d*   The mare may be lying down at this stage, but may get up and walk round the box, especially if excited.

    *e*   The foal's forelegs should be the next thing to appear, probably clearly visible inside the bag about a quarter of an hour after the start of labour.

    *f*   This is, in any case, the time for the attendant to enter the box and approach the mare, speaking soothingly to her.

    *g*   If more than twenty minutes have elapsed without further progress, it is probably an abnormal presentation. The vet should be called and by gently inserting a hand washed in mild disinfectant and lubricated with olive oil should be able to ascertain the reason and straighten the legs or head into the correct position.

    *h*   Only if the attendant is highly experienced, should he intercede himself in this way.

vii  Foaling—second stage:
Normally, by this stage, the mare should be alternately straining and resting with her attendant and possibly an assistant in the box with her:

    *a*   The nose and then the head should follow the legs quite smoothly.

    *b*   The shoulders, which come next, are the most difficult part and though it is always advisable to leave it to the mare, it may be thought desirable to give her some help.

    *c*   The forelegs may be gripped in thick towelling and as the mare strains a gentle downwards pull exerted, which should cease as soon as the mare stops straining.

    *d*   Steady pulling when the mare is not straining will do no good and might even damage the mare and foal.

    *e*   Only a little assistance is generally required, and as soon as the shoulders are passed the foal will generally slide out without much further effort.

viii Foaling—third stage:
The attendant should now be supporting the foal as it comes out of the mare:

a   He must remember that as long as the foal is inside the membranous bag it is breathing through the umbilical cord, but as soon as the bag is ruptured it must begin to breath normally.

b   If the bag is ruptured while the foal is still not clear of the mare, there can be a danger that its ribs will be constricted so that it is unable to breathe, but fortunately this is rare.

c   When delivery is complete, the bag should be slit with the fingers and pulled clear of the nostrils and head: and the foal should be encouraged to breathe, if it does not do so at once, by pressing the hindribs and belly at regular intervals.

d   The foal should then be dragged round to the mare's head to allow her to lick it; this also breaks the umbilical cord, as in nature. The mare should then be left in peace until she feels like rising.

e   Although the umbilical cord generally breaks naturally as above, it is sometimes necessary to cut it with scissors and, in any event, this may be done as a precaution against navel ill or joint evil (see p. 344).

f   A ligature should be tied tightly round the cord about an inch below the foal's belly: two ligatures are often tied, one a couple of inches lower, and the cut made between them: the foal's navel is then liberally daubed with iodine on a cottonwool pad.

g   N.B. In normal circumstances with an ordinary delivery the whole process should take only around forty minutes or so.

ix  After the foaling:
Presuming all is well with her, the mare should be left alone, as indicated above, to lick the foal:

a   Should she show no inclination to do this it may be advisable to rub salt on the foal to encourage her; otherwise it may be necessary to dry it off with a towel or soft hay.

b   In any event, the mare will probably be on her feet within half an hour and she should then be given a bran mash and a drink of water.

c   The after-birth may be hanging down and, if so, should be tied up to prevent the mare, or foal, treading in it.

d   It should be allowed to come away by itself, which it usually does in an hour or two: if it fails to do so within four hours the vet should be called: it should never be forcibly removed.

e   The box should quickly have the worst of the soiled bedding removed and fresh straw brought in and placed on top.

*f*    The attendants should then withdraw again and keep a watch on the mare and foal once more; this is one of the few occasions when the upper door of the box might be closed to maintain warmth.

*g*    After struggling to its feet and falling down a few times, the foal will probably find the teats of its own accord.

*h*    If it fails to do so after a reasonable time, it may be necessary to go in and direct its head to the right place.

x    After-foaling complications:
Although in 90 per cent of the cases everything is normal, there are certain after-foaling complications which may arise.

*a*    A very weak foal may not be strong enough to drink, and it is important that it is fed within the first two hours.

*b*    If it is too weak to stand upright, the best plan is to milk off gently some of the mare's milk supply and feed it to the foal direct, either with a bottle and teat, or failing that a teaspoon; it may even be advisable to add a little brandy.

*c*    Another difficult case is when the mare steadfastly refuses to allow the foal to feed: in which case it is necessary to intervene.

*d*    The mare should be bridled and a leg held up while the attendant helps the foal to suck, meanwhile the mare should be soothed and gentled as far as possible.

*e*    A quarter of an hour later another attempt should be made to induce her to accept the foal and this will probably be successful, although cases occur of twenty-four hours or more passing before the mare will accept the foal willingly.

*f*    If the foal has not passed the 'foetal dung' within a few hours, it is necessary to give it a dose of two tablespoonfuls of liquid paraffin, if weakly, or castor oil, if strong, and administer an enema of warm soapy water with a little olive oil added to it.

*Section 7*    *The Care of the mare and foal*
After the foaling, in the normal course of events, the mare and foal should remain in the box for a few days.

i    Putting-out at grass:
On the first fine sunny day, they may be let out for a short while in the nearest suitable paddock:

*a*    The time allowed out each day should be steadily increased until they are out all day.

*b*    In a fortnight, or three weeks, the mare and foal should be sleeping out in a paddock with a suitable shelter box available.

ii    Handling the foal:
From the very earliest stages the foal should be accustomed to handling.

    *a*    When the mare is led out an attendant should lead the foal out alongside, at first with a stable rubber round its neck and an arm round its quarters.

    *b*    In this way, the foal will soon learn to lead quite docilely without any real trouble.

The Foal: First Lessons in Leading

iii    The mare in season:
Between the fifth and ninth day the mare should come into season again:

    *a*    If it is desired to breed from her again, it will probably be advisable to do so as soon as possible and lose no time.

    *b*    It may be decided to send her to the stallion with the foal at foot at once, as soon as it is felt safe to do so.

    *c*    Whether this is after two or three days, or after a fortnight, or three weeks, entirely depends on their condition.

iv    At four weeks:
In about a month, the mare may be put to light work again if desired and the foal may be allowed to run with her.

   *a*   The foal should not be allowed to take too much exercise.

   *b*   Nor should the foal be allowed to suckle when the mare is hot and tired.

   *c*   About this time, the foal will have begun to nibble grass and will also have started to nibble at hay and other foods fed to the mare.

v   During hot weather:
If the months from June onwards prove exceptionally hot and fly-ridden, it may be desirable to keep the mare and foal in during the day and put them out in the evenings.

   *a*   A good thick day bed should be provided for the foal to lie on in the stable during the day.

   *b*   Due account should be taken of the weather and they should not be put out during very heavy rain or thunderstorms.

vi   At six months—weaning:
By about six months, the weaning process should be started:

   *a*   The best method is generally a gradual weaning over a week or so, with the periods of separation gradually extended.

   *b*   Or it may be accomplished simply by an abrupt separation of the mare and foal. But

   *c*   They will require careful penning, out of earshot of each other, and the foal, especially, should be watched to see that he does not damage himself trying to leap out to rejoin the mare.

   *d*   The mare will require her feed cut down and some of the milk taken off her to prevent mastitis or the formation of painful lumps in the udder; a little gentle massage may be required.

   *e*   In either case, the foal is best kept with a companion, if possible, of about his own age.

*Section 8   The yearling and on*
From the point of weaning onwards, the youngster's education should be steadily and constructively continued, but the pace must never be forced too hard; the diet is also important.

i   Worming and feeding:
All foals inevitably become infested with worms, and after weaning the youngster will require worming as a matter of course. He should then be fed liberally.

   *a*   The best hay available should be provided and he should have an hour or two at grass each day.

b  Non-heating foods are best, but in the case of thoroughbred and Arab youngsters (*N.B.* not ponies) 1–3 lbs. of crushed oats with linseed and occasional doses of cod liver oil is desirable.

ii  Training the youngster to lead:
Simply by accustoming the youngster naturally to stable manners, to leading well in a head-collar and to general handling, he very quickly becomes amenable to further training:

a  If training has been carried out from the earliest stages, as suggested above, this follows merely as an extension.

b  He should be led round the manège rails, or indoor school walls, at first at a walk, later at a trot, to accustom him to keeping his quarters in, and neither to pull unduly nor lag behind.

c  The trainer should hold the lead rein firmly, but not pulling on the head-collar and should lead the youngster with the shoulder level to his, while all the time talking encouragingly to him.

d  Pulling on the lead rein will almost certainly have the opposite to the desired effect, and cause the youngster to pull against it.

e  Should the youngster try to pull back, either the trainer or an assistant behind, should simply tap the quarters very gently and thus cause him to move forward at once. There should be no noise, fuss or bother, merely gentle encouragement.

f  Should the youngster forge ahead too fast, or play up, he must be allowed to get it out of his system and the lesson then continued: he will soon learn to lead quietly—about twenty minutes at a time should be the limit to start with.

g  Practise should be given in leading from both sides, and he must learn to lead at a walk and a trot, and also to halt and to move ahead as required.

iii  Stable manners:
The youngster should be regularly handled and stroked all over in the stables as a matter of course; this will accustom him to grooming later on and train him to stand still, move over, or back, thus acquiring good stable manners.

a  In the box, by merely pushing him gently on the shoulder and quarters, while giving the quiet command 'Move over', the youngster may quickly be taught a valuable lesson.

b  This may be carried an important stage further by standing in front of the youngster and pushing gently back against his chest and giving the quiet command 'Move back'.

c  These, and the additional commands 'Stand' and 'Steady', will be quickly understood and accepted, and like the above are invaluable training for the future.

iv The care of the feet:

The youngster must also be accustomed to having his feet picked up and inspected daily as well to having a regular monthly pedicure:

a If the blacksmith calls regularly, he should be asked to check the youngster's feet, rasping or paring them down, as required, as well as tapping them with the hammer, thus generally preparing the way for shoeing at a later date.

b If the blacksmith does not call regularly, the youngster's feet must still be trimmed to prevent them growing misshapen, and to ensure that he will not readily be frightened of being shod in due course.

v Discipline:

The youngster should not be unduly petted and pampered, but should be treated with affectionate commonsense and gentle firmness:

a One school of thought maintains that titbits should never be fed as being liable to encourage bad habits and possibly leading to the youngster being unnecessarily spoiled.

b If the youngster is allowed to expect tibits, it can certainly lead to bad habits, but, here, as elsewhere, in any form of animal training, common sense and a sense of proportion are required: individual circumstances must vary.

c Especially where a youngster has had no previous handling, the quickest way of gaining his confidence may be through his stomach.

d Should the youngster become overfamiliar, or uppity, however, he should be firmly, but gently, disciplined, e.g. nuzzling or nibbling in a friendly way can quickly get out of proportion and should be checked if it shows signs of doing so.

e In most instances of mischievous misbehaviour, a verbal scolding will be enough, but care must be taken that it is not repeated, or is checked beforehand.

f Patience and firmness and still more patience are necessary with the youngster at all times.

vi The degrees of training:

The mistake must not be made of overdoing it and expecting too much from the youngster too soon:

a By the simple stages suggested above, the youngster may gradually be brought half way to being a made horse without any real effort.

*b* Training in lunging, (also spelt lungeing and longeing), may be given as a yearling and the two year old may be accustomed to the bit, the bridle and the saddle.

*c* Full making and schooling should not generally be started before the youngster is four years old and sufficiently grown to withstand the weight of the rider safely.

*d* Much must depend on the breed and the individual youngster concerned, as well as on the trainer.

vii Castration:
Unless required as a stallion for breeding purposes, the young colt must be castrated, i.e. gelded:

*a* It is inadvisable to castrate at six months or so when the youngster is being weaned, or even beforehand, as is sometimes practised: this is likely to be too early a shock to the system.

*b* It is more commonly left until the colt is a year old, when the male characteristics may start to become aggressively and precociously noticeable with mares and fillies.

*c* If the youngster can be kept away from fillies or mares, there may be no harm done in leaving the castration until he is a full two years old, when the male characteristics of conformation are more fully formed.

*d* To leave the operation any later, even though it is quick and simple, is not advisable.

*e* Nor should it be left until the hot weather when the flies are very bad, as it is advisable to turn the youngster out afterwards to allow the wound to drain freely.

*f* The operation should in any event be performed by the vet, and his advice as to timing should be taken.

viii Further education:
No opportunity should be missed of increasing the youngster's education:

*a* He should be walked out and introduced to traffic and accustomed to unusual noises and sights by degrees.

*b* He should also be accustomed to strange horses and dogs, and every opportunity taken of preparing him for his future life.

*c* If he has not been introduced to the horse box, and travel in this way, an early opportunity should be taken to accustom him to it, preferably in the company of an experienced horse.

*d* The younger he is when accustomed to walking up the ramp and entering the box as a matter of routine the better.

e   When he is due to be lunged, or exercised seriously, he should be clipped out and accept that also as a part of his education.

f   Finally, he must be shod and learn to accept that and his new shoes without fuss or bother.

g   Only then is the youngster ready for making and schooling, but by then he is already well on his way to being made a horse and his schooling will be comparatively simple.

### Section 9   The Teeth and Ageing

By studying the teeth, it is possible to gauge the horse's age. The following is a guide (for parts of the teeth, see pp. 23–24):

i   Temporary teeth:
The milk teeth are small and white and have a pronounced neck: They appear as follows:

a   Birth, or soon afterwards: the two Centrals appear in each jaw.

b   4–8 weeks: the two Laterals appear in each jaw.

c   8–10 months: the two Corners appear in each jaw.

d   12 months: all temporary teeth are in wear.

ii   Permanent teeth—up to 5 years old:
The permanent teeth are larger than the temporaries and without such an obvious neck, nor are they as white:

a   2¼–2½ years the Permanent Centrals begin to replace the Temporary Centrals.

b   Rising 3: the Incisors in both jaws meet at the front edges when the mouth is closed.

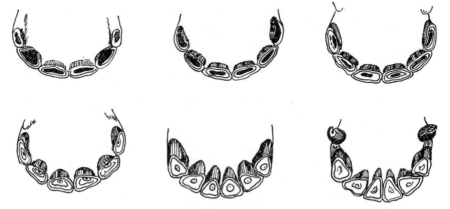

Teeth: (*Top l. to r.*) i. 4 years. ii. 6 years. iii. 8 years. (*Bottom l. to r.*) iv. 12 years. v. About 17 years. vi. About 20 years

c  3 years: the Permanent Centrals are in wear.
d  3½ years: The Permanent Laterals appear.
e  4 years: the Laterals and Centrals are level and in wear at the front edges. The Mark extends across the Table.
f  4½ years: the Corner Milk teeth are replaced by Permanents.
g  4½ to 5 years: the Canines appear.
h  5 years: the Corners are in wear on the front edge only. All teeth are present and the mouth looks neat.

4 years old

iii  From 5 years old onwards:
a  6 years: all are fully developed and in wear: the Marks in the Centrals are becoming smaller. The Upper Corner Incisors extend further beyond the Lower Corner Incisor at the back.

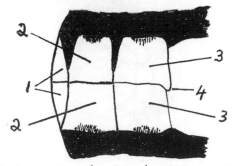

Side view of Incisors: 1. Centrals. 2. Laterals. 3. Incisors. 4. Notch at 7 years

b  Rising 7: the Tables of the Centrals are becoming triangular assuming the shape of the Fang as they wear down. The Marks on the Corners are oblong and show the least wear.
c  7 years: the Corner Incisor in the upper jaw shows a notch where it projects over the corresponding tooth in the lower jaw. The Marks in the Laterals show signs of wearing out.

271

d   Rising 8: in the Centrals, the Fanghole begins to show as a line in front of the Mark. The Marks in the Corners are becoming smaller.

e   8 to 8 off: all Incisors are becoming triangular.

f   9 years: from now on the teeth become longer and lose their neat vertical appearance: the angle at which the upper and lower jaws meet becomes less and the teeth project forward.

The Mouth of an Old Horse

iv  Galvayne's Mark or Groove:

This is a yellowish-brown groove on the outside of the Upper Corner Incisor, which starts from the gum and works downwards with age:

Galvayne's Groove

though not found in all horses, it is a rough guide to age from 10 years onwards as follows:

a   10 years: Galvayne's mark appears.

b   15–16 years: it extends from the gum half way down the tooth.

c   20–21 years: it is the full length of the tooth.

d   25 years: the mark is half grown out, i.e. in the lower half of the tooth only.

e   30 years: the mark grows out completely and disappears.

# PART III
## Making and Schooling

Making and schooling the young horse, like training the rider, must be divided into a series of lessons, as follows:

A   The Preliminary Training: Dismounted
B   The Intermediate Training: Mounted and Dismounted
C   The Advanced Training: Mounted

*Section 1   The Principles of Training*
All animal training is based on the principle of slow progression, one step at a time. The trainer should only advance at a pace that suits the animal and should never be hurried.

i   The training methods:
    By simple association of ideas, rewarding success and scolding failure, by using the horse's own natural instincts, e.g. his gregariousness, by regular repetition and routine without boredom, by patience, by kindness and by sternness when required, the trainer may achieve a high standard of control.

    *a*   The trainer must know beforehand exactly what he is trying to achieve, also the methods most likely to succeed and the likely reactions of the animal.
    *b*   Certain resistances to training are always liable to arise and the trainer must know them and be able to distinguish between them and reactions due to lack of understanding, boredom or too intensive training.

ii   Out-thinking the horse:
    The trainer must always out-think the horse and never allow the youngster to realise that he has won any battle of wills.

    *a*   Even if the trainer has failed to make the youngster do as he wished,

273

he should always end each lesson with some action correctly performed, however simple.

*b*  Once the trainer has decided on the cause of his failure, i.e. incomprehension, obstinacy, boredom, etc., he must take steps to ensure that it is not repeated and that the next lesson is successful.

iii  Self-control:
The trainer must NEVER lose control of his temper:

*a*  It can do no possible good and may do much harm.

*b*  If he feels in danger of doing so, he should return the youngster to the stable until he has recovered himself.

iv  Apparatus:
The use of apparatus, such as dumb jockeys or bearing reins, to achieve quick results is entirely wrong:

*a*  It is likely to result in incorrect head carriage and cramped movement, as well as deadening the mouth.

*b*  Direct control by the trainer, both mounted and dismounted, with recourse to as few such artificial means as possible is likely to have far better results.

*Section 2   The Theory and Practise of Schooling*
The theory and practise of schooling are as follows:

i  The preparations:
For any lesson of any length the preparations should be the same.

*a*  The horse should be quietly led into the school, or manège, there he should be expected to stand while the saddle and bridle are inspected, and the girth, throat-lash and curb-chain all checked.

*b*  The stirrups may then be lowered and the rider may mount, but the youngster must not be allowed to move until the rider wishes him to do so.

*c*  For the first ten minutes or so, the horse should merely be exercised to loosen up his muscles and get into the correct receptive frame of mind.

*d*  A figure of eight at the walk, then a serpentine at a trot, then walking out in circles. After each correct exercise, the youngster should be patted and verbally encouraged; he should also be allowed a minute or so's walking on a loose rein.

*e*  Before each exercise, the youngster must be collected, to prepare him for what is to come, but must never be allowed to anticipate; nor should any movements be so routine that he imagines he knows what is coming in advance; he must be kept interested and controlled.

*f* If the horse does not do what is required, the reasonable answer is that the trainer has failed to put it to him correctly and another means of doing so should be considered and attempted.

*g* In each lesson, it is always advisable to work in a repeat of previous lessons to ensure they are not forgotten and are steadily improved. During the middle of the lesson, when the youngster is at his most receptive, bring in any new work that it is required to teach him: this may be repeated very briefly again just before going in, if possible, correctly.

*h* Never repeat any lessons until the horse gets tired of them. This is especially the case with anything he already does well: slow and steady progress is the best way to improvement, not constant repetition.

ii The timing:
The timing of any lesson is most important.

*a* For the first ten or fifteen minutes, the horse may be exercised to set him in a receptive frame of mind.

*b* For the next ten minutes, the youngster may be worked steadily at a collected and extended trot, in a series of figures, and possibly jumping at intervals.

*c* He should then deserve a short rest of three to five minutes walking on a loose rein.

*d* The next period is spent teaching the youngster whatever new lesson is required to be impressed on him, e.g. the half pass, and twenty minutes may be spent on this. Keep varying the directions, varying the number of paces each time, trotting round the school collectedly for a few paces, halting and then repeating the process, always allowing a brief respite between each exercise. Make much of him on each occasion he does well.

*e* He may now have another ten minutes slow work at the walk on a loose rein, with possibly one or two jumps over poles on the ground taken with the office given.

*f* He is next given some repetition of work done previously: back reining, turns on the hock, and similar points performed correctly. One or two jumps may be added for variety.

*g* Finally, he is walked round for five minutes to let him cool down and a last half pass at the walk for a few paces in either direction, before taking him in to the stable.

*h* There he may be given a titbit before being groomed and made comfortable: the total time has been close on an hour and a half, which is just about right.

iii Hacking:
Hacking also should be made both interesting and a lesson for the youngster:

a No opportunities should be missed of putting lessons to use, i.e. opening gates, with half pass, turns on haunches, etc.

b No route should ever be allowed to degenerate to the stage where the youngster thinks he knows exactly where to change pace; variety is essential here, also.

*Section 3   A Theoretical Training Schedule*
It is, of course, impossible to decree in advance exactly how the training of any particular animal will go—too much depends on individual circumstances—but a theoretical training schedule, over a six month period, might be as follows:

i The preliminary training:

a 1st week: Handling the youngster, picking up his legs and gaining his confidence: accustoming him to the head-collar: oats feed 1–2 lbs. a day.

b 2nd week: Lunging, at the walk and possibly also at the trot. Increasing confidence. Increasing exercise. Oats, 3 lbs. a day.

c 3rd and 4th weeks: Lunging, now at canter. Pole on ground may be added, and also jumping free, if desired. Oats up to 4 lbs.

d 5th and 6th weeks: Lunging continued. Bitting and backing also carried out. Horse accustomed to saddle and rider on his back. Oats up to 5 lbs. a day.

e 6th and 7th weeks: Initial hacking begun to accustom youngster to weight of rider. Also, lunging continued. Oats up to 6 lbs. a day by this time.

f 8th to 9th weeks: Further hacking continued: only aim so far to gain propulsion and muscle youngster. Lunging still continued. Oats up to 7 lbs. a day.

g 10th to 12th weeks: Schooling indoors, mounted and dismounted, begun. First three months completed with advanced schooling still to come. Muscled youngster now ready to begin schoolings.

ii The advanced training:
This again must advance at the pace of the individual horse, but might be something as follows:

a 13th to 14th weeks: Collected walk and halt. Flexion. Hacks. Indoor school work, or manège, in double bridle. Oats 7 lbs.

*b* 15th to 16th weeks: The collected trot. Rein back and turns. All indoor school or manège work at this stage. Oats 7 lbs.

*c* 17th and 18th weeks: The full pass and half pass. Jumping. Repetition of previous training. Oats 7 lbs.

*d* 19th week to 22nd week: The collected canter. Jumps. Repetition of previous work. Oats 7 lbs.

*e* 22nd week to 28th: Change of leg at canter and jumping, with outside work occasionally interspersed. Oats 9 lbs. daily.

iii The application:

This must, of course, vary from horse to horse, depending on innumerable factors, but it is given here so that the reader may attach at least a theoretical time schedule to the ensuing training programme:

*a* The training programme which follows should take at least six months and possibly longer.

*b* It is never advisable to push any training too hard, or it will be found the pupil begins to make mistakes and react against the discipline.

*c* Some horses will find certain items on the programme easy, and others will find them hard.

*d* The trainer must be guided by each horse and take it on at its own pace, as suggested in the following sections.

*Section 4 The Preliminary Training: Dismounted*
*The First Stage*

The first stage of preliminary training, dismounted, is accustoming the youngster to being handled, to wearing a head-collar and to being led, all of which should be satisfactorily completed by careful handling from foaling onwards. However, it is necessary with unhandled youngsters, which have just been allowed to run wild, or semiwild.

i The unhandled youngster:

As the unhandled youngster is now stronger, more self-willed, and probably highly suspicious of man, his preliminary training, even the question of his preliminary handling, becomes that much more difficult.

*a* With particularly wild youngsters, it is generally advisable to let them settle down first in their loose box and become accustomed to stable routine before trying to gain their confidence.

*b* Entering the box and quietly sitting down and reading a book, taking no notice of the youngster at all, will usually cause curiosity to overcome fear in the end.

*c* Once the youngster makes the first approaches, a judicious titbit and

277

soothing use of the voice, combined with gentle handling, should be enough to break the ice.

d    Quiet handling in the box, while accustoming the youngster to the trainer's voice and presence, is the next stage.

e    Accustoming the youngster to the head-collar is simply a matter of gentle perseverance and patience: thereafter leading in hand soon follows, using the same training methods outlined above (pp. 267–270).

f    More time and patience will naturally be required with the unhandled youngster than with the foal or carefully handled yearling, but, given time, the results achieved should be the same.

ii    The results of the first stage:
The results of the first stage of dismounted preliminary training should be a mannered youngster.

a    The youngster should lead well in hand; should change from a walk to a trot on command; should halt, or start again, readily on command.

b    He should have confidence in his trainer and should have begun his general education, becoming accustomed to traffic, and to sights and sounds outside the stables.

c    He should now be ready for the second stage of his dismounted preliminary training, which includes lunging, bitting and backing.

*The Second Stage*
The second stage of the dismounted preliminary training includes lunging, bitting and backing, and an examination of the various tackle required.

i    The lunging tack:
The tack required for lunging (*N.B.* also spelled lungeing or longeing), the second stage of the dismounted preliminary training, is as follows:

a    The lunge line, or rein, is of webbing or lampwick, about twenty-five feet long, with a quick release catch, or strong leather buckle, at one end and a loop at the other.

b    The lunge whip should be four and a half feet long, of cane, steel or fibre glass centre bound with gut, and with a light six foot lash.

c    A strong leather head-collar: this may be preferred to a lunging cavesson with a padded nose-band reinforced with metal, which may jerk a youngster's nose painfully. *N.B.* The lunge line should be attached to the underside of the head-collar, not to the side, or the top of the nose-band.

d    Protective bandages with cottonwool or other padding, brushing boots and overreach boots to prevent any danger of injury.

ii Lunging—outline:
The trainer stands in the centre of the manège and circles the youngster round him at the end of the lunge line.

a    With the aid of the voice and the whip, the trainer starts the horse moving forward freely and halts him as desired.

b    With the aid of the voice and the whip the trainer alters the youngster's paces from a walk to a trot or canter.

c    After a period varying from about fifteen minutes to start with, and eventually extending to forty-five minutes, he halts the horse and reverses the direction of movement.

d    This allows for equal muscular development and prevents the horse becoming one-sided.

e    Lunging exercises the youngster and encourages free forward movement.

Lunging: too far behind (*left*); correct (*centre*); too far in front of horse with whip in wrong hand (*right*)

 *f*  Lunging also improves the youngster's balance and this suppleness and builds up and strengthens his muscles.

 *g*  By forcing the youngster to move in a continuous circle, it supples him laterally and flexes his ribs and neck, as well as bringing his hindlegs under him.

 *h*  Lunging is the best exercise for any horse which may have contracted bad habits, e.g. faulty head carriage due to bad schooling.

iii  Lunging—The first stage: at the walk
An assistant is desirable at first to lead the youngster round in a circle at a reasonable distance out from the trainer.

 *a*  The trainer should pivot round with the horse, holding the lunge line taut and trailing the whip point on the ground behind the horse's quarters.

 *b*  The first few lessons should be conducted at a walk simply to accustom the youngster to the idea.

 *c*  It is also desirable to accustom him to the sight of the whip which may seem very alarming to him at first.

 *d*  The commands 'Waw-awlk' and 'Haw-alt', or any variation, should be given in a particular intonation of voice which should always be adhered to thereafter.

 *e*  As soon as he is walking out well in one direction, the youngster may be halted and brought into the centre for a feed, titbit or to be made much of, as preferred, and then turned round and started off for an equal time in the opposite direction.

 *f*  Only when he is moving out well at a walk and starting and halting on command should the trainer move on to the next stage.

 *g*  Much must depend on the trainer, the youngster and the degree of training achieved hitherto.

iv  Lunging—The second stage: the trot and canter
To encourage the youngster to trot the command 'Ter-ot' may be given with a special intonation.

 *a*  The whip may also be lifted and may be cracked, if desired, but should not touch the horse.

 *b*  Should the youngster begin to canter, the trainer should slow him down gently, repeating the command and keeping the lunge line taut.

 *c*  When the youngster slows down, he should be encouraged to keep trotting before eventually being slowed to a walk and then halted.

 *d*  As indicated above, the youngster should then be exercised at the same pace for a similar period in the opposite direction.

*e*    The best paces for exercise and improving balance and suppleness are a fast walk and steady trot, but a controlled canter is also good.

*f*    This should be encouraged with the use of the command 'Can-tar', which should be given individual intonation, as well as by raising the whip and possibly cracking it behind the youngster.

*g*    The intonation for each command should be clearly distinguishable, as it is to this the youngster will react, not to the words, which, of course, mean nothing to him.

v    Constantly turning into the centre when lunging:
As with any form of training, the horse may develop certain forms of resistance to lunging and these should be known beforehand, with their appropriate counters.

*a*    One of the most tiresome forms of resistance to lunging is when the horse develops the habit of constantly turning in to the centre.

Lunging: Correct. Quarters outside track (*wrong*). Quarters inside track (*wrong*)

*b*    This is generally due to indiscriminately providing titbits, which should be fed only if earned by good work, not automatically provided each time the horse turns into the centre.

*c*    In effect, the horse has been trained to act in this way and cannot justly be blamed: it is the trainer's fault entirely.

*d*    The horse should be prevented from turning in by keeping the whip pointed at his shoulder or behind his girth.

*e*    When he shows any sign of turning in, he should be verbally checked and urged on with a touch of the whip behind the hocks.

*f*    Should he turn in despite this, then simply turn him straight round and set him going at once in the opposite direction.

*g*    On no account allow him to stop, or, worse still, feed him, or the habit will become even more deeply rooted and harder to eradicate.

vi    Other resistances to lunging:
The other commoner resistances to lunging which may be encountered

(and, like those above, they are primarily due to bad handling) are as follows:

*a*   Breaking excitedly into a near-gallop can very readily prove an effective resistance with a weak trainer.

*b*   It is probably due to mishandling the whip and ineffectual control following the horse's reactions.

*c*   This is purely a question of control and the trainer must not allow himself to be dragged about off-balance or lose his nerve.

*d*   The weight should be leaned against the lunge line and the whip kept down.

*e*   As soon as the horse slows to a canter, the command 'Can-tar' may be repeated, and as the horse tries to slow to a trot the whip may be raised.

*f*   The horse's reactions should be carefully gauged and finally, as he wishes to trot, the command 'Ter-ot' may be given and he may be eased. Do not, however, let him decide the pace at any time.

*g*   Rearing may be cured by touching under the belly with the whip and is generally due to light-heartedness, though it may be persisted in if found to intimidate a weak trainer.

*h*   Kicking out, or bucking, may be dealt with by verbal scolding if persisted in, but should generally be ignored as merely an exhibition of high spirits.

vii  The results of lunging:
Lunging teaches the youngster to respond to the trainer's voice commands and to alter pace to them alone:

*a*   It also helps to build muscle and generally balance and supple the young horse.

*b*   The youngster not yet ready for backing may be exercised and schooled by lunging to the stage where he is quite ready for it.

viii Jumping:
To balance the youngster further, and to build up his muscles, there is no harm in starting him jumping at this stage. This may be done in two ways:

*a*   The youngster may be lunged over a jump, or he may be turned down a jumping lane and encouraged to jump free.

*b*   The jumping lane need only consist of an outer railing or wall on each side for some fifteen or twenty yards with one or two jumps set across it.

*c*   In either case, the youngster should only be expected to leap over a pole lying on the ground in the first instance.

*d* He may be led up to it and allowed to inspect it beforehand and then, finally, led over it, first at a walk, then at a trot.

*e* The jump may then be raised to six inches and the youngster shown it again and the performance repeated. If necessary, he may be given a lead over it by another horse.

*f* It will only be a matter of a few days before he is jumping eighteen inches, and for the moment that should be sufficient.

ix Intermediate steps before backing:
Bitting, bridling and fitting a saddle are necessary intermediate steps before backing the young horse.

*a* The youngster should be lunged with bit, bridle and saddle; thereafter, backing is the final stage before being ridden.

*b* At one time, long-reining was another intermediate stage commonly practised, sometimes with the use of a dumb jockey and bearing reins as well (see xi and xii below), but this is now unusual.

x Bitting:
Bitting is accustoming the youngster to accept the bit without objection and is a further step towards making the schooled horse.

*a* The first step is to measure the youngster's mouth (see p. 73), and make sure that a suitable mouthing bit is available.

*b* A mouthing bit used to accustom the youngster to the feel of a bit in his mouth may be either a broad wooden bar type bit, or else a keyed bar—or snaffle—bit with long cheekpieces.

*c* Some trainers prefer the broad wooden bar type, which is light and mild, and prefer to leave this on the youngster in the stables for some time to accustom him to it.

*d* Other trainers prefer the keyed bit, bar or snaffle, which will encourage the youngster to play with the keys and tends to keep him preoccupied rather than fussing with the bit: this also tends to keep the mouth moist, which is desirable.

*e* What may suit one youngster and one trainer may not suit others, and it is probably wisest to see what seems to suit the individual youngster best.

*f* A useful tip is to smear the bit with syrup to encourage the youngster to accept it willingly.

*g* The youngster should also be lunged with the bit in his mouth to accustom him to it further.

*h* Thus, the youngster may be bitted at any period in the second stage of dismounted training, and if it is desired to use the long reins on the youngster they may then be used.

xi   The long reins:
The long reins are a matching pair of reins similar to the lunge line, some twenty-five feet long, of webbing or lampwick, with stout buckles at one end and a strap and buckle at the other to join them.

a   When used, they should be buckled direct to the cheekpieces of the bit.
b   They are generally led through rings mounted on a back pad, held in place by a surcingle, but the back pad may be dispensed with altogether.
c   In the early stages, the horse is simply lunged in the manège in the normal way with the long reins, first one way and then the other.
d   The next stage is walking round the school with the youngster being driven in front on the long reins.
e   It is possible to use the reins as if riding, i.e. feeling the horse's mouth as if on his back, not exerting a steady pressure as in driving.
f   Due to the natural drag of the length of rein, it is, however, very easy, unless great care is taken, to make the horse's mouth either one-sided or dead. Experience is important, and long reins are better omitted unless the trainer is sure of his skill.
g   Most horses trained in this way would have been better made and schooled from the horse's back, always assuming the trainer to be a finished rider.
h   By long-reining, a youngster's training may be carried a stage further before it is fit to be ridden: it is also one way an adult can school a pony unable to stand their weight.

xii  The dumb jockey, bearing reins and side reins:
The dumb jockey, in effect, is an extension of the long rein pad fitted with a cross-piece, to which are affixed bearing reins or side reins exerting continuous pressure on the bit unless the head is held as required: the apparatus is used with long reins.

a   The whole principle is artificial and ill-conceived resulting in incorrect flexion and incorrect head carriage, also, very probably, a dead mouth.
b   Apparatus of this nature has no part in making and schooling a horse and should not be used by any modern trainer.
c   The use of side reins with a body roller and pad is sometimes recommended when lunging the youngster, but, as with the use of bearing reins, can have thoroughly undesirable effects.
d   The side reins are attached to the cheekpieces of the bit and with a rubber insert are attached to the body roller.

*e*  They are supposed to keep the head straight and maintain the correct head carriage, but, inevitably, this interferes with the correct lateral movement of the horse when turning in a circle.

*f*  If adjusted too loosely to affect the issue one way or another, they are clearly useless anyway.

*g*  If adjusted too tightly, they may do untold damage to the mouth and correct head carriage.

*h*  All such mechanical devices are best left well alone, since they can only, at best, achieve a cramped imitation of correct head carriage and may do a great deal of harm.

xiii Backing:
Backing is the last stage of the preliminary dismounted training before the mounted making and schooling can begin. It is simply the process, once the youngster has been accustomed to the saddle on his back, of accustoming him to the weight of the rider.

*a*  The numnah, or pad, may be placed on the horse's back first and, once he is accustomed to that, the saddle may follow.

*b*  Once accustomed to it in the stable, it may be lightly girthed and the youngster lunged in it with bridle and bit as well.

*c*  While an assistant holds the youngster's head, the trainer may then lay his weight across the saddle for a few seconds, dismounting before the youngster has had time to become restive.

*d*  If this experiment is accepted calmly the trainer may repeat it for a longer period; the youngster may then be lunged.

*e*  On the next occasion, the trainer may actually mount briefly and allow the youngster to grow accustomed to his presence on his back, soothing him all the time with his voice.

*f*  The final stage is for the trainer to mount and allow the assistant to lead the youngster round with the trainer mounted and reins in hand.

*g*  The first mounted lessons then follow in due course, though regular lunging should still remain an important part of the youngster's curriculum.

*Section 5    The Intermediate Training: Mounted and Dismounted Outdoor Work*
The early mounted schooling should aim at accustoming the green youngster to his rider and the outside world, as well as muscling him, suppling him and preparing him for more advanced training.

i  The object:
The object at this stage should not be schooling so much as muscling,

suppling and balancing the youngster, and accustoming him to his rider's weight.

a    He should be accustomed to the use of the legs to provide impulsion, and also the pressure of the legs to make him halt, as well as the appropriate aids with the reins and voice, but that is as far as the schooling should go at this stage.

b    He should be accustomed to his rider mounting and dismounting, both in the indoor school, or manège, and the open, and he must learn to accept this without attempting to move.

c    The youngster should have plenty of steady walking, especially across country, both uphill and downhilll, with his hocks well under him, which will help to muscle him and prepare him for more advanced work.

ii    The bridle and bit:
At this stage of schooling, it is essential only to use a snaffle-bridle: the double-bridle is too severe.

a    The double-bridle may be used in serious schooling later on, but at this stage it is too easy to make mistakes and damage the youngster's mouth, however good the rider may be.

b    Too early use of the double-bridle may cause the youngster to get 'behind the bit', 'over the bit', or 'over-bent', i.e. flexing the neck too much. If this happens, the youngster will then have to be reschooled.

c    Even the ordinary snaffle, with its nutcracker action, may prove too severe for some horses' sensitive mouths, more especially those with free movement.

d    A broad bar snaffle, a vulcanite snaffle or rubber snaffle may be more suitable in such cases.

iii    Humouring the youngster:
When things go wrong at this stage, it is important to humour the youngster rather than try to create instant obedience.

a    When the youngster shies, baulks, or otherwise reacts quite unexpectedly and unpredictably, as he often will, at some totally innocuous object, such as a stone by the roadside, he should not be scolded in any way.

b    Rather than try to force him past it using legs and voice and making an issue of the matter, it is important at this stage to humour him.

c    Let the trainer dismount at once and lead him up to the object to examine it, smell it, paw it or snort at it as he wishes.

*d*   Then take him back and remount and urge him gently past it and thereafter there should be no more trouble, at least with that particular object.

*e*   By this means, the youngster's horizons will be broadened and, so long as no issue is forced, he will not develop any resistances or aversions to traffic or wayside objects.

*f*   By riding in fields adjacent to heavy traffic on main roads, he may become accustomed to this also without trouble.

*g*   Whenever possible, the trainer should take the advantage in outdoor work of letting the circumstances teach the youngster some important lesson for the future.

*Schooling Indoors: Mounted*
The early lessons in the school, or manège, should also chiefly be with a view to muscling, suppling and balancing the youngster.

i   The aids to advance and to halt:
The youngster must be taught the meaning of these, but should not otherwise be schooled at this stage.

   *a*   To advance: the heels are used behind the girth and the reins eased slightly.

   *b*   To halt, or reduce speed: the youngster is collected with pressure from both legs, and the reins are felt more strongly until the change is made.

ii   The aim:
The aim of the schooling at this stage should be to improve the youngster's balance and impulsion.

   *a*   The young horse should be urged to step out freely, and the rider should concentrate on keeping the youngster's body straight.

   *b*   Turns at this stage should be made by moving the rein to the side required, not pulling back, and possibly losing impulsion. At the same time, the opposite rein should be moved against the neck, i.e. 'neck-reined'.

   *c*   The various school exercises, the serpentine, circles in corners, figures of eights, and others, should be carried out at a walk without skimping, but at this stage only at a walk: it is too early to expect collected trotting.

   *d*   The horse must be made fit and brought into condition before any real work can be expected of it, even simply bearing the rider's weight for long.

iii   Easing the youngster:
The youngster must never be overtaxed, and it is important to watch out for signs of strain.

    *a*   If sweat forms on his neck in little beads, he is being overtaxed—healthy sweat merely damps the neck and does not form globules—and he should be eased off at once.

    *b*   Any work at the trot should be conducted while posting to ease the pressure on the youngster's back, and the diagonals should be frequently changed to avoid any danger of one diagonal becoming overworked.

    *c*   The youngster at this stage is like an athlete being trained, and his preparation must be gradual. Equally, it must vary from horse to horse and what suits one may not suit another.

    *d*   The bulk of this initial training, however, is better outside; only a small part should be in the school or manège.

*Schooling Indoors Dismounted*

Some of the more important points of training may now be instilled while dismounted, if preferred to mounted schooling.

i    The rein back:
It is advisable to practise the rein back first alongside a wall of the manège to help keep the youngster straight.

    *a*   The trainer should stand in front of the horse with the reins held in one hand beneath the jaw.

    *b*   The lunging whip may be held in the other hand to simulate the leg aid and keep the quarters straight.

    *c*   Gently encourage the youngster to lower its head and flex its jaw, at the same time touching the flank with the whip and saying 'Back' in firm tones.

    *d*   Almost certainly, the horse will take a pace backwards with no difficulty and he should then be made much of by the trainer.

    *e*   No more should be demanded from him on that occasion, but on the next occasion two strides may be taken with an interval for praise between them.

    *f*   Do not let the youngster move his whole head back to escape the action of the bit, i.e. get behind the bit.

    *g*   Do not overdo this training at the start.

ii   Teaching flexion:
Flexing exercises can be carried out dismounted and are much favoured by some trainers.

a   The snaffle-reins are held in the left hand in front of the horse's nose: the curb-reins in the right hand below the jaw.

b   The curb-rein is pulled gently until the horse yields its jaw and bends its head from the poll.

c   The snaffle-rein is used to prevent any lowering of the head, or bending it back too far.

d   This exercise should not be overdone, and it is wise to be content with very slight movement at first.

iii   Turning on the forehand:
This is a simple movement to teach the youngster while dismounted:

a   The reins are held and the trainer faces the horse while holding the forehand still.

b   The quarters are urged round in whichever direction is required using the lunging whip to stimulate the leg on the flank.

c   Since most youngsters are in any event heavy in the forehand, it is inadvisable to practise this movement unduly.

iv   Lunging over jumps and free:
Further lunging over jumps, and free in the jumping lane, may be carried out with a view of muscling and balancing the youngster:

a   The jumps may now be put up to two feet and the youngster should be enjoying them.

b   Free-jumping may also be increased, if there is a suitable jumping lane available.

## Section 6   *The Advanced Schooling: Mounted*
Once the youngster is judged to be sufficiently muscled, suppled and balanced, his serious schooling can begin.

## *The Double-Bridle*
For the youngster's serious schooling, most of which will take place in the indoor school, or manège, the double bridle is essential:

i   The fit:
It cannot, of course, be overstressed that the fit must be perfect, neither too large nor too small.

a   Any sign of pinching the lips, or being too large and sliding across the bars of the mouth, causing one-sided mouth, must obviously be avoided.

  *b* With a good fitting double-bridle the youngster will generally accept it quite quickly.

  *c* The curb-chain may be leather or rubber covered to prevent undue pressure in the chin groove.

ii The action and use:
  The action has already been examined at length, (pp. 67–69), but with the youngster certain points must be remembered regarding use.

  *a* For most purposes the snaffle-reins will be sufficient in the early stages; the bit-reins will be barely employed at all.

  *b* Undue use of the bit and curb may have very severe effects on the youngster's sensitive jaw and may cause him to get 'behind the bit' or 'overflexed'.

iii The snaffle and drop Nose-band:
  As mentioned above (p. 75) there are those who advocate the use of the snaffle and drop nose-band for schooling, even for advanced school work:

  *a* Although the combination of snaffle and drop noseband is undoubtedly a very useful one, it cannot compare with the effect of a double-bridle in sensitive hands.

  *b* The delicate degrees of feeling, and the exact placing of the horse's head, may be very much more readily achieved with the double-bridle.

  *c* On the other hand, if the trainer is dubious of his ability to use the double-bridle effectively enough in the first instance, he might be wisest to use the snaffle and drop nose-band throughout, then later school the horse with the double-bridle.

*Flexion and the Collected Walk and Halt*
These are bound up with each other as follows:

i Flexion:
  This is the action of the horse when it relaxes, or flexes, its lower jaw to the pressure of the curb, while carrying its head correctly with the neck high and bent at the poll.

  *a* When the horse has its head straight, correctly held and the jaw relaxed, this is known as 'direct flexion'.

  *b* When turning at a collected pace with the inner rein felt more strongly and the horse's head slightly turned in that direction, this is known as 'lateral flexion'.

  *c* If the jaw is open, but the head carriage is incorrect, e.g. overbent, this is not correct flexion. In this instance, the youngster is getting 'behind the bit', a bad fault, since it means the rider has no control: the youngster should be urged forward by strong leg pressure at once.

ii   The collected walk:
The youngster must be sufficiently free moving and responsive to the legs and ready to flex his jaw willingly enough before teaching the collected walk:

Before Flexing

a    When carrying out the exercises recommended above at a walk, the occasional flexion will be felt unmistakably as the lower jaw gives to the bit.

Flexed

b    This indicates the youngster is ready to be taught flexion properly at a collected walk.
c    He must be impelled forward with the legs and held back with the reins, until his nose drops and his jaw relaxes.

*d* He should then promptly be rewarded by dropping the reins and walking on.

*e* By degrees, the number of paces at a collected walk may be very gradually increased, then the youngster should be urged on at an extended walk with loose rein.

This is very tiring for youngster and trainer and progress must be very gradual, but eventually he should be able to walk round the school once or twice at a collected walk.

iii The collected halt:
This is a natural follow-on from the collected walk.

*a* The youngster should be taught to stand with the head held correctly and jaw flexed.

*b* He is then ready for any movement that may be required of him.

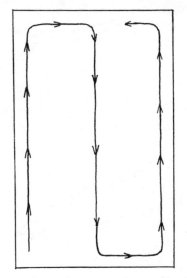

Using right angle turns to change direction

*The Collected Trot, the Rein Back, the Turns*
The next stage in advanced schooling include the above, as follows:

i The collected trot:
The collected trot improves the youngster's balance and combined with regular changes of direction causes him to use his quarters more, giving a freer action and a lighter forehand:

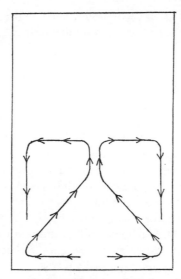

Reverse Changes of Hand

a   From trotting at a normal eight miles an hour, the youngster must now be slowed down to a trot of about six miles an hour.

b   The youngster's hocks must be forced under him with increased leg pressure, thus forcing him up to the bit and raising his head carriage slightly.

c   This is a very tiring exercise for the young horse, and should not be carried out at first for more than a dozen or so paces.

d   The pace may then be altered to an extended trot of about ten miles an hour and the youngster encouraged to trot in the varied school exercises already practised at a walk.

e   The pace should be varied frequently and the youngster sometimes halted, then moved on again in another direction.

f   The legs are all important both in urging the youngster forward and keeping the quarters from flying out at the turns.

g   Neck-reining should still be practised, but the reins may now be given direct pressure for change of direction

h   After these exercises, the youngster should be allowed to walk or trot quietly with a loose rein, stretching out his head and neck as he wishes to ease the tired muscles.

ii   The rein back:
The rein back, or back-reining, is amongst the most important suppling and

balancing exercises for the youngster, encouraging him to get his hocks underneath him and lightening his forehand. It should be taught mounted as follows:

a    The youngster should be halted facing the wall of the school or manège, and made to stand collectedly.

b    Both legs are then closed firmly behind the girth, a little further back than normally applied.

c    At the same time, a slight even pressure is applied to each rein simultaneously and the voice command 'Back' is given.

d    The youngster will then generally back a pace without further trouble, or the need for a dismounted assistant as often recommended.

e    No more than one pace should be expected on the first occasion and the youngster should be made much of by the rider, but then should promptly be collected again and set moving forward.

f    He may then be halted again and another backwards step made; the number taken should be gradually increased, but always varied to avoid it becoming a habit only to take a certain number.

g    The youngster should be kept straight by the pressure of the legs: he should then always be moved on again afterwards at a collected pace.

h    He may be halted, then backed, from any pace, then urged on again: this is an excellent balancing exercise.

iii    The turn on the forehand:
The turn on the forehand is the first occasion a single leg aid is used:

a    The youngster should be halted along side the wall of the school or manège: the wall to the horse's left side at first.

b    Using pressure on both reins to prevent forward movement, the left leg should be used with considerable pressure behind the girth, the right leg remaining inactive.

c    The horse will not understand what is required and his head should be turned slightly towards the wall, while the whip may be applied smartly once or twice just behind the rider's leg.

d    This will almost certainly have the effect of forcing the youngster to take a step or two with his quarters away from the wall.

e    This should be accepted as sufficient and he should be made much of, then walked round the school and the lesson started again on the opposite side of the school or manège.

f    The whip should be discontinued as soon as it is no longer required, and very soon the youngster will be able to make a complete turn either way on the forehand.

*g* This should always be done at the halt as highly dangerous on the move.

*h* Once it can be performed successfully, the turn on the forehand should seldom be executed being a useless form of exercise for the horse.

iv The turn on the hocks:

The turn on the hocks, or haunches, is the next lesson to be taught the youngster. It teaches him to get back on his hocks when turning; a most important aspect of training.

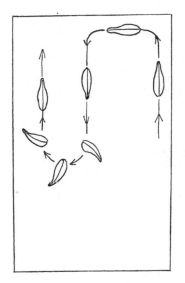

Turn on the Haunches

*a* To teach this, initially, it is desirable to have the youngster halted in a corner of the school or manège, one wall on the horse's left, the quarters in the corner.

*b* The right rein is pulled in a sideways direction and the left rein supports this by neck-reining.

*c* The right leg remains static, but the left leg applied in front of the girth presses the horse towards the right and this may be enforced with a touch of the whip on the left shoulder.

*d* The horse cannot move backwards and is in any event impelled forwards if he tries this, and therefore hesitantly moves a pace or so to the right with his forehand.

*e* The body weight should be slightly backwards pinning the right hindquarter so that the youngster is forced to pivot on it.

*f* The horse is then made much of and walked round the school to practise the same lesson on the other side.

*g* The lesson must next be practised in the open, as the horse grows more accustomed to it, but, as with the turn on the forehand, this must be a gradual process and should not be hurried.

*h* The natural tendency in the open is for the youngster to move his forehand one way and his quarters the other, i.e. turn on the centre, but this must be resisted and the quarters held firmly in position with the hocks collected well under the horse.

*The Full Pass or Passage*

The full pass, or passage, is the movement of the horse sideways without any forward progression: it is extremely useful and practical and improves the horse's collection, bearing and suppleness.

*i* The aids:
Although difficult for the horse to perform, the passage is, in practise, readily enough understood by the horse. The aids to move to the right when the youngster is halted are as follows:

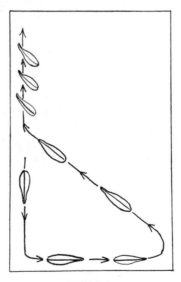

Full Pass

*a* The right rein should be pulled sideways and in practically the same instant the left leg should be applied behind the girth, to push the horse's quarters to the right and the rider's weight should be slightly inclined to the right.

b   N.B. This is the first use of the diagonal aids, i.e. the opposing leg and rein, which are much used in advanced schooling.

c   The opposing rein, i.e. the left rein, should neck-rein to the right and later on the neck-reining and slight pressure of the right rein will be sufficient.

d   The right leg must provide impulsion and keep the horse up to his bit; it must also control the sideways movement and prevent the horse moving too rapidly to the right.

e   N.B. The side steps should be steady and even: the horse should cross the left legs in front of and across the right legs.

f   The horse's head should be very slightly flexed in the direction of the movement and the forehand must always lead the quarters, otherwise the horse will be behind his bit.

g   For both the above reasons, the rein aid should slightly precede the leg aid.

h   To move to the left, the aids are reversed and the horse's movements are similarly reversed.

ii   Teaching the full pass:
The method of teaching the youngster the full pass may be as follows:

a   Halt the youngster facing the wall of the indoor school or manège, and apply the aids as outlined above: he will then take a hesitant step or two sideways.

b   He should at once be made much of and walked round the school or manège before being halted again and the aids reversed to obtain the same results in the opposite direction.

c   N.B. At this stage, it may be best to take the youngster on to learning the half pass, which will now come easily, and perfect that at a walk before returning to perfect the full pass.

d   The next stage is to turn the youngster round facing the centre of the school or manège, and continue the practise, gradually increasing the number of steps taken.

e   The youngster should never be asked to do too much, and the lessons should be interspersed amongst other forms of schooling, particularly including the half pass (see p. 299).

f   The horse should always be passaged an equivalent distance in each direction to maintain an even balance, and not more than a dozen steps should be expected without a rest.

g   The feature to aim at, in particular, is a quick and easy change from passaging in one direction to passaging in the other; this is known as 'the counter change of hand'.

h  The horse should be halted from the walk, trot or canter, and passaged three or four paces in one direction, then three or four paces in the other, possibly with a turn on the centre in between. The forward movement may then be continued: this is an excellent suppling and balancing exercise.

iii  Common faults:
There are certain faults which are likely to arise which should be avoided.

a  It is a common fault in riders to hold their opposing leg, i.e. the leg not providing pressure, stiffly away from the horse, thus failing to exercise correct control or provide impulsion to keep the horse up to his bit.

b  If the horse's head is not turned towards the direction of the movement, i.e. away from it, the horse is behind his bit and the whole benefit of the exercise is lost.

c  Care must be taken with this and other movements that the youngster does not begin to anticipate the aids; even though this indicates willingness to please, it must not be allowed: he must be made to wait for the correct application of the aids before moving.

d  The horse should not be at a direct 90° angle when passaging but the head should be slightly preceding the hindlegs.

iv  Terms used in the passage:
There are certain technical terms used to describe the horse's or rider's actions when passaging.

a  When moving at full pass, or half pass, the horse is said to be moving 'in two tracks', i.e. the fore- and hindlegs each move parallel to the other.

b  When the horse's head is facing the wall of the indoor school or manège, he is said to be moving with 'shoulder out'.

c  Conversely, when the horse's head is facing into the centre of the indoor school or manège, he is said to be moving with 'shoulder in'.

d  A horse may thus be passaged to the right or left, with shoulder in or out.

e  N.B. The above terms are widely understood and accepted in this country, but originated as the result of an incorrect translation and understanding of the continental terms 'renvers' and 'travers'; these terms have a quite different meaning referring to a flexing exercise not 'in two tracks', hence, are not interchangeable with the British terms.

*f*   When the horse is changed from either pass or half pass in one direction to pass or half pass in the other, it is known as the 'counter change of hand'.

*g*   The turn of the head in the direction of the movement is known as 'lateral flexion'.

## The Half Pass

The half pass is a sideways movement in two tracks also, but the horse should gain as much ground forward as to the side, hence, moving at about 45° to the direction in which he is facing. It is easier for the youngster to execute than the full pass, so some trainers prefer to start with it, but this is a matter of opinion.

i   At the walk:
Once the youngster has begun to master the full pass successfully, it is time to start teaching the half pass.

*a*   The aids are the same as for the full passage, except that the inner leg pressure is stronger to cause forward movement with each stride and similarly the pressure felt on the right rein is less.

*b*   As with the full pass, the progression should be gradual and equally divided between right and left.

*c*   Starting with two or three steps, the number may be increased to around a dozen, until the youngster can half pass across the school or manège.

*d*   Once he can successfully pass freely from left to right and change from one direction to the other, i.e. 'the counter change of hand', practise may take place anywhere, in the school or out of it.

*e*   It is probably best at this stage to continue more intensively with the full pass until that also is mastered.

*f*   Like the full pass, this is a valuable exercise as well as being extremely useful, e.g. opening gates, etc., but note the faults in 4iii above.

ii   At the trot:
Once the half pass has been mastered at the walk, it may be practised at the trot:

*a*   The aids are the same, with increased impulsion and collection, and the rider must sit with the horse, weight slightly inclined in the direction of movement.

*b*   The horse should have little difficulty in understanding what is required if the trainer applies the correct aids.

*c*   The full passage at the trot should not be attempted, at least at this stage, being more correctly a high school movement, as is all fast work on two tracks.

## The Collected Canter

The canter is the most difficult pace for the horse to perform collectedly and should be the last to be taught.

i  Striking off with the desired leg leading:
Since the horse is already collected at the walk and trot, there should be no real difficulty in obtaining a collected canter at once.

    *a*   To strike off with the off-fore leading, start the youngster from a walk moving into a corner to the right. i.e. clockwise.

    *b*   The aids are the left, or outside, leg giving firm impulsion behind the girth, and the right, or inside, leg giving impulsion on the girth to force the horse forward. The feel stronger on the right rein; i.e. a diagonal aid.

    *c*   To accentuate this for the youngster, it is necessary to raise the right rein upwards, to raise and, hence, lighten, the forehand and by moving the hands to the left increase the weight on the near-fore and lighten the off-fore.

    *d*   This should force the youngster to lead off with the off-fore leading and the head correctly flexed.

    *e*   Should he somehow strike off wrongly, or merely trot, then he must be halted and the lesson started again until successful.

    *f*   To obtain the near-fore leading, the aids must be reversed. *N.B.* See p. 119 on lateral aids for the canter.

    *g*   A steady collected canter a few times round the school should be enough, and then the horse should be halted and cantered in the reverse direction.

    *h*   Steady slow progression will ensure the correct leg is used as desired.

ii  Exercises at the canter:
It is important, once the horse has learned to lead off with the correct leg as desired at the canter, to exercise the horse correctly.

    *a*   To start with, circles round the school are sufficient, then the size of the circles is reduced, helping to increase the horse's balance and collection.

    *b*   Once the circles are quite small, the aids for the half pass may be given at the canter and the horse taken across the school collectedly at the canter: to side step from left to right the off-fore must be leading and vice versa.

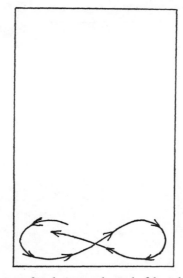

Figure of Eight Using the End of the School

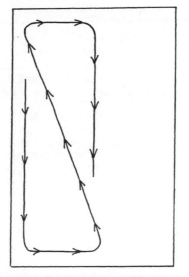

Figure of Eight Using Half the School

c   It is important at this stage not to canter false, or to lead with the wrong leg at any time, in order not to confuse the youngster; hence, after crossing the school at the canter, the horse must be halted and walked, not cantered into the corner incorrectly.

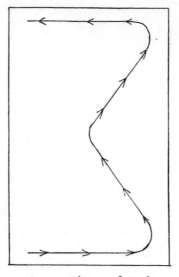

Counter Change of Hand

*d* When cantering round correctly, the horse must be halted; made to walk collectedly for a few paces then started off again on the correct leg as before.

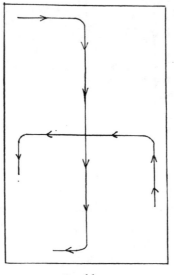

Doubler

*e*  The direction is, of course, reversed and similar lessons are given in the other direction to ensure that the youngster knows the aids automatically without any mistakes.

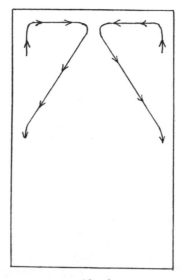

Half Volte

*f*  The number of paces at the canter may be progressively reduced to about six or so, then the horse may be halted and started on the other leg, but not yet taken into a corner cantering false. The object at this stage should merely be changing the leg correctly to the aids when starting to canter.

*g*  By this time, the youngster should be cantering very collectedly and well; slowly with an even collected stride, hocks well under and good head carriage bent at the poll and good flexion.

iii  Change of leg at the canter:

The change of leg at the canter should be done in the air and the sequence should be as follows:

*a*  By this time, the trainer should be cantering with the inside rein felt very slightly more strongly, so that the jaw can be felt flexing at each stride: the impulsion should be maintained by the inside leg, but the outside leg, or diagonal aid leg, will be in contact behind the girth supplying pressure and ensuring that the correct leg is leading.

*b*  To change the leg, the aids must be reversed. Thus, when cantering to

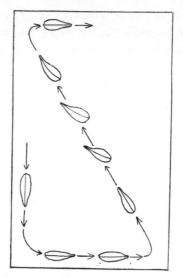

First Lesson in Changing Leg at the Canter

the left, the horse must be collected firmly with the right leg closed behind the girth, the left rein felt more strongly and the left leg closed behind the girth.

c   The youngster must be ridden on a diagonal across the school or manège, and, as he goes into the opposite bend at the precise moment when he is swinging out his leading near-fore in front, clearly visible from the rider's viewpoint, the aids must be reversed, as above.

d   To ensure that the youngster changes behind as well as in front it is as well to make the leg aid change a fraction earlier than the hands change.

e   The horse should then be halted and made much of, then collected and walked round the school, before repeating the lesson in the opposite direction.

f   Gentle repetition will soon ensure that the horse changes leg correctly as required.

iv  Faults that may occur:
However careful one may be, inevitably faults may arise and the commoner are as follows:

a   If the youngster shows he is upset at any point in this training, the trainer knows that he is forcing the pace too much and should ease off for a short while.

b   The start to the canter must be made absolutely straight: if the rider applies his outside leg too far back, or pushes it, as for a side step or pass, i.e. lacking impulsion, the start will not be straight.

c    The youngster must be kept perfectly straight while changing and should not be thrown off balance, i.e. by change of rider's weight, or pulling his head, as by using lateral aids.

d    The change must be made both in front and behind, as above, but, if not successfully completed behind, the rider will feel the awkwardness of the pace and the youngster must be checked to a halt and started again correctly.

*Jumping*

The youngster may have been already lunged over jumps without the rider and may also have been jumped free in the lane, without fuss or excitement, or he may be completely inexperienced. His jumping training, with rider, should in any event start soon after he has begun the balancing exercises recommended on pp. 287–289.

i    The preliminaries—stage one:
The preliminaries are very similar to those recommended for lunging, i.e. the use of a pole on the ground.

a    The youngster may be walked over a pole lying on the ground, preferably one painted white and, thus, particularly noticeable.

b    The first few times he is walked over it, the youngster may lift his legs exaggeratedly, but he will soon grow to pay no attention to it.

c    At this stage, the trainer should start to teach 'the office', or aids to jumping, i.e. close the legs behind the girth at the exact moment the horse takes off.

d    The youngster should then be patted and made much of when he steps neatly over the pole, but taken back at once if he fails and put over it with stronger pressure from the legs.

 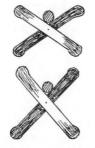 

Cavaletti: A Cavaletto    Side view of Cavaletti    Some uses of Cavaletti

    *e*    Once this is achieved at the walk, the pole may then be taken at a trot, still receiving the office on each occasion, but not being encouraged to leap in any way.

    *f*    The next stage is to take the pole at the canter in the same way without fuss or bother and without leaping: only when this has been successfully completed should the first jumps be taken.

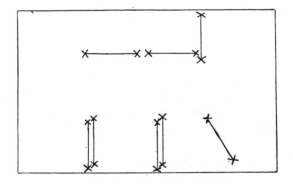

Uses of Cavaletti in the School

ii    The preliminaries—stage two:

The next stage is also similar to that recommended for lunging, i.e. the jumps are raised to six inches or a foot at first.

    *a*    These jumps should be set in the open and the horse taken over them a number of times during the course of each day as a matter of routine.

    *b*    Cavaletti, or poles with a cross at one end, which make two variable heights, are useful practise for this stage.

    *c*    These little jumps, a foot, or eighteen inches high should be all that is required for a fornight or so.

    *d*    By the end of a fortnight or three weeks, the youngster should be leaping eighteen inches or two feet perfectly, without wings to the jump and without fear, enjoying himself.

    *e*    From this point onwards, the jumps should not be raised, but should be spread progressively, i.e. a bar should be placed progressively further in front of the jump, first one foot, then up to three feet, with a corresponding bar on the far side of the jump.

    *f*    In this way, the youngster can be progressively stretched and will soon be leaping quite a height in order to stretch the distance required.

    *g*    From this point on, variety is important and the horse should be allowed to see the jumps before being asked to leap them: i.e. a fallen tree, a brightly coloured row of barrels, etc., but still not raised unduly in height, only in width.

iii   The final stages:
The horse has thus been prepared for jumping without any real effort and without fuss: he should enjoy his work.

*a*   From now onwards, he may be taken at a variety of fences or obstacles, but never sickened of jumping by too much of it.

*b*   It is only essential that he must have confidence in his rider and that the rider shall not jab him in the mouth at any time, if possible.

*c*   The greater the variety that the youngster can be given, the better, but once he has made a good clearance do not continue *ad nauseam*.

*d*   Water, banks and similar obstacles should be accepted in turn, and it is important above all that they should never be rushed. This does not mean to say, on the other hand, that the youngster should not be allowed sufficient momentum.

*e*   With water, especially, it is generally important to allow the horse to spread, and by approaching too fast the horse may not be given time enough to do so and instead is jumped into the obstacle.

*f*   The rider must assist the horse by calculating the best take-off speed and point, and assist the horse by arriving at that point at the best speed.

*g*   It goes without saying that he will ride with a forward seat ready to help the horse should he peck.

*h*   With the conclusion of his jumping training, the youngster is now a usefully schooled horse ready for work and a pleasure to ride.

# PART IV
## Practical Preparations

*Section 1    For Hunting*

The schooling recommended above should be quite sufficient to make a useful hunter, but certain further preparations should be made, as follows:

i    The youngster should be accustomed to hounds:

    *a*    The usual method of accustoming a horse to hounds is to 'walk' hound puppies for the hunt, i.e. care for them during puppyhood.

    *b*    By this means, the young horse grows up accustomed to the sight and sounds of hounds.

    *c*    When hacking, they should, if possible, be exercised together for their mutual benefit.

    *d*    If hound puppies cannot be 'walked' to the mutual benefit of the young horse and the hunt, the best answer is to take the youngster cub-hunting to accustom him to hounds by degrees.

    *e*    When cub-hunting, there is not such a large field and there is generally more room to manoeuvre, thus the youngster can be acclimatised gradually to hounds, as well as the sound of the horn and other hunting sounds and sights.

ii    The youngster should also be acclimatised to crowds and to the presence of many other horses, such as are liable to be encountered at the meet:

    *a*    As above, cub-hunting is generally the best way of gradually preparing him for the season to come.

    *b*    A visit to the local agricultural show, even if not shown, may be good preparation for the general excitement of the meet.

iii    The youngster must be accustomed to company when hacking, or when leaping across country:

    *a*    If possible he should be hacked with several other horses, not just stable companions.

308

*b*  They should gallop on while he is made to take his own time or direction.

*c*  He should be accustomed to leaping fences with horses on either side of him.

*d*  He should be made to open and shut gates, while the others canter on without him.

*e*  He must be acclimatised to having other horses milling round him at gates or other obstacles, and checked if he shows the slightest sign of kicking.

iv  The normal preparations for any hunting season are:

*a*  The horse must be brought into the stables, clipped and trimmed and brought into condition by regular exercise.

*b*  A few days before hunting, the shoes should always be checked and renewed, if necessary.

v  The normal preparations for any hunting day are:

*a*  The horse may receive the normal early morning feed, possibly earlier than usual to allow time for digestion, but no hay afterwards.

*b*  The horse must be well groomed and, if hacked to the meet, care must be taken to ensure that the horse does not arrive hot and sweating: whether boxing or hacking to the meet allow plenty of time to ensure punctuality.

*Section 2  For Showing, Gymkhanas and Show-Jumping*
The schooling recommended above is enough to prepare the youngster sufficiently for the first two as well as for the novice classes in show-jumping, but certain points should not be overlooked.

i  For showing:
For a show, the youngster should be turned out in a show saddle, a double-bridle, or pelham, and should be particularly well groomed.

*a*  He should be neatly trimmed and glossy, with plaited mane, and should be a little on the fat side rather than in hard condition.

*b*  It is well to exercise him a good while before his class is due, so that he can then be given a final grooming and preparation, as well as a rest, before he is due to enter the ring.

*c*  The horse should be taken unhurriedly to the collecting ring about ten minutes or so before the class is due, and there quietly walked round after reporting to the ring stewards.

*d*  In the ring, he should be kept well up to his bit, walked, trotted and cantered, as requested, and shown at his best in each pace with the minimum of effort visible on the part of his rider.

e　When called in, the judge may then ride the youngster, so it is important that he is accustomed to strangers riding him and accepts the judge gracefully.

f　He will then require to be off-saddled and trotted up and down, and, again, it is desirable that he should be well under control, especially on the turn, not sprawling out widely.

g　To accustom the youngster to the crowds and strange noises round the ringside, it is generally advisable to take him to a show first without showing him before introducing him to the show ring.

ii　For gymkhanas:
The gymkhanas at local shows, or organised by local riding clubs or pony clubs, are much more relaxed affairs than shows, but it is as well to prepare the horse in advance.

a　Although the schooling recommended above should be quite sufficient, it is as well for the horse and rider to get in some practise at speedy mounting and dismounting from both sides.

b　Speedy saddling and off-saddling and mounting and dismounting bareback is another thing to be practised; and in neither case should the horse or pony be allowed to vary from its training to stand still when being mounted or dismounted.

c　Do not let the excitement of the competitions in a gymkhana spoil months of careful training: both before and after the gymkhana give the horse some intensive training.

d　Practise in bending, in reining-back, in fast trotting and steady cantering from a walk, in the pass and half pass, will all be useful, but do not allow the excitement of the moment to result in slovenly work: ensure afterwards that the movements are all practised and perfected once more.

e　Gymkhanas can be fun and good practise for the youngster and rider, but they can also be ruination to months of training if the rider allows himself to be carried away and forgets to apply the correct aids, or applies them badly: ensure this does not happen and if any mistakes are made ensure that the horse is promptly reschooled.

iii　For show-jumping:
The training recommended above should be sufficient for the horse and rider to compete in the novice classes with a reasonable chance, but certain points must be remembered.

*a* The rider must join the British Show Jumping Association (B.S.J.A.) under whose rules all show-jumping is run and the horse must also be registered with them.

*b* Preparation should consist of checking the jumps the youngster is likely to encounter and, as far as possible, duplicating them in practise.

*c* Preparation should not consist of jumping the youngster until he is heartily sick of the sight of jumps, or of using a 'rapping pole' of any other device supposed to 'encourage' the horse, but generally having the opposite effect.

*d* As with showing, it is advisable to introduce the youngster to the atmosphere and acclimatise him gradually, by taking him, if possible, to a show beforehand, or to a gymkhana or riding club or pony club event.

*e* In the first instance, it is advisable only to enter the simplest events and not expect the youngster to jump against time, or for that matter to make a clear round first time out. As with everything else practise is required.

*f* More advanced show-jumping, like advanced dressage is a highly specialised aspect of horsemanship and, as such, outside the scope of the young horse and rider.

Jumps: Plain Rails     Rails over Oil Drums     Picket Fence

*Section 3   For Dressage and Horse Trials*

Although the training recommended above for the youngster may be sufficient for him to compete in the most elementary dressage tests, the more advanced tests and horse trials are, like more advanced show-jumping, highly specialised and professional aspects of horsemanship.

i Dressage:

Dressage tests are a series of movements performed in an enclosed arena (forty by twenty yards up to elementary level) lasting from six to fifteen minutes according to the degree, or grade, of test being performed.

*a* The grades of test in Great Britain are: Preliminary, Pony Club, Novice, Elementary, Medium, Prix St Georges and Grand Prix (the last two are international tests as set by the Federation Equèstre Internationale: F.E.I.).

311

*b* The tests are generally performed from memory, but a 'caller' may be allowed.

*c* The F.E.I. rules define the various dressage categories as follows:

Ordinary walk: A free regular and unconstrained walk of moderate extension. The horse should walk energetically, but calmly, with even and determined steps, distinctly marking four equally spaced beats.

Collected walk: The horse moves resolutely forward, with his neck raised and arched. The head approaches the vertical position . . . good hock action. . . . Each step covers less ground and is higher than at the ordinary walk . . . the hindfeet touch the ground behind the footprints of the forefeet.

Extended walk: The horse should cover as much ground as possible without haste and without losing the regularity of his steps. The hindfeet touch the ground clear beyond the footprints of the forefeet. The rider lets the horse stretch out his head and neck without, however, losing contact, the head being carried in front of the vertical.

Ordinary trot: The horse goes forward freely and straight, engaging his hindlegs with good hock action on a taut, but light, rein, his position being balanced and unconstrained. The hindfeet touch the ground in the footprints of the forefeet.

Collected trot: The neck is raised, thus enabling the shoulders to move with greater ease in all directions, the hocks being well engaged and maintaining energetic impulsion, notwithstanding the slower movement. The horse's steps are shorter, but he is lighter and more mobile.

Extended trot: The horse covers as much ground as possible. He lengthens his stride, remaining on the bit with light contact. The neck is extended and, as a result of great impulsion from the quarters, the horse uses his shoulders, covering more ground at each step without his action becoming much higher.

Ordinary canter: The horse, perfectly straight from head to tail, moves freely, with a natural balance. The strides are long, even and the pace well cadenced. The quarters develop an increasing impulsion.

Collected canter: The shoulders are supple, free and mobile and the quarters very active. The horse's mobility is increased without any loss of impulsion.

Extended canter: The horse extends his neck. The tip of the nose points more or less forward, the horse lengthens his stride without losing any of his calmness and lightness.

Rein back: The walk backwards, the legs being raised and set down simultaneously in pairs.

Pirouette: A small circle on two tracks, with a radius equal to the length of the horse, the forehand moving round the haunches. At whatever pace the pirouette is executed, the horse should turn smoothly, maintaining the exact cadence and sequence of the legs at that pace. The forelegs and outside hindleg move round the inside hindleg which forms the pivot and should return to the same spot each time it leaves the ground.

Passage: A slow, shortened, very collected, very elevated and cadenced trot. It is characterised by a pronounced engagement of the quarters, a more accentuated flexion of the knees and hocks and the grace-elasticity of the movement. Each diagonal pair of legs is raised and put to the ground alternately, gaining little ground and with an even cadence and prolonged suspension.

Piaffe: A collected trot on the spot. The horse's back is supple and vibrating. The haunches with active hocks are well engaged giving great freedom and lightness to the action of the shoulders and forelegs. The neck is raised, the poll supple, the head perpendicular, the mouth maintaining light contact on a taut rein. The alternate diagonals are raised with an even, supple, cadenced and graceful movement, the moment of suspension being prolonged.

d    Do not be put off by the above from entering the simplest dressage tests, if there is an opportunity of doing so. The horse, trained as recommended, should be capable of performing creditably.

e    Once the rider knows what is required, he will find that preparation for dressage is simply a matter of schooling in the manner to which he should already be accustomed.

f    The piaffe and passage belong more strictly to the high school work and are highly specialised, and are not included in the simplest grades of test.

g    N.B. Advanced high school work includes the pass at the trot and canter, and the artificial 'airs' known as: 'the Spanish Walk', the Spanish trot', the 'Passage' and 'Piaffe'.

ii    For horse trials:
Horse trials may vary from one, to two, or three day events and are generally sufficiently specialised to be beyond the scope of anything but the highly trained horse and rider.

a    The aim is to include a dressage test of medium standard, a speed and endurance test in five phases and a show jumping test.

b    The speed and endurance test covers an overall distance of about seventeen miles in a three day event. It is divided into five phases:

Phase A: Roads and Tracks at a speed of 240 metres per minute.
Phase B: A steeplechase over about two and a half miles over ten to a dozen obstacles Timed.
Phase C: Roads and tracks at a speed of 240 metres per minute. There is at this stage a compulsory halt of ten minutes while the horse is checked and passed fit to continue by vets.
Phase D: Cross-country over five miles with thirty or so fixed obstacles, sited to test the courage, judgment and skill of horse and rider. Timed.
Phase E: A final straight mile gallop on the flat.

c   On the final day of the three day event, the show-jumping takes place to demonstrate the horse is fit enough to complete a tricky show-jumping course after the previous day's effort.

Jumps: Double Oxer          Hog Back                    Triple Bar

d   The British Horse Society is the governing body for such trials, and they are marked on a system of penalties and bonus points.

Stone Wall

e   In one day events, the dressage is ridden first and then either the cross-country, or show-jumping, as decided by the organisers.

f   Although these trials cater for novice, intermediate and open horses, it should be appreciated that this applies only to the horses. The riders are highly experienced and no novices.

g   By consistent training on the lines indicated, there is no reason why the young horse of good conformation and action should not be brought up to a standard sufficient to compete in such a trial.

h   It should be emphasised that the rider should have achieved a sufficiently high standard, and that the horse and rider must both be fit enough; this is no test for a part-time rider.

# PART V
## Driving

Driving a single horse in harness is a comparatively simple task for anyone, but driving two or more horses together is a specialist task which no one should attempt without considerable training and experience.

*Section 1    The Single-Horse Vehicles*
The vehicles which can be drawn by a single horse may be divided into two main categories, i.e. two- and four-wheeled.

i    The two-wheeled vehicles:
The two-wheeled vehicles, loosely termed 'traps', may be divided into several types.

a    The float: The prototype of them all. A simple country vehicle consisting of a flat platform on two wheels with shafts attached: used for transporting milk churns and light loads by small farmers.

b    The gig: The simple one-horse cart, with two wheels, a seat for two or three people with back supports, of varied designs. The principal means of transport for most country people before the motor car. Includes such varieties as Tilbury, etc.

Gig

*c*   The dog-cart: Basically a gig with two seats back to back, to carry four people, also a deep-slatted boot which was originally used to carry sporting dogs, as the name implies.

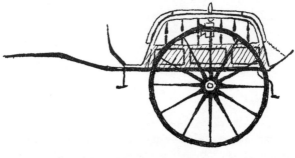

Dog Cart

*d*   The governess-cart: Basically a gig with entrance by a door at the back and seats on both sides: primarily intended for children and governess, as the name implies.

Governess Cart

*e*   The Cabriolet: A high, hooded vehicle with a platform behind for diminutive 'tiger', or attendant. Seldom seen outside museums today.

ii   The four-wheeled vehicles:
The only four-wheeled vehicle which may be drawn by a single horse is a phaeton, but there are many varieties, with the only point in common being that the front wheels are smaller than the rear wheels:

*a*   The Stanhope, is a town vehicle generally drawn by a single horse.
*b*   The park phaeton, is a specially low slung phaeton intended for ladies driving in the park, and is also generally drawn by a single horse.

*Section 2   The Harness*
The harness for driving is as follows:

i   The bridle:
   The parts of the bridle and their fitting are as for the riding bridle, except for the possible use of blinkers:

   a   The leather may be black rather than brown and will require polishing.
   b   Blinkers, or blinders or winkers, are a rigid leather addition to the bridle intended to confine the vision of the harness horse to prevent shying: only necessary on rear horses of tandems, or four in hands (i.e. wheelers), to protect their eyes from the reins of the horses in front.
   c   If worn, the blinkers must be quite rigid and at least an inch from the eye.
   d   On a single horse, they are quite unnecessary and only used due to custom.

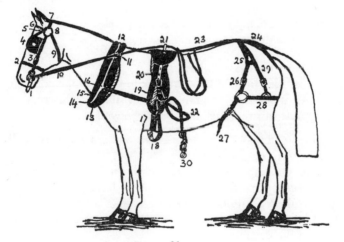

Parts of harness

1. Bit, driving bit. 2. Noseband. 3. Cheekpiece. 4. Blinker. 5. V-strap. 6. Browband. 7. Crownpiece. 8. Rosette. 9. Throatlash. 10. Reins. 11. Driving ring. 12. Hames strap. 13. Afterwhale of Collar. 14. Hames. 15. Forewale of collar. 16. Tracebar. 17. Girth. 18. Bellyband. 19. Shaft tug. 20. Back band. 21. Rein terret. 22. Trace. 23. Back strap. or Crupper strap. 24. Crupper. 25. Split Cross strap. 26. Loin strap. 27. Breeching strap. 28. Breeching Webb. 29. Quarter strap. 30. Hooking-in chain.

ii   The collar:
   The collar should be oval at the base and pointed at the top and may be split for convenience in putting it on. It is through the collar that the horse bears its weight.

<ol type="a">
<li>It is generally stuffed with rye straw and lined with leather or felt.</li>
<li>It should be long enough to allow the hand to pass between it and the horse's breast.</li>
<li>It should also be possible to pass the hand between the neck and the top of the collar.</li>
<li>It should not be tight, or pinch in any way, nor should it be overlarge and rock from side to side.</li>
<li>If pressed to one side, it should allow one finger to be inserted all the way down the shoulder.<br>
It should be pressed firmly against each shoulder to ensure that the after-wale is clear of the horse; if it is not, the collar needs restuffing.</li>
</ol>

iii The hames are of metal, joined by straps at the top and bottom to fit the shape of the collar exactly between the fore- and after-wales:

<ol type="a">
<li>The traces are attached to the hames about two-thirds of the way down the collar.</li>
<li>If the hames are not bent to fit the collar exactly at all points, the collar will press unduly and may gall the horse.</li>
</ol>

iv The breast-strap or breast-collar:
These may be used in light harness work in place of the collar and hames: the traces are attached to this broad leather strap which crosses the breast, and it is against this that the horse bears the weight:

<ol type="a">
<li>The breast-strap fits across the breast and is kept in place by a neck-strap in front of the withers.</li>
<li>If the breast-strap is set too high, it will cut into the gullet at the breast, and especially broad breast-straps should have a groove, or dip, cut in them to allow the gullet freedom.</li>
<li>If the breast-strap is set too low, it will interfere with the free movement of the shoulder.</li>
</ol>

v The back-pad or harness saddle:
This should fit in the same manner as a riding saddle and be placed in position in the same manner: its purpose is to hold the 'terrets' or metal guide rings for the reins, also to support the shafts through special leather loops known as 'tugs'.

<ol type="a">
<li>The back-band slides freely through the back-pad and carries the 'tugs' on either side through which the shafts pass.</li>
<li>The back-pad is held in position by a girth and the back-band is attached by a belly-band done up looser than the girth.</li>
</ol>

c   It is customary to give the belly-band a twist round the shaft on the off-side behind the stop on the shaft before doing it up, to keep the shafts at the correct angle.

vi  The traces:
The traces should be of equal length of stout leather attached to the hames or breast-pad at one end, and stretching to the trace-hook, or attachment, on the vehicle at the other end.

a   They must be sufficiently long to give the horse full clearance of the footboard.

b   When hooked in position, they should keep the points of the shafts roughly level with the hames.

c   It is through the traces that the horse pulls the load, hence they must be even and secure.

vii  The breeching:
The breeching should hang horizontally over the quarters and is intended to assist the horse to hold back a heavy load when going downhill, or in backing.

a   It must not allow the harness-pad to be pushed forward when backing, or interfere with the movement of the quarters.

b   The adjustment is by the quarter-strap and loin-strap, and it should fit twelve to sixteen inches below the root of the tail and allow the width of a hand between it and the thigh.

c   Although often used, it is not strictly necessary in light harness work.

viii  The crupper:
The crupper fits under the dock of the tail and is connected to the saddle-pad by a back-, or crupper-, strap: its purpose is to keep the back-pad in position.

a   It should be well padded and should fit properly under the tail.

b   The crupper-strap connecting to the back-pad should not be too tight and should allow two fingers at least to pass between it and the horse's croup.

c   With heavy draught horses, it is not strictly necessary as the breeching fulfills the same function.

d   With heavy draught horses, it is desirable to have a side-strap on the crupper which can be easily adjusted.

Section 3   *Harnessing-up and Putting-to*
The harness should be fitted as follows:

i   The collar:
The collar must be put on first.

    *a*   It should be held upside down and stretched apart, unbuckling, if of the split variety, before being slipped over the horse's head.

    *b*   Once over the head, it should be turned the right way round and placed in position, being checked for fit, bearing in mind that collar-galls are mostly due to friction from the movement of the shoulders.

    *c*   *N.B.* It is only at the top of the neck, in front of the withers that galls are likely to arise from pressure.

    *d*   The hames and traces are often put on already attached to the collar.

ii    The Pad, crupper and breeching:
The pad, crupper and breeching, if used, are next.

    *a*   These should be put on, crupper first, with the back-pad placed slightly behind its correct position at first, until the crupper and breeching are in place, it is then adjusted.

    *b*   The girth should be buckled up, but should allow two fingers to be inserted behind it quite easily.

iii    The hames and traces:
The hames and traces, if not fitted with the collar, come next.

    *a*   They should be fitted home in the grooves between the fore- and after-wales of the collar.

    *b*   The hame-strap should be pulled as tight as possible.

    *c*   The traces should be loosely knotted in figures of eight and allowed to dangle from the hames for the moment.

iv    The bridle and bit:
The bridle and bit are next to be fitted.

    *a*   The curb-chain, if one is worn, should be carefully adjusted at the same time.

    *b*   The blinkers, if they are worn, should also be carefully checked for fit to make sure they do not rub against the eyes.

v    The reins:
The reins are the last item before putting-to:

    *a*   They should be passed through the terrets, or metal rings on the back-pad.

    *b*   They should be buckled to the rings of the bit and the spare end coiled through the off-side terret.

vi    Putting-to, i.e. harnessing to the vehicle:
The horse should next be led out quietly to the vehicle and drawn up with his back to the shafts.

*a*   The shafts should then be raised and the vehicle drawn forward until the points of the shafts can be passed through the tugs, which come up against the stops on the shafts.

*b*   The traces are then hooked into position and the breeching, if used, is buckled round the traces and into the slots in the shafts.

*c*   The belly-band is then buckled up, being given a turn round the shaft on the off-side to keep the shafts at the correct level.

*d*   The harness is all then quickly checked over for the last time.

vii   Checking the balance:
It is desirable to check the balance of a two-wheel vehicle by adjusting the load if possible; a sliding seat simplifies this.

*a*   Overweighting in front will force the shafts down and bring weight on the horse through the saddle.

*b*   Overweighting behind will force the shafts upwards and prevent a direct pull.

*c*   When the balance is correct there should be a gentle up and down movement of the shaft tug when trotting and a very slight play in the shafts.

*Section 4   Driving*
The control of the horse from the vehicle through the reins, voice and whip.

i   Mounting the vehicle:
The vehicle should be mounted from the off-side.

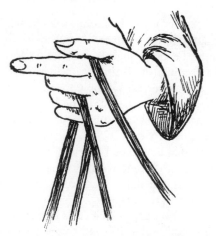

How to Hold the Driving Reins

*a*    The reins should be taken from the off-side in the right hand, near rein under the forefinger and off-rein under the third finger.

*b*    The trap should then be entered from the off-side and the reins transferred to the left hand.

*c*    The near-rein should be over the forefinger and the off-rein between the second and third fingers, the ends of the rein passing between the third and fourth fingers and being gripped by them.

*d*    Thus, with the hand upright, thumb pointing to the right, the horse can be turned to the left by tilting the wrist upwards or to the right by turning it downwards.

ii   The driving position:
The driver should sit straight and upright with feet and knees together.

*a*    The left forearm should be horizontal, with the back of the hand to the front, wrist rounded and flexible.

*b*    The whip should be carried in the right hand at the point of balance pointing to the left, with the forefinger free to pick up and shorten the reins as required.

*c*    The purpose of the whip is to keep the horse up to his bit, and it should normally be drawn back, not flicked, between the collar and pad with a stroking movement.

iii  Driving:
A steady contact should be kept on the reins always; they should never be jerked.

*a*    To start the horse moving, the mouth may be felt lightly and the horse lightly touched with the whip or 'clicked' with the tongue.

*b*    The hand may be eased slightly when the horse moves, but steady contact must continue at all times.

*c*    When turning a corner, check the pace and allow plenty of room for the vehicle to turn the corner after the horse.

*d*    Pressure on the rein towards which the turn is being made must be increased as required.

*e*    Sudden halts should be avoided whenever possible, but strong pressure on the horse's mouth is required if it is necessary.

*f*    Once the horse has halted, the pressure should be eased immediately to prevent him starting to back.

*g*    If it is required to back the vehicle, it is best to dismount and guide the horse from his head, unless it is only for a pace or two.

*h*    When going up steep hills, the driver and passengers should dismount to ease the horse, and he should not be trotted down steep hills or his legs may be damaged.

iv  Signals when driving:
The old driving signals involving the use of the whip have now been dropped as too complicated for modern usage: the normal driving signals have replaced them.

 *a*  Arm out to the right, fully extended, to signal a right turn.
 *b*  Arm out to the left, fully extended, to signal a left turn.
 *c*  Arm extended to the right, palm down and moved up and down, to signal intention to slow down or halt.
 *d*  Arm out to the right from the shoulder and bent upwards from the elbow, palm forwards, the familiar signal for 'HALT'.

N.B. These are the highway code signals for riding also.

## Section 5  *Unharnessing*
On the return to the stables, unharnessing should take place as follows:

i  Halt by the coach-house:
The pony and trap should be halted as near to the coach-house as possible.

 *a*  The whip is then housed in its socket holder and the driver should dismount from the off-side.
 *b*  The spare ends of the reins are then coiled in the off-side terret.

ii  Removing the harness:
When removing the harness the first step is to unbuckle the breeching from the shafts.

 *a*  The belly-band should then be unbuckled and the traces unhooked and loosely coiled in figures of eight.
 *b*  The horse is then led forward out of the shafts, and the shafts eased out of the tugs as he moves forward.

## Section 6  *Training for Driving*
The training for driving initially parallels that of training for riding.

i  Initial training:
The initial training in handling and leading, both in the stable and outside, are exactly similar to those given above (pp. 277–278).

 *a*  The youngster must be trained to lead easily at a walk and trot as required.

    *b*    He must also learn good stable manners.

ii   Preliminary schooling:
The youngster's preliminary schooling on the lunge line also closely parallels that of the riding horse.

    *a*    He must be taught to walk and trot to voice commands on the lunge line and to respond to the whip.

    *b*    He is then trained on the long reins; it is through the use of the long reins that the harness horse receives his preliminary schooling.

    *c*    Once the trainer is satisfied with his progress, the youngster may be introduced to harness work.

iii  Schooling to harness:
The next stage of the youngster's education is the schooling to harness, thereafter to draught work.

    *a*    In the first place, the harness is fitted on the youngster by degrees until he is accustomed to being long-reined in it.

    *b*    The first training in the shafts should be in a stoutly constructed vehicle and the youngster should at first be led round to accustom him to the weight and feel.

    *c*    Only when the youngster is thoroughly accustomed to the feel of the vehicle, should a driver mount behind the horse, and the training, with a load aboard, may then be repeated until the youngster accepts it quite calmly.

    *d*    The final stage is taking the youngster gently through his paces from the vehicle in an enclosed space, e.g. large flat field or similar enclosed area.

    *e*    As with any other youngster, the schooling is still far from complete at this stage and the horse must be gradually accustomed to the various more advanced aspects of his work, e.g. travel at night, by lamplight, work in heavy traffic, if necessary, etc.

# PART VI
## The Commoner Vices and Cures

Horses are not born with vice, but develop vices as a result of bad handling of one sort or another, and prevention is both better and easier than cure.

*Section 1    The Stable Vices*
Certain vices, while not necessarily restricted to the stables, are more common there and are generally due to bad stable management, i.e. thoughtless, careless or weak handling.

*Crib-biting*
A crib-biter grips any available stable fitting, such as the manger, between his teeth and at the same time gulps air: this vice constitutes an unsoundness and is more of a disease than a vice.

i    The signs:
     The crib-biter will often gulp down air until its belly swells, then stretch its neck and belch with a grunting noise before grasping the manger, or similar object, between its teeth again.

     a    By this constant biting the horse's teeth are worn down and irregular, resulting in faulty digestion and colic.
     b    A confirmed crib-biter will inevitably be in poor condition, however much it is fed; it will also have badly worn teeth.

ii   The causes:
     The vice may stem originally from boredom in the stables with insufficient exercise and interest.

     a    It may start, according to one theory, with the horse licking the walls of the box, or a salt lick fixed in the box.
     b    It may be due to inadequate food, lacking minerals, or bulk, or some other dietary deficiency.

    *c*   It may be due to internal parasites.

    *d*   It may be due to copying another horse.

iii   The cure:

It is always advisable to treat the cause first, rather than the vice, but, if of long-standing, it is probably incurable:

    *a*   If due to a dietary deficiency, it should be corrected at once.

    *b*   If due to internal parasites, they should be removed at once.

    *c*   If due to copying another horse, it should be removed.

    *d*   If due to boredom and insufficient exercise or interest, then the horse must be kept exercised and interested.

    *e*   If none of the above effect a cure and the habit appears of long-standing, all the stable fittings should be soaked in creosote.

    *f*   If this has no effect, all the fittings must be moved and the horse left in a bare stable and fed from a portable manger which is removed at once after feeding.

    *g*   If it still continues, a muzzle may be the only answer except when the horse is being fed.

    *h*   Plenty of work, exercise and interest, as well as sound stable management are the best preventatives and may go a long way towards a cure. But, if of long-standing, it may well be incurable.

## Wind-sucking

This is a vice generally associated with crib-biting, but may be a separate vice on its own; it also constitutes an unsoundness and is more of a disease than a vice.

i   The signs:

The wind-sucker will suck down air with a backward jerk of the head, often until its belly is swollen: it will then arch its neck and pass the wind with a grunting sound.

    *a*   The direct effect is certain to be poor condition, as with a crib-biter.

    *b*   Colic and indigestion are also likely to be side effects.

ii   The causes:

Similar to crib-biting, with which it is often associated.

iii   The cure:

As with crib-biting, it is always best to treat the cause, rather than the vice, but a wind-sucker of long-standing like a crib-biter of long-standing may well defy cure. Preventives are:

*a*  A 'flute-bit' or hollow tube bit, perforated with holes like a penny whistle, may be attached to a normal head-stall: it is fitted so as to prevent the horse closing his mouth to suck air and must be worn permanently except for feeding and work.

*b*  A device known as a 'gullet-plate' and 'cribbing-strap', i.e. a broad strap buckled tightly round the gullet, may be effective.

## Weaving

The weaver constantly swings his head, neck and forehand to and fro, from side to side, sometimes extending this to rocking from foot to foot, lifting first one fore foot then the other.

i  The signs:
Weaving is instantly identifiable and the horse fails to put on any condition due to the constant exercise it takes.

ii  The causes:
The cause is almost certainly a nervous habit contracted due to boredom and lack of interest.

*a*  It may also be hereditary.
*b*  It may also be copied.

iii  The cure:
One of the likeliest cures for a weaver is to keep the horse outside, possibly in a New Zealand rug.

*a*  If the vice is being copied from another horse, remove the originator promptly.
*b*  It is essential, in any event, to provide as much work, exercise and interest as possible.
*c*  Any unnecessary idle periods in the stables should be avoided.
*d*  When in the stable, a salt lick or hay net, or something to keep the horse occupied, is important; in this case, it is unlikely to lead to crib-biting or wind-sucking.
*e*  Pillar-reins to prevent lateral movement of the head are sometimes recommended, but, like muzzles, flute-bits and similar devices, these are aimed at the vice not its cause.

## Kicking

Kicking can be a tiresome vice in the stables and one that should not be overlooked.

i   The causes:
The causes of kicking may vary from boredom to disturbance of some kind,
e.g. objection to darkness, rats, grooming, strange horses, etc.

   *a*   Some horses undoubtedly enjoy the sound their kicking makes against
partitions or posts.
   *b*   Itchy heels may be the cause of kicking, or just objection to being
handled on the part of the youngster.
   *c*   Kicking may begin as pure mischievousness and end as a vice, if the
groom or attendant is not sufficiently firm.
   *d*   Once the horse appreciates that it has gained some point by kicking,
e.g. made the groom desist from grooming the ticklish underbelly, it
has in effect been encouraged to repeat the offence.

ii   The cure:
As with any other vice, the cure is only to be found once the cause has been
pin-pointed:

   *a*   If the kicking is due to boredom, or disturbance of any kind, as listed
above, remove the cause.
   *b*   If the horse is apparently just enjoying making a noise, pad the post or
partition so that the noise is deadened.
   *c*   If due to weak handling, this must be corrected promptly before the
vice gets any worse: firmness is essential with a kicker, and prompt
retaliation will probably prevent repetition.
   *d*   Care must be taken to distinguish between fear, or sexual causes, such
as in-season mare, from congenital kicking: punishment will do no
good in such cases.
   *e*   Punishment, if given, should consist of no more than a rap on the leg,
expecially as raised to kick; if standing close to the kicker it is unlikely
to be able to do any harm.

*Biting*
A really confirmed biter, who lays back his ears and does his best to savage either
his groom, or another horse, is fortunately rare.

i   Causes:
Biting generally starts simply as a mischievous habit, but it can quickly
develop into a tiresome habit.

   *a*   It should never be aggravated by teasing of any sort.
   *b*   When grooming, make allowances for ticklish parts, but maintain
firmness and do not allow the horse to force an abrupt conclusion.

ii  Cure:
With the really congenital biter, of attendants and other horses, a muzzle is
about the only answer.

  *a*  A sidestick, i.e. a stout stick attached to head-collar and surcingle, may
  be used to prevent lateral movement and, hence, permit grooming and
  handling.
  *b*  As with any other vice, prevention is better by far than cure: nip any
  incipient biting firmly in the bud.

*Other Minor Vices*
There are various other minor stable vices, tricks, or bad habits, which should
be checked before they are allowed to develop:

i  Barging through doorways:
This is a tiresome habit, without quite qualifying as a vice, but not generally
difficult to cure.

  *a*  It is due to weak handling in the first place, and is liable to result in
  injury to the horse if not checked.
  *b*  One really firm demonstration that it will not be allowed is usually
  sufficient to cure all but the worst cases.
  *c*  Repeated firm, but gentle, handling will overcome the worst cases in
  time.

ii  Crowding in the box:
Some horses develop the tiresome habit of deliberately crowding the groom
over into a corner, or against the wall of the box.

  *a*  As with barging through doorways, this is a tiresome habit, due to
  weak handling, and not generally hard to cure.
  *b*  As above, one really firm demonstration that it will not be allowed is
  usually sufficient.

iii  Tearing clothing:
This is the sort of bad habit that starts through boredom and bad management, and if allowed can develop into a tiresome vice.

  *a*  It is generally caused by ill-fitting, old, or ragged clothing being put
  insecurely on the horse.
  *b*  All clothing should be in good repair and securely fastened, then the
  habit is unlikely to arise.

iv  Bed-eating:
This scarcely constitutes a vice, but can become a tiresome habit and is hard
to cure once started.

    *a*   It is probably due to lack of bulk in the food originally, or to dietary deficiencies.

    *b*   Alter the diet to ensure sufficient bulk.

    *c*   Alter the bedding to something inedible, such as peat moss.

v   Getting cast:
Though scarcely a bad habit, or vice, some horses do seem more prone than others to getting cast, i.e. lying down in their box and getting so close to a wall that they cannot rise:

    *a*   It may be due to the box being too small.

    *b*   It may be due to rolling in the box with colicky pains.

    *c*   If the box is large enough and it happens more than once, check the horse's general health: it may be due to abdominal stones.

    *d*   It can sometimes be extremely awkward getting the horse to its feet again and, hence, if it happens frequently, can be very tiresome. Look for the cause and remove it if possible.

vi  Dung-eating:
In no sense a vice, but such a habit indicates a depraved appetite, due probably to a dietary deficiency.

    *a*   Check the diet and remedy if necessary.

    *b*   Check for internal parasites and dose if required.

*Section 2   Outdoor Vices: Mounted or Dismounted*
*Rearing*
Rising up on the hindlegs, either in a half-rear, or right up vertically in a full-rear.

i   The reaction:
Rearing can be very frightening for the novice and unless promptly checked may develop into a tiresome and dangerous vice.

    *a*   The horse should be given his head and the rider's weight should be thrown forward on his neck.

    *b*   If he goes very near the vertical, the rider should slip his foot out of the right stirrup, and hold with his right arm round the neck, ready to slip off to the left. The rider must remember to hold onto the right rein, not the left, or he may pull the horse over on top of him, if he has to step clear.

    *c*   When the horse rears, the reins must never be pulled. If this is done, the horse may come right over backwards and damage the rider: this is the cause of most cases of a horse going over and is due to the rider panicking.

*d*   There is no need for panic, since the rider will feel the horse going over if it is going to and with the right foot out of the stirrup it is merely a question of stepping to one side out of the way and holding on to the right rein.

The Rear

ii   The cure:

Like any other vice the only real way to cure it is to find the cause and cure that, thus preventing recurrence. However, there are cases when the vice has become too confirmed to be cured, although this is fortunately uncommon.

*a*   A horse that frequently rears for no apparent reason may sometimes be cured by riding out in a numnah or blanket and deliberately pulling him over on soft sandy soil or similar surface: a saddle should not be used, or the tree may be broken or the horse damaged.

*b*   Another method is to flick the horse under the belly between the legs with a whip: the horse will then drop down to protect himself.

*c*   The horse should not be hit over the poll with the butt of the riding crop, or otherwise abused, even if the rider has been taken by surprise and his nose has been damaged or is bleeding. In no circumstances, should any horse be punished while the rider is in a temper.

*Bolting: Running Away*

Bolting, or running away, with the bit firmly held in the teeth and the jaws locked.

i   The reaction:
Bolting can also be very frightening for the novice, and this too may become a dangerous vice.

   *a*   If there is room to let the horse go, this is probably the best course, if possible, over heavy going, e.g. over plough land, or up a steep hill.

   *b*   When the horse flags and wants to stop, keep him going, preferably over harder conditions than normal. This may well result in a cure.

   *c*   If the horse must be stopped quickly, try giving him his head suddenly to make him drop the bit, if it is held between his teeth: pull him up by a firm decided pull and then relaxation of the reins.

   *d*   Never freeze solid and panic, or worse still maintain a steady pull on the reins: this will only make him pull all the harder.

ii   Causes and cure:
There may be a variety of causes.

   *a*   One of the commonest causes is a heavy-handed rider and a sensitive-mouthed horse.

   *b*   A sore mouth, a badly fitting bit, or bridle, extreme fear, or something wedged in the teeth causing the horse pain, may all also lead to isolated cases of bolting.

   *c*   In isolated instances, find the cause and the horse is unlikely to bolt again.

   *d*   If it appears to be a confirmed vice, and there is no obvious cause for it, try a bitless bridle, or milder bit, before taking extreme measures.

   *e*   Reschooling in skilled hands may be the only cure.

## Baulking

Baulking consists of halting firmly and obstinately and refusing to move onwards.

i   Causes:
The root causes of baulking are often obscure and hard to find, but may frequently stem from defective vision, or nervousness or some past experience:

   *a*   Defective eyesight may cause the horse to fear something quite unnecessarily.

   *b*   Nervousness, or atavistic fears, may result in obstinate halting of this kind.

   *c*   There is generally some reason, or some object, which causes the obstinate refusal, as, for instance, a small stream or ditch, or log, or similar obstacle.

ii   Cure:

There is never any point in forcing the horse forward under duress, or beating it, or otherwise punishing it for baulking.

a   If the cause of the baulking can be clearly ascertained, dismount from the horse and try to lead it up to the cause to examine it.

b   If there is no clear reason for the baulking, again dismount and simply turn the horse round and walk back a short distance, before turning round again and walking back.

c   By turning the horse round, walking him about and encouraging him verbally, the horse's attention will probably be distracted and there will be no further trouble.

d   Persistent baulking is probably due to defective vision and a vet should be consulted.

## Shying

Shying is a sideways or backwards reaction away from some object, which has temporarily frightened, or alarmed the horse.

i   Causes:

As with baulking, there is frequently some obscure root cause of shying, such as a fright experienced as a foal and half remembered, or again defective vision or nervousness.

a   The horse has poor side-vision and something seen out of the corner of the eye, especially something moving, may often cause a horse to shy unexpectedly.

b   Nervousness and atavistic fears may also have their effect.

ii   Cure:

If the cause of the shying can be easily pin-pointed, the horse should be shown it and allowed to examine it, if possible.

a   It is generally best to let the horse smell, paw, or otherwise examine the object in his own time, without forcing him forward or punishing him.

b   The idea is to show him that the object is harmless and not to associate it in his mind with punishment or pain which might only make him shy all the more next time.

c   Prevention is the best cure for shying, and the horse should be checked before he actually starts to shy. The experienced rider will note by his flickering ears and tensing body that he is thinking of shying and will collect him and ease his head away from the object rather than towards it: the likelihood is that he will then not shy in the first place.

    *d*    Punishment for shying is worse than useless and only likely to make matters worse.

*Other Vices or Bad Habits*

Certain other vices, or bad habits are commonly encountered, as follows:

i    Pulling:

This is a tiresome habit, which may have been caused, in the first instance, in a variety of ways.

    *a*    Causes may vary from nervousness, lack of balance, a heavy-handed rider, a horse heavy in front, a badly fitting bit or bridle, an unsuitable bit, a sore mouth, or something wedged in the teeth.

    *b*    The cure is, as with any vice or bad habit, to ascertain the cause and if possible remove it or alleviate it.

    *c*    If nervousness, patience is required to overcome it; if lack of balance, balancing exercises; if heavy hands, a fresh rider with lighter hands; if heavy in the forehand, plenty of suppling exercises, rein-backs, etc.; if unsuitable bit, change it; etc.

ii    Tongue over the bit:

Some horses develop the tiresome habit of getting their tongue over the bit and sometimes even lolling it out of their mouths in a most unsightly manner, although it does little actual harm:

    *a*    It is often caused by too tight a curb-chain, or heavy hands lacking relaxation, or by careless, overhasty schooling.

    *b*    It is generally curable with a mild bit and light hands, but a flat leather port sewn over the mouthpiece of the bit may effect a cure: it is also advisable to make sure that the curb-chain is long enough.

iii    Fighting the bit and tossing the head:

This is another tiresome habit, but generally easily enough cured.

    *a*    It may be due to an unsuitable, or badly fitting, bit or bridle, to a sensitive mouth or heavy, niggling hands, or due to a wet neck from sweating.

    *b*    Cure by removing the cause: if the head-tossing is due to a wet neck, the best cure may be a standing martingale.

iv    Poking the nose:

This may be due to faulty conformation, but is more generally due to poor hands or poor schooling.

    *a*    If the cause is faulty conformation, a standing martingale may be necessary.

*b*   In the case of poor schooling, correction by a trainer with good hands should soon effect a cure.

v   Jogging:
This perpetual refusal to settle down to a walk and persistent jiggling trot can be very tiresome.

*a*   It may be due to too much heating foods and insufficient exercise, to badly fitting bit, bridle, sensitive mouth, or heavy niggling hands, or bad schooling.

*b*   Cure by removing the cause or by reschooling in the hands of a competent trainer.

vi   Running backwards:
This is really a form of baulking or jibbing, and if allowed to develop into a vice can be serious, as well as dangerous:

*a*   Initially, it may be due to a sensitive mouth, ill fitting or incorrect bitting, heavy, insensitive hands and incorrect use of the aids.

*b*   Correct by finding the cause and, if necessary, reschooling.

vii   Circling when being mounted:
This is yet another bad habit due to weak handling and should not be allowed to develop.

*a*   The horse's head should be turned towards the rider and the near-side of the head-stall held firmly with the left rein short.

*b*   Only when he is thus prepared, should the rider mount and the horse will be unable to circle away, especially if held against the wall of a building or similar position.

*c*   Careful, firm handling and schooling for this, as for most other bad habits, will soon effect a cure.

viii   Barging through gateways:
As with barging through doorways in the stables, this is simply a matter of firm handling.

*a*   The horse should not always be allowed off immediately on entering a field when being taken out to grass.

*b*   Walk some way into the field, then turn and walk back. Vary the place and routine of removing the head-collar or halter on each occasion; do not allow the horse to anticipate your actions.

ix   Refusal to box:
This is a very tiresome habit, due entirely to bad initial training or subsequent bad handling, or both:

*a*  Assuming there is no time factor involved, no attempt should be made to force the horse in with ropes, or by blindfolding it or using other devices: these may be successful, but are only postponing the solution to the problem.

*b*  The best method is to position the horse box so that the loading ramp is as near level with the ground as possible.

*c*  The example of a stable companion leading the way will usually be sufficient, but in difficult cases may not, at first, be enough.

*d*  Cover the ramp with straw and remove the central partition if there is one and coax the horse in with a feed, as if into an ordinary box. The sight of a stable companion eating a feed will generally overcome any suspicions.

*e*  Once the horse has overcome its fear and been rewarded, it should be led back to the stables. Repeat the performance after a day's pause and by degrees the resistance to boxing should be overcome.

*f*  At all times avoid noise, shouting, or evidence of excitement or bad temper; these are amongst the contributory factors to this common bad habit.

x  Refusal to be caught:
This can be a very tiresome habit indeed due entirely to bad initial training, or subsequent bad handling, and requires care and patience to overcome it.

*a*  The horse should always be fed and rewarded when coming to be handled.

*b*  It should not always be led into the stables, or worked immediately on being caught.

*c*  The horse, or pony, (it is usually a pony) should not be allowed to associate being caught with something unpleasant, e.g. being galloped incessantly and jogged in the mouth by a bad rider.

*d*  A small enclosure may have to be built by a gate, so that a separate gate, or pole, may be slid into place behind the pony when it comes in the first instance, but this should only be required if the pony has become really wild.

xi  Jumping out of the paddock:
This can be another extremely tiresome habit and one that can be very hard to cure.

*a*  The object is usually to find company, so the presence of a companion may cure it.

*b*  Making the paddock horse-proof is another obvious answer, but there are some horses or ponies (it is usually a pony) who will find their way out of anything.

# PART VII
# Ailments and Injuries

*Section 1 Diseases: Internal*
*Anthrax*
A short, fatal, notifiable and highly contagious disease causes by a bacillus.

i  Symptoms:
    The symptoms are alarming and obvious, but of such brief duration, only a few hours, that if the horse is outside the chances are that it will be found dead. The symptoms are:

    *a*  Swelling of throat and neck accompanied by great pain.
    *b*  A very high temperature.

ii  Incurable.

iii  Call vet and inform police.

*Arthritis*
May occur anywhere from the shoulder, or stifle, to the foot; it is a common disease in old horses. Causes unknown.

i  Symptoms:
    It may be very hard to diagnose in the early stages:

    *a*  The horse may be lame on one day and sound the next.
    *b*  The lameness will gradually increase until the horse can no longer be worked.

ii  The disease eats away the bone and is incurable.

*Asthma*
Fortunately, a rare disease in horses, but when it does occur is generally chronic: at more or less regular intervals the breathing is laboured and difficult.

337

i The cause is uncertain, but:

    a It may be due to stuffy insanitary stables. Or
    b It may be due to dusty fodder.

ii There is no known cure. But

    a It is advisable to check ventilation and sanitation.
    b All fodder should be fed damped.


## Azoturia
Or Monday Morning disease

i Cause:
It is due to a horse being fed its normal ration of corn, but having no exercise, as it might at the weekend: hence, Monday Morning disease.

ii Symptoms:

    a The horse's hindquarters are stiff and the hindlegs may drag.
    b The muscles of the loins may become very hard and tense.
    c The horse's breathing will quicken and he may start to sweat.
    d The muscles may be seen quivering and the horse may fall down and
      be unable to rise.
    e If any urine is passed, it will be coffee coloured.
    f The temperature will be about 103°F.
    g Pneumonia and death may result, but mild cases recover quickly.

iii Cure:

    a Prevent by altering diet accordingly when resting.
    b In the event of an attack, return horse to stable, in horse box if necessary,
      and give warm enema.
    c Send for vet and apply hot blankets to loins.
    d Food should be of a laxative type.


## Bronchitis
An inflammation of the bronchial tubes.

i Cause:
There are three chief causes:

    a Exposure to cold, particularly after heavy exercise when exhausted.
    b Infection by bacteria.
    c Irritants, e.g. thistle down the wrong way.

ii   Symptoms:
A harsh cough which increases when exercised. Also

*a*   A thin watery discharge from the nostrils, which later becomes thick.
*b*   A rise in temperature to 105°F.
*c*   Discharge from the eyes and mucous membrane turns dull red.
*d*   The pulse is fast and the breathing quick and effortful.

iii   Cure:
As with all cases of discharge from the nostrils, the vet should be called at once.

*a*   There should be plenty of fresh air available, but no draughts. Check ventilation.
*b*   Warmth is important and should be provided by rugs and bandages.
*c*   Rub the throat with liniment.
*d*   A eucalyptus inhalation will ease the horse but
*e*   N.B. Do NOT drench, or ball, as either may cause the horse to choke, and could cause pneumonia.

### Cold in the Head
Similar to the human cold in the head; caused by exposure or infection.

i   Symptoms:
There is a thin discharge from the nostrils which becomes thick. The coat will be dull and lifeless, staring.

*a*   The horse will probably both cough and sneeze.
*b*   He may water at the eyes and his temperature will be a little high.

ii   Cure:
The important thing is to rest the horse at once and avoid work, which may lead to pneumonia or other complications.

*a*   A laxative diet should be provided.
*b*   Check the temperature regularly, and if it does not drop to normal within a few days it is a sign of complications.
*c*   Add a pinch of nitre to the water.
*d*   Keep the stable well ventilated and the horse well rugged.
*e*   Provide eucalyptus inhalations.
*f*   Call vet if in any doubt.

### Colic
One of the commonest horse diseases, although it should be avoided by good

feeding and stable management, this is similar to stomach ache, or flatulence, in human beings:

i    There are two recognisable types of colic:

    *a*    Spasmodic colic, milder and less serious variety.
    *b*    Flatulent colic, more severe, when a vet may be advisable.

ii    Cause:
Both types of colic have similar causes, as follows:

    *a*    Injudicious watering after a heavy feed.
    *b*    Mouldy hay or fermented grain.
    *c*    A sudden change of diet or of temperature.
    *d*    Bad teeth causing poor digestion; or infestation of worms.
    *e*    Over-feeding or a stoppage in the stomach.
    *f*    Stones in the kidneys, bladder or bowels.
    *g*    Sand in the stomach.
    *h*    Twisted gut.

iii    Symptoms:
The symptoms are similar for both types, merely varying in severity:

    *a*    The horse turns round, looks at his stomach and kicks at it, whisking his tail.
    *b*    He is off his food, uneasy and possibly breathing heavily.
    *c*    He may break into a sweat, and the pulse will be very fast.
    *d*    The mucous membrane of the eye may be inflamed.
    *e*    He may strain to pass urine or faeces.
    *f*    He may lie down and get up again repeatedly and roll about violently.
    *g*    The belly may be swollen and the horse in obvious pain.

iv    Cure:
Whether, in fact, a cure is possible depends on the cause of the attack and its severity. Normally, however, it is simple enough to cure, but colic should never be treated lightly since it may be symptomatic of a serious, possibly fatal illness.

    *a*    If the attack starts outside the stables, the horse should be returned to his box and encouraged to stale, i.e. pass urine, by shaking straw under him and whistling.
    *b*    The horse should be well bedded-down and allowed to lie if he wishes, but must be prevented from injuring or casting himself: (see p. 330), he may be best walked around if showing signs of being extremely restless.

c   The horse should be drenched: a colic drench should be available, but a pint and a half of linseed oil with two tablespoonfuls each of brandy and turpentine added makes a ready substitute.

d   ·A warm enema may also be administered.

e   If relief does not seem to be experienced, a hot rolled blanket should be applied far back under the belly.

f   If the drench appears to have no effect within an hour, call the vet.

g   If the attack is due to stones in the bladder or intestine, or to a twisted gut, the attack may well prove fatal.

## Concussion
Similar to that suffered by humans:

i   Cause:
Due to a blow, such as knocking the head against a low doorway or beam.

ii   Symptoms:
The symptoms are similar to those experienced by humans.

a   Unconsciousness, which may be brief or last some time.

b   Involuntary action of bowels and bladder.

c   Breathing effortful and irregular.

d   The pupils of the eyes are dilated.

e   On recovering consciousness, the horse may be paralysed.

iii   Cure:
The vet should be sent for at once:

a   The horse should be kept absolutely quiet.

b   Ammonia, or a similar stimulant, may be held under the nose.

## Congestion of the Kidneys
The condition is as follows:

i   Cause:
Due to failure of the kidneys to excrete impurities. Or

a   May be due to fermented grain or mouldy hay, or other bad fodder.

b   May be the result of fever or other illness.

c   It may also result from an injury to the loins.

d   It may be the result of a severe chill.

ii   Symptoms:
The horse tends to be stiff, particularly in the hindquarters.

a   The loins are tender under pressure.

*b*     The urine is lighter coloured than normal.

*c*     The horse passes more urine than normal.

iii    Cure:
The horse should be rested.

*a*     He should also be kept warm and well rugged.

*b*     The diet may be changed.

*c*     Linseed mashes may be fed extensively.

*d*     If the cause is bad fodder a laxative should be given, otherwise not.

## Congestion of the Lungs

Is due to the lungs filling with an abnormal quantity of blood, and may be followed by pneumonia.

i     Causes:
May be caused by excessive exercise while the horse is unfit and is sometimes seen when a horse is ridden to a standstill, e.g. at the end of a long hunt. Also:

*a*     Exposure to bad weather.

*b*     Bacteria.

*c*     Irritants, e.g. a drench which has gone the wrong way.

ii    Symptoms:
The symptoms are alarming, as follows:

*a*     The nostrils are distended, the flanks and chest heaving with every breath.

*b*     The horse stands with legs outstretched and head and neck extended.

*c*     The horse will stagger and may fall if made to move.

*d*     The pulse is weak and the mucous membrane of the eye a dull blue.

*e*     The horse may break into a cold sweat.

*f*     The temperature may rise as high as 106°F.

iii    Cure:
The vet should be sent for promptly.

*a*     The horse should be placed in a well-ventilated box and warmly rugged.

*b*     He should be fed nutritious and laxative food, not bulk.

If affected in this way in the open, e.g. the hunting field:

*a*     The horse should be turned head to wind.

*b*     All constrictions, girths, throat-lash, etc., should be loosened.

*c*   A coat should be placed on his back and he should be rested for at least half an hour before trying to move him.

*d*   Box home as soon as possible.

*e*   In any event, a long period of convalescence is likely.

### Contagious Pleuro-Pneumonia

Uncommon, but highly infectious, due to bacteria in the air, food or water from an infected horse, with an incubation period of from two to seven days.

i   Symptoms:
The horse may not go off his food at first, but will be listless and may have a cough.

*a*   The appetite will disappear and the breathing become rapid and effortful.

*b*   The temperature may rise as high as 106°F.

*c*   A thin watery discharge from the nostrils will become thick and brown.

*d*   The mucous membrane of the eye will be bright red.

*e*   There is a swelling under the chest and the horse may grunt.

ii   Cure:
Immediate isolation is most important, and the vet should be called at once.

*a*   If not diagnosed promptly, it is unlikely the horse will survive.

*b*   Invalid foods, such as steamed hay, gruels, fresh grass, linseed mash, boiled oats and similar easily digested fodder, should be fed.

*c*   Eucalyptus inhalations may be given for relief.

*d*   The crisis will usually be about the sixth day, but a long convalescence will follow.

### Influenza

In the horse, this is quite different from human kind and may be either a mild variety, which lasts about a week, or a severe variety, or pinkeye, which is at its most critical about the end of the first week. Both are highly infectious and contagious.

i   Symptoms:
In both varieties, the temperature is high and the horse is exhausted: the vet should be called at once.

*a*   In the mild variety, the eye is dirty yellow, but in the severe variety, or pinkeye, it is bright red.

*b*   The legs, muzzle and belly may be swollen: the severe variety may often develop into pneumonia.

343

ii Cure:
The first step is isolation of any affected horse: it is advisable to call the vet.

a Draught-free ventilation and rugging well are important.
b Inhalations of eucalyptus, and invalid foods, are necessary.
c Check temperature regularly and nurse carefully.
d Best prevented by keeping horses in good condition, as most likely to attack horses when debilitated.
e It is essential to burn all infected bedding, also thoroughly disinfect clothing, box and grooming kit, or anything else which may have been in contact with an infected horse.

## Joint Evil, Joint Ill or Navel Ill

A disease affecting the foal from birth to eighteen months and caused by infection through the navel or from the mare's milk.

i Symptoms:
Varying depending on the age contracted and nature of the attack.

a There may be a reluctance to suckle.
b The temperature of the foal may rise to 103°F.
c The joints may swell, particularly hock and knee.
d The navel may swell and abscess.
e There may be marked stiffness and lameness and a tendency to lie down.

ii Cure:
If contracted, the chances of the foal surviving are small:

a The principal counters to joint evil are precautionary and consist of thorough disinfecting of the foaling box, etc. (see pp. 260–261).
b It is less common in mares foaling in the open.
c Disinfecting the navel at birth and sanitary conditions are the best precautions (see pp. 263–264).
d The vet should be called at any suspicion of the disease.

## Laryngitis

An inflammation of the lining of the throat, similar to sore throat in humans.

i Symptoms:
The horse will have a cough and difficulty in breathing.

a The throat will appear swollen.
b The horse's breathing will sound harsh.

*c*    There will be a discharge from the nostrils and, in severe cases, the throat may be blocked and the horse choke to death.

ii    Cure:
The vet should be called and an injection given.

*a*    The horse must be kept warmly rugged in a well-ventilated stable.
*b*    The throat may be rubbed with liniment.
*c*    Electuary should be smeared on the tongue as directed.
*d*    Gruels, linseed tea and similar invalid foods should be fed.
*e*    When the horse is able to digest more solid foods, bran mashes, green meat and damped hay should be fed.

## Pleurisy

An inflammation of the pleura or lung membrane generally caused by infection.

i    Symptoms:
The horse is off its feed, unwilling to move and obviously in pain, but generally will not lie down.

*a*    The temperature may be as high as 107°F.
*b*    The breathing is excessively fast and so is the pulse.
*c*    Both eyes and nose may discharge.

ii    Cure:
Death may follow in two or three days unless the vet is called at once.

*a*    The horse should be kept warmly rugged in a well-ventilated box.
*b*    Four tablespoonfuls of Epsom Salts and a pinch of nitre may be added to the drinking water daily.

## Pneumonia

Inflammation of the lungs due to bacteria, exposure to bad weather and over-exercise, i.e. riding horse to a standstill. A common complication with influenza, or strangles, or due to general debility.

i    Symptoms:
The head is outstretched and breathing fast and difficult, but the horse generally will not lie down.

*a*    The temperature will rise and the pulse is rapid.
*b*    The horse may have a cough and shivering attacks.
*c*    There may be a thin nasal discharge, which may turn brown.

ii    Cure:
As with congestion of lungs, influenza, or pleurisy and similar pulmonary

diseases, the horse must be warmly rugged in a well-ventilated stable and the vet called at once.

a   Four tablespoonfuls of Epsom Salts and a pinch of nitre may be added to the drinking water daily.
b   Eucalyptus inhalations may be given.
c   Careful nursing is important.

### Rheumatism

Rare in horses and, like arthritis, difficult to diagnose as the horse may be lame in one limb and then another.

i   Cure:
It is due to excess uric acid in the blood and hence green food is essential:

a   A laxative diet is also desirable.
b   The horse should be warmly rugged and embrocation rubbed into the affected joints.

ii   The horse may be exercised gently.

### Shivering

Is an incurable progressive disease generally following a severe fall or serious illness.

i   It is a nervous disease characterised by spasmodic involuntary muscular twitches.
ii   The hindlegs generally seem out of control and backing is difficult: touching the back may cause involuntary cringeing.

### Staggers or Megrims

A brain affection causing sudden loss of balance, equivalent to human fainting.

i   Cause:
Like 'tight-lacing' in a Victorian heroine, it may be due to poor circulation caused by tight harness, throat-lash, collar, etc.

a   May also be due to a weak heart, or brain congestion.
b   Or to incorrect feeding and impaired digestion, or worms.

ii   Symptoms:
The horse will stagger and fall to the ground.

a   Attacks are periodical with intervals of months, or even years; they occur invariably when working.

*b*   The attack will generally last about five minutes and the horse will then get up and seem dazed.

iii   Cure:
Ascertain the reason for the attack and treat accordingly:

*a*   If due to worms treat for worms.
*b*   If due to ill-fitting harness remove, etc.

## Stones

May be in the kidneys, bladder or intestines.

i   In the kidneys:
Unless both kidneys are affected, unlikely to cause trouble:

*a*   Symptoms are colic pains after work and repeated attempts to stale, tenderness over loins and gritty or sandy traces in the urine.
*b*   Cure by providing plenty of fluids, and add a spoonful of bicarbonate of soda to every bucket of water.

ii   In the bladder:
Large stones may cause colic pains and stiff movements and increasing in size with age may cause abrupt death.

*a*   The urine may tend to dribble continuously and be mixed with blood, also may smell strong and be very yellow.
*b*   Call in vet if suspected as an operation may be possible.

iii   In the intestines:
These are due to lime salt deposits in the bowels and can be very large, but it is the medium-size stones which may shift and cause a stoppage which are the most dangerous. The symptoms are repeated attacks of colic, which finally may prove fatal.

## Strangles

An extremely contagious disease caused by streptococci which attacks the nose and throat of young horses; generally under six years old.

i   Symptoms:
The first signs are generally dullness and thin watery discharge from the nostrils, which turns thick and yellowy.

*a*   The temperature rises to 105°F.
*b*   The mucous membrane of the eye will turn reddish.
*c*   The horse may start coughing and the glands in the throat will swell, becoming hot and tender.

347

d    These glands will later soften and burst.

e    Abscesses may also form on joints.

f    Should the streptococci enter the bloodstream abscesses may form internally and cause death (known as 'bastard strangles').

Strangles

ii    Care:

Call in the vet at once and isolate immediately, as well as burning all bedding, disinfecting grooming kit, rugs and stable.

a    Rug warmly in well-ventilated isolation box.

b    Give eucalyptus inhalations.

c    Swellings should be encouraged to burst and drain, being then treated as ordinary wounds.

d    Invalid fodder should include steamed hay, linseed mashes, green meat and gruels.

e    The disease will last from a month to two months, depending on its severity: the convalescence should be very gradual.

f    The wind is often affected.

*Tetanus*

A disease caused by bacillus gaining entry through a wound.

i    Symptoms:

The temperature rises to 103° or more and:

a    There is a general stiffening of the limbs.

b    The membrane of the eye extends over the eyeball.

c    Finally, the jaw becomes locked.

ii    Cure:

a    Immunity can be obtained by preventive injections.

*b*  Once the symptoms develop, the prognosis is hopeless.

## Worms

Worm infections are common enough.

i    Red worm:
     The red worm is the worst parasite affecting the horse in the British Isles.
     It is a blood-sucker and passes through the wall of the bowel into the blood
     vessels.

   *a*  The symptoms are severe loss of condition, dropped abdomen, dry,
        staring coat, irregular bowel action and evil-smelling diarrohoea.
   *b*  A microscopic worm count of the droppings is required to decide the
        degree of infestation.
   *c*  Call the vet for treatment, which is comparatively simple, but depends
        on the worm count.

ii   Round worm:
     The common intestinal worm found in most animals: white, round and
     about a foot in length.

   *a*  A large infestation may cause loss of condition and intermittent colic
        or bowel irregularity.
   *b*  Call in the vet, who will probably recommend starvation for twenty-
        four to thirty-six hours and saline stomach pump.

iii  Whip worms:
     These worms are about $1\frac{3}{4}$ inches long and very thin, found only in the
     rectum.

   *a*  They cause a sticky discharge from the anus and the horse will probably
        rub his tail badly.
   *b*  A saline solution of one handful of salt in a gallon of warm water
        should be given as an enema.

iv   Stomach bots:
     Not strictly worms, but the larvae of the gad-fly, which are laid on the
     horse's legs as eggs and ingested when licked by the horse, duly hatching out
     in the stomach.

   *a*  A heavy infestation may result in staring coat and loss of condition:
        they may be noticed in the dung.
   *b*  Prevent by clipping legs if many eggs are seen, or by singeing them.
   *c*  Internal infestation may be cured by a drench of 1 pint of linseed oil
        with two tablespoonfuls of turpentine.

349

*Section 2   Diseases: External—Contagious*

*Acne*
A highly contagious skin eruption of scattered pimples arising near the withers: dab with cottonwool soaked in antiseptic.

*Canadian Pox*
A highly contagious skin eruption of clusters of pimples, which may arise any-where on the body, but generally behind the elbows.

*Itchy Mane and Tail*
May be due to a parasite, or to worms, or blood condition: only contagious if due to a parasite.

i   The horse will rub the mane or tail.

ii  If due to worms, treat accordingly (see above), if due to blood condition, feed bran mashes and alter diet.

iii If due to parasite, treat as mange (see below).

*Lice*
May be found in horses out at grass or in poor condition. They cause the horse to lack condition with blotchy coat and he may be seen to rub against posts or trees.

i   The lice may be seen in the coat, especially in sunlight.

ii  Treat with any powder recommended by the vet: a second application will be required after ten days to deal with any eggs that have hatched out in the interval.

*Mange*
Parasitic mange must be reported to the local authorities as it is highly con-tagious.

i   There are three kinds of parasitic mange:

    *a*   Sarcoptic, which may occur on any part of the body, but is usually found on the neck and withers. This is by far the most serious variety: it is extremely hard to eradicate.

    *b*   Soroptic, due to a different form of mite, although found in similar parts of the body to sarcoptic: it is easier to eradicate.

    *c*   Symbiotic: this is generally confined to the legs or root of the tail.

ii  The symptoms for each are the same:

    *a*   Extreme irritation of the skin in the affected area.

    *b*   The horse will show signs of pleasure when scratched with a stick.

    *c*   The skin grows thick and wrinkled and the hair eventually falls out leaving small crusts in the affected area.

iii  Cure:

Isolate immediately and call the vet.

    *a*   The bedding should be burned, the stable and rugs disinfected.

    *b*   Clip out the horse if not already clipped and burn the hair.

    *c*   Treat as recommended by vet.

### Ringworm

An extremely contagious skin disease due to a fungus.

i   It may be contracted from strange horses, strange boxes, strange clothing, harness, or saddlery.

ii  The symptoms are circular raised patches of hair, generally on the neck or shoulders.

    *a*   The hair falls out, leaving greyish crusts on the bare skin.

    *b*   The horse rapidly loses condition and the contusion spreads quickly:

iii  Isolate the horse; all gear and tackle should be disinfected rigorously.

    *a*   If the coat is long it should be clipped and the hair burned.

    *b*   The patches should be washed thoroughly.

    *c*   The patches should then be painted with iodine, or as recommended by the vet.

### Section 3  Diseases: External—*non-contagious*
### Cracked Heels: or Mud Fever

Inflammation of the skin of the heels: also possibly legs and belly.

i   Cause:

Due to excessive mud and wet, but more prevalent in some areas than others.

    *a*   Washing the legs and heels destroys the natural oil and leaves the skin dry and predisposed to crack.

    *b*   If the legs are left to dry naturally under flannel bandages after exercise and are then brushed out, the complaint is unlikely to occur.

ii  Cure:

Wash the legs with warm water and soap.

    *a*    Then dry thoroughly and apply soothing lotion recommended by the vet.

    *b*    To prevent: rub vaseline in the legs and heels before exercise.

*Eczema*

Eczema is an inflammation of the skin consisting of an eruption of small pimples, which may discharge.

i    It may take one of two forms:

    *a*    Weeping eczema: in which the pimples exude a liquid causing matting of the hair and general irritation of the skin.

    *b*    Dry eczema: in which the scale flakes off and leaves dry skin.

ii    It is caused by dirt, irritants in the skin or indigestion.

    *a*    In the heels, or bend of the knee or hock, it may be dry and scaly, followed by ulcers.

    *b*    These may be painful and cause lameness.

iii    Cure by cleaning the affected areas and applying zinc ointment, also stop all heating foods and feed bran mashes.

*Grease*

Commonest in heavy draught horses in badly managed stables, but also found in light horses if cracked heels are ignored:

i    Appearance:
Cracked heels fill with a cheeselike growth.

    *a*    A foul-smelling watery liquid may be discharged from them.

    *b*    The skin may erupt in small swellings.

ii    Cure:
The legs should be clipped and the vet consulted as this can be hard to cure.

    *a*    A 1 per cent solution of zinc chloride may be used to damp them daily.

    *b*    They should be kept bandaged and padded to assist the circulation.

    *c*    They should not be washed.

*Humour*

A pustulous skin condition caused by overheated blood. Pimples may appear anywhere on the body: and may be cured by cutting down the corn fed and feeding laxative bran mashes.

352

*Heel bug*
This generally only affects thin-skinned well-bred horses, and the heels appear swollen and painful, causing lameness. Treat with sulphanilamide ointment or as directed by the vet.

*Nettlerash*
Also known as 'urticaria': when small areas of skin are raised: due to insect stings, or bites, or diet changes: may be anywhere on the body and patches varying in size up to 2 inches across. Treat with bran mashes and reduction of heating fodder.

*Warbles*
Uncommon in horses, but due to the maggot of the warble fly, which is laid as an egg in the summer.

i    Warbles not under the saddle or harness, are not serious and may be left to ripen naturally, but when they are must be dealt with as soon as possible.

    *a*    Fomentation should be applied to help the maggot to grow.
    *b*    When ready to emerge through the skin a small hole will be observed in the centre of the lump caused by the warble.
    *c*    This may be squeezed out with the thumbs, but, unless experienced, this may be best left to the vet.
    *d*    The cavity left should then be disinfected and painted with iodine.

ii    If a warble bursts under the skin, the pressure of saddle or harness will cause a swelling and veterinary attention will be required.

*Warts*
Ugly growths on the skin, most frequently found on the nose or face, or inside of the hindlegs or sheath.

i    Although unsightly are harmless unless under harness when they may be rubbed.

ii    It may be necessary to ask a vet's advice, but,

    *a*    A silk thread tightly tied round the base of a wart and retightened daily may cause it to drop off from lack of blood.
    *b*    A stick of caustic potash applied carefully each day may dissolve the wart.

*Section 4   Injuries*
*Abscess*
A concentration of pus in a cavity beneath the skin, which may be chronic, or acute:

i    Cause may be:

    *a*    A thorn, or splinter of wood, or glass, etc.
    *b*    Bacterial infection.
    *c*    Disease, e.g. tubercular.

ii    Treatment in acute cases is generally hot fomentations.

    *a*    Veterinary lancing may be required.
    *b*    If in doubt, the vet should be called in.

### Broken Knees

If the injury to the knee or knees, is deep, the vet should be called at once.

i    There is considerable danger with an open joint.

    *a*    Also the blemish may be greatly reduced if expert advice is quickly available.
    *b*    The wound should be cleaned with warm water and a little disinfectant.
    *c*    It should be dusted with a distinfectant powder.
    *d*    The horse's head should be tied up to prevent him dirtying the wounds.

ii    If the skin is not broken, but only the hair removed no treatment should be necessary.

### Brushing and Speedy Cutting

These result in injuries, due to the hoof of one leg striking the opposing leg.

i    Brushing occurs on the inside of the fetlocks, either fore or rear:

    *a*    It is generally due to faulty conformation.
    *b*    It may be due to poor condition.
    *c*    Or it may be due to poor shoeing.

ii    Speedy cutting occurs below the knee on the inside of the leg and is due to the same causes.

iii    The injury should be treated as a bruise, or a wound.

    *a*    The horse should be shod with three-quarter shoes.
    *b*    If necessary, he should be brought into better condition.
    *c*    If required, brushing boots may be worn to prevent repetition.

### Cataract, Conjunctivitis and Corneal Opacity

All of these may be the result of injury to the eye, caused by a blow.

i    Cataract:
This is opacity of the lens and may be tiny or may obscure the entire lens. As well as being caused by a blow, it may be the result of some other eye disease or due to heredity.

ii   Conjunctivitis:
This is an inflammation of the membrane covering the eye and, as well as being caused by a blow, may be due to a cold, or the presence of a foreign body in the eye.

iii  Corneal opacity:
The cornea, which should be transparent, may show a speck or be opaque; like conjunctivitis, it may be due to a blow, a cold or the presence of a foreign body.

iv  Conjunctivitis and corneal opacity:
In both these, tears are present and the eye will be kept closed to protect it from the light.

    *a*   The eye should be examined for any foreign body and if any is seen it must be carefully removed.
    *b*   The eye should be bathed in boracic lotion and the eyelid smeared with vaseline.
    *c*   The horse should be in a darkened box.

v    Corneal opacity and cataract:
To check for these, hold the flame of a gaslighter close to the eye in a darkened box.

    *a*   The flame will be reflected on the surface of the cornea and both surfaces of the lens.
    *b*   The inner image on the lens will be upside down.
    *c*   When the light is moved, the upside down image moves in the counter direction.
    *d*   If the lens and cornea are healthy, the images are clear and distinct, if not, they will be blurred or, in very bad cases, the reversed reflection will not be visible.
    *e*   The condition is incurable.

*Fistulous Withers*
An abscess above the withers between the shoulder blades.

i    Cause:

    *a*   An ill fitting saddle or harness.

    *b*   A bite by another horse or a blow.

ii   Symptoms:

    *a*   A pain in the withers followed by a swelling which may burst.

    *b*   The swelling may subside, but the pain remains.

iii   Cure:

Call the vet as soon as suspected: the condition is serious.

    *a*   A course of antibiotics may cure the condition.

    *b*   An operation may be necessary, but if neglected the prognosis is poor.

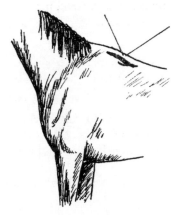

Fistulous Withers

*Nose Bleed*

Bleeding from the nose is the result of a broken blood vessel. It will generally stop of its own accord, but may recur. Bathe the nostrils with cold water; if from one only, plug with cottonwool.

*Opthalmia*

An inflammation of the eyeball, which may be due to a blow or to infection. It should be treated as is conjunctivitis, above: but generally develops into a cataract.

*Overreach*

Caused by the toe of the hind-shoe striking the heel, or back of the coronet of the foreleg; may also occur on the fetlock or higher.

i   It may be due to heavy going at fast paces, or jumping.

ii   If likely to occur, overreach boots should be worn.

iii  The injury may vary greatly in severity, but should be treated as wounds: iodine should be applied at once, if possible.

*Sitfast*
A hard painful swelling on the horse's back, due to pressure from an ill-fitting saddle, or harness, or continued pressure on a half-healed sore:

i  Symptoms:
A lump appears and gets larger and more painful the longer it is left.

*a*  In the case of an old sore, a hard dry skin forms over it.
*b*  This then comes off and leaves the sitfast.

ii  It must be cut out by a vet and then treated as an open wound.

*Wounds*
Wounds are dealt with on pp. 235–236.

*N.B.* Wounds near joints:

If a wound is near a joint and there is any sign of yellow flow from it, there is danger that this is synovial fluid or joint oil; in this case, call the vet at once. All wounds near joints are potentially more serious than others.

*Section 4  Lameness: In the Feet*
*Due to Bad Shoeing*
Lameness originating from bad shoeing results from a number of causes.

i  Bruised sole:
This may be caused by a badly fitted shoe, but is more generally due to treading heavily on a sharp stone.

*a*  The result is injury to the sensitive sole of the hoof, and which penetrates the outer wall.
*b*  The symptoms are heat and pain in the foot causing lameness: pressure on the sole with the shoeing pincers will cause the horse to wince.
*c*  Remove the shoe and poultice the foot until the inflammation and soreness have gone.
*d*  The horse should be carefully reshod with a light, flat, seated-out shoe.

ii  Contracted heels:
Due to lack of frog pressure, one or both heels may be contracted.

*a*  This may be due to the blacksmith paring the frog, or the bars of the foot (see pp. 162 and 174).
*b*  It may be due to shoeing with calkins that are too high.

    *c*    Or to the horse having been lame for some time, and not having carried weight on that foot.

    *d*    The sole should be rasped down at the heels to encourage frog pressure.

    *e*    The horse should be shod with tips only.

Half Shoe

iii    Corn:

A corn in a horse is similar to that in a human and caused by undue pressure of the shoe; due primarily to bad shoeing.

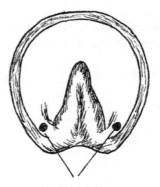

Seat of Corns

    *a*    It is in effect a bruise of the sensitive sole caused by the shoe, and, therefore, unlikely in unshod horses.

Half Shoe: Tip

*b*   Corns appear in the sole at the angle formed by the bar and the wall where the horn is thinner.

*c*   The treatment consists of removing the shoe, paring out the corn to remove the pressure and reshoeing with a three-quarter shoe.

*d*   If there is any pus found, an antiseptic poultice should be applied.

iv   Nail binding:
This is caused by nails being driven too close to the sensitive laminae of the foot:

*a*   The blacksmith should sense his error and check at the time (see pp. 169 and 175).

*b*   The symptoms are pain, lameness and heat in the foot.

*c*   The cure is remove the shoe and apply hot antiseptic poultices for two or three days, and rest.

v   Pricked sole:
May be caused by the farrier driving a nail into the sensitive sole, or by a nail picked up when exercising.

*a*   If due to the blacksmith, it is poor workmanship, even if the horn of the hoof is very thin (see p. 169).

*b*   The symptoms are heat and pain in the hoof, as in iv above, also lameness increasing in intensity.

*c*   The shoe should be removed at once and the puncture enlarged to ensure good drainage.

*d*   The vet may prescribe penicillin, or antibiotic injections, and, if the horse is not immunised, he may give an anti-tetanus injection.

*e*   Antiseptic poultices should be applied daily.

*f*   When the horse trots sound, a piece of tow may be inserted and either kept in place with a bar shoe, or with Stockholm tar.

vi   Seedy toe:
The middle layer of horn becomes separated from the sensitive layer underneath and a soft horn forms in the space between.

*a*   It may form anywhere in the wall of the foot, but is chiefly found in the toe.

*b*   One of the principle causes is excessive pressure on the wall of the foot due to tightly hammered or bulging toe clips, or tightly hammered clenches or nails.

*c*   It is generally discovered by the blacksmith when shoeing, due to lack of grip for the nail.

*d*   The horse will only go lame when the area concerned is large.

*e*   The affected horn should be pared away and dressed with Stockholm tar and tow. Reshoe to avoid bearing on the bad section of the foot.

*f*   The coronet should then be blistered to encourage new growth.

*g*   It is advisable to call in the vet, rather than leave it to the blacksmith if it is a bad case.

Seedy Toe

## Due to Injury or Lack of Care

i   Brittle feet:
These are caused by excessive dryness of the horn.

*a*   This is due to exposure to sand and sea water.

*b*   Fresh growth should be stimulated by blistering the coronet.

*c*   The horn should be oiled daily and kept clear of water.

ii   Canker:
Generally only found where horses are kept in very insanitary stables or in marshy area.

*a*   It is a softening of the horn forming a cheeselike growth with a foul smell.

*b*   It starts in the frog extending to the sole and the horn.

*c*   There is liable to be considerable pain and lameness.

*d*   It requires prompt veterinary attention and may require an operation to cure effectively.

iii   False quarter:
This is a horizontal crack in the hoof due to an injury to the coronet, such as a tread.

*a*   This checks the secretion of the horn.

*b*   The treatment is to blister the coronet to encourage fresh horn growth.

iv   Laminitis:

A most serious disease involving inflammation of the sensitive laminae under the horn of the hoof. More common in front than behind, and more common in flat feet.

Result of Acute Laminitis

*a*   It is due to hard work when unfit, or to galloping, either on the roads, or, when turned out to grass, on hard ground.
*b*   Too much heating food and not enough exercise may also cause it.
*c*   Too much weight being placed on one foot, i.e. if the other is injured, especially if the horse's diet has not been suitably altered to laxative.
*d*   It may follow a bad attack of colic, or foaling.
*e*   The symptoms are abnormal heat in the feet and obvious pain, evidenced by sweating and groaning.
*f*   The horse may move, when forced to do so, on its heels with his back arched and the temperature may be as high as 106°F.
*g*   Call the vet as an injection may be helpful.
*h*   Feed bran mashes, give an aloes ball and apply poultices.
      Encourage to lie down with plenty of bedding.

v    Navicular:

Incurable and fatal, this is a corrosive ulcer on the navicular bone, generally confined to the forefeet.

*a*   Too much fast work, or fast work on hard surfaces, causing concussion, especially after a long rest, are likely causes.
*b*   Contracted heels and short upright pasterns are more prone to navicular.
*c*   Lack of frog pressure, is liable to cause navicular: hence high calkins may result in the disease.
*d*   Navicular may be hereditary.
*e*   It is slow to appear and hard to detect, but the first signs are generally

pointing of a forefoot: if the alternate hindfoot is not rested also this is a bad sign.

*f*   The horse may be lame when setting out, but it will wear off with exercise or soft going, but there will be heat in the foot afterwards.

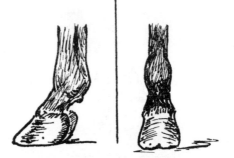

The Effects of Navicular Disease on the Feet

*g*   The lameness will increase with time, and the horse will become pottery and inclined to stumble. The foot will become contracted at the heels and the sole concave.

*h*   The horse is in pain, is dangerous to ride and there is no cure: the kindest thing, once diagnosed by the vet, is to have the horse put down. Temporary relief may be had by keeping the horse on a clay bed, but it is only temporary.

vi   Quittor:
This is a fistulous sore on the coronet, which may be due to a variety of causes:

*a*   A tread from another horse, or an overreach.
*b*   Due to pus working upwards from a suppurating corn, or
*c*   From a suppurating sandcrack, or
*d*   From a picked up nail which has been overlooked.
*e*   There will be pain and lameness followed by discharge.
*f*   Apply an antiseptic poultice and call the vet.

vii   Sandcrack:
This is a crack in the wall of the hoof running downwards from the coronet, sometimes to the ground, sometimes only part way.

*a*   The sandcrack may or may not cause lameness.
*b*   It may not be visible near the coronet but spreads further down the wall of the hoof.

*c*   It is generally due to a tread or overreach.

*d*   It may also be caused by rasping the wall of the hoof.

*e*   Remove the pressure from the crack and, if at the toe, shoe with quarter clips.

*f*   The crack may be isolated by making a groove with a hot iron, to prevent it extending to new horn; or a clasp may be put across it.

*g*   Fresh horn growth should be stimulated by blistering the coronet.

*h*   If it suppurates, the horn must be cut away to allow the pus to drain.

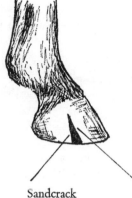

Sandcrack

viii Thrush:

Thrush is an inflammation of the frog similar to canker, but restricted to the cleft of the frog.

*a*   It is chiefly found in insanitary poorly mucked-out and badly drained stables.

*b*   It is liable to be a chronic condition, generally found in the hindfeet rather than the front.

*c*   It may cause lameness.

*d*   The smell, as with canker, is foul and unmistakable.

*e*   The cleft of the frog is soft and spongey as with canker.

*f*   Wash out and disinfect the foot: pare out the frog and apply Stockholm tar, salt and tow to the cavity. Renew the dressing twice daily.

*g*   Ensure that the horse stands on clean straw and is thoroughly mucked-out and cared for: caught before becoming chronic, as it should be, it is easily cured.

*In the Forehand*

i   Knee spavin:

This is a bony growth on the inner side, or at the back of the knee:

363

a   It is much less common than a hock spavin and more serious, though not hereditary.

b   It may be caused by a blow or a strain.

c   The knee will swell, but the horse may not go lame at first.

d   The horse will be unable to bend the knee and will move with a circular swing of the leg.

e   If the leg is bent at the knee, he will show signs of pain.

f   Treat by blistering.

ii  Shoulder lameness:
Generally caused by the horse landing badly over a jump, slipping, or falling with his forelegs spraddled.

a   The horse will trot short and slight swelling and heat may be noticeable.

b   The treatment is rest, application of liniment and massage.

c   Cold water may be applied to the shoulder with a hosepipe twice a day for about an hour.

iii Capped elbow:
A bruised and swollen point of the elbow caused by lack of bedding, uneven flooring or, more frequently, the heel of the shoe when lying down.

Capped Elbow

a   There may be temporary heat, pain and lameness at the time, but this is not likely to last long.

b   If the swelling is hard, the capped elbow is chronic.

c    If very large it points to an abscess which must be lanced.

d    For horses prone to capped elbows, plenty of bedding and three-quarter shoes should prevent recurrence.

e    A sausage boot, i.e. a stuffed leather ring, strapped round the coronet may also be used to prevent recurrence.

iv   Splint:

This is a bony enlargement of the cannon bone, generally on the inside of the forelegs, but sometimes on the outside. Seldom seen in the hindlegs:

Splint

a    Generally caused by the leg being jarred on a hard surface and, unless causing lameness, nothing to worry about.

b    Before they are six years old most working horses acquire some splints: after that age rarely, unless due to a blow.

c    While forming, a splint may cause spasmodic lameness, but once set they do not generally cause trouble unless interfering with a tendon or ligament; in the hind leg, they seldom cause lameness.

d    If they are high up under the knee, they are known as a 'knee splint', and this is the least desirable place for them.

e    To locate a splint, pick up the leg and press the fingers down the splint bone until the horse winces.

f    Cold water bandages and cooling lotion are generally sufficient, but it may be felt necessary to treat with liniment or to blister it.

*In the Hindquarters*

i    Bog spavin:

A soft and puffy swelling, generally chronic, on the inside and front of the hock, which does not necessarily cause lameness.

a    It is generally due to a strain, but is most frequently found in straight hocks.

   *b*   If it does cause lameness the horse will carry the leg and swing it clear of the ground.

   *c*   Treat by rest and massage with liniment.

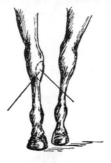

Bog Spavin

ii   Bone spavin:

A bony growth just below and inside the hock joint, which is not serious unless it causes lameness.

   *a*   It may be due to faulty conformation, e.g. sickle hocks, especially when under strain, such as jumping in heavy going, or due to excessive concussion or working too hard too young.

   *b*   The horse may drag the toe and shorten his stride, also appear to drop his hip as the lame leg comes to the ground; it may result in inability to bend the hock properly at a trot.

   *c*   A hard bony enlargement will develop.

   *d*   Treat by rest and raise the heels of the shoe.

Dropped hip

iii  Broken pelvis:
This is fortunately not common, but it is possible for it to be broken unobserved.

  *a*  It may happen by slipping on a smooth surface, by falling severely, or in jumping, or most frequently in passing through a narrow doorway, or by hitting a gatepost.
  *b*  The horse may be very lame and there may be a swelling between the legs.
  *c*  A creaking sound may be heard at the break itself.
  *d*  Complete rest in slings is the only possible treatment.

iv  Capped hock:
A damaged or swollen hock with either a swelling each side of the hock and lameness or an unsightly swelling on the point of the hock without lameness.

Capped Hock

  *a*  It is generally caused either by kicking in stables, or insufficient bedding.
  *b*  Treat with massage and liniment or a mild blister.
  *c*  Provide more bedding, or a hock-boot, to avoid repetition.

v  Curb:
A thickening of the tendon, or ligament, at the back of the hock, about 4 inches below the point of the hock, caused by strain and commonest in sickle hocks.

  *a*  It may not cause lameness, but if it does the horse goes on the toe and rests the heel at a stand.

  *b* Treat by raising the heel with calkins, or wedge heels, and apply cold water.

  *c* A mild blister may be sufficient, but firing may be recommended for a permanent cure.

  *d* *N.B.* False curb is merely an unduly large head of the metatarsal bone showing, and is neither a fault nor an unsoundness.

Curb

vi Occult spavin:

A growth between two bones of the hock, more serious than a bone spavin and more difficult to detect since there is no outward growth.

  *a* The cause is strain, or concussion and more likely to occur in sickle or cow hocks.

  *b* Treatment is rest and raise the heels of the shoe: blister, or pin-firing may help.

vii Stifle lameness:

Lameness in the stifle which may be due to a sprain or dislocation.

  *a* It is noticeable from behind as a horse trots away, since the same quarter will be slightly raised and the step slightly shorter.

  *b* If it is sprained, treat as an ordinary sprain with liniment.

  *c* If dislocated the vet must be called.

viii Stringhalt:

A nervous disease causing the horse suddenly to snatch up one or both hindlegs when walking, sometimes when trotting.

  *a* Sometimes it is barely noticeable.

  *b* In bad cases, the horse may almost kick himself.

  *c* There is no cure.

ix Thorough-pin:

A distension of the tendon sheath above and on either side of the point of the hock.

*a*  If it is small, no treatment is required.
*b*  If large, rest and blister.
*c*  Although technically an unsoundness, it seldom causes a horse to go lame.

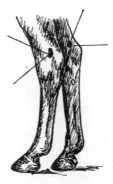

Thoro'pin

*General*

i  Ring-bone:
A bony enlargement of two types, known as low ring-bone and high ring-bone.

*a*  A low ring-bone is round the top of the hoof.
*b*  A high ring-bone is round the pastern bones.
*c*  It may be caused by a blow, but is most common in horses with straight pasterns and the result of concussion.
*d*  The symptoms are heat and enlargement.
*e*  Rest and call a vet.

ii  Sessamoiditis:
An inflammation of the sessamoid bones just above and behind the fetlock joint.

*a*  It is caused by faulty conformation, such as turned out toes or upright pasterns.
*b*  The horse will go lame off and on with varying degrees of heat noticeable.
*c*  The treatment is rest and a blister, but a cure is uncertain.

iii  Sidebone:
A bony growth which may form on either lateral cartilage of the foot and

369

may be hereditary, or caused by a blow, a tread, over high calkins or narrow feet.

*a*   A hard lump may be noticeable and heat in the coronet at the heel.
*b*   If the horse is not lame, no treatment is required, but if lame call a vet.

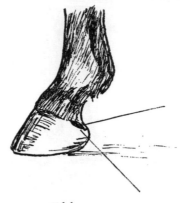

Sidebone

iv   Sore shins:
Inflammation of the membrane over the cannon bone caused by galloping on hard ground.

*a*   Results in heat and swelling.
*b*   Requires massage and rest, or possibly a mild blister.

v   Split pastern:
A fracture of the pastern, which is likely to cause extreme lameness:

*a*   It may require X-rays to diagnose it definitely.
*b*   Send for a vet if it is suspected.
*c*   It is believed to be caused by the tendons contracting together instead of alternately and does not necessarily occur at a fast pace.
*d*   It is usually treated with plaster of paris and a soft sawdust bed rather than slings.

vi   Sprains:
Generally in the forelegs, but occasionally in the hind-, sprains are caused by abruptly halting a horse, by all its weight landing on one leg, by too much galloping, especially on hard or heavy ground, by leaving the toes over-long, through defective conformation, by accidental slipping on ice, or concrete, etc.

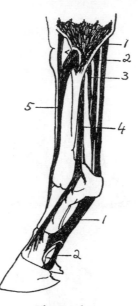

The Tendons

1. Perforatus Tendon. 2. Perforans Tendon. 3. Check Ligament. 4. Suspensory Ligament. 5. Extensort Tendon.

Sprained Tendons

*a*   The symptoms are heat, swelling pain and lameness.
*b*   Rest the horse and apply cold water bandages.
*c*   In bad cases, blistering or firing may be required if a recurrence is likely.

vii  Windgalls:
Soft painless swellings around the fetlock:

371

Swollen Fetlock

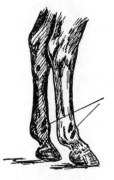

Wind Galls

a   They are caused by strain and overwork.
b   Though unsightly they are not harmful and will not cause lameness.
c   Cured by rest. Removing strain by calkins may help. Blistering is scarcely worth while, except for show purposes.

*Section 5   Wind Affections*
These may be due to affections of the throat, or of the larynx, or of the lungs: they may result in the horse 'making a noise', but it does not follow that all noises are indicative of unsoundness.

*Broken Wind*
Or heaves, so termed because there is a noticeable double exhalation, visible in the heaving flanks.

i    Cause:
It is due to a breakdown of the air vesicles of the lungs, through overstrain.

     *a*    This may be the result of respiratory disease, i.e. asthma, bronchitis, a chronic cough, pleurisy or pneumonia, etc.
     *b*    Or through excessive exercise after heavy feeding, particularly bulk feeding.

ii    Symptoms:
These generally start with a cough and slight nasal discharge.

     *a*    The cough grows shorter and the breathing laboured after any exertion.
     *b*    The double exhalation, noted above, becomes obvious.
     *c*    The horse eventually develops a large stomach and the flanks fall away.

iii    There is no cure, but it is advisable to call the vet for advice on treatment.

## High-blowing
A distinct sound made by a horse when galloping, but during exhalation only.

i    It is due to excessive flapping of the false nostril and is not a disease.

ii    Unlike whistling, or roaring, it disappears as the speed is increased.

## Thick in the Wind
This is generally a temporary condition, but as long as it lasts is an unsoundness.

i    It may be the result of bronchitis, or of the horse being grossly fat.

ii    The horse should not be given fast or severe work in this condition or it may lead to whistling.

## Whistling
The horse makes a high-pitched whistling sound when galloped.

i    It is due to an affection of the throat or larynx resulting from paralysis of the left vocal cord.

ii    It is serious in that it generally leads to roaring.

iii    It is sometimes possible for a horse to be an 'intermittent whistler', i.e. making a noise on some occasions and not on others, but this generally leads to whistling proper.

## Roaring
A deep noise made when the horse is trotted, cantered, or galloped, resulting in the horse being very distressed.

i   Once the condition has become established, it grows progressively worse, i.e. whistlers become roarers and steadily deteriorate.

    *a*   In the early stages, it may be hard to detect.
    *b*   A fit horse will make less noise than an unfit horse.

ii   The only remedy is an operation on the vocal cord allowing more room for air in the throat.

    *a*   The sooner the operation is carried out the more chance there is of success.
    *b*   Even if it is not completely successful, it is likely to allow the horse to be worked thereafter.

iii   Roaring can have a markedly bad effect on the heart, and it is advisable to check the heart. Signs of heart weakness are:

    *a*   Inability to stay and tiring easily.
    *b*   Irregular pulse and loss of condition.

*Testing for Soundness of Wind*
The horse may be tested inside and outside the stables.

i   Inside the stables, the horse may be held by the head, while an apparent threat is made to hit him in the ribs with a stick.

    *a*   The theory is that if he grunts when the stick comes forward this may be regarded as a sign of unsoundness.
    *b*   It is advisable to have an expert on 'grunts' present.

ii   Outside the stable, the normal method is to trot and canter the horse in circles in both directions: halt and listen; then gallop and listen again.

# PART VIII
## The Horse Inside Out

*Section 1    The Stomach, Lungs and Heart*

i    The Nasal Cavity:
     This is the first division of the respiratory tract:

   *a*    It extends from the nostrils to the pharynx.
   *b*    The doubling of the skin at the nostrils provides false nostrils for easy
          distension.

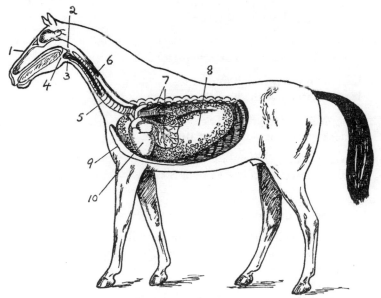

The Respiratory System

1. The Nasal Cavity. 2. The Pharynx. 3. The Larynx. 4. The Epiglottis. 5. The Trachea, or Windpipe. 6. The Oesophagus, or Gullet. 7. The Bronchi and Branches. 8. The Lungs. 9. The Sternum, or Breastbone. 10. The Heart.

ii  The Mouth:
The roof of the mouth is formed by the hard and soft palates.

a   The hard palate is thick and membranous with fifteen to twenty ridges, or bars, running across it.
b   The hard palate is succeeded by the soft palate.
c   The muscular and membranous soft palate prevents the horse breathing through the mouth and forces vomit to pass through the nose.

iii  The Pharynx:
The pharynx lies at the base of skull.

a   It is at the rear of both mouth and nose.
b   It is common to both the respiratory and alimentary tracts.

iv  The Larynx:
Is a short tube below the pharynx at the start of the trachea:

a   It is formed of cartilages: the thyroid, cricoid, two arytenoids and epiglottis, held together by muscles.
b   It contains the vocal cords.
c   The epiglottis acts as a valve at the entrance to the larynx to prevent food getting down the trachea.

v   The Trachea or Windpipe:
An almost cylindrical tube extending from the larynx to the chest.

a   It is about thirty inches long.
b   It terminates near the base of the heart by dividing into two bronchi.

vi  The oesophagus or gullet.
This extends from the pharynx to the stomach:

a   It is muscular and membranous with thick walls.
b   It passes down the centre of the neck above the trachea.

vii  The Bronchi and Branches:
The branches of the larynx:

a   These subdivide into smaller branches called 'bronchioles'.
b   They then terminate in infundibuli, from which spring the air cells of the lungs.

viii  The Lungs:
There are two, which fill the chest cavity.

a   They are spongey and elastic capable of considerable distention and contraction.

*b*   They are covered with a fine membrane called the 'pleura'.

ix   The Sternum, or Breast Bone:
In the centre of the body, this forms the floor of the chest cavity.

*a*   It consists of six bony segments united by cartilage.
*b*   It has eight depressions for cartilages of the true ribs.

x   The Heart:
The central pump of the body, conical in shape and weighing about 6 lbs.

*a*   It has four cavities, the two lower called 'ventricles', the two upper called 'auricles'.
*b*   It is a large hollow involuntary muscle situated between the lungs and enclosed in a protective envelope known as the pericardium.

xi   The Diaphragm:
A muscular and tendinous structure which forms a partition between the thoracic and abdominal cavities.

*a*   It is convex in front and concave behind.
*b*   It is the chief muscle in respiration.
*c*   If the horse is called on for severe effort with a full stomach, the diaphragm is liable to be ruptured.

xii   The Spleen:
A ductless gland situated around the curvature of the stomach.

*a*   It is a spongey reddish brown, or purple, organ.
*b*   It is often found enlarged in cases of illness: in anthrax it is both enlarged and ruptured.

xiii   The Stomach:
The stomach is placed behind the liver towards the left side of the body:

*a*   Its fluid capacity is about 3 gallons.
*b*   In shape, it is somewhat crescentic with the outlet near the opening.
*c*   The inlet is known as the 'cardiac orifice' and the outlet into the duodenum as the 'pyloric opening'.
*d*   It has three linings: the outer, peritoneum; the centre, muscular; the inner, mucous membrane.
*e*   The interior is in two parts, the left pale and hard, the right soft and red.
*f*   Near the cardiac orifice, the internal lining is puckered so as almost to obliterate the opening, hence the horse cannot vomit.

xiv  The Duodenum:
The first portion of the small intestine:

    *a*    It is twelve finger breadths in length.
    *b*    It starts at the pyloric orifice of the stomach.

xv  The Liver:
The largest gland in the body: lying between the diaphragm and the stomach, almost in the centre of the body.

    *a*    It secretes bile which it discharges into the intestine.
    *b*    The horse has no gall bladder.

xvi  The Large Colon, or Double Colon:
This forms the forward portion of the large intestine:

    *a*    It lies largely on the right side of the abdomen.
    *b*    It is about ten feet in length, folded into four parts.

xvii  The Caecum:
Lies immediately beyond the small colon:

    *a*    It is the first part of the large intestine.
    *b*    It is about three feet long.

xviii  The Small Intestine:
Extends from the pyloric orifice of the stomach to the caecum:

    *a*    Is divided into the duodenum, the jejunum and ileum.
    *b*    It is about seventy-two feet long.

xix  The Small Colon:
A continuation of the large colon.

    *a*    Continues to the base of the caecum.
    *b*    Is about ten feet long.

xx  The Rectum:
The terminal part of the large intestine.

    *a*    Leads from the small colon to the anus.
    *b*    Is about eighteen inches long.

xxi  The Anus:
The rounded orifice below the tail.

    *a*    The rear opening of the intestinal canal.
    *b*    It is closed by a muscle, the sphincter ani.

xxii The Kidneys:
There are two, one each side of the centre line of the body, below the lumbar vertebrae.

*a*   They are the glands concerned with urination.
*b*   They are kept in place by fibrous tissue, fat and the pressure of the intestines.

xxiii The Bladder:
This is a muscular membranous sac in the pelvic cavity.

*a*   It contains the urine.
*b*   When full, it extends to the abdomen.

xxiv The Urethra:
This is a long membranous tube.

*a*   It extends from the bladder to the apex of the penis in the male, or the vagina in the female.
*b*   It carries the urine from the bladder.

*Section 2   The Skeleton*

i   The Head:
This is generally divided into:

*a*   The cranium, or skull:
*b*   The face:

ii   The lower jaw:

*a*   The largest bone in the skull.
*b*   It articulates with the temporal bone on each side.

iii   The Atlas, or First Cervical Vertebra:

*a*   Is in the form of a ring with two wings, which can be felt just behind the ears.
*b*   It articulates with the occipital bone and axis, or the second cervical vertebra.

iv   The Axis, or Second Cervical Vertebra:

*a*   It has a long body with an odontoid, or toothlike, projection in front, on which the head rotates, hence its name.
*b*   It provides attachment for muscles.

v   The Cervical Vertebrae:
They are seven in number, forming the neck:

a   They are the largest in the spinal chain.
b   Each articulates with its neighbours.

vi  The Backbone:

a   This reaches from the skull to the tail.
b   It is composed of five regions, the cervical, dorsal, or thoracic, lumbar, sacral and occygeal.

vii The Dorsal and Lumbar Vertebrae.
There are eighteen dorsal and six lumbar vertebrae.

a   In the dorsals, the neural spines are marked and, up to the fourth or fifth, form the withers of the horse, decreasing in length thereafter.
b   Each has a corresponding rib with which it articulates.
c   The bodies of the lumbar vertebrae are flatter and longer and have no corresponding ribs.

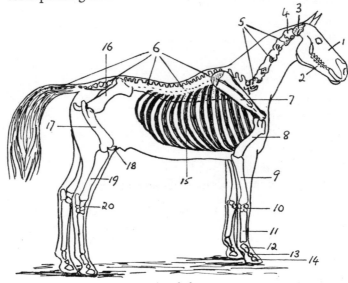

The Skeleton

1. The Skull, or Cranium. 2. The Lower Jaw. 3. The Atlas Bone. 4. The Axis, or Second Cervical Vertebrae. 5. The Cervical Vertebrae. 6. The Backbone. 7. The Scapula, or Shoulder Blade. 8. The Humerus. 9. The Radius. 10. The Knee, or Capral Bones. 11. The Metacarpus, or Cannon. 12. The First Phalanx, or Pastern Bone. 13. The Second Phalanx, or Os Coronae. 14. The Third Phalanx, or Os Pedis. 15. The Ribs. 16. The Croup Bones. 17. The Femur or Thigh Bone. 18. The Petella. 19. The Tibia. 20. The Tarsal Bones.

viii The Sacrum:

- *a* This is formed of five bones which are fused in the adult horse into one.
- *b* They are roughtly triangular in shape.

ix The Coccyx, or Tail Bones:

- *a* There are between fifteen and twenty.
- *b* They are very small in comparison with the other bones of the back.

x The Scapula, or Shoulder Blade:
This is a broad, roughly triangular bone on the outer side of the ribs.

- *a* It is broad and flat at the upper extremity.
- *b* It tapers to a neck and terminates in a hollow bulging head which fits over the humerus.

xi The Humerus:
This is a short strong bone articulating with the radius.

- *a* The upper end is rounded to fit into the concavity of the scapula.
- *b* The lower end has two condyles or knuckle type projections, which fit on the radius.

xii The Radius:
This is a long bone with a slight bend to the front:

- *a* The upper end is flattish with depressions to receive the condyles of the humerus.
- *b* The lower end has hollows and ridges to fit the bones of the knee.
- *c* The bone of the arm, fused to the lower rear end is the ulna, forming the point of the elbow.

xiii The Knee, or Carpal Bones:
These correspond with the human wrist:

- *a* Seven bones make up the group: scaphoid, lunar, cuneiform, unciform, magnum, trapezoid and trapezium (projecting backwards).
- *b* These are all small, articulate with one another and with the radius and ulna above and metacarpus below.

xiv The Metacarpus, or Cannon:
Consists of one large bone running from knee to fetlock, also one small bone on each side, the small metacarpal, or splint, bones.

- *a* The large round, cylindrical, upper end has depressions to fit the carpal bones and the lower end has two condyles to articulate with the pastern bone, or os suffraginis.

*b*    The splint bones articulate with the carpals at the larger upper end and terminate about two-thirds down the cannon at the 'button of the splint'.

xv  The First Phalanx, or Pastern Bone:
This is a rounded cylindrical bone.

    *a*    It articulates with the os coronae, or second phalanx.
    *b*    It is about one-third the length of the cannon.

xvi  The Sessamoids:
There are two, small, triangular prism-shaped bones behind the pastern joint.

    *a*    They are attached to the lower end of the cannon and the upper end of the first phalanx.
    *b*    They absorb some of the stress of the fetlock joint.

xvii The Second Phalanx, or Os Coronae:
This is of the same shape as the first, but shorter.

    *a*    The upper end has a projection to fit into the first phalanx.
    *b*    The lower end articulates with the coffin bone and the navicular bone.

xviii The Third Phalanx, or Os Pedis:
The shape of the os pedis, or coffin bone, is like the hoof.

    *a*    The bone is porous in appearance.
    *b*    In front, there is a triangular projection for the tendons and, behind, a pair of winglike projections to which the lateral cartilages are attached.

xix  The Navicular Bone:

    *a*    It is a boat-shaped bone.
    *b*    It lies behind the Os Pedis and between it and the Os Corona.

xx  The Ribs:
There are eighteen, attached to the backbone above and the breastbone below.

    *a*    The first eight are true ribs, the remainder are false ribs.
    *b*    They are all attached to the backbone by a joint and the breastbone by a cartilage.
    *c*    The false ribs are only connected to the breastbone through being connected to each other.

xxi  The Croup Bones:
Each is formed by the fusion of ileum, ischium and pubis.

a    These meet in a cup called the 'acetabulum', which receives the head of the thigh bone.

b    The ileum bone articulates above with the sacrum and also forms a projection, the haunch.

c    Each joins the opposite side below to form the pelvic girdle.

xxii The Femur, or Thigh Bone:
The most powerful bone in the body:

a    The upper end has a well-formed neck and head which fits into the acetabulum.

b    The lower end has two large condyles to articulate with the tibia.

xxiii The Patella:

a    A spongey bone which moves over the lower end of the femur.

b    It forms a part of the stifle joint.

xxiv The Tibia:
A triangular bone running from the femur to the hock.

a    On the outer side, a rudimentary bone called the fibula is attached.

b    The upper end is shaped like a low cone.

c    The lower end has two grooves into which the backbones fit.

xxv The Tarsal Bones:
There are six in number, placed in two rows.

a    Astralagis and calcis are on the top row.

b    Cuboid magnum, cuneiform magnum and cuneiform parvum form the lower row.

c    Astralagus is pulley shaped and fits into the lower end of the tibia.

d    Calcis has a tuberosity which forms the point of the hock.

xxvi The Cannon, First Phalanx, Sessamoid, Second Phalanx, Third Phalanx, etc. are the same as the corresponding bones in the forelegs.

*Section 3*    *The Deep Muscles*

i    The Temporal:
A small thick muscle attached to the lower jaw.

a    It closes the lower jaw and aids mastication.

b    When only one muscle acts, it produces lateral movement.

ii   The Longus Colli:

  *a*   Powerful muscles running below the cervical vertebrae.
  *b*   Their action is to bend the neck downwards.

iii  The Sterno-hyoid:

  *a*   A long muscle running under the surface of the neck close to the trachea or windpipe.
  *b*   It acts on the larynx and hyoid bone.

iv   The Scalenus:

  *a*   Runs from the last four cervical vertebrae to the first rib.
  *b*   Its action is to flex the neck, or when stationary assist the breathing.

v    The Rhomboideus:

  *a*   Is in two portions, the cervical portion and the dorsal portion, each inserted in the scapula.
  *b*   Their action is to pull the scapula upwards and forwards.

vi   The Longissimus Dorsi:
This is the strongest muscle in the body.

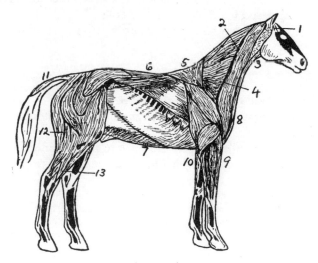

The Muscles

1. The Temporal. 2. The Longus Colli. 3. The Sterno-hyoid. 4. The Scalenus. 5. The Rhomboideus. 6. The Longissimus Dorsi. 7. The Rectus Abdominis. 8. The Biceps. 9. The Extesnor Suffraginis. 10. The Deep Flexor. 11. The Coccygeal. 12. The Semi-Membranosus. 13. The Flexor Metatarsi.

<dl>
<dd>a  It extends from the ileum, dorsal and lumbar spines, to the ribs, cervical and dorsal vertebrae.</dd>
<dd>b  It extends the spine, aids respiration and raises the neck.</dd>
</dl>

vii  The Rectus Abdominis:
This is a broad band from the breast bone to the pelvis.

<dl>
<dd>a  Its action is to aid respiration.</dd>
<dd>b  It also aids defecation, micturition and parturition.</dd>
</dl>

viii  The Biceps:
A very powerful muscle.

<dl>
<dd>a  This extends from the lower extremity of the scapula over the front of the humerus to the radius of the forearm.</dd>
<dd>b  It chiefly flexes the elbow joint, but also extends the shoulder joint.</dd>
</dl>

ix  The Extensor Suffraginis:

<dl>
<dd>a  It extends from the elbow joint over the knee and fetlock joints.</dd>
<dd>b  Its action is to extend the foot forwards.</dd>
</dl>

x  The Deep Flexor:

<dl>
<dd>a  A strong muscle extending from the humerus, radius and ulna to the os pedis.</dd>
<dd>b  It flexes the knee, fetlock and pastern joints.</dd>
</dl>

xi  The Coccygeal:
The tail muscles.

<dl>
<dd>a  Four in number from the lumbar and sacral regions.</dd>
<dd>b  They depress the tail and pull it to one side.</dd>
</dl>

xii  The Semi-Membranosus:

<dl>
<dd>a  A very large muscle extending from the ischium to the femur and patella.</dd>
<dd>b  It extends the hip joint and aids in rearing.</dd>
</dl>

xiii  The Flexor Metatarsi:

<dl>
<dd>a  A powerful muscle extending from the femur and tibia to the metatarsus.</dd>
<dd>b  Its action is to flex the hock.</dd>
</dl>

*Section 4  The Superficial Muscles*

i  The Auricular Muscles:
There are four principal muscles in this group:

  *a* To turn the ear forward.
  *b* To turn the ear back.
  *c* To pull the ear down to the neck.
  *d* To pull the ear down and outward.

ii The Masseter:

  *a* On the outer surface of the lower jaw.
  *b* The action closes the lower jaw.

iii The Orbicular:
There are three principal pairs in this group:

  *a* One pair open the eye.
  *b* The others close the eye.

iv The Muscles of the Lips and Nose:

  *a* There are five muscles used in opening and closing the lips and providing lateral movement.
  *b* There are four muscles concerned with opening and contracting the nasal passages.

v The Mastoido-Humeralis:

  *a* Runs from the head down the spinal column, over the shoulder and is attached to the humerus.
  *b* Brings the forelimb forward, or, if the horse is standing, lowers the head, or pulls the head to one side.

vi The Latissimus Dorsi:

  *a* A broad muscle which passes downwards and forwards over the chest.
  *b* Its action is to flex the shoulder joint.

vii The Scapular Muscles:
The depression each side of the scapula is filled with muscles.

  *a* Their action is to extend and abduct the shoulder joint.
  *b* These are the group concerned with the condition known as 'shoulder slip', i.e. shoulder lameness (p. 233).

viii The Extensors of the Arm:

  *a* These are powerful muscles originating from the humerus and extending down to the ulna.
  *b* Their action is to extend the fore-arm.

ix The Extensor Metacarpi:

  *a* This extends from the humerus to the cannon.

*b*    It extends the limb below the knee.

x    The Extensor Pedis:

*a*    This muscle extends from the humerus and radius to the os pedis.
*b*    It extends the foot and cannon.

xi    The Intercostals:

*a*    These muscles lie between the ribs.
*b*    Their function is to aid the breathing.

xii   The Fascia Lata:
This muscle arises from the sacral spines and the angle of the hip.

*a*    It spreads over the hip and leg to the femur.
*b*    It provides the muscles of the hip with attachment.

xiii  The Gluteus:

*a*    There are three gluteal muscles, each very powerful.
*b*    They abduct the thigh and are brought into play when the horse rears.

xiv   The Rectus Femoris:

*a*    A powerful muscle extending from the ileum to the patella.
*b*    The action is to flex the hip, and also to extend the stifle joint.

xv    The Vastus Externus:

*a*    Another powerful muscle extending from the femur to the patella.
*b*    Its action is to extend the stifle.

xvi   The Gastrocnemius:

*a*    A very powerful muscle extending from the femur to the calcis.
*b*    Its action is to extend the hock joint.

xvii  The Flexor Pedis Perforans:

*a*    This muscle extends from the rear of the tibia to the os pedis.
*b*    Its function is to extend the pastern and fetlock joints and to extend the hock.

xviii The Extensor Pedis:

*a*    This muscle extends from the femur down the front of the hock into the os pedis.
*b*    It helps to extend the fetlock and pastern joints and also the hock.

# GLOSSARY

Abscess: A concentration of pus in a cavity beneath the skin of a horse, which may be chronic, or acute, and caused by:
1 A thorn, or splinter of wood, glass, etc.;
2 Bacterial infection;
3 Disease, e.g. tuberculosis.
Treatment is generally hot fomentations unless veterinary lancing is required: consult vet if in doubt.

Acne: A highly contagious skin eruption of clusters of pimples near the withers of a horse. Dab with cotton wool soaked in a weak carbolic or antiseptic solution.

Action: A horse's ease, or otherwise, of movement, which should be free and even, equal on all limbs, straight and without twisting in or out. Of the curb, or curb-bit, or bit causes the horse to flex its jaw.

Action lessons: A method of training the horse by associating actions with the voice, physical commands, or rewards.

Age; ageing: Of the horse, may be told by the teeth.

Aged: Of a horse more than eight years old, after which age becomes difficult to gauge accurately.

Aids: To the control of the horse: see pp. 100–103.

Airs: Artificial paces other than the natural walk, trot and canter.
Principal artificial airs are: Spanish Walk, Spanish Trot, School-Walk, Passage, Piaffe.

Albinos: A recognized breed of horses, originating in the U.S.A., foaled white but turning golden dun.

Alcock Arabian: An eighteenth-century foundation stallion to which every grey thoroughbred's pedigree can be traced.

Alfalfa, or lucerne: A cloverlike plant, useful for fodder: see p. 218.

Alterative: A medicine which improves a horse's condition: see pp. 226–227.

Amble: Of a horse: to lift its feet on the same side together, i.e. a form of slow single-footing.

American Saddle-horse: Recorded since 1839, of average height 15–15.3 h.h.

Anglo-Arab: Any Thoroughbred-Arab cross.

Ankle boot: A protective boot worn by a horse to prevent brushing: see pp. 194–195.

Anthrax: An incurable, fatal and notifiable disease, caused by a bacillus. Symptoms: painful neck and throat swellings, high temperature and death within a few hours.

Appaloosa: A spotted breed of pony found in U.S.A. originally bred for war by the Nez Perce Indians.

Appetite: A horse's inclination to satisfy hunger, or otherwise, which may be used as a pointer to fitness and feed requirements.

Approved mare: A mare selected to be one of the forty or so covered by a particular stallion.

Arab: A breed of horse originating in Arabia, famous for endurance, pure breeding and intelligence.

Arm: The forethigh of a horse, from the elbow, beneath the chest to the junction of the knee.

Arthritis: An incurable disease in a horse, causing lameness. Hard to detect at start and chiefly found in old age; it may attack the bone anywhere from the stifle or the shoulder to the foot.

Astride: With legs on each side, the commonest method of riding, as opposed to side-saddle.

At bait: Of a horse which stands in stable during the day with food.

Australian nose-band: A rubber strap slipped over the bit rings and joined over the nose by junction to the brow-band. It exerts pressure on the nose and prevents the tongue being over the bit.

Azoturia: Otherwise Monday Morning Disease, thought to be caused by a day without exercise and full corn ration: the horse is stiff in the loins, sweating and runs a temperature. Give a warm enema and rest. Severe cases can cause death.


Back: Of a horse: see pp. 34–36.
To accustom a young horse to mounted rider: see pp. 284–285.

Back-pad: A harness-saddle, fitted as riding saddle and held in place by girth: see pp. 318–319.

Back-rein: To cause the horse to back by use of the reins and aids: see pp. 115 and 293–294.

Balance: Steady equilibrium: in horse may be improved by schooling; in rider depends on confidence and practise.

Balding girth: A plaited leather girth, designed to avoid galls.

Balearic: A distinctive breed of horse found in Majorca, with slender legs, a thick neck, a Roman nose and an upright mane.

Balk: Of a horse, to refuse a leap.

Ball: To administer physic to a horse in ball form: hence: balling.

To form lumps of ice in the shoes of a horse, when riding in snow, prevented by greasing the soles well beforehand.

Ballotade: A high-school air in which a horse half rears off its hocks and lands collectedly on four legs.

Bandages: These may be woollen to keep horse warm; or pressure, of nylon/terylene, for sprains and strains, for keeping dressings in position, or to prevent injuries; or cold-water bandages soaked in cold water for strains: pp. 190–193.

Bang: To cut the end of a horse's tail squarely with shears; hence, bang-tail: see pp. 181–182.

Bank: A method of fencing with an earth mound, common Ireland and the West Country. A common show-jumping obstacle.

Barrel: The body of the horse from behind the forearms to the loins.

Barren mare: A mare incapable of breeding.

Bars: The part of the horse's mouth without teeth, between the tushes and molars where the bit rests: see pp. 23 and 66–67.

The bars dividing the sole of the foot from the frog: see p. 162.

Bar-shoes: Shoes having the heel connected under the frog to relieve pressure, or in case of injury: see p. 173.

Basuto: An extremely hardy breed of S. African pony.

Bay: A colour of a horse, varying from near brown to near chestnut, notable for black mane and tail: see p. 41.

Bearing-rein, or check-rein: A fixed rein sometimes used on harness horse, or for training to cause the neck to arch like side reins undesirable: see p. 284.

Bedding: For a horse, may be straw, peat moss, sawdust, bracken, etc. See pp. 198–204.

Bed down: To arrange a horse's bedding for the night, hence, bedded-down, implying all well for the night: see pp. 203–204.

Behind the bit: Frightened of the bit, unable to bear the pressure on the bars of the mouth, hence, overflexed and out of control: see p. 286.

Bellyband: A part of the harness, a loose strap running through the pad holding the shaft tugs, keeping the shafts in position: see pp. 318 and 317.

Bending exercise: Weaving a horse between evenly spaced poles at various paces to test reaction to leg pressure and neck-reining.

Bishop: To file down the teeth of an aged horse, hollow the centre and burn black to emulate the teeth of a 5–6 year old. Once common amongst unscrupulous horse dealers; said to be named after one Bishop.

Bit: Or curb-bit, when used in conjunction with the bridoon, or snaffle to make up a double-bridle: see p. 66.

To insert the bit in the horse's mouth: see p. 69.

Bite: Of a horse, to attempt to savage another horse, or human: a vice best prevented by a muzzle.

Black: Melanistic pigment throughout the body, coat, limbs, mane and tail, see p. 42.

Black-brown: Where the dominant colour is black with a brown muzzle: see p. 42.

Blaze: A white marking between the eyes of a horse extending down the face the whole width of the nasal bones: see pp. 45–46.

Blemish: A mark left on a horse either by injury or disease.

Blinkers, or blinders, or winkers: Rigid leather addition to harness bridle: see p. 317.

Blister: To set up a counter-irritant, producing severe inflammation intended to draw blood to the affected area and expedite healing.

Blood horse: A Thoroughbred: see pp. 49–50.

Body: The trunk: a horse may be said to have 'depth of body', i.e. a deep chest conformation: see pp. 34–36.

Body brush: A grooming brush of short stout bristles with a webbing loop across the back, used in conjunction with a curry comb for removing scurf and dirt: see pp. 150–151.

Bog spavin: A soft and puffy swelling on the inside of the hock, caused by strain. Treat by rest and painting iodine: see pp. 365–366.

Bolt: Of a horse: to run away uncontrollably with the bit in its teeth.
To gulp food, due to teeth decay or greed: see p. 208.

Bone: Measured by the amount below knee or hock: see pp. 31 and 40. Hence, plenty of bone: good bone.

Bone spavin: A bone growth inside and just below the hock joint, which need not be serious unless it causes lameness: see p. 366.

Bore: Of a horse: to lean heavily on the bit.

Bots: The eggs of the gad fly which are laid on the horse's legs and when licked off hatch in the horse's stomach: effect is worms in large numbers, but otherwise not injurious. Cure linseed oil drench; starve for twenty-four hours if horse badly affected: see p. 349.

Box: To lead a horse into a horse box; hence, loosely, good boxer, difficult boxer: see pp. 269 and 335–336.

Box foot: A hoof with a small frog, high heel and upright wall: see p. 33.

Boy's horse: A horse suitable for a boy, generally used in negative form to indicate a strong puller or difficult ride not suitable for a boy, or novice.

Bran: The husk of grain separated from the flour in the milling: see pp. 225–226.

Bran mash: Horse feed of damped bran: see p. 226.

Break: To tame, or teach horse discipline (Obs. Mod: usage: school), hence,

halter break, i.e. accustom to halter, break to voice, saddle, traffic, etc.

Breast-cloth, or breast pad: Used in very cold countries to prevent the horse's breath condensing on the breast, which can cause pneumonia; buckled below the collar and forms useful protection from the cold.

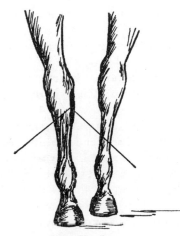

Bone Spavin

Breast-collar, or breast-straps: A light harness pad held in place by a neck strap used in place of a collar and less likely to cause injury: see p. 318.

Breeching: A broad leather band suspended behind a horse's hindquarters to take the weight of a vehicle on halting, down slopes and backing. Should fit 12–15 inches below the root of the tail. Only necessary for heavy cart work. Complete breeching consists of crupper, breeching body, breeching straps and hip straps: see p. 319.

Breed: To raise horse: see pp. 250–266.
A particular strain, or type of horse recognized as pure bred. There are over 100 recognized breeds and types of horse. See pp. 47–54.

Breeder: One who rears horses, a stud-owner.

Breeding: The pedigree of a horse, hence, 'shows his breeding'.

Breton: A breed of French draught horse raised in Brittany and hardy good workers.

Bridge: The bridge of hands, or crossed reins across a horse's crest to prevent the body falling forward, over jumps, or steep slopes. Used in steeple-chasing: see p. 94.

Bridle: The head-gear of a riding or driving harness: see pp. 65–67 and 317.

Bridle-bracket: A wall bracket designed to hold the bridle.

Bridle-hand: The hand holding the reins, generally the left.

Bridle-head: The part of the bridle crossing the poll, joined to the cheeks and of which the throat-latch is part.

Bridoon: The small snaffle-bit which makes up part of the double-bridle.

Brittle hoof: A hoof with easily split horn, due to lack of care, heredity, or bad shoeing. Treat by blistering the coronet to stimulate growth and by oiling daily.

Broken knee: Any open injury to the knee of a horse is so named. It may be caused by a fall on a hard surface and is advisable to call in vet; the injury and marking may be reduced.

Broken wind, or heaves: Overdistention and breakdown of the air vesicles of the lung of a horse caused by strain; may be the result of pneumonia, respiratory disease, or excessive bulk feeding. There is a noticeable double exhalation visible in the heaving flanks, hence, heaves: The horse develops a large belly and its flanks fall away; there is no cure but it is not hereditary.

Brood mare: A mare used for breeding purposes: see pp. 251–255.

Brow-band: A strap joining the two side straps of the head-stall: see p. 65.

Brown: A colour recognized by the colour of the horse's nose: see p. 42.

Bruise: Contusion caused by a blow, not always obvious in a horse: the treatment is cold fomentations.

Bruised sole: Contusion to the sensitive sole of a horse's foot, caused by treading on a sharp object: the symptoms are heat, pain and lameness: see p. 357.

Brush: Implement, generally of bristles set in wood, for grooming horses. There are three kinds. Dandy brush: generally of stiff fibre used for removing hard caked mud from the coat: see p. 151. Body brush: of short stout bristles for removing dirt and scurf: see pp. 150–151. Water brush: with softer bristles for damping mane and tail: see p. 151.

Of a horse: to strike the fetlock, coronet, or hoof of the opposite foot with the inner side of the hoof or shoe.

Brushing boots, or Yorkshire boots: Made by saddlers in a variety of ways; to prevent injury by brushing: see p. 195.

Buck: Of a horse: to arch its back.

Buttock: Of horse: the back of the thighs: see pp. 37–38.

Byerly Turk: A stallion imported to England in 1689, which had a great effect on English thoroughbred breeding.


Cadence: A dressage term denoting the rhythm of a horse, its balanced movement and rhythmical airs.

Calkins, or calks: Projections on the underside of the heel of the shoe: see pp. 170–171.

Camargue horse: A breed of horse, generally greys about 14 h.h., found in southern France.

Canker: A rare disease resulting in softening of the horn of the hoof, with a cheeselike growth and foul smell. Generally caused by bad drainage or marshy conditions and requires veterinary treatment.

Cannon bone: The shin bone of a horse: see pp. 31.

Canter: A pace of three time with a fourth silent beat. The pace set by the pilgrims on horseback to Canterbury, hence known as the 'Canterbury gallop': see pp. 109–110.

Cantle: The raised rear part of the riding saddle: see p. 57.

Capped elbow, or Shoeboil: A swollen point of the elbow, generally caused by lack of bedding when lying down; see pp. 364–5.

Capped hock: A damaged or swollen hock, may be caused by lack of bedding, or kicking in the stable: see p. 367.

Carriage: The head, tail, body and deportment and bearing of the horse: see pp. 26–41.

Carty: Of any draught horse, or similar type; derogatory in connection with a thoroughbred cross.

Cast: To throw a horse to the ground by use of special hobbles; or of a horse which has lain down in the stables, or fallen down, and is unable to rise: see p. 330. Of horse's coat: to shed it.

Cataract: An opacity of the lens of the eye, possibly hereditary, or the result of a blow, or disease; incurable: see pp. 354–356.

Catch hold: Of a horse: to take charge of its rider and bolt.

Castrate: To emasculate a male horse. Alt. geld, hence, gelding: see p. 269.

Cavesson: A strong leather head-collar, used for lunging: see p. 77.

Chaff: The remains left after threshing corn, or less correctly. Chopped hay, or straw, useful to provide bulk with oats: see pp. 219–220.

Chaff-cutter: A machine used to chop hay or straw.

Champ: Of a horse: to work the bit in the mouth, to take hold of the bit and play with it.

Change of leg: The act of altering the leading leg at the canter: see pp. 303–305.

Check-rein: See bearing-rein.

Cheek: The sidepiece of a bit: see p. 66.

Cheekpiece: The part of the bridle to which the bit is attached: see p. 66.

Chestnut: A whole colour of a horse: see p. 42. A horny outgrowth on the inside of the forelegs, above the knee; on the inside of hindlegs, below the hock.

Chill: A cold often the result of lack of grooming after exercise.

Chin groove: An obvious cleft beneath a horse's chin in which the curb-chain should lie: see p. 24.

Chop: A mixed feed of chopped hay, crushed oats, etc. (colloq.).

Churn barrel: (Colloq.) A well-ribbed-up animal, especially a brood mare with well-sprung ribs and a large belly.

Cinch: (U.S.A.) Girth.

Clean-bred: Of any animal of any breed with no impure blood in the pedigree.

Clean leg: A horse's leg free from blemishes, splints, etc.

Clench, or clinch: The point of a horseshoe nail when hammered through the hoof, twisted off and hammered down into place: see pp. 169-170.

Cleveland Bay: A pure-bred type of carriage horse: see pp. 48-49.

Clicking, or forging: The noisy action of a horse caused by striking the toe, of the forefoot with the toe of the hindfoot: generally occurs when the horse is weak, unfit, or going loosely and uncollected. Cure is to collect the horse, have its shoes attended to.

Clip: To remove the winter coat of a horse when bringing it in for work generally in October or November and early in the New Year to remove growth, but not after April-May when the spring coat appears: Three types of clip common: trace-high, clipping only belly and upper parts of leg; right-out, when the whole horse is clipped; hunter's clip, generally leaving saddle patch and legs unclipped: see pp. 176-181.

Clips: Of shoeing: to hold shoe in place: p. 170.

Close-coupled: Of a horse with a short, deep and compact body, with well-sprung ribs.

Clothing: Rugs, used to prevent a clipped horse catching a chill in the stable, may be day, or night rug: see pp. 185-188.

Clydesdale: A breed of heavy horse originating in Clydesdale: see p. 48.

Coachman's elbow: The salute when driving a coach, given by raising the whip to eye level across the body, hence, 'raising the elbow'.

Coat: The skin of the horse; should be shining and glossy.

Cob: Any horse between 14-15 h.h. of sturdy build; only the Welsh cob is a separate breed: see pp. 51 and 53.

Cold: In the head of the horse is similar to a human cold, with sneezing and discharge from the nose, cough, watering eyes, a dull coat and slight temperature. Caused by chill, neglect, or contagion. Treat with bran mashes and linseed, inhalations of eucalyptus: see p. 339.

Cold-back: A condition which may cause the horse to buck, or kick, when the saddle is first put on: warm the saddle beforehand to avoid this: see p. 60.

Cold-bit: An unwarmed, frozen, bit should not be inserted in the horse's mouth: see p. 71.

Cold-blooded breeds: The breeds originating from N.W. Europe and parts of N. Asia, as opposed to warm-blooded breeds from the Orient and Mediter-

ranean. Generally a large-headed, heavy-boned and coarse type.

Cold shoe: To nail a shoe on a horse's foot without shaping and heating beforehand.

Colic: May be of two kinds: spasmodic colic caused by an abrupt change of temperature or food, or watering after a grain feed, or nervousness; Symptoms kicking at abdomen, tail whisking: treatment drench and enema: see pp. 339–340. Flatulent colic: caused by bad food, fermented grain, sudden change of diet, or bad teeth; symptoms similar to spasmodic colic, but belly swollen and constant pain; may be advisable to call vet; give drench and enema.

Collar: Fits over head and takes weight of the load when horse moves forward: see pp. 319–320.

Collar gall: A sore generally caused by friction of ill-fitting collar: see pp. 235 and 320.

Collect: To shorten the horse's pace, by light pressure of the hands while driving the hindquarters forward by leg pressure, hence, a collected horse is said to be on the bit and in front of the legs, see pp. 106 and 290–292.

Colostrum milk: The first milk from a newly foaled mare is colostrum and is important to the foal for the purifying and disease-resistant qualities it contains; the foal should suck this within two hours: see pp. 263–264.

Colt: A young entire, i.e. uncastrated, male horse, from the stage of weaning from his dam to the time when he is either castrated or goes on to become a stallion: see p. 47.

Common: common bred. Lacking quality, coarse.

Concentrates: see Nuts.

Condition: Implies good working condition, i.e. the body hard, but well covered with flesh, a firm neck, a silky and glossy coat, a bright eye, and good appetite, digestion, dung and urine, as well as good spirits.

Confidential: Implies an old man's horse with no tricks; dead quiet.

Conformation: The build and manner in which a horse is formed: see pp. 21–41.

Congestion: Abnormal accumulation of fluid in a part of the body of the horse. Of the kidneys: may arise from shock, loin injury, or a chill. An increased amount of light-coloured urine is passed and the quarters are noticeably stiff: rug warmly, change diet and feed linseed mashes. Of the lungs: due to bacteria, exposure or hard exercise when unfit; the horse stands with its neck and head outstretched and falls if made to move; its breathing is very exaggerated and its flanks heave, while there is a rapid rise in temperature; the condition may arise from being ridden to a standstill and the immediate treatment in the open is to stand the horse with its head to wind, remove all constricting straps, place a coat over its back and keep as warm as

possible. Do not move for at least half an hour; later keep in a warm airy box and feed laxative food. Send for vet: see pp. 342–343.

Conjunctivitis: Inflammation of the membrane covering the eye, due to cold, foreign matter, a blow, or whip lash: tears are visible and the eye is swollen. Examine the eye for a foreign body, bathe and smear the eyelid with vaseline or a similar ointment and keep the horse in a dark box: see pp. 354–355.

Connemara: Breed of hardy pony found in Western Eire: standing 13–14 h.h. see p. 53.

Constipation: The failure of the horse's bowels to operate due to faulty feeding or lack of exercise; put on soft laxative foods and, if necessary, give an enema.

Contact: The link formed by the reins between the hands of the rider and the horse's mouth; should be light, but positive, the lighter the better. Hence, light contact, light hands, light mouth: see p. 102.

Contracted heels: A condition where the walls of the foot are contracted on one or both sides of the heel, due to lack of frog pressure; may be due to the blacksmith paring the frog, making calkins too high, or may be due to lameness preventing the horse putting weight on the leg: see pp. 357–358.

Coper: (Colloq.) A dealer in horses; often incorrectly used in derogatory sense.

Corn: A bruise on the sensitive sole of the foot, due to bad shoeing, or to the shoes being left on too long. Remove the shoe, pare the corn and, if necessary, poultice; then reshoe with three-quarter shoe: see p. 358.

Coronary band, or coronary cushion: The bulge above the coronet at the base of the pastern: see p. 32.

Coronet: The lowest point of the pastern immediately adjoining the hoof.

Cough: A violent noisy involuntary expulsion of air from the lungs, caused by a chill, dry dusty feeding, bad health, or contagion. Treat with electuary, warmth and rest; isolate.

Cow kick: A forward kick with the hindlegs.

Cow hocks: Inward turning hocks resembling those of a cow: see p. 39.

Cracked heel; or grease: see grease.

Crib-biting: A vice consisting of grasping the manger or similar object in the teeth and generally swallowing air at the same time; caused by boredom or imitation in stables. Causes indigestion, colic and deformation of teeth; remove stable fittings, or heavy creosote, etc.: see pp. 325–326.

Croup: The rump of the horse: see pp. 36–37.

Crupper: A padded loop of leather fitted round the root of the horse's tail buckled either to a D at the back of the saddle, or the rear of the harness-pad, to keep them in place if necessary: the crupper-strap should allow

Cow Hocks

two fingers to pass between it and a horse's croup: see pp. 80 and 320.

Curb: To flex the lower jaw of the horse by use of the bit, or curb-bit and curb-chain, which acts on the bars of the mouth when contact is made more positive, i.e. by pressure on the curb-rein.

A thickening of the tendon, or ligament, at the back of the hock, about 4 inches below the point of the hock, caused by strain and most common in sickle hocks: may not cause lameness, but if it does the horse goes on the toe and rests the heel at stand: treat by resting the heel with calkins and apply cold water.

N.B. False curb is caused by the head of metatarsal bone being unduly large and is not a fault or unsoundness.

Curb-chain: A chain used in conjunction with a curb-bit, fitting across the chin groove and attached to the hooks on the cheekpieces of the bit; it should be twisted right-handed to lie flat and should be thick to avoid causing sores: see pp. 66–67.

Curb-strap or lip strap: Fastened to each cheekpiece of the bit and holding the curb-chain in place: A curb-strap or lip strap may sometimes be used in place of the chain with a very tender skinned horse, which objects to the chain: see p. 67.

Curby hocked: Implying that the hocks have curbs.

Curry comb: A metal plate with blunt teeth on one side for cleaning the body brush of accumulated scurf when grooming; held by wooden handle, or by loop on back of hand: see pp. 150–151.

Daisy-cutter: (Colloq.) A horse with such a low action that it goes near to the ground, i.e. does not raise its legs.

Dales pony: A breed of native pony found in Yorkshire: see p. 53.

Dam: The mother of a horse.

Dandruff: Scurf, removed from a horse by the body brush: see p. 149.

Dandy brush: See Brush: pp. 150–151.

Dapple-grey: Of a horse, grey with darker spots of seasonal origin: see pp. 42–43.

Darley Arabian: A famous foundation stud horse born in 1702 and imported in the early eighteenth century: Many famous Thoroughbreds trace back to him: see p. 49.

Dartmoor pony: A breed of pony native to Dartmoor, whose height does not exceed 12·2 h.h. A popular children's pony: see p. 54.

Debility: Weakness, or lack of condition, due to disease, poor horsemastership, or similar cause.

Deep through the girth: (Colloq.) Deep-chested.

Derm: The true skin, or inner skin, of a horse, full of blood vessels and nerves, which extrudes layers of cells, which form the outer skin, or epidermis: these, in turn, dry up on the horse and cause dandruff.

Destroy: To kill humanely. The bullet should be aimed through the brain at the intersection of lines from the base of each ear to the opposite eye.

Diagonal aids: Provided by a rider's opposite hand and leg to make a horse move diagonally, i.e. left rein pressure and right leg pressure moving hindquarters over at the same instant, or vice versa: see p. 103.

Diarrhoea: Frequent evacuation of fluid faeces, caused by sudden changes of diet; a chill on the stomach; excitement; red worms; or indigestible matter in the intestine. Find the cause and remove it.

Dipped back: A back where the dip between the withers and the loins is pronounced: common in old age; also known as 'sway back': see pp. 34–35.

Direct impulsion: Making a horse move forward by pressure of the legs behind the girths, easing contact on the reins and using the voice. see pp. 106 and 287.

Dished face: (Colloq.) A concave-shaped frontal appearance of the face: see pp. 24 and 52.

Dishing: Throwing out the forefeet sideways, moving badly in front, with an untrue action, not straight: see p. 33.

Dismounting: The act of alighting from a horse: see p. 97.

Disunited: Of a canter; with the wrong rhythm and wrong legs together: see p. 110.

Dock: The root of the tail. To cut the tail short, now illegal.

Doer: Of a horse: Good or bad, an animal which thrives well or badly; a good doer readily puts on flesh and condition, a poor doer does not, hence, does badly.

Done: Of a horse which is exhausted, or alternatively, of one that has been groomed.

Donkey feet: See 'Box feet'. Narrow, upright feet, generally with contracted frog: see p. 33.

Dorsal stripe: A continuous black stripe from neck to tail, common in many northern and Asian breeds.

Double-bridle: A bridle consisting of a bridoon, or snaffle, and bit, or curb-bit: see pp. 64–71.

Double-jump: Two fences, or rails, set far enough apart to compel a horse to jump in between them and out again in two movements.

Drain: A channel constructed to lead off liquid sewage; of two kinds in stables— underground or surface: see p. 138.

Draught horse: A horse accustomed to drawing loads in harness: see p. 48.

Drench: To administer liquid medicine to a horse: see pp. 236–237.

Dressage: The training of a horse in obedience to the aids and collected paces: see pp. 311–313.

Ds: D-shaped metal fittings attached to a saddle, to which flasks, packs, etc., can be fitted.

Dumb jockey: A wooden mechanism, adjusted with bearing reins to simulate a rider while lunging a young horse; a harmful device: see pp. 284–285.

Dump: To rasp away the front of the toe when shoeing in order to make the foot fit the shoe rather than the shoe fit the hoof; an inexcusable but common practise when shoeing: see p. 174.

Dun: Black coloration of the skin of a horse: see p. 42.

Dung: The faeces of a horse, which should be moderately soft, well formed and brittle, light in colour, moderately damp and free from odour or slime: see p. 209.

Dung-eating: A vice indicating depraved appetite due to incorrect diet, lack of salt, or stomach acidity: check cause and cure: see p. 330.

Ears: The organs of hearing, acute and sensitive, which should be pricked and erect; when laid back are indicative of temperament and are generally a useful guide to a horse's attitude of mind: see p. 25.

Ear-stripping: The action of gently pulling the ears of a horse, while standing in front of it to warm them when they are cold or to dry them when they are wet; the condition of the ears is an indication of the temperature of the body and when the horse is being groomed after work, this is most important; correctly performed the horse enjoys it: see p. 158.

Eczema: Non-contagious inflammation of the skin, characterized by very small pimples which may discharge; often limited to one small area, it may be caused by dirt or indigestion; it may be either a dry eczema with a scaly effect, or a wet eczema with liquid causing matting of the hair, in the heels, or bend of the knee or hock, which can cause ulcers and may be very painful. To treat stop heating foods, put horse on bran mashes, clean the affected part and anoint with zinc ointment: see p. 352.

Eggbutt snaffle: A snaffle with special hinges to the rings designed to avoid pinching the horse's lips: see pp. 71 and 75.

Elbow: The upper joint of the foreleg: see pp. 29

Embrocation, or liniment: A liquid used for fomenting strains in tendons, bruises and bumps; must be always available for horse first aid: see pp. 237 and 240.

Emphysema: See broken wind.

Enema: The injection of a warm soapy fluid into the rectum by means of a syringe. The rectum should be emptied by hand, well greased, and the syringe, also greased, gently inserted. About 3½ gallons may be slowly pumped in and kept for 10 to 15 minutes by holding the tail down: see p. 349.

Enteritis, or inflammation of the bowels: May be caused by feeding a horse grain when it is hot and tired, by a chill, or by eating frozen roots, or mouldy hay: symptoms are similar to flatulent colic, but the horse may lie on its back, which is a very bad sign; call vet.

Entire: A stallion, or entire horse, i.e. one which has not been gelded: see pp. 47.

Epidermis: The outer skin: see Dermis.

Equine: Pertaining to horses.

Equitation: Horsemanship, or the art of training a horse to use and develop his muscles in absolute harmony with his rider's wishes so that they attain perfect equilibrium at all times and all paces.

Ergot: A rough pad of flesh at the back of the fetlock: see p. 31.

Escutcheon: The point below the point of the hips, down the flanks, where the direction of hair growth changes.

Ewe-necked: A condition when the neck appears to be concave rather than convex at the arch of the crest, as in a sheep: see pp. 26 and 27.

Exhaustion: Loss of strength due to exercise, best cured by gentle quick grooming, loose rugging and a small warm feed, such as linseed mash.

Exmoor: A distinctive pony breed found in Exmoor: see p. 52.

Eye: The organ of vision, and generally a sound means of telling a horse's character: see p. 25.

Face: Of the horse, that part between the poll, the eyes and the muzzle, including the forehead: see p. 24.

Facepiece: A decorative brass harness piece suspended from the bridle found in heavy draught breeds.

Fairly hunted certificate: A certificate which must be signed by an M.F.H. to the effect that a horse has been hunted, which must be registered at Weatherby's prior to entering point-to-points or steeplechases.

Falabella: A breed of Argentinian miniature horse standing 30 inches high, named after the family who developed them.

False canter: A canter with the wrong leg leading: see p. 110.

False nostril: A flap of skin sometimes found inside the top of the nostril, which may give rise to 'high blowing': see p. 373.

False quarter: A horizontal crack in the hoof caused by injury to the coronet checking horn growth. Treat by blister to encourage horn growth and remove shoe pressure.

False ribs: Those ribs to the rear of the eighth rib.

Far: A local term in the north country for the offside of an animal.

Farcy: Glanders. A notifiable disease. See Glanders.

Faroe Islands pony: A pony breed similar to the Icelandic.

Farrier: A blacksmith, or shoeing smith, hence, farriery.

Fault: To notice blemishes, weaknesses, in appearance, conformation, or temperament, hence, 'fault free', 'faulty'.

Favour: Of a horse, to indicate lameness by not placing weight on an injured limb, hence, 'favouring a leg'.

Feather: Long hair on a fetlock, especially heavy breeds.

Feather-edged: Of a shoe, used on a horse with a tendency to brush against the opposite leg: see p. 173.

Federation Equestre Internationale (F.E.I.): The international body governing horse shows.

Feed: Provide with food, hence, 'off his feed'.

Fell pony: A breed of moorland pony found in the north-west: see p. 53.

Felloe: The outer section of the wooden wheel rim, to which the spokes and tyre are fitted.

Fetlock joint: The joint between the cannon bone and the pastern: see p. 31.

Fetlock boots: See brushing boots.

Fever: A sick condition when the temperature rises above the normal 100·5F., generally accompanied by a high pulse and breathing rate.

Fever in the feet: See laminitis.

Fiddle-headed: Of a horse, having a large plain, coarse, carty head.

Figure of eight: Schooling exercise for a horse in the manège, in the shape of a figure of eight: see pp. 123, 124 and 301.

Filled legs: Swollen legs, usually caused by a lack of exercise, or overfeeding which can be reduced by massage and bandages.

Filly: A young female horse less than four years old: see p. 47.

Fire: To treat a damaged tendon, or joint of a horse, by cauterizing it with a red-hot iron: outdated method of veterinary treatment.

Firing-irons: The implements used for the above operation.

Fistulous wither: An abscess on the wither, penetrating between the shoulder blades, generally caused by an ill-fitting saddle tree, or due to a blow, or bite from another horse, or to contagious abortion virus. Symptoms are pain and swelling, possibly bursting. Call vet: see pp. 355–356.

Fitzwilliam girth: A double girth, one of webbing, one of leather, now uncommon.

Five-gaited: (U.S.A.) For a horse with normal gaits of walk, trot and canter, plus an amble, between a walk and a trot, and a broken amble, a single-footed pace: see rack.

Fjord pony: A Norwegian pony, notable for its colour between cream and dun, with a distinctive black dorsal stripe.

Flag: Of a horse, to lose vigour after a hard gallop, or easily when in poor condition.

Flank: That part of a horse below the loins and behind the ribs, extending downwards towards the belly: see p. 36

Flat-boned: Of a horse's legs and knees, with a good, clean, hard appearance.

Flat-catcher: (Obs.) A good-looking horse with a hidden vice or weakness.

Flat feet: Large feet with sloping walls in front and low heels.

Flat-footed: Of a horse which goes on its heels rather than its toes, due to the lowness of the wall of the hoof. Caused by bad shoeing.

Flat-sided: Of a horse whose ribs are not well rounded, or well sprung.

Flatulence: or wind: caused generally by indigestion. Treat with bicarbonate of soda.

Flea-bitten: Descriptive of an aged grey horse with a spotted coat.

Flecked: The effect caused by small groups of white hairs showing through the coat irregularly on any part of the horse.

Flemish: A breed of Belgian heavy horse, much imported to this country since the fourteenth century, so that there is Flemish blood in most heavy breeds in Britain.

Flex: The horse flexes when he relaxes his lower jaw to the pressure of the curb-bit, with his head correctly held neck high and bent at the poll: see pp. 290–291.

Flexion, direct: Is obtained by obtaining impulsion with the legs and retaining slight pressure on the curb-bit to cause the horse to flex: see pp. 290–291.

Flexion, lateral: Is obtained in a similar manner except that the pressure is increased on one rein as required to cause the horse to turn its head in that direction as it flexes: see p. 290.

Float: A utility two-wheeled vehicle with low platform, suitable for a pony: see p. 315.

Flute-bit: A perforated hollow bit, intended to prevent wind-sucking: see p. 327.

Fly-cap: A net cap over the horse's ears to protect it against flies on the head, neck and ears.

Fly link: The curb-chain link through which the lip strap is passed.

Fly sheet: A cotton, or net sheet worn over the back and quarters in the stable as a protection against flies.

Flying change: A change of leg at the canter, both front and hind, in the air at the precise moment when all four legs are in the air.

Foal: Of a mare: to give birth: see pp. 260–264.

A colt, filly, or gelding up to the age of twelve months.

Foal-heat: The mare's first heat after foaling, generally from the seventh to fifteenth day subsequent: see p. 265.

Foaling-time: The time when a mare is due to foal: see pp. 260–261.

Fodder: A term used for any feeding stuff commonly fed to horses. Also forage.

Foot-board: Where the driver's feet rest on a horse-drawn vehicle.

Forage: See fodder.

Forearm: The part of the foreleg from the elbow to the knee, which contains the bones known as radius and ulna: see p. 29.

Forehand: All that part of the horse from the withers forward: see p. 21.

Forelock: The part of the mane extending forward between the ears and hanging over the forehead.

Forge: Of a horse: to let the hind-shoe make contact with the foreshoe when trotting, making a clicking sound: due to fatigue. Slovenly riding, i.e. lack of collection, or possibly youth. May be helped by shoeing.

Forward seat: A balanced seat on the horse so that shoulder, knee and ankle remain in line with the weight forward rather than back on the horse's loins: see pp. 99–100.

Founder: Laminitis: see p. 361.

Four-in-hand: A team of four horses consisting of two wheelers and two leaders.

Four time: A pace of four time is any pace marked by four hoof beats in each stride.

Frederiksborg: A Danish breed of horse for work and saddle standing 16 h.h.

Free-mover: A horse that moves freely, showing power and good shoulder movement and stepping out well.

Fresh: Descriptive of a horse when excitable and short of exercise.

Friesian horse: A Dutch breed of heavy horse also used for riding.

Frog: A wedge-shaped portion of elastic horn between the bars of the foot, expanding laterally when carrying the weight of the horse: see pp. 33–34.

Frog-cleft: A natural cleft in the widest part of the frog.

Front: That part of a horse in front of the rider, hence, good front, good rein, good outlook.

404

Frost studs: Detachable studs to fit the shoes of a horse in slippery conditions: see p. 171.

Full brother, or sister: progeny with the same dam and sire.

Fuller: To make a groove in the ground surface of a horseshoe, to take the heads of the nails and to grip the ground, as well as to make the shoe lighter: desirable in shoes for light horse, or hunter: see p. 168.

Full mouth: A horse at six years of age, when all its adult teeth are present: see p. 271.

Full pass: A movement when the horse moves sideways without gaining any forward ground, as opposed to a half pass when the horse moves sideways and forwards: see pp. 115–116.

Gad fly, *Gastrophilus equi:* A two-winged insect which lays its larvae on horse's legs. The bots are ingested, if not removed and continue their life cycle in the horse's stomach: see p. 349.

Gag-bit: May be of several kinds, aiming, by means of pulleys, or similar devices, to bring pressure of the jaws: sometimes used with rogue horses, or by horse-breakers, as a last resort.

Gag-reins: Reins applied to a gag bit, usually running through the bit itself.

Gait: The pace of a horse: a horse normally has three, but see five-gaited.

Gaited-out: At gait, horse gait; of a horse pastured for payment.

Galiceno: A breed of horse established in the U.S.A. 12–13.2 h.h., hardy and docile.

Gall: A sore, caused most commonly by ill-fitting harness, girths, or saddles: see p. 235.

Gallop: A horse's fastest pace: a pace of four time: see p. 111.

A stretch of ground suitable for galloping a horse.

Galloway: A breed of horse once common in S.W. Scotland standing about 14 h.h.

Galvayne's Mark, or Groove: a brownish groove on the corner incisor tooth appearing generally but not always at the age of ten and reaching the bottom of the tooth at twenty; it is thus a useful gauge of a horse's age after nine years.

Garron: A term usually applied to the powerful native horses of the Highlands used for deer stalking and similar work: see p. 52.

Gaskin, or second thigh: Muscular development from hock to buttock, visible from behind: see p. 39.

Gay: Of a horse when its head and tail are carried well and its walk is spirited.

Gelderland: A Dutch breed of riding and coach horse.

Gelding: A castrated male horse: see p. 47.

General Stud Book: Started in 1791, it includes the breeding of all thoroughbred stock.

Gentle: To speak to, and handle, a horse soothingly and with understanding, especially in case of fright, or with young horses.

Gestation period: The period in the womb between conception and birth, about 11 months in a mare: see p. 257.

Get: (Colloq.) Progeny of a stallion.

Get under: To approach too close to a jump.

Get up: To rise: achieved by horse by raising its hindlegs first with its forelegs stretched in front.

Gidran: A Hungarian breed of saddle horse about 16 h.h.

Girth: The measurement around the horse's body from behind the withers to the lowest point: see p. 35.
  The band of leather, nylon, webbing, or cotton cord, used to stretch round the horse's belly to hold the saddle in place: see p. 61.

Girth galls: Injuries caused by lack of care in fitting the girth, by soft condition or by dirty girths. Treat with healing ointment and do not work until cured.

Girth-sleeve: A rubber, or sheepskin cover for the girth to prevent galls.

Girth-straps: The straps on the saddle to which the girth or girths are fastened, generally three in number.

Girth-up: To secure the saddle in place by means of the girth: see pp. 62–63.

Give a leg up: To help to mount by holding leg for the spring.

Glanders, or farcy: a contagious and fatal notifiable disease, that can be communicated to man. Symptoms are discharge from the nose, a lump under the jaw and sores and abscesses on the nose or legs. It may be a while developing, but it is highly contagious, hence, important to call a vet early in cases of discharge from the nostrils.

Godolphin Arabian: A famous arab stud horse imported in 1791 and in many thoroughbred pedigrees.

Going: The ground over which a horse travels: thus, when wet, heavy going, when frosty, hard going.

Gone in the wind: Indicates unsoundness in the wind.

Good hack: The words imply a warranty that the horse is sound in wind and eyes, is quiet to ride and not lame.

Good hunter: These words imply a warranty that the horse is sound in wind, eyes and action, quiet to ride and capable of being hunted.

Good nick: (Colloq.) In good condition.

Good roof, top: (Colloq.) The good line of a horse's back.

Goose rumped: Of a horse, when the slope from the highest point of the quarters runs steeply down to the root of the tail.

Goose Rumped

Go short: To go lame.

Gothland pony: A breed of Scandinavian pony, 12–14 h.h., generally brown, bay, or chestnut.

Governess cart, or car: A low-hung, light, two-wheeled trap for a pony, seating four persons facing each other, with an entrance door at the rear.

Grain: The corn of a cereal; for a horse, oats is accepted as the most suitable grain.

Grass: Herbage of many varieties suitable for grazing, e.g. foxtail, timothy, meadow fescue, cocksfoot, etc. Hence, 'turning out to grass', 'at grass'.

Grass sickness: A sudden, generally fatal, gastric disease, which attacks horses at grass between April and September, but generally confined to Scotland. The symptoms are listlessness, followed in some cases by nasal discharge and constipation, finally death. Call a vet.

Graze: Of a horse, to feed on grass.

Grazing: The act of eating grass, or the pasture which is about to be grazed, hence, good grazing, bad grazing: see p. 211.

Grease: A chronic skin ailment commoner in heavy breeds. Generally caused by dirty stables and lack of care; cracks in the heel fill with foul smelling cheesy matter. Treat by clipping the hair and applying a mild astringent.

Green: Applied to horse, means not yet fully trained, hence, green youngster.

Green feed: Grasses, lucerne, clover, etc., fed in lieu of hay, freshly cut. Also termed green meat: see p. 216

Grey: Of a body coat, a varying mosaic of black and white hair on the black skin: as the age increases so the coat turns whiter in colour.

Grey ticked: White hairs sparsely distributed amongst the coat in any part of the horse.

Groom: Male or female who attends to the requirements of the horse when in stables.
To clean and brush the coat of a horse, or pony, hence, the grooming kit, brush, etc.: see pp. 149–159.

Groningen: A type of Dutch dual-purpose saddle and draught horse.

Grow out: Of a horse, to exceed the height limits laid down for a breed, or type.

Gruel: Oatmeal and boiling water, mixed to a paste, generally about 1 gallon of water to 1 lb. of oatmeal, or, in the case of linseed gruel, about 1 lb. of linseed, soaked and brought to the boil: salt should be added for a tonic to feed tired horses.

Grullo: (U.S.A.) Mousey colouring in a horse, or a horse of mousey colouring.

Grunt to the stick: By pretending to hit a horse a blow in the stomach with a stick while in the stables, it is sometimes possible to induce the horse to grunt, which may, or may not, be an indication of unsound wind, hence, grunts, grunting.

Gymkhana: Originally, Anglo-Indian, now generally accepted as mounted sports, such as musical chairs, bending, etc., controlled by the British Gymkhana Association.

Habit: The costume worn by a female riding side-saddle.

Hack: A light type of riding horse. The controlling body for Show Hacks is the British Show Hack and Cob Association.

Hackamore: A bitless bridle, with a single rein. Two metal cheeks act on the chin and nose: see p. 76.

Hackney: A harness horse, or pony, with a characteristic high-stepping action. Breed Society: The Hackney Horse Society.

Haflinger: A sure-footed Tyrolean mountain pony breed: 14 h.h.

Hairy: Of a horse's heels, indicates draught horse blood, hence, hairy-heeled.

Half-bred: Indicates a mixture of breeding, possibly one side Thoroughbred.

Half-sister: But of the same dam, by a different sire.

Half-halt: A brief check in movement to prepare a horse for a change of pace or direction, or jump, or similar act.

Half-pass: A movement whereby the horse moves diagonally forward and sideways, forehand leading quarters, on two tracks, head flexed in the direction of the movement, at a walk, or trot, or canter: see p. 118.

Halt: To stop. Aids are a slight pressure of the reins, with the legs behind the girth: see pp. 107 and 292.

Halter: A head-stall, or simple noose, with a lead of rope, or leather, used for leading, or temporarily tying up a horse.

Hames: Detachable metal arms linking the traces and the collar: see p. 320.

Hames-strap: The strap fastening the hames at the top and thus holding them in their place between the fore- and after-wales in the collar.

Hand: The unit, equalling 4 inches, by which the height of the horse is normally measured. Abbreviated: h.h.

Handle: To accustom a young horse to a halter and human beings, both to their presence and voice and actions. This is the first step in schooling a youngster: see p. 265.

Hand-rub or strap: To groom the horse by hand alone, rubbing the coat with the palm: see p.156.

Hands: The contact between the horse's mouth and a rider is maintained by the rider's hands, sensitive contact being maintained through the fingers, hence, good hands, light hands, heavy hands, etc. see pp. 104–105.

Handy: Of a horse, indicates an ability to turn quickly at speed and immediate reaction to a light rein, hence, handiness.

Hang on the hands: Of a horse, when insufficiently schooled, or tired, to lean on the bit.

Hanoverian: A German breed of riding and harness horse.

Hanoverian bit: Any bit with a double-jointed and ported mouthpiece which is not attached to the cheeks.

Harness: The equipment to enable the horse to draw a vehicle, which varies in type and according to the vehicle: see pp. 317–320.

Harness room: The room where all the equipment for the horse, for driving and riding, is kept. It should be dry and of an even temperature. See tack room: see pp. 144–145.

Haw: The third eyelid of a horse.

Hay: Dried grasses, used as a staple diet for bulk feed, specially old hay over a year old. New hay under a year old should not be fed: see pp. 216–219.

Hay grasses: Those grasses which make hay. Useful grasses are, cocksfoot, crested dogstail, foxtail, meadow fescue, rye grass, rough and smooth stalk meadow grass, sweet vernal, timothy and yellow bent grass: see pp. 216–219.

Hay net: A net of creosoted cord with a purse neck, which can be stuffed with sufficient hay for the horse's requirements and hung at a convenient height from the ground to prevent the hay dust falling in the horse's eyes: see pp. 141 and 219.

Hay tea: A mild tonic brew for sick horses: prepared by pouring boiling water

on a bucketful of the best hay and allowing it to soak under a cover. It should be fed when the liquid is cool.

Head: All that part forward of the neck, which should be seen to be balanced and light to carry: see p. 22.

Head carriage: The position of the head and neck combined, hence, in a horse of good conformation good head carriage, or conversely bad h-c: see pp. 26–27.

Head-collar: Or head-stall: an unbitted leather bridle, for leading a horse, or tying up in a stall. Generally with a brow-band and metal buckles for adjustment. There are many varieties.

Health: The condition of the body evidenced by an alert head carriage, a bright eye, cocked ears, the body well filled, but the skin supple and shiny, the droppings firm.

Heart room, plenty of: Indicating deep girth and chest, allowing plenty of room for the heart and lungs: see p. 35.

Heat, to be on, or in: Of a mare, or filly, in season, to be ready for introduction to the stallion for breeding: see p. 257.

Heaves, or broken wind: The appearance of a double exhalation which is noticeable in the flank movement of a horse.

Heavy horse: Any large draught horse: e.g. Shire, Clydesdale, etc.: see p. 48.

Heel: The lower rear part of the wall of the hoof of a horse: see p. 33.

Heel boot: A rubber, or leather boot over the heel to prevent a cut from the hind toe: see p. 195.

Heel bug: A swollen, painful heel: a form of dermatitis, cured by sulphanilamide ointment.

Herring-gutted: Of a horse with a flat-sided, weedy body and concavity from girth to quarters. It can be the result of ill-treatment or lack of care: see p. 36.

Hidebound: Of a horse with a staring coat and its ribs showing prominently.
Generally the result of a lack of care and exercise.

High-blower: A horse which has a false nostril and gives a sound like a wind defect at a gallop: see false nostril. The sound disappears as the speed increases, unlike roaring, hence, high blowing: see p. 373.

Highland pony: The largest and strongest native breed. Breed Society: The Highland Pony Society.

High school: The art of riding as practised in the Spanish Riding School at Vienna, hence, high school horse, i.e. one trained in the classical airs: piaffe, levade, capriole, etc.

Hindquarters: The part of the body between the rear of the flank and the root of

the tail, downwards to the top of the gaskin. Abbr. quarters: see pp. 36–37.

Hinny: The off-spring of a stallion on a she-ass.

Hip-down: Of a horse which has suffered permanent injury due to a fracture of the external projection of the pelvis at the angle of the haunch, generally termed the joint of the hip. This is a common injury caused by careless leading through doorways.

Hip-straps: The straps supporting the breeching over the rump.

Hippophil: A horse-lover.

Hippophobia: Fear of horses.

Hireling: A hired horse.

Hitch-up: (Colloq.) To harness a horse.

Hobble: To fasten the legs of a horse, to prevent it straying, or to cover a mare, or for an operation to prevent it kicking.

Hobbles: May be of various kinds and materials: they are best made of leather with rings for a short length of rope: a fore- and hindleg, or both forelegs may be hobbled to prevent trotting.

Hobday: To effect the operation on the larynx for the relief of roaring, perfected by Sir Frederick Hobday.

Hobson's choice: No choice at all: after a sixteenth-century Cambridge horse-keeper named Hobson, who hired out his horses in strict rotation without regard to any preference expressed by his clients.

Hock: The joint on the hindlegs between the second thigh and the cannon: see pp. 39–40.

Hock boot: A shaped leather pad with straps fitting over the hock to prevent a capped hock: see capped hock: p. 194.

Hock lameness: Lameness due to an injury on the hock, usually detected by turning the horse in a small circle.

Hog: To clip a horse's mane: see pp. 183–184.

Hogged mane: A mane clipped down to the crest; to stay neat it requires clipping again once a week: see pp. 183–184.

Hollow back: A noticeably dipped back, from withers to loins, symptomatic of old age, but may be due to weakness: see p. 399.

Holstein: An old German breed of riding horse.

Hood: A light cloth used for covering the ears, head and neck of a clipped-out horse, when travelling in cold weather; also termed 'head-cap': see pp. 185–186.

Hoof: The horny outer covering of the foot, which grows downwards from the coronary band: see pp. 32–33.

Hoof pick: A blunt hooked implement used for removing the caked mud, dirt, stones and similar obstructions from between the sole of the hoof and

the frog, which might otherwise cause lameness: see p. 153.

Hopples: Straps exclusively used in pacing harness, being loops adjusted to allow the correct length of pace between the front- and hindlegs and permit only lateral pacing.

Horn: The outer surface of the hoof, also known as the 'wall of the hoof'.

Horse: A herbivorous quadruped with solid hooves, a long mane and tail, widely distributed throughout the world, chiefly used for draught and riding purposes'
An adult male of the species.

Horse box: A means of conveyance, by road, or rail, for one or more horses.

Horse coper, or dealer: A buyer and seller of horses.

Horseman, or woman: One who rides a horse, by inference, well, or a farm-worker who has care of horses.

Horsemanship: The art of riding a horse.

Horsemaster: One who is skilled in all matters concerning horses.

Horse sense: (Colloq.) Common sense.

Horse shoe: A metal bar shaped to the foot of the horse and nailed in place. see pp. 168 and 172–174.

Horse sick: Of pastures which have been too intensively grazed by horses and are generally heavily infected with red worm: see pp. 211– 212.

Horsey: (Colloq.) Connected with, or apparently connected with, horses.

Humane killer: A captive bolt-type, approved, pistol for killing animals, old or injured horses.

Humour: A pimply skin condition caused by overheated conditions of the blood and cured by cutting down corn and seeing the bowels are opened.

Hunter: A horse suitable for hunting, generally in part, or wholly, Thorough-bred, classified by show standards as from 14·2 h.h to 17. h.h. from small to heavy weight. It has five show divisions: small, ladies, light-weight, middle-weight and heavy-weight: see p. 50.

Hunter trials: Competitive events, usually over a course planned across suitable hunting obstacles, either team or individual entries generally being judged against time and performance.

H.I.S.: Hunters Improvement and National Light Horse Breeding Society, founded in 1885 to improve and promote the breeding of hunters and other horses for riding and driving.

Hybrid: A cross between a horse and an ass.

Hyracotherium, or Eohippus: A mammal of the Lower Eocene period, possibly an ancestor of the horse.

Icelandic pony: Stands 12–13 h.h. and is extremely hardy, stocky, docile and friendly.

Icterus, or jaundice: Characterized by loss of appetite, hard droppings, a staring coat, dark urine, yellow gums and mucous membrane of the eye. Call the vet.

Impulsion: Forward movement created by the muscular power of the hindquarters springing from the hocks and caused by the riders judicious use of hands and legs.

Inbreed: To mate closely related animals, progeny to dam, sire to progeny, brother to sister.

Incisors: The biting teeth in front of a horse's mouth, by which the horse's age may be estimated: see p. 23.

India-rubber snaffle: A snaffle bit of rubber, generally with a chain running through it to prevent it being bitten through: see p. 71.

Indirect-rein, or neck-rein: The rein opposite to the direction in which the horse is required to move: by pressure on this rein the well-schooled horse can respond as if to the direct rein.

Influenza: Of two kinds, mild or severe: the latter also known as 'pink eye'. In both, there is a high temperature and discharge from eyes and nostrils; in severe cases, the eye is bright red. The causes are unknown, but it is highly infectious, so treatment includes isolation and thorough disinfection of stables. Call vet.

In foal: Of a mare when pregnant.

In front of the bit: Of a horse which hangs on the hand and pulls.

In hand: Of a horse when led: also, in show classes, generally of mares and foals, or stallions, which are led by hand rather than ridden.

In the book: Of horses registered in the General Stud Book.

Iomud: A Russian breed of horse of great endurance from Turcoman.

Itch, or mange, or scabies: Irritation of the skin or hair of a horse, caused by a minute mite. Only three kinds of affect a horse: Sarcoptic, Soroptic and Chorioptic. The symptoms are considerable itching, wrinkling of the skin, and possibly sores; diagnosed by putting a scraping under a microscope. It is a notifiable disease of a highly contagious and infectious type: isolate the horse, call the vet and thoroughly disinfect.

Itchy mane and tail: May be due to the above, soroptic mange, worms, or a disordered blood condition.

Jackass: A male ass.

Jaundice: See Icterus.

Jaunting car: An Irish two-wheeled horse-drawn vehicle in which the passengers sit back to back facing the sides of the road; a type of gig.

Jennet, or genet: The offspring of a horse sire and a female ass.

Jib: or baulk: to refuse to move forward, sometimes running backwards

instead: and in consequence more serious in a saddle horse. In a saddle horse, circling in tight circles before pushing it forward may be effective. In either saddle or harness horse, it may be advisable to lead the horse forward to examine whatever is causing it to jib. Use of the whip and force are not advisable. See p. 333.

Jig: To trot at a short paced uncomfortable trot, produced by a high-spirited or under-exercised horse when being forced to walk against his will.

Job in the mouth, or jab in the mouth: A deliberate or involuntary sharp jerk on the bit in the horse's mouth.

Jodhpur boots: Elastic sides or buckle-over boots to wear under jodhpur breeches; generally brown.

Jodhpur breeches, or jodhpurs: Riding breeches extending to the ankle and worn with jodhpur boots, which originated in the state of Jodhpur in India.

Jog: To trot at a short-paced trot similar to, but less uncomfortable than, jigging.

Joint-ill, or joint evil: a disease which may attack a foal up to about eighteen months and is due to infection through the navel contracted at birth, generally in dirty foaling conditions. The symptoms are a reluctance to suckle, a temperature and swelling of joints. Call the vet. The prognosis is poor. Outdoor foalings are seldom affected and sanitary foaling conditions in the box are the best preventive. See p. 344.

Joint oil, or synovial fluid: The fluid which lubricates the bone surfaces in a joint: see pp. 235–236.

Jointed bit: A bit having a jointed centrepiece.

Jowl: The part of the horse's head within the lower jaw bones.

Jump: To clear an obstacle on horseback, hence, show jump, to clear obstacles in the show ring: hence show-jumper, show-jumping, good jumper, poor jumper etc.

Jumper's bump: A noticeable bump on the croup which for no good reason is supposed to enhance a horse's jumping ability: see p. 36.

Jumping lane: A narrow fenced passageway used to teach horse and rider to jump by means of fences and obstacles placed at varying distances along it: see p. 147.

Jutland: A breed of horse originating in Jutland, of sturdy medium size, used principally for draught work, generally chestnut, brown, or bay.


Kabarda: A Russian breed of horse found in the Caucasus, about 14.3 h.h., generally bay. It is agile and used for pack work and riding.

Karabair: A Russian breed of horse with Arab blood, bred in Uzbekistan.

Karabakh: A predominantly Arab breed of Russian riding horse found in the Caucasus.

Kathiawari: A hardy breed of horse found in the Kathiawar Peninsula, North-West Pakistan.

Keep: Grazing for horses.

Keratoma: A horny growth on the inner wall of the horn of the hoof, caused by excess activity of the horn producing laminae, generally as the result of an injury, or puncture. It may cause inflammation and lameness and pus may discharge. Remove all pressure and call a vet.

Keyed bit: A mouthing bit with metal attachments shaped like keys, which the horse can play with and which help to produce saliva and so a soft mouth.

Kiang: A species of wild Asiatic ass found in Tibet.

Kick: Of a horse, to strike out with the hoof.

Kicker: A horse noted for the vice of kicking, which may be marked out hunting by tying a red bow to its tail as a warning.

Kicking strap: A strap running through the loop at the top of the crupper and buckled to both ends of the shafts; only used in the case of a habitual kicker.

Kick over the traces: To succeed in getting a leg over the trace and so to throw off all control.

Kineton nose-band: A device attached to the bridle to bring pressure to bear on the nose before bearing on the bars of the mouth, which can be of aid on a strong and determined puller.

Kladrub: An Austrian breed of horse, of Spanish origin, notable for its height, up to 18 h.h. with a Roman nose and a heavy crest and action.

Klepper: A breed of horse, said to be Estonian in origin and crossed with Arabs, standing about 13-15 h.h. They are strong and of considerable endurance.

Knabstrup: An old Danish breed of spotted horse, developed after the Napoleonic Wars.

Knacker: A buyer of horses for slaughter, hence, knacker's yard—a place full of old horses about to be slaughtered.

Knee: The joint between the forearm and the cannon bone on the forelegs.

Knee-cap: A covering for the knee, generally of felt reinforced with leather, fastened with a top strap, which must be tight, above the knee, and a loose strap below the knee. It provides protection when travelling, or walking on icy surfaces against damage caused by slipping; a stouter version may be used for jumping practise.

Knee-roll: A pad, or roll, of leather forming the forward edge of the saddle flap, to enhance the rider's grip.

Knuckling over: Of a horse when the fetlock joints, both fore and hind, collapse

forward in action, or protrude obviously forward at a stance. The condition is generally caused by overwork and the treatment is rest.

Konik: A Polish term meaning 'small horse' and covering several breeds of Polish horse.


Lameness: A limping or halting movement, which may be due to many causes, injury to a hoof, etc., and which is detected best in a trot. If lame in front, the horse will raise its head when the unsound leg is put to the ground and lower it when the sound leg is put to the ground. If lame behind it will drop its croup as the sound leg is on the ground and lower its head as the injured hindleg and diagonally opposite foreleg are on the ground.

Laminitis: An inflammation of the sensitive laminae of the inner wall of the hoof, which may be caused by lack of work and rich feeding, too much hard work on hard ground, especially when unfit, due to flat feet, after foaling, or after a bad attack of colic. The treatment consists of removing the shoes, feeding bran mashes and providing plenty of bedding. If the attack is severe, send for the vet as antihistamine injections may be helpful.

Lampas: A condition associated with cutting permanent teeth: the roof of the mouth is swollen. Give a laxative and Epsom Salts in the drinking water to improve the blood condition.

Laryngitis: Similar to a sore throat in humans: in a horse may be a serious disease. The throat may be swollen and the harsh sound of the breathing noticeable: it may lead to choking and death: treat by keeping warm and giving eucalyptus inhalations and electuary. Rub the throat with liniment and feed gruels, green food and damped hay.

Latvian horse: An all-purpose Latvian breed of heavy horse.

Laxative: A medicine to loosen the bowels: commonest for a horse are bran mash, Epsom Salts, linseed oil, or aloes ball.

Leading leg: The foreleg leading at the canter.

Leading rein: A rein attached to a bridle, or head-collar, for the purposes of leading a horse.

Leathers: May refer to leather breeches, but generally taken to mean shortened version of 'stirrup leathers'.

Leery: (Colloq.) Indicating hesitation or doubt on the part of a horse which is not actually jibbing.

Lepper: (Colloq.) A jumper, e.g. a good lepper.

Leucoderma: White patches sometimes appearing on the hairless parts of a horse: they are due to a lack of pigment and are not detrimental, except to the appearance.

Levade: A high-school movement whereby the horse raises its forelegs from

the ground and tucks them inwards while bending deeply on its hind-quarters.

Lice: Parasitic insects infesting the hair and skin, commonly found only on horses in poor condition with long coats. The coat appears blotchy and the horse rubs itself, leaving bare patches. Clip out and groom thoroughly, if possible, and treat with D.D.T.

Light in hand: Of a horse which bends his head at the poll, drops his nose and flexes his jaw to the actions of the rider's hands and legs.

Light in the bone, or short of bone: Of a horse, when the bone below the knee, or hock, seems narrow, suggesting possible weakness.

Linchpin: The pin which holds a vehicle's wheel in place, passing through the end of the axle tree: now rare.

Lippizaner: An Austrian breed of horse, originating from the famed Lippiza Stud founded in 1580. Used exclusively by the Spanish School of Riding in Vienna; they are generally greys, with strong quarters, heavy shoulders and neck and small heads.

Lip-strap: A narrow leather strap fastened to the ring on one cheek of a curb-bit, passing through the centre link provided on the curb-chain and buckled to the ring on the other cheek of the curb-bit, to prevent the curb-chain hanging too far down the chin, or the horse taking hold of the cheek of the bit in its teeth. It also prevents the bit being inverted should the horse suddenly toss its head violently upwards.

Lisk: The point in the groin where the hairs divide in different directions.

Litter: Straw bedding.

Liverpool bit: Any type of driving bit with a circular cheek and a central mouthpiece.

Livery stable: A stable which takes horses at livery, i.e. cares for the horses of others at a price agreed per week; it generally also has horses for hire.

Lockjaw, or tetanus: A disease caused by the tetanus bacillus in a wound entering the bloodstream, generally through punctures. The symptoms are that a horse is outstretched, with its limbs stiffened, and is in a nervous state: keep the horse quiet and send for a vet at once.

Loins: That part of the back behind the saddle on either side of the spine: see pp. 35–36.

Long in the tooth: Said of an aged horse.

Long rein: To drive a young horse by means of two long reins while the trainer is following on foot behind: used by some trainers prior to backing a youngster.

Lonsdale girth straps: Specially long straps, extending below the saddle flap to use with a short girth to remove the bulk from beneath the rider's thigh.

Loose box: The horse's stable, as opposed to stall, where the horse can move

around freely and lie down and rise without hindrance. Is generally about a minimum of 10 feet by 12 feet by 12 feet, having a half door: see pp. 139–140.

Loose rein: A rein hanging loose without contact between the rider, or driver, and the horse's mouth.

Lop-eared: Of a horse whose ears droop downwards, giving a slack appearance, as opposed to prick-eared, with an alert look: a lop-eared appearance is not a fault.

Lose flesh: Of a horse, to grow lean and debilitated; this may be due to worms, poor management, or difficulty in feeding due to dental or digestive trouble.

Lot of horse in a little room: Describing a compact, short and close coupled horse, generally of a cob type.

Lozenge: A round leather guard, fitting between the bit and a horse's mouth, to stop the formation of a sore, or to check one-sidedness, or improve the fit of the bridle.

Lucerne: A cloverlike plant high in nitrogenous content. See also Alfalfa.

Lundy ponies: A breed of pony on Lundy Island, descended from New Forest mares and foals and a Thoroughbred stallion, originated in 1928.

Lunge: To circle a young horse on a single long rein round the trainer at various paces, in either direction, from the old term 'longe'.

Lunging rein: A rein, generally of webbing or lampwick, about 25 feet long, which may have a swivel to fit the cavesson and a loop at the other end.

Lunging whip: A lengthy whip, generally of light cane, or with a steel core, bound with leather or gut, and a long but light thong: see p. 278.

Lymphangitis, or Azoturia, or Monday Morning Disease, or Big Leg: An inflammation of the lymphatic vessels of the legs, which generally attacks the hindlegs, especially of working horses. Symptoms are swelling of the limb, which may be considerable, extreme lameness and shivering. Put the horse on bran mashes and Epsom salts, and call vet: he may prescribe anti-histamine. It is advisable not to cut exercise abruptly for horses prone to the disease: this is generally regarded as the reason for the attacks, hence its nickname.

Made horse: A horse which has been fully trained for riding or driving.

Made hunter: A horse which has been trained for safe cross-country work and accustomed to hounds and hunting.

Maiden: Of either a mare which has never been put to a stallion, or a mare carrying her first foal.

Maize: Grain common in the U.S.A. and many other parts of the world: it should not be fed to young horses and is best mixed with other grains, crushed or split, as it is very heating: it is less flesh-forming than oats.

Make: To school a young horse and train it; hence, 'make and break'.

Makes a noise: The term indicates a possible unsoundness in the wind such as whistling, or roaring.

Mallein test: A test for the detection of glanders in horses.

Mallenders: Grease behind the knees, a chronic inflammation behind the knee joint with a watery discharge: a common complaint in out-of-condition draught horses. Change the diet, add a mild laxative and dress the area with a lotion. See sallenders.

Mane: The long hair growing from the crest of a horse.

Manège: An enclosed area, possibly covered, used to school a horse and rider.

Mange: A contagious notifiable skin disease which has three varieties: 1 Sarcoptic: 2 Soroptic: 3 Symbiotic: Sarcoptic is the most serious because of its highly contagious and infectious qualities; it occurs on any part of the body, but generally on the neck and withers. Soroptic is due to a different mite, but appears similar, although easier to treat and eradicate. Symbiotic is chiefly confined to the legs and root of the tail. All result in intense irritation of the skin: isolate at once and notify a vet.

Manger: A receptacle of varied design; a stable fixture for feeding the horse. It must be wide enough and deep enough to allow a horse to eat comfortably, but not waste food by pushing it on to the floor, and it should be placed at a convenient height and have its front sloped in towards the wall to prevent any vice such as the horse rubbing its mane beneath the manger: should be of porcelain or metal with rounded edges so that it can be readily cleaned and no corners to secrete stale food or dirt. Wood readily rots and is therefore a bad material for mangers.

Manipur: A breed of pony bred in Assam, standing up to 13 h.h. of Arab-Mongolian origins; ideal for polo.

Manure, or horse dung: Makes a particularly fine garden fertilizer, very good also for mushrooms.

Mare: A female horse of four years or upwards, or a female of related species.

Martingale: A piece of harness attached to the girth and affecting the movement of the horse's head, via the reins or bridle. Of three kinds:

1. A standing martingale: attached to the girth and the rear of the nose-band and so adjusted that it catches the horse's nose when the head is raised beyond the horizontal.

2. A running martingale: is branched and through the rings at the end of each branch the reins are passed, so preventing the horse from carrying the head too high. In a double-bridle the bit-reins are passed through the rings.

3. A Cheshire martingale is branched and attached directly to the bit rings by snap hooks: this is highly dangerous and not to be recommended. There are subdivisions of these types, including the Irish martingale which is

simply two loops, or rings, carried under the neck through which the reins are passed. It is sometimes called a pair of spectacles, or rings.

Martingale ring: A rubber ring fitting round the martingale strap at the point where it is held in position by the neck-strap to keep the neck-strap in the correct position.

Martingale stop: A leather stop fitted to each rein about a foot from the bit to prevent the rings of a running martingale from snagging in the bit or in a tooth.

Marwari: A breed of horse found in the Marwar area of Rajputana.

Mash: See linseed and bran.

Measuring stick: A measure, generally of wood, with a sliding arm at right-angles measured in hands and inches to give the exact height of a horse.

Mecklenburg: A German breed of saddle horse.

Megrims, or staggers: An affection of the brain resulting in loss of balance and falling: due to defective circulation, or digestion, or worms, or brain seizure. It may be periodical, but generally occurs when the horse is working: the horse sways and falls, then rises in a dazed state. Call in a vet.

Metacarpal: The cannon bone of the foreleg.

Metacarpals: The two small bones behind the cannon, which sometimes become attached to it by bony deposits known as splints.

Metatarsal: The cannon bone of the hindleg.

Mierzyn: A Polish native breed of pony about 14 h.h.

Molars: The grinding back teeth in a horse's mouth.

Monday Morning Sickness: See lymphangitis.

Mongolian: Of a type of pony found in a wild or domesticated state in Mongolia.

Morgan: A breed of light general purpose horse, 14–15 h.h. found in the U.S.A. and descended from a famous sire, Justin Morgan, foaled in Vermont in 1789.

Mounting block: A platform, generaly about 30 inches high with two or three steps on which a rider stands to mount his horse.

Mouth: To accustom a young horse to the bit in its mouth. Consists of the horse's lips, tongue, teeth and roof, also bars. Also, that part of the bit adjacent to the tongue and bearing on the bars of the mouth; hence, a horse which can be ridden collectedly, with gentle pressure of the bit on the bars of the mouth is said to have a 'good mouth'.

Mouthing bit: A bit generally of wood with keys, to cause the youngster to play with it and accustom him to having a bit in his mouth.

Muck out: To clean out a horse's stable removing the soiled bedding and dung.

Muck sweat: A lathered and sweaty condition after severe exercise.

Mud fever: Similar to chapped hands in a human being, consisting of inflam-

mation of the heels, legs and sometimes belly, due to mud and wet. Wash well, rinse and dry thoroughly and apply zinc lotion: the condition seldom occurs when a horse's legs are left unclipped.

Mule: The progeny of a mating between a jack ass and a mare: mules are sterile.

Mule feet: Feet which are small of frog, with high heels and boxy appearance; also termed 'donkey feet'.

Mullen mouth: The half-moon mouth of a bit.

Mustang: A wild horse found on the western plains of U.S.A. and in South America, now generally used as a range horse.

Mutton fisted, or ham handed: Of a rider whose hands are heavy and who lacks feel for a horse's mouth.

Muzzle: That part of the head including the nostrils, lips, gums and teeth. To cover the muzzle with a leather or similar guard to prevent biting, dung-eating or similar stable vices; may also be of wire mesh or fibre glass.

Nag: An old English term for a horse.

Nagsman: A highly skilled horseman who improves a horse by schooling it while riding: he is generally a professional employed by a stables.

Nail binding, or shod too close: The state caused by a nail driven too close to the sensitive laminae of a horse's foot: symptoms are heat in the foot, lameness and pain: treat by removing the shoe and poulticing the foot.

Nappy: Of a horse which exhibits stubborness or refuses to obey aids, or to pass a particular place.

Narrow: Of a horse, not filled out, generally in front, when its chest is narrow and the forelegs close together, or behind, when its croup and thighs lack muscle.

Nave: The wooden centre of the wheel from which the spokes stem.

Navel ill: See joint ill.

Navicular bone: The small boat-shaped bone at the back of the foot behind the pedal bone.

Navicular disease: A chronic inflammation of the navicular bone, caused by concussion and generally only found in the front feet. The symptoms are lameness and pointing of the foot to rest. No satisfactory cure is known.

Neapolitan nose-band: A metal loop encircling the nose with metal shanks, similar to a hackamore and very severe.

Near-side: The lefthand side, looking towards the horse's head.

Neck-rein: The rein opposite to the direction in which the horse is required to move. See indirect rein.

Neck-strap: The circular leather strap at the base of the neck through which the martingale passes: may be used as support when learning to jump.

Neigh: A horse's cry implying recognition, pleasure, or mating instinct.

New Forest pony: A breed of pony found in the New Forest, Hampshire, of a height not over 14·2 h.h. It is a good riding type.

Nicker: A brief, quiet neigh of pleasure: at the approach of food, or a person known and liked.

Nicking: The cutting of certain tail muscles to cause a higher tail carriage, only common in the U.S.A.

Niggle: To play with the bit in a horse's mouth to distract its attention or to prevent a bad habit, such as biting.

Nonius: A Hungarian breed of horse, generally dark bay.

Norwegian horse: A dun horse with a black dorsal stripe found in Norway. There are two types: the Fjord in the west and the Gudbrandsdal Valley further east; it is up to 14·2 h.h. in height.

Nose-bag: A portable feeding device, attached to the bridle to allow a horse to eat oats, etc.

Nose-band: A part of the bridle worn under the cheeks and above the bit. If a standing martingale is worn, it is attached to the rear of the nose-band. It should be adjusted to allow two fingers to enter between the band and jaw.

Nose-band, drop: A nose-band fitting round the muzzle below the bit to prevent the horse opening its mouth.

Notifiable disease: An infectious or contagious disease which must be reported to the police or government department concerned.

Novice: A show horse which has not won a specified amount of prize money.

Numnah: A felt or sheepskin pad cut into the shape of saddle, but slightly larger, to be worn underneath the saddle to prevent pressure in cases of a sensitive back.

Nut-cracker: (Colloq.) A horse which grinds its teeth.

Nuts: concentrated foods of varying value. Proprietary brands reliable. e.g. Pegasus Nuts used as hay substitute by B.S.J. Team in Mexico due to poor quality of Mexican hay. Useful for horses with broken wind unable to eat hay.

Oat-crusher: A machine used for crushing oats and generally installed in large stables where oats are stored in bulk in hoppers. Generally used once a week to supply the amount required for the week, it thus checks the amount used accurately.

Oats: Grain grown in a cool climate as food for man and horses. White oats are best and should be a year old before being given, rolled or crushed. Oats are a stimulating food, of which up to 14 lb. a day is required by a horse working hard: see pp. 220–222.

Obedience: Submission to the aids and response to a rider's wishes and commands.

Obvinka: A strong breed of Russian pony standing 13 h.h. to 14 h.h.

Occipital crest: The bony enlargement between the ears at the top of the head: see Poll.

Occult spavin: A growth occurring between two of the bones of the hock, just below the joint and on the inner side. No enlargement is visible, but a horse probably goes lame: it is difficult to detect, and can be serious.

Odd-coloured: Of a horse with more than two colourings making irregular body markings.

Odd feet: Differing sizes of feet in the same horse, due to malformation, possibly the result of illness causing a lack of growth. The horse is not necessarily unsound, but merely has a blemish in its appearance.

Oestrus: The period when the mare is ready for the stallion, in season, on heat, generally from nine days after foaling and thence every three weeks or so during the spring to summer months.

Off: Used after a horse's year of age to indicate that the age is now passed, e.g. three off.

Off-side: The righthand side of the horse, looking towards the head from the back.

Office: (Colloq.) A jumping term, e.g. giving the office, which means applying the aids at the final positioning of the horse immediately prior to a leap.

Oldenburg: A heavy breed of German blood horse standing 17 h.h. with certain 'heavy' characteristics, such as a heavy head and coarse neck and feet. The breed matures early, but lacks hardiness.

On: Used as in, 'On his toes', of a fidgety horse eager to go and unwilling to walk.
'On the bit', of a horse with a light, but definite hold of the bit, not to be confused with leaning on the bit.
'On the leg', of a horse long in the leg, i.e. too light in the chest, not deep-chested and lacking substance.

Onager: A breed of ass found in Asia, Persia and N.W. India.

One-sided: (Colloq.) Of a rider who rides with his weight noticeably to one side of the horse: or; of a horse's mouth, which is noticeably less responsive on one side, generally due to the rider's heavy-handedness or to bad bitting. Find the cause and rest and bit carefully, or the mouth may become permanently calloused.

Opacity of the cornea: A disease in which the eye is swollen, probably kept closed, and may become dim and cloudy, due to a cold, foreign matter or a blow. Examine the eye carefully, remove any foreign matter, bathe with a boracic lotion and keep the horse in a dark box on a laxative diet.

Open: A horse's heels: a mistaken practise of some blacksmiths is to cut the horn at the angles of the heels to 'leave room for the foot to expand': the

423

practise has exactly the opposite effect and should never be allowed.

Ophthalmia: Inflammation of the eyeball due to a blow or infection. An extremely painful condition, its prognosis is poor: often followed by a cataract or loss of sight, it should be treated as should opacity of the cornea.

Orlov, or Orlovsky Trotter: A Russian breed of trotting horse, originated by Count Orlov in 1777 and now a heavy and a light breed.

Over at the knee: Of a horse in which possibly due to too much work, or possibly to conformation, there is a noticeable forward curve at the knee: it is a show fault only.

Overbent

Overbent: Of a horse showing an excessive bend at the poll: also overcollected.

Overcheck rein: A rein used on trotting harness running from the bit to a pad to hold the head up.

Overreach: A wound in the heel, or the back of the coronet, caused by the hind-shoe striking the foreleg, which may occur on the fetlock or even higher: most often caused when galloping in deep-going, it may be prevented by bevelling the toes of the hind-shoes and setting the shoes well back. In horses subject to this, overreach boots should be worn.

Overreach boots: Circular rubber boots slipped over the hoof, sometimes laced, to prevent injury.

Override: To ride a horse too hard for too long a period or at too fast a pace when unfit.

Overshot: Of a horse whose upper teeth fit over its underjaw. Also: parrot mouth.

Oyster-footed: Of a horse with feet notable for their flat appearance and with regular concentric ridges, which may be natural or the result of laminitis.

Pacer: A horse which moves with the same legs on each side instead of with diagonal legs, as does a normal trotter: common U.S.A., also known as an ambler.

Packhorse: A horse used for carrying a pack.

Pad: The centrepiece of harness, across the horse's back.

Paddock: An enclosed grass field generally well sheltered and used for rearing young horses, or for mares in foal.

Pad-saddle: A felt saddle with no tree of which certain versions may be made with a leather tree for exercise: it may be used with a saddle and tree to prevent sores.

Palomino: In U.S.A., the name for any horse of a particular golden colour, with a white mane and tail. The society in this country is The British Palomino Society.

Panel: The cushioned pad of a saddle between the girth straps and the horse.

Pannade: The technical term for the curvet: a horse's leap with its fore legs together and its hindlegs raised before its forelegs reach the ground.

Parrot mouth, or overshot jaws: Whereby the incisors or the top jaw meet beyond those of the lower jaw, leading to digestive difficulties due to an imperfect bite.

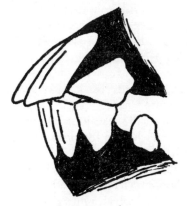

Parrot Mouth

Part-bred Arab: A horse, other than a thoroughbred, with a strain of Arab blood in it. A register of part-bred Arabs is kept by the Arab Horse Society.

Pass: Either a full-pass, when a horse moves sideways without gaining any forward ground, or a half-pass when a horse moves forwards and sideways.

Passage: A high-school air when the horse is trotting as if on air; a well-cadenced regular movement with a marked moment of suspension.

Passmore and Cole bar: A safety stirrup bar device to allow the stirrup leather to be released in the event of the rider falling and so to avoid him being dragged.

Pastern: The part of the horse's leg between the fetlock joint and the coronet; it is undesirable that it should be too straight.

Past mark of mouth: Of a horse whose age can no longer be told accurately from the teeth marks: i.e. aged.

Patch: A noteworthy area of colouring different to the general body colour of the horse.

Patent safety: (Colloq.) A term for a horse, generally a hunter, accepted as a safe and comfortable ride.

Peck: A stumble, generally on landing after a jump, but it may well be at any gait.

Pedal bone: The crescent-shaped bone inside the hoof, which with the navicular bone and the lower coronet bone forms the foot joint.

Pelham bit: A bit combining the action of a double-bridle, or both curb-bit and bridoon, in one.

Percheron: A heavy draught horse which stands 16–17 h.h. originated in France and imported to this country after 1914–18 war: see p. 48.

Periople: A thin secretion-like varnish covering the exterior of the wall of the hoof, secreted by the perioplic ring on the coronary band.

Petachial fever: An acute feverish condition accompanied by purple bleeding from the mucuous membranes of the eyes and nose. Generally the aftermath of another disease. Its prognosis is poor. Call a vet.

Phaeton: A four-wheeled personal carriage.

Piaffe: A high-school term for passage on the spot.

Piebald: Of two colours, generally black and white or brown and white, in large and usually distinct patches.

Pig-eyed: Of a horse with small mean-looking eyes.

Pillar reins: Special reins attached to the posts of a stall to hold a horse when backed into the stall.

Pillars: A method of schooling a horse between two pillars still used in the Spanish Riding School in Vienna, but otherwise not in general use today. The end posts of a stall to which pillar reins may be attached.

Pin-fire: To use hot pointed irons to stimulate the growth of tissues: seldom used in modern practise.

Pink-eye: see influenza.

Pinto: A horse of multi-coloured, or piebald, or skewbald, type in the U.S.A.

Pin-toed: Of a horse with inward turning toes; it is not as serious a fault as outward turning toes which may lead to dishing and injury as the fet strikes the inside leg.

Pinzgauer: An Austrian heavy horse breed of 15–16 h.h.

Pipe-opener: (Colloq.) A short gallop with a view to clearing a horse's wind.

Pirouette: A high-school movement turning on the haunches at a canter.

Plaited mane: A mane which has been plaited in five or six plaits for appearance in the show ring.

Plaited reins: Reins with plaited strands of leather at the hand part to provide a better grip when slippery with sweat or rain.

Plaiting: crossing the forelegs in action due to faulty conformation with likelihood of injury unless brushing boots are worn.

Plaiting

Plantar cushion: A thick, fibrous fatty cushion above the frog, inside the hoof, acting as a shock-absorber.

Pleurisy: An inflammation of the membrane of the lung, or pleura, generally caused by bacterial infection, or as a complication of influenza, or a similar disease. Pain, sweating and fever are the symptoms. Call vet.

Pneumonia: Inflammation of the lung by a chill or exposure, undue work when unfit, or the result of another illness. The horse has a high temperature and breathes fast: nursing and care are most important. Call vet.

Point a leg: To rest a foreleg with the toe pointed; this indicates lameness or damage to foot or leg; it is one sign of navicular disease.

Point of the loin: The highest point of the body to the rear of the saddle.

Point of the shoulder: Above the shoulder, between the lower end of the shoulder blade and the upper arm.

Points: The various external features making up the conformation of the horse: see pp. 21–41.

Point to point: A race, originally over natural country, of about 3½ miles, limited to horses which have been hunted regularly and fairly with a recognized pack of hounds.

Poll: The part of a horse's head between the ears.

Poll evil: A soft painful swelling between a horse's ears generally caused by a blow on the top of the head: treat as an acute abscess, but due to the difficulty of draining, call a vet.

Poll-pad: A pad attached to the head-collar when the horse is travelling to avoid the danger of poll evil in a horse box.

Pommel: The forward raised part of the arch of a saddle. In a side saddle, there are two pommels, the top pommel which is fixed and the lower, or leaping pommel, which is detachable.

Pony: A horse of a small breed, generally no more than 13–14 h.h. By show standards a pony is limited to 14·2 h.h. and under.

Port: A curve of varied size in the mouthpiece of a bit to allow room for a horse's tongue: see p. 66.

Post: To rise in the saddle at a trot.

Pregnancy: The carrying of a foal in the womb, the period of gestation is 11 months.

Prick-eared: Of a horse with short pointed ears giving an appearance of alertness.

Pricked sole: The result of the blacksmith driving a nail into the sensitive part of the sole of the foot, or of treading on a loose nail: the symptoms are lameness and heat in the foot: remove the shoe and poultice if necessary.

Prime: Of a horse between six and ten years of age.

Proppy: (Colloq.) Of a straight-actioned horse with lack of flexion at knees and pasterns.

Pulled tail: A tail which has had the hairs pulled from the side of the dock to give a slim neat effect.

Puller: A horse which takes the bit and pulls due to insensitive handling having ruined its mouth.

Pulse: The heart beat: in a horse normally between 36 and 42 beats per minute. Best felt inside the forearm where the radial artery crosses the bone of the elbow joint, or between the angle of the lower jaw and the lower incisors.

Purgatives: A means of clearing the bowels for curative reasons: bran mashes and Epsom Salts are mild laxatives. Severe purgatives, such as aloes balls, should only be given on vet's advice and after feeding nothing but bran mashes for forty-eight hours.

Purging: Diarrhoea, which may be caused by an abrupt change of diet, excitement a chill, or red worms.

Put down: To kill humanely: due to illness, accident or old age. A point should be chosen at the intersection of an imaginary cross between the eyes and opposite ears.

Put to: (Colloq.) To harness a horse to a vehicle.


Quality: Of a horse: an appearance of nobility and excellence of conformation combined with blood and bone.

Quarter: The part of the hoof between the heel and toe.

Quarter horse: (Colloq. U.S.A.) An all-round stock and riding horse, standing from 14–15 h.h., particularly fast in a quarter-mile sprint.

Quartering: A brief method of grooming without removing rug and roller: first the quarters, then the forehand are groomed in turn.

Quarter marks: Patterns, such as diamonds, raised on a horse's quarters by brushing the hair in the reverse direction to the growth, producing a pattern or design. Also: Marks in a manège at the quarter and three-quarter distances along the side, to aid in schooling.

Quarters: (Colloq.) The hindquarters, those parts between the flank and the base of the tail and the gaskin.

Quarter strap: A harness strap holding the breeching in place over the quarters.

Quidding: The act of dropping partially chewed food from the mouth, caused by malformed teeth, or teeth in need of attention.

Quittor: A fistulous sore on the coronet caused by a blow, an overreach, a suppurating sand crack or a neglected nail. Pain, lameness and discharge are the symptoms: send for a vet.


Race, or Rache: A thin white mark down the face.

Rack: A single-footed pace, in which each foot comes down alone at speed in turn.

Racking boots: U.S.A. term for overreach boots especially used on five-gated horses.

Rack-up: To tether a horse to a ring in a wall.

Rag: (Colloq.) A group of young colts.

Ragged hips: Prominent hip bones, due to poor feeding or poor condition.

Rake: (Colloq.) See rag.

Ralli-cart: A two-wheeled trap, generally with curved sides, which resembles a dog-cart, but with shafts continuing through the floor to the rear.

Ram-headed: Of a horse with an outward curved profile, the opposite of dish-faced.

Rangy: Of a horse with size and scope for growth.

Rasp: A long-handled file, used on a horse's teeth, of several sizes and varieties. Also applied to the file used by the blacksmith to keep the horse's feet to size for shoeing.

Rat-tail: A tail with little hair on the dock.

Ray: A dorsal stripe.

Razor back: A prominent backbone.

Rear: Of a horse: to rise on its hindlegs: the rider should lean forward and pull on one rein to turn the horse round in a circle.

Reducing paste: Vinegar and Fuller's Earth make a common mixture to reduce filled limbs.

Red worm: A bowel parasite causing loss of flesh, a dry coat, dropped abdomen, anaemia. Call vet.

Rein-back: To make a horse step backwards a few paces by means of the correct leg aid with the reins so held that the horse's head is correctly flexed.

Reins: The leather straps running between the rider's hands and the bit. Generally half an inch to an inch thick and of various materials, but commonly leather, plain or plaited, fastened by stitching, buckles or hook studs.

Rein-stops: Leather pads fitted to the reins about 10 inches from the bit to prevent the running martingale catching on the rein buckle or a tooth.

Remouth: To remake a mouth spoiled by heavy hands, i.e. to start the process of mouthing from the beginning as with a young horse.

Renvers, also known as 'quarters out': A movement in two tracks with the head and shoulders of the horse parallel to the manège wall and its loins and quarters bent outwards.

Rhenish: A heavy draught horse from the Rhine Province.

Ridden regularly: Of a horse which is quiet to ride.

Ride: To sit on a horse's back and by seat, balance, lightness of hand and harmony of movement and understanding, to achieve complete unity with the horse, as well as mastery at all paces and in all circumstances.

A broad swathe either cut through a forest or deliberately left when planting.

Rider: One who when mounted controls his horse by means of the aids with the minimum of fuss and the maximum of effect, achieving the ultimate in unity and harmony with his mount.

Riding school: An enclosed area, which may be open or roofed, used for exercising and schooling horses and riders.

Rig: A horse in which one or both testicles have not come down into the scrotum: castration requires a veterinary operation. A rig may show stallion propensities and can be tiresome with mares, as it may be able to put them in foal.

Ring-bone: A bony enlargement of two types: if round the top of the hoof,

Ringbone

it is known as 'low ring bone'; if round the pastern bones, it is known as 'high ring bone'. Common in horses with straight pasterns, but may be caused by a blow. The symptoms are heat and swelling. Rest and call vet.

Ringworm: A very contagious skin disease caused by a fungus. Raised circular patches of hair, generally at first on the neck and shoulders, flake away leaving bare grey-white crusts: isolate and disinfect clothing, stables and saddlery: dress with iodine on patches.

Rise to the trot: Or trot light: to rise to alternate beats at the trot.

Rising: Of a horse's age: nearly. Thus, a horse approaching six years is said to be rising six.

Roach-backed: Of a horse when its prominent convex spinal column is visible.

Roadster: (U.S.A.) A light harness horse.

Roan: Of a horse when its colour is affected by an admixture of white hairs giving a lighter effect: it may be a blue roan when the body colour is black, a bay or red roan when the body colour is bay, a strawberry or chestnut roan when the body colour is chestnut.

Roarer: A horse which makes a noise when galloping due to a condition of the larynx.

Rogue: A vicious horse.

Rogue's badge: In the hunting field a red ribbon tied round the tail to warn others of its kicking propensities may be so termed.

Roller: A girth with two pads for either side of the spine, to keep a day or night rug in place.

Roller mouth: A bit with mouthpiece rollers to prevent a strong horse taking hold.

Roman nose: A convex line of face, common to Shire horses.

Rough off: To prepare a horse for going out to grass by easing off the corn and by gradual hardening, such as the removal of rugs and omission of grooming.

Rough shoe: To insert studs, or frost nails, in a horse's shoes, to facilitate movement in icy conditions.

Round action: The action of a horse which does not have much free movement and fails to cover much ground.

Round-up: The collection of cattle, sheep, or horses, generally cattle in the U.S.A. for sale, or for selection of stock. It is common amongst moorland and mountain breeds in Britain.

Rowel: A wheel at the head of a spur, now very little used.

Rubber: A square of linen cloth used for grooming: a duster.

Rub down: To groom a horse which is sweating, or wet, with straw and afterwards with a dry stable rubber.

Rug up: To rug a horse in stable either for the night or for the day.

Russ: A breed of Swedish pony found on the island of Gatland.

Saddle: A seat for the rider on a horse's back, to ease both horse and rider developed from about the 4th century. Generally of leather, concave shaped, with side flaps and stirrups, it is held in place by a girth round the horse's belly: see pp. 55–60.

Saddle cloth: A rectangular cloth, placed under the saddle.

Saddle galls, or saddle sores: Sores on the back in the area covered by the saddle. Generally caused by badly fitting saddle, uneven padding, bad riding, or riding an unfit, soft horse too soon and too hard. Basically due to lack of care: the cure is rest and treatment with salt water and sulphanilamide powder, then antiseptic ointment.

Saddle-horse: A recognized breed of American riding horse: also a wooden stand on which a saddle, or saddles, can be placed for cleaning or storage.

Saddle mark: The shape of a saddle left in a natural position when clipping out a horse: see pp. 177–180. Also a patch of white hair in the saddle area, generally left by a saddle gall.

Saddle soap: A soap made specially for application to leather with a damp sponge, designed both to clean and preserve all types of leather harness.

Safety catch: A hinged end of the stirrup bar designed to release the stirrup leather if the rider falls: various designs of special bars were made, but are seldom used today.

Sallenders: A disease similar to mallenders only at the front of the hock: treat as for mallenders.

Salt lick: A lump of rock salt, or a shaped block of salt with minerals added, hung in a field, or stable for horses to lick, thought possibly to be a contributory cause of crib-biting.

Sand colic: A type of colic occasioned by grazing in sandy soil by the sea where grazing may be mixed with sand.

Sand crack: A crack in the hoof wall running from the coronet downwards, possibly caused by an injury to the coronary band by a tread on the inside of the coronet. It can also be caused by rasping the outside of the hoof and damaging the periople so that the horn becomes hard and brittle. Treat by removing the pressure, shoeing with quarter clips and blistering the coronet to stimulate fresh growth: it may require a clasp across the crack, or isolating the crack with a hot iron to prevent it spreading.

Sanfoin: A grass which makes fine hay.

Sausage boot: A stuffed leather ring strapped round a horse's coronet to prevent a capped elbow, caused when the horse is lying by the heel of the shoe on the elbow joint.

Sausage Boot

Savage: Of a horse, to bite another horse, or human.

Sawdust: May be used as bedding for a horse, but the drains must first be blocked and layers spread thickly for comfort: it heats in contact with urine: see p. 207.

Schleswig horse: A medium heavy breed of carthorse bred in Schleswig Holstein.

School: Any area, open or fenced, or covered, used for training and schooling horses and riders. To exercise and train a horse with or without rider.

Scurf: Exfoliation of the epidermis causes dandruff or scurf in the horse's coat: regular exercise and grooming, plus the addition of a little linseed oil in the feed should remove any excess.

Seat: Of a rider, the rider's position in the saddle.
The dipped part between the pommel and the cantle of a saddle.

Second thigh, or gaskin: The part of the horse's hindleg between the stifle and the hock, which should be visible as muscular development from behind: see p. 39.

Seated shoe: A shoe with a bevelled edge used to avoid contact with the sole in cases of flat feet and dropped sole: see p. 174.

Seedy toe: A foot ailment resulting from separation of the middle horn layer from the sensitive layer beneath, and in the space a soft horn forms. Generally caused by a blacksmith hammering the toe clip too tightly, or by laminitis, it is usually first found by the blacksmith when shoeing, as lameness only results when the condition is well developed. The affected area must be pared away and dressed with Stockholm tar and the coronet blistered to encourage the growth of new horn.

Serve: To mate a mare with a stallion, hence, service.

Service boots: Heavy felt-covered boots to strap on the hindfeet of a mare being served, to prevent her damaging the stallion by kicking.

Sessamoiditis: An inflammation of the sessamoid bones just above and behind the fetlock joint caused by faulty conformation, such as turned out toes, or upright pasterns, resulting in the horse going lame on and off with varying degrees of heat. The treatment is rest and blister, but a cure is uncertain.

Shafts: The poles, generally ash, between which a horse is harnessed in a single horse vehicle.

Shagya: A Hungarian breed of Arab descent.

Shannon bone: The cannon bone in the hindleg.

Sheepskin nose-band: A nose-band with a thick sheepskin covering over the front, preventing the horse from seeing shadows in front, hence, sometimes termed a 'shadowroll'.

Sheltie: (Colloq.) A shetland pony.

Shetland pony: The smallest of the pony breeds in Britain: see p. 51.

Shire: The largest and best known of the English heavy draught-horse breeds: see p. 48.

Shivering: A nervous affliction exemplified by muscular contractions: the hind-legs seem out of control and the horse has great difficulty backing. The disease is progressive and incurable and may result from illness or a bad fall: see p. 346.

Shoe: To fit a horse with shoes, hence, shod.

Shoe boil: (Colloq.) A capped elbow.

Shoeing block: A tripod occasionally used in certain tasks in shoeing a horse.

Shoeing forge: A forge where only shoeing horses is involved: also termed a 'farrier's shop'.

Short-coupled: Of a horse which is deep of body, short of back and with well-sprung ribs.

Short of a rib: (Colloq.) Of a horse with a noticeable space between the last rib and the point of the hip: a weakness, as the horse is too long in the back.

Shoulder galls: Injuries caused by badly fitting harness collar, similar to saddle galls: see pp. 235 and 320.

Shoulder lameness: Lameness in the shoulder as a result of a fall, or strain when jumping. Test by pulling the leg forward and back once or twice to check for signs of pain; when trotted uphill the signs of lameness much more noticeable.

Shy: Of a horse, to start at some small object, or noise; can be a bad vice if unchecked; may be due to defective eyesight, nervousness or temperament.

Shy feeder: A horse with a poor appetite, having to be encouraged to eat.

Sickle hocks: Malformed weak hocks, slightly resembling a sickle: see pp. 40 and 252.

Sickle hocks

Side-bone: A bony growth, which may form on either lateral cartilage of the foot and may be hereditary, or caused by a blow, a tread, overhigh calkins, or narrow feet: a hard lump is noticeable, also heat in the coronet at the heel: if the horse is not lame no treatment is required, but if lame call a vet.

Side-reins: Reins attached to the roller or pad, sometimes used for training purposes but undesirable: see pp. 284–285.

Sight unseen: (Colloq.) As in 'bought sight unseen', i.e. on a written or verbal description.

Silage: Grass preserved with molasses as fodder, not often used for horses: see pp. 224.

Single-foot: A very fast walk when only one foot is on the ground at a time.

Sire: In breeding, the father of a horse; should be chosen for his excellence and ability to sire good stock, hence, 'proven sire', i.e. one which has sired good offspring.

Sitfast: A swelling on the back, hard and painful, caused by an ill-fitting saddle, or pressure on a partly healed sore; a lump forms which will grow if neglected. It should be cut out by a vet, as, if the roots are not removed, it will not heal; it must then be bathed and allowed to heal properly.

Skeleton-bridle: A bridle used in harness without blinkers.

Skewbald: Of a horse with irregular areas of white and any colour other than black.

Skip: A wickerwork, rubber, or plastic basket sometimes used in stables for removing droppings.

Skirt: The lower part of the saddle covering the spring bar for the stirrup leathers: see pp. 55 and 57.

Slack in the loins: Of a horse with weak loins.

Slings: A harness used solely for supporting or raising a sick or lame horse formed by a broad belly canvas kept in position by a breast-collar and breeching, suspended from pulleys to an overhead beam.

Slug: Term of contempt meaning lazy animal requiring constant encouragement to move.

Snaffle-bit: A bit formed one by jointed, or unjointed mouthpiece, which latter may be straight or half-moon, i.e. curved. The cheekring may be circular or D-shaped: see pp. 71 and 72.

Snaffle-bridle: A bridle with a snaffle-bit.

Snatch at the bit: Of a horse to play with and toss the bit, a vice caused by incorrect mouthing, which should be checked by careful schooling.

Snip: A single white mark in the region of the nostrils of varied size and position: see pp. 45–46.

Sock: A white mark from the coronet to a short way up the leg: see pp. 44–45.

Sore back: A condition caused by ill-fitting saddlery, poor horsemastership, riding unfit horses, etc. The horse must be rested until fit.

Sore shins: Inflammation of the membrane over the cannon bone caused by galloping on hard ground and resulting in heat and swelling: requiring massage and rest, or possibly a mild blister.

Sorrel: (Common usage in U.S.A.) Meaning a light shade of chestnut, or dark red roan.

Soup plates: (Colloq.) Large round feet, generally out of proportion to the size of the horse.

Spanish fly: A common name for the blister Cantharides.

Spanish Riding School of Vienna, or Imperial Riding School of Vienna: The school famed for its Lippizanner stallions and classical riding.

Spanish Walk: A spectacular artificial air whereby the horse stretches its forelegs out straight at a walk, but not a recognized high-school movement.

Spavin: See bog spavin, bone spavin, occult spavin.

Spay: To remove the ovaries from a mare.

Speedy cutting: Injury to the hock, cannon bone, or knee, caused by a blow from the opposite foot, generally due to weakness, or lack of condition. Treat as for a cut, or bruise. Fit speedy cut boots.

Splash board: An oblong of wood or leather to act as a shield in front of the driver's feet on a horse-drawn vehicle.

Splint: A bony enlargement on the cannon, or splint bones, generally on the inside of the forelegs and seldom in the hindlegs: it is generally thrown out after six years old as the result of a blow. It may cause lameness at the outset, but once set does not usually interfere with the horse. Treat with cold-water bandages: a persistent case may need pin-firing.

Sprains: Generally in the forelegs, but occasionally in the hind, are caused by abruptly halting the horse, by all its weight landing on one leg, by too much galloping, especially on hard or heavy ground, by leaving the toes overlong, through defective conformation, or by accidental slipping on ice or concrete, etc. The symptoms are heat and swelling and pain: in bad cases blistering or firing may be necessary if a recurrence is possible.

Spring tree: A saddle tree with two tempered steel lengths running from head to cantle, providing resilience and strength.

Spurs: An artificial aid attached to the heel of the boot of ancient origin and many kinds and designs; blunt spurs or those with rowels clipped should be used.

Stable: A building in which a horse, or horses, is housed. It should be well drained, airy without being draughty and light: see pp. 133–140.

Stable management: The maintenance of cleanliness in the stable and the care of the horses within, as well as that of all harness and saddlery.

Stable rubber: A linen cloth used in grooming, a duster.

Staggers: See megrim: see pp. 346–347.

Stale: Of a horse, to pass urine: see p. 230.

Stallion: A horse of four years or more, entire, i.e. ungelded.

Stall: A compartment for a horse, open at its rear end, so that the horse must be haltered; the disadvantage is lack of freedom of movement.

Standard bred: The American breed of trotting and pacing horse, on average 15·2 h.h.

Stand back: To take off some way from a jump.

Star: A white mark on the forehead: size, shape and position may vary considerably and should be included in the description: see pp. 45–46.

Star-gazer: A horse which holds its head too high and hence does not look at its jumps, which can be dangerous, as it tends to jump blindly.

Staring coat: The dull appearance of the hair when the horse is out of condition, ill, or suffering from worms: see p. 229.

Stifle: The junction of the patella and the tibia in the hindleg, equivalent to the knee joint: see p. 38.

Stifle lameness: Lameness in the stifle, which may be due to a sprain; it is noticeable from behind as the horse trots away, since the lame quarter will be slightly raised and the step will be shorter. If sprained, treat with fomentations; if dislocated, call the vet.

Stirrup-iron: A metal hoop in which the rider's foot rests. Of ancient origins, the style, patterns and metals used may vary: see pp. 62–63.

Stirrup-leathers: See leathers: see p. 63.

Stocking: White marking on the leg, extending from the coronet to the knee or hock: see pp. 44–45.

Stops: The metal blocks on the shafts of a horse-drawn vehicle which keep the harness in the proper position: see p. 321.

Strangles: An extremely contagious disease of the throat and nose which may spread to swellings in the body caused by the streptococcus of strangles. The infection may be from fodder, infected paddocks, or mangers, etc. The symptoms are a noticeable apathy and dullness, a rise in temperature and unhealthy red mucous membrane of the eye. The discharge at the nostrils turns thick and yellow, there is a sore throat and coughing and the glands beneath the throat turn hot and swell, later soften and burst. Most frequent in horses under six years of age, the disease should be treated by immediate isolation, rigorous disinfection, burning bedding, etc. Keep the horse warm and give eucalyptus inhalation, cleanse its nostrils and smear the abscesses with stimulating liniment as they must not be allowed to burst internally, or once in the blood stream death follows. Food should be easily digestible and soft. The disease takes four to six weeks and a long convalescence, of at least two months, follows; the wind is often affected. Antibiotics can be very effective.

Strap: To groom a horse.

Strapper: A groom.

Stringhalt: A nervous disease causing the horse suddenly to snatch up one or both hindlegs when walking or sometimes when trotting. Sometimes barely noticeable, but in bad cases the horse may almost kick itself: incurable.

Stripe: A narrow white mark running vertically down the face, not wider than the nasal bones: see pp. 45–46.

Stud: A place where horses are kept for breeding.

Stud book: A record of pedigree stock.

Stud groom: The leading groom of a stud.

Suffolk horse, or Suffolk Punch: A famed heavy draught horse bred in East Anglia, which stands about 16 h.h. and is very strong: of chestnut colouring: see p. 48.

Super-purgation: Overpurging, the result of an overdose of physic or of physic administered without due preparation. Give 1–4 drachms of chlorodyne and $\frac{1}{2}$ oz. of bismuth. As constipation may follow when purging has ceased, give small doses of Epsom Salts in mashes.

Surcingle: A webbing strap passing over the saddle, or over a rug, or numnah, to keep it in position on the horse's back.

Swan neck: A neck of a horse in which there is a tendency to ewe neck in the lower part: see p. 27.

Sway backed: Of a horse whose back is perceptibly sunken behind the withers and short of the loins, due to a wrench, overloading, or old age.

Sweat flaps: Flaps to prevent both the buckles from causing discomfort to a horse and, as the name implies, sweat from staining the saddle or rider: see pp. 55 and 57.

Sweat-rug: a string rug put on under a reversed top rug when a horse has been sweating. Easily washed and dried. Should not be used as an excuse for failing to dry a horse thoroughly.

Sweat-scraper: A part of the grooming equipment: a semicircular strip of metal with a handle, which can be used for quick removal of excess sweat on a horse returning sweating to a stable. (*N.B.* No horse should be returned to the stable sweating.)

Sweet itch: A spring and summer disease with irritation of the crest, withers and croup resulting in rubbing and bare patches appearing, often accompanied by bleeding. Stop green foods, of all kinds, and apply healing ointment: a very distressing affliction akin to hay fever or allergy in humans, mostly affecting ponies.

Switch tail: An undocked tail, with the hairs pulled to a point.

Synovial fluid: See joint oil.


Tack: (Colloq.) An abbreviation for tackle, or harness, and the accepted stable term for saddlery, hence, tack room, tack cleaning, etc.

Tail: The term includes the dock and hair: see p. 38.

Tail bandage: Should be of cotton, preferably not elastic, worn to keep the tail neat and clean, specially when travelling. Alt., a special leather tail guard may be worn.

Take hold: Of a horse: to take the bit in its teeth and pull against the rider, or driver.

Take-off: The point from which a horse leaves the ground when leaping, hence, the take-off side of an obstacle.

Teeth: There are twelve molars, or grinders in each jaw of the horse, and six incisors or biting teeth, also two tushes, or canine teeth, generally absent in mares: age can be told by the incisors; see pp. 22–24.

Temperature: In a horse normally 100·5°F. rectal reading.

Terrets: The rings on the pad through which the driving reins pass: see pp. 318 and 320.

Tetanus: A disease caused by the bacillus tetani which gains entry through a wound. The temperature rises to 103° or more and there is a general stiffening of the limbs, while the membrane of the eye extends over the eyeball, and finally the jaws become locked. The disease can be avoided by preventive injections, but once the symptoms develop it is generally hopeless.

Thick in the wind: Hoarse due to being fat and out of condition. The hoarseness may result in whistling, or may be temporary only, but is regarded as an unsoundness while it lasts.

Thoroughbred: (Accepted abbrev.: T.B.) The purest bred and best known of all English breeds.

Thorough-pin: A distension of the tendon sheath above and either side of the point of the hock: if it is small no treatment is required; if large, rest and blister. Although technically an unsoundness, it seldom causes a horse to go lame.

Throat-lash, or throat-latch: A narrow buckled strap running under the throat and preventing the bridle slipping over a horse's ears: it should allow three fingers between it and the horse's throat: see p. 65.

Thrush: Inflammation of the frog generally found in the hind-feet and caused by bad drainage, or poor mucking out of the stables. It may cause lameness and is easily detected by the smell; the cleft of the frog is spongy; wash and pare away decay, then fill the cavity with Stockholm tar and a wad of tow; stand the horse on a clean dry floor.

Tied in below the knee: Of a horse where the measurement of the leg below the knee is less than that further down; this means lack of bone and is a bad fault.

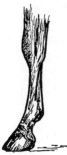

Big Knee caused by injury and tied in below the knee

Tied in under the hock: As above, but in the hindlegs.

Timor: A breed of pony common in Australia and New Zealand, originating from the Timor Island. Used for stock work chiefly, it is strong in the back and quarters, intelligent and sure-footed, and found in various colours.

Tips: Shortened shoes to protect the toes of a horse at grass on stony soil: see p. 172.

Tit: (Colloq.) A term of contempt for a small horse.

Tittup: (Colloq.) To jig on the toes, at a fidgety false gait, neither a walk, trot, nor canter.

Tongue over the bit: Of a horse with the bit not lying on the tongue and providing control as should be the case so that the head carriage is uncontrollable.

Tooth rasp: A file with a long handle for removing sharp edges on teeth, especially molars, which may affect eating: see p. 231.

Touched in the wind: (Colloq.) Slightly affected in the wind.

Trace high clip: See clipping.

Traces: Two lengths of strong leather used in draught harness.

Tracheotomy: An operation to the throat to assist the breathing, or to stop roaring, by inserting a tube in the trachea, or windpipe, about 10–12 inches from the angle of the throat. The tube, of plated metal, should be cleaned out twice or more weekly, but if there is any danger of it being under water the tube must be corked securely, or the horse will drown.

Trap: Any two-wheeled horse-drawn vehicle.

Trave: A wooden cage for shoeing awkward horses, which may be termed more fully a 'shoeing trave'; seldom seen today.

Treads: Of a horse, bruises or cuts on the coronet caused by the shoe of the opposite hoof, or by another horse; treat as wounds.

Trot: A pace in which the horse moves from one pair of diagonals to the other, i.e. a pace of two time.

Trot light: See rise to the trot.

Trot out: Trot faster than normal.

Tubed: Of a horse with a tube inserted in its throat as the result of a tracheotomy.

Tucked-up: Of a horse with a tightly drawn up belly giving a thin appearance between loins and ribs, generally pointing to illness, overwork, or bad horse management.

Turn-out: (Colloq.) A two- or four-wheeled horse-drawn vehicle.

Turned-out: (Colloq.) Put out to grass, not kept in the stable, generally during the summer: see pp. 210–215.

Twisted gut: A fatal condition when the membrane (the mesentery) holding the coils of the stomach in place snaps, due to a fall on a full stomach, a violent purgative, or colic. The symptoms are a high temperature, constant bowel movement, fast breathing and acute pain. Put down as soon as the condition is diagnosed.

Twisted snaffle: A pattern with the bar turned to provide a serrated edge with a more powerful effect.

Twitch: A rope loop fixed to a wooden handle, which is used to restrain a

horse by placing the loop over the horse's muzzle and twisting it until it is
tight to distract the horse's attention from shoeing, a minor operation, etc.
Not to be recommended.

Undershot: Of a horse whose incisors do not meet properly because the lower
jaw protrudes further than the upper jaw: the ability to eat is affected.
Unnerved: Of a horse which has had the nerves to its feet severed to prevent
suffering in the case of a chronic foot disease, such as navicular.
Unseen: See sight unseen.
Urticaria: Or nettle rash: small lumps suddenly appearing over the body, which
come and go suddenly, due to a dietary or other allergy.

Veterinary boot: A leather boot to protect the foot.
Veterinary certificate: A certificate of soundness, a declaration of the physical
state of the horse when examined by a veterinary surgeon; this must
include mention of all defects and where none are found the horse is
considered sound.
Veterinary surgeon: A member or Fellow of the Royal College of Veterinary
Surgeons.
Vice: Any bad habit acquired in a horse.

Waist of the saddle: The narrowest part of the saddle.
Wall: Of the hoof, that part visible when the hoof is on the ground, i.e. the
quarters and heel.
Wall eye: A bluey eye surrounded by white, the condition due to a lack of
pigment, but not a blemish.
Warbles: A species of fly which lay their eggs in the skin of the horse: the
maggots form hard lumps in the spring, often in the saddle area, but hot
fomentations allow the maggots to be squeezed out; the hole then left has
to be dressed.
Warranty: See good hack/hunter. There is no case at law in the case of an
unsound horse, unless there is evidence of an express warranty, or of fraud.
Warts: Unsightly skin growths occurring most frequently on the nose, belly
and sheath. Fine thread bound tightly round the base may cause them to
drop off in time, but they are only harmful if in the way of tack, or malig-
nant growths.
Water brush: Part of the grooming kit: a brush with longer bristles than the
grooming brush, damped and used on the mane and tail.
Weaving: A stable vice. The horse rocks from side to side continuously: due
to boredom: see p. 327.

Weed: A term of contempt for a horse of weak conformation, hence, weedy, weediness.

Weight-carrier: Generally taken to mean a horse capable of carrying 15 stone or more.

Well let down: Of a horse's hocks, when they are long and low, and drop vertically to the ground.

Well ribbed-up: Of a horse's ribs, flat in front but swelling behind the saddle. Also well sprung.

Welsh Cob: A famed breed of cob, standing 14–15 h.h., strong and bold jumpers: see pp. 53 and 54.

Welsh Mountain pony: Indigenous to Wales and one of the nine breeds of Mountain and Moorland pony, 12 h.h. with dished face and small neat head: see p. 54.

Welsh pony: A combination of cob and pony standing 12·2–13·2 h.h.

Weymouth bit: Generally a straight mouthpiece and port with cheeks varying in length, it is worn with a thin jointed snaffle to make up a double-bridle: see p. 72.

Whinny: A horse's call denoting pleasure.

Whistling: An affection of the larynx, due to partial paralysis of the vocal chords, resulting in a type of roaring in a higher pitch, which often leads to roaring.

White face: Where the white covers the forehead and the front of the face down towards the mouth: see p. 46.

White line: The line of union between the wall of the hoof and the sole of the foot; it shows how much the blacksmith has in which to place his nails: see pp. 161–162.

Whole coloured: Of a horse in which there is no hair of any other colour except one on any part.

Windgalls: Soft painless swellings round the fetlock, caused by strain, or overwork; unsightly but not harmful, they are cured by rest.

Wind-sucker: A horse which sucks in air and swallows it, similar to, and sometimes resulting from, crib-biting. It is a difficult vice to cure: remove all fittings from the horse's box and muzzle it: secure a strap tightly round the throat: see pp. 326–327.

Winter out: To keep a horse out of doors throughout the winter.

Wisp: A grooming aid of hay or straw, coiled in a rope form, then in a figure of eight shape, used to stimulate circulation: see p. 152.

Withers: The withers start at the base of the crest and should be highest at the top point of the shoulder and gradually slope into the back.

Wolf teeth: Small rudimentary teeth which may appear just in front of the first upper molars: they can interfere with the bit in which case they should be removed, but are otherwise harmless.

Worms: Common parasites of varying types and degree of danger: see p. 349.

Yaw: Of a horse, to push its head down and forwards when being ridden, i.e. fighting the bit.

Yearling: A colt, or filly, one year old, but not yet two: see p. 47.

Zeeland horse: A Dutch horse, of early origins. A useful draught horse of great stamina.

Zemaituka: A pony breed of ancient origin found in Lithuania and renowned for its staying power and good feet.